INTERNATIONAL LIBRARY OF NEGRO LIFE AND HISTORY

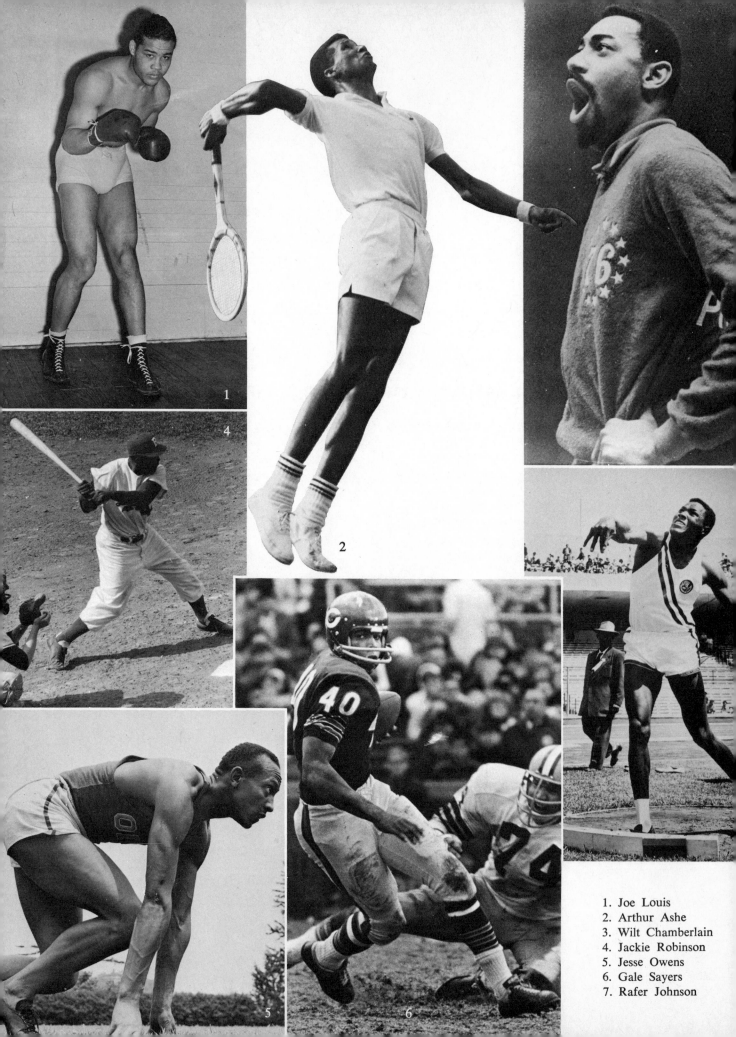

1. Joe Louis
2. Arthur Ashe
3. Wilt Chamberlain
4. Jackie Robinson
5. Jesse Owens
6. Gale Sayers
7. Rafer Johnson

INTERNATIONAL LIBRARY OF
NEGRO LIFE
AND HISTORY

THE BLACK ATHLETE

Emergence and Arrival

BY
EDWIN B. HENDERSON
AND
THE EDITORS OF *SPORT* MAGAZINE

PUBLISHERS COMPANY, INC., NEW YORK, WASHINGTON, LONDON

under the auspices of
THE ASSOCIATION FOR THE STUDY OF NEGRO LIFE AND HISTORY

13

To

THE BLACK ATHLETE

Editor-in-Chief, CHARLES H. WESLEY

Research Editor, PATRICIA W. ROMERO

Production Editor, ALLAN S. KULLEN

Art Director, ARCHIE MIDDLETON

Copy Editor, DAVE SENDLER

Editorial Coordinator, ALLAN S. KULLEN

Preface

THE Association for the Study of Negro Life and History joins with Publishers Company, Inc., in presenting this new series of volumes which treat in detail the cultural and historical backgrounds of Negro Americans. This association, a pioneer in the area of Negro history, was founded in Chicago on September 9, 1915, by Dr. Carter G. Woodson, who three years earlier had been awarded the degree of Doctor of Philosophy in American History from Harvard University.

In 1916, Dr. Woodson began publishing the quarterly *Journal of Negro History*. In 1924, Negro History Week was launched, and since that time it has continued on an annual basis in the month of February, falling between the birth dates of Abraham Lincoln and Frederick Douglass. The *Negro History Bulletin* was first published in 1926 to serve both schools and families by making available to them little-known facts about Negro life and history.

During the fifty years of its existence, The Association for the Study of Negro Life and History has supported many publications dealing with the contributions of Negro Americans to the growth and development of this country. Dr. Woodson wrote several books which have served as standard texts in schools throughout the nation; and as a result of his scholarship and dedication, others became interested in disseminating factual studies which would put the Negro in true perspective in American history.

With this fact in mind, we gratefully acknowledge the contributions of these previous scholars, which have aided us in the preparation of this *International Library of Negro Life and History*. Our grateful acknowledgment is also expressed to Charles W. Lockyer, President of Publishers Company, Inc., whose challenging approach has made possible this library.

We cannot acknowledge individually all the contributions made by others, but our gratitude goes also to the institutional staffs of the Library of Congress, the Schomburg Collection of the 135th Street New York Public Library, the Moorland Room of Howard University, the National Library of Medicine, the National Archives and Record Service, the New York Historical Society and the Cincinnati Historical Society, for the use of books, papers and pictures which have made this study possible.

It is a well-known fact today that few Americans are aware that the Negro people have a long history of proud achievement. Because the standard sources of world history have failed to include their contributions, an honest account of the many outstanding roles that Negroes have played in the mainstream of world culture is long overdue. The material in each of these volumes makes this knowledge available to the American people.

CHARLES H. WESLEY

Washington, D.C.

Foreword

THIS VOLUME is the result of the efforts of several persons who have worked toward its completion. Among these is Edward Bancroft Henderson, who has pioneered as both an author and a participator in the field of athletics. A native of Washington, D.C., he attended its public schools, the Miner Teachers College, Howard University, Columbia University and Harvard University. He taught Physical Education and Health in the public schools of the District of Columbia and became director of its Department of Health, Physical Education and Safety for Negro High Schools. He served on the Boards of Directors of the Washington NAACP and the Citizens Committee on Race Relations and was co-editor of the official *Handbook of the Inter-Scholastic Athletic Association of the Middle Atlantic States,* the Spaulding Athletic Annual.

In 1939, Henderson authored *The Negro in Sports,* published through the Association for the Study of Negro Life and History. The book represents a serious effort to put before the youth of our country the story of the contributions of a few outstanding black athletes.

Joining Henderson in the creation of this current volume, *The Black Athlete,* were the editors of *Sport* magazine, under the direction of Al Silverman. *Sport* was founded in 1946, the year in which Negroes significantly began to overcome the barrier of the color line in athletics. Throughout the years, *Sport* has provided in-depth coverage of the black athlete—his problems, his strivings, his achievements and his contributions to sports in America.

As with all publications, it takes the efforts of many people to put together the final product. We are grateful for the able assistance of the following people who helped create this book: Joel Bender and Andy Carra, for their editorial contributions; Allan Kullen for handling the task of picture selection and placement of illustrations; and Mary Eldridge, for proofreading the entire manuscript. A special word of thanks goes to the wire services, especially to Maurice Davy of United Press International, for his untiring efforts in finding the photographs we needed for this volume.

CHARLES H. WESLEY

Washington, D.C.
September, 1968

Table of Contents

INTRODUCTION xi

CHAPTER

ONE   The Old Days and the New 1

TWO   Boxing Shows the Way 7

THREE   Race to Glory 31

FOUR   Too Good—Too Soon 55

FIVE   The Milestone—Jackie Robinson 69

SIX   Stars on the Diamond 85

SEVEN   Modern Basketball—The Negro Domination 117

EIGHT   Kings of the Ring 157

NINE   Football—The New Success 199

TEN   Breakthrough—Track, Tennis and Golf 241

BIBLIOGRAPHY 275

PICTURE CREDITS 298

INDEX 299

Introduction

THE YEAR 1946 became a milestone in the history of the Negro in American sports. That single point in time has nothing to do with the athletic skills of Negroes; there were great Negro athletes prior to that year, just as there have been since. The year is important because it was then that the white men who operate major professional sports in this country finally began to see the inevitable light. They brought into their brand of professional baseball and football a few Negro players. It took a long time for some of the owners to make that move. Now none of them holds back; any who did would be left behind in the competitive race because everyone else is doing it.

I had the good fortune to be the man chosen to "break the color barrier" in baseball. It was a burden and a challenge—but a tremendous honor. I was fortunate to be in the right place at the right time. God gave me the gift to play major league baseball and I was young enough. Perhaps most important, I came to the attention of a courageous man who was in a position to do something about the evils of segregated sports. He was, of course, Mr. Branch Rickey, who was then president of the Brooklyn Dodgers.

Since white men control sports—as they do almost everything else in the nation—the Negro usually has had to rely on them to offer him an opportunity. That is, after all, what we need—opportunity. Sometimes the white man does this out of his own self-interest; sometimes, because he knows it is right. In Mr. Rickey's case, it might have been a combination. But when a man takes the first big step, he must be a big man—and Mr. Rickey was.

Mr. Rickey had taught school, practiced law, made political speeches, coached football and baseball teams, and both played and managed in major league baseball. He was also a deeply religious man. He did not drink, he did not swear, and he never went to a baseball game on Sunday. He had seen the rotten fruits of racial bias in the country. He knew it was wrong and he knew it must change. He knew in his heart that he must do what he could to change it.

The inroads that World War II had made on the available supply of white players gave him an opportunity to seek new sources of talent. He quietly assigned scouts to watch Negro players, many others besides myself. But even his colleagues in the Dodger administration and his own family, who were in on the closely guarded secret, warned him to move cautiously. Those who do not remember those days cannot conceive of the situation. Mr. Rickey pretended that he was interested in us as players for an all-Negro team he would field, the Brown Dodgers. It was not until after he had signed me to a Dodger contract that he could disclose the secret.

I shall never forget the first interview I had with Mr. Rickey in his office in 1945. I am a normal man with the feelings of any normal man. If anything, my competitive instincts are so sharp that I will eagerly challenge any man who challenges me. But Mr. Rickey made entirely clear to me that day that I could not behave normally. Racial epithets would be hurled at me, and baseballs and spikes would be hurled at me too. The white players would be testing me, some because of an innate bias, but justifiably too in many cases, to see if I would measure up. On my ability to measure up to the challenge would depend not only my future but the future of my race in baseball; my race's future too, perhaps, in other sports—and even in all of American life.

Before my major league career had ended, Mr. Rickey had been proven right in every way. I was severely tested. Hard as I tried, I lost my temper occasionally, and there were nasty stories about racism in baseball. One team even threatened to strike, to refuse to play the Dodgers with me on the team. But Mr. Rickey correctly judged that I could play major league baseball; and that other Negroes could too. He correctly judged that once this fact was proven, others would follow his lead, and soon the race issue would disappear.

In just a little over two decades, the color line has all but been eliminated from the playing fields of major professional sports, the diamond, the gridiron, the court. We have not journeyed into paradise, for little has been done in the front offices, the executive suites of sports. There are no more Branch Rickeys around. But the lesson of sports cannot be lost on the rest of society. ,

No one in the world of sports ever asked that the Negro receive special or favored treatment. Nobody shortened the baseline when I was trying to steal a base; nobody moved in the fences for Willie Mays, or shortened the field for Jim Brown, or lowered the basket for Oscar Robertston. And nobody asks that the Negro receive special treatment in life. All we asked for in sports was the chance to perform under rules making us equal to everyone else, the chance to compete against everyone else, to prove ourselves.

Sports has been a valuable tool for the American Negro. He has suffered prejudice in this area just as in all the others. But youngsters today can look up to Negro sports heroes, just as boys have always looked up to sports heroes. We in sports, I am proud to say, have proved beyond any reasonable doubt—as if we ought to have to prove anything—that the Negro American is every bit as good as anyone else in any field of endeavor.

But so far, our triumphs have come on the playing fields. There is one major area left in the world of sports for the Negro to enter. That is in the field of administration. The Negro makes the all-star teams, the all-pro teams, the All-American teams. But where are the Negro managers and club owners?

Basketball made a major stride when Bill Russell became coach of the Boston Celtics; he had led his team to the world championship often as a player and now he has done so as a coach. Jim Gilliam is a coach with my old club, the Los Angeles Dodgers. But there are no Negro head coaches in professional or major-college football, and no Negro managers in baseball's major leagues.

That breakthrough, too, must come soon. There are now assistant coaches in football and coaches in baseball. There is no more reason to believe that a Negro manager would favor Negro players over whites than there is truth in the reverse. No one who knows anything about sports doubts that many Negroes are qualified to make the decisions on running a team.

Still, there are no Negro team owners. One reason is that not many Negroes have the financial resources; those who do may not be interested or, again, may not have been given the opportunity. But that time will come. There is no reason that it shouldn't come.

I am a fortunate man. The fact that I could play major league baseball has enabled me to provide a comfortable life for my family, has led to new and better career opportunities, has given me a measure of fame. I owe thanks to a great many people, especially to Mr. Rickey. But Mr. Rickey, I am certain, would agree that neither he nor anyone else gave these things to me. What he did was to offer me the opportunity that every American should have. The rest I had to earn on the fields of competition.

The history of the Negro in sports is in many ways a microcosm of the history of the Negro in America. For a long time our talents were hidden or ignored. When we received the opportunity, we showed that we would compete and could excel. That is all the Negro is asking, in sports or in society— the opportunity.

JACKIE ROBINSON

New York City
July, 1968

In the "old days," the Negro athlete could compete only with all-Negro teams—either in all-Negro colleges or in all-Negro leagues. Regardless of his ability, he was denied recognition on a national level because of the color of his skin. But today, skin color plays a relatively unimportant role in the world of sports. An example of this is the great defensive line of the Los Angeles Rams, the "Fearsome Foursome." Three of these men are black (from left to right), Roger Brown, Lamar Lundy and Deacon Jones. They, along with teammate Merlin Olsen, are still set apart from their competitors—but this time it's because of their ability, not the color of their skin.

CHAPTER ONE

The Old Days and the New

SINCE the Negro is barely over a century out of slavery in the United States, perhaps it should not seem strange that he is barely two decades out of effective bondage in the world of athletics. Yet somehow this particularly rankles. Sports has always symbolized, theoretically at least, the American dream of sportsmanship and fair play.

The unfairness of discrimination in sports seems evident to thinking people today. So much is different from a few short years ago. And this may offer a clue to why segregation came so easily: people didn't think about it for a long time; they simply accepted it. Most puzzling of all, they accepted segregation in certain areas of sports and not in others. In the days when no Negro could play major league baseball or football, a Negro could be heavyweight boxing champion of the world, as Jack Johnson was by 1908 or Joe Louis by 1937; could be the first jockey to win three Kentucky Derbies, as Isaac Murphy was by 1891; and could warm the hearts of his coun-

trymen by winning four gold medals at the Olympic Games, as Jesse Owens did at Berlin in 1936.

It is a moot question how long segregation might have remained effective in major American sports had not a wise and decent human being named Branch Rickey signed Jackie Robinson to a baseball contract in 1945. Surely the barriers would have fallen sometime. But without the courage and foresight of Branch Rickey, they might have stood for years more. And all the significant contributions of sports toward changing the racial atmosphere of American life, toward wiping out the barriers of segregation in so many other areas, would have been postponed significantly.

In the past few years, the color of a man's skin has become of relatively little importance in the world of athletics. In perhaps no other field, with the possible exception of show business, has the Negro been able to assert himself with such success, to reach the top with such ease, as in sports. Whatever is lacking in the life of the American Negro, sports stands as an example of what might be.

Everyone knows that it was not always so. The major professional sports of baseball, football and basketball were entirely segregated until after World War II. Golf and tennis were just beginning to break the barriers in the 1960's. Sports were, even then, segregated almost entirely in the colleges and high schools of the South.

In the days when segregation of sports was almost unnoticed as an evil, when it was accepted as a fact of life except in such activities as boxing or track and field, Negroes competed among themselves. The great baseball teams like the Homestead Grays and the Kansas City Monarchs played in Negro leagues; they didn't get a crack at the New York Yankees. The great Negro basketball players performed for the Harlem Globetrotters or the New York Rens.

The list of Negro athletes who never could know the recognition of the modern era is almost endless; our knowledge of them is limited by the lack of attention they received. There are authoritative baseball men who believe, for example, that Josh Gibson was the greatest baseball catcher of all time, yet he was born, like the flower in Thomas Gray's *Elegy,* "to blush unseen, and waste its sweetness on the desert air" of Negro leagues.

That is one of the reasons this book is important. It is important to mature Negroes and whites, who need to be reminded of a little-remembered time when lack of equal opportunity was the accepted standard. It is important, too, to young Negroes and young whites, who may never have heard what it was like in those days. Whatever the problems that exist today, they are at least problems that arise from progress. Not too many years ago, the major problem was hopelessness.

The year 1946 was the milestone of change. It marked the entrance into "white" profes-

sional baseball of Jackie Robinson in the minor league system of the Brooklyn Dodgers. But that same autumn, in the All-America Conference, the then-new major league of professional football, Bill Willis and Marion Motley became stars with the Cleveland Browns. By 1947, the year that Jackie Robinson moved up to the Dodgers, another far-sighted man, Bill Veeck, signed Larry Doby to a contract with the Cleveland Indians, making him the first Negro to play baseball in the American League. Other teams soon followed. Before long, no team dared hold out.

These men and those who followed them were the fortunate ones. All it took was the opportunity for men like Willie Mays, Henry Aaron, Roy Campanella and Frank Robinson, among others, to make good in baseball; for Jim Brown, Dave Robinson, Jim Parker and Buddy Young in football; for Bill Russell, Wilt Chamberlain, Elgin Baylor and Oscar Robertson in basketball, and so many others. Some of the new young stars of the 1960's were born in the year 1947, when Jackie Robinson and Larry Doby entered the major leagues. That, ironically, was the year that Josh Gibson died.

All it took was the opportunity, but Negro athletes have seized that opportunity with a thrust out of all proportion to their numbers. Only one American in eight is Negro, but Negroes make up more than one-quarter of the regulars on major league baseball teams, more than one-third of the regulars on professional football teams, more than half of all the players in major league professional basketball. When all-star teams are selected, the ratio of Negroes to whites is even higher.

Thus, now that the Negro athletes' success is so convincingly demonstrated, it has become fashionable to ask: Is the Negro any different from the white man that he should so excel? The answer is, resoundingly, yes. Not necessarily different in ways that come quickly to mind, but different in ways that arise from his life in the United States.

First, perhaps, it would do well to examine the question of physical differences. The issue is unsettled, and might always be; for all the study that has gone into the subject, scientists continue to disagree. This year, the Los Angeles *Times* put the question of physical differences as it concerns sports to a group of men qualified to make judgments.

One was Vince Lombardi, the successful coach and now general manager of the Green Bay Packers, a white man. He said: "I think Negroes are more naturally endowed. They have more quickness. I think their physique has a great deal to do with it. They're built differently. Their muscular development is longer. Their muscles are not as bunched. They've a longer type of muscle. This gives them greater spring and more quickness."

A second was A. S. (Jake) Gaither, the winning football coach at Florida A&M College, a Negro. He said: "I can't prove it scientifically, but it apparently is a fact that the Negro is faster. And he apparently has better natural coordination. He responds to rhythm. Now as I said, I don't have any scientific support for this other than the fact that the Negro has excelled."

Bill Rigney, a white man who has managed both the San Francisco Giants and the California Angels, said: "I think physically the Negro is a little bit stronger. I think he has a little more stamina. I think he has an extra amount of rhythm too. I can't remember a good Negro player who didn't have a good swing—a swing so natural that if you were going to paint a swing that's the way you'd paint it. There have been white guys with picture swings too. But the Negro has more of a good, fluid motion about him. You notice there seem to be very few Negroes who can't run. It just seems they're wound a little tighter."

Bernie Casey, a Negro and a star pass-catcher in the National Football League, said:

"I have formed some of my own conclusions which I could not substantiate medically. First, the Negro was brought to this country as a physical specimen, a physical thing, to work the land. He was right away involved in physical labor. And he was involved in sports by the white slave owner. This started a pattern of physical excellence. If one Negro did outrun another, he got a few gratuities. If he became the fastest buck in the county, he might be given less work to do or some other reward. So competition gave him an out, and it has continued that way through the years. Also, the Negro evolved in a warm climate, a climate conducive to being outdoors a great deal. So he may have been involved in more physical activity [in his African days] than the white. Negroes tend to be longer limbed and they tend to be more supple. They seem to have more flexibility of body."

In these and any number of similar statements from sports authorities, there appears to be something of an instinctive feeling that the Negro may be slightly different physically than the white man; at the same time, no one has confidence that he can prove it. But that brings us to a better explanation of why the Negro has excelled. It seems clear that if there is a difference, and in some way the Negro is physically superior, the difference is slight enough to defy flat proof. That leads to other possible explanations—explanations with which everyone who knows sports would agree—about why the Negro has reached his current stature in the athletic world.

They can be divided into two reasons, or treated as one, for they involve the same basic factor—the treatment that the Negro has undergone in the United States and his life now, however improved it might be. To state the issue swiftly, in the vernacular of sports: the Negro is hungrier.

The circumstances are obvious. The Negro in the United States has always found his opportunities so limited that when he finds a chance to succeed he goes at it with immense effort. In the period after World War II, the opportunities began to open in sports, and Negroes did, indeed, battle to take advantage.

Here is how Jake Gaither of Florida A&M described it for the Los Angeles *Times*. "Why does the Negro excel in sports? I just think he's hungry. He was denied the opportunity to excel so long that when he got the opportunity he approached it with a lot more intensity than other athletes. He's just had a keen desire to excel."

Bernie Casey commented: "This has been one way the Negro has found to open doors which perhaps might have been closed to him if he weren't an athlete. And being an athlete gives him a certain amount of status, because people, black or white people, respect a man who is physically superior. They may not respect him as a man, but they respect him as an athlete."

Another Negro athletic star, Tom Hawkins of basketball's Los Angeles Lakers, said: "From an early age you identify with people who have been successful. From a Negro standpoint, those people would be in sports and entertainment. There have been isolated examples in other fields, for instance, Booker T. Washington. But on a large scale, Negroes identify wth people in sports and entertainment.

"I've read and talked to people about the physical difference between Negroes and whites. But I don't buy it [as an explanation of the Negro's excellence in sports]. I think it's a matter of personal and physical experience that has brought the Negro to the position he has today. Let's take it from the social standpoint. When you're a kid, you want something to do that will relax you and be rewarding. But years ago there were many places the Negro couldn't go. Restaurants and places of entertainment. So if I'm not at one of those places, maybe I'm out playing football or baseball or shooting at a basket.

All those hours devoted to sports are bound to show up in differences in players. I think if you take two individuals, one black and one white, who are somewhat equally endowed physically, and put them through the same playground experiences and the same sort of training programs, it would be very difficult to tell which was the superior athlete when they matured."

These views state what any qualified observer can see. Again excepting the entertainment world, no other endeavor offers the Negro a chance to earn as much money or gain as much public acclaim as sports. For football and basketball players in particular, sports not only offers these prospects but an intermediate opportunity to receive a college education he might not otherwise be able to afford. The training of college and the recognition of an athletic career provide for athletes stepping stones to possible successes in other fields after their days on the playing field are over.

There is yet another, tangential factor to be considered, however, when one studies the Negro's excellence in sports. The fact is that not only are a disproportionately high number of Negroes competing in big-time athletics, but an even more significant number are stars, the outstanding players in their fields. To cite one figure: Jackie Robinson was the first Negro to become the National League's most valuable player. That was in 1949, and of the nineteen awards made since then, twelve have gone to Negroes.

The reason here is not merely ability. It is, again, and perhaps surprisingly, discrimination. For all the opportunities that the Negro receives in sports, discrimination is still present, and to the athletes themselves, blatant. It is difficult to document, for no coach would admit this publicly, but Negro athletes contend firmly that they must be better than a white athlete to win a position on most teams; if they are only equal in ability, the

Negroes will not be on the team. So it is not surprising that they often excel.

The classic illustration of discrimination is the fact that in major league professional football there are no Negro quarterbacks. The quarterback runs the team on the field and must be followed by all other players. But although there have been Negroes successful in college as quarterbacks, when they have come to the professional ranks they have without exception been shifted to other positions. Similarly, professional football authorities rate the other key leadership positions as offensive center and guard and defensive middle linebacker. There are almost no Negroes playing any of these positions.

Besides this discrimination in terms of leadership, Negro athletes contend that there is a quota system on most teams, again a charge that is almost impossible to document. But instances can be cited in which a Negro athlete is shifted to another position that a Negro is already playing; this has the effect of forcing two Negroes to battle for a job, instead of allowing both of them to be regulars if they could both prove themselves superior to whites. From these circumstances it is not difficult to see why the Negro athlete is "hungrier" than his white counterpart.

Finally, there is an entire major area of sports in which the Negro has barely made any progress. That is in the administrative and leadership areas off the playing field. White athletes of intelligence and athletic instinct are almost certain to be offered jobs as coaches or managers when their playing days end. The same is not true for Negroes, a situation that Jackie Robinson and others have pointed out over and over. Many Negroes have tried without success to obtain these administrative positions.

A start has been made. Bill Russell, one of the greatest basketball performers of all time, was named in 1966 to coach the Boston Celtics, the most successful of professional teams. He led the Celtics to the world championship in 1967–1968. Jim Gilliam is a coach with the Los Angeles Dodgers of the National League in baseball. A few Negroes have been named assistant coaches of college football teams in recent years. Buddy Young, the former Baltimore Colts star, is an administrative assistant to the commissioner of professional football; and Monte Irvin, the fine former outfielder of the New York Giants, has been appointed to the staff of the commissioner of baseball. The opportunities seem now to be increasing slightly, but they are still few.

It seems beyond dispute that Negroes undergo discrimination in sports as they undergo discrimination in every area of American life. But if sports is as important a part of American life as many people think, if it is some kind of microcosm, then perhaps there is reason to be hopeful. For years, discrimination in sports was far worse than it is today; for years, the attitude was blatantly segregationist in most areas of sports. Now it is not. And if Negroes still must be better to succeed, and if they still do not receive the leadership opportunities that whites do, at least there is progress here as well.

The history of the Negro in American sports is a checkered one, often dramatic, often sad, often triumphant. This books tells that story in human terms. It chronicles the careers and lives of the Negro men and women who have been outstanding on the playing fields of this country and the world. It is unlike some other histories because it will need to be revised so frequently. For the story of the Negro in American sports is ever-changing. It will, in the years to come, be ever more triumphant.

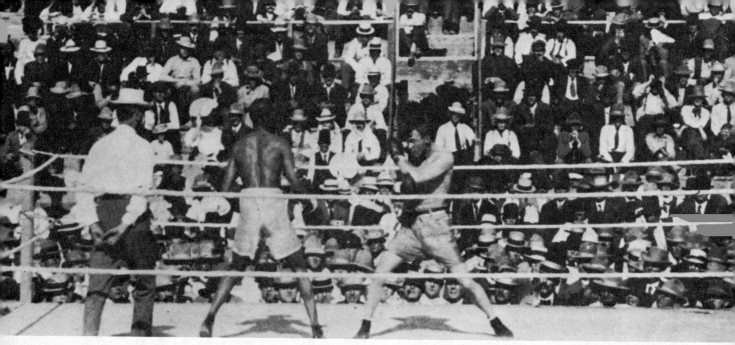

The Joe Gans–"Battling" Nelson fight won by Gans in the 42nd round.

Joe Louis

Henry Armstrong

CHAPTER TWO

Boxing Shows the Way

THROUGH all the long, segregated years of American sports—ended finally by World War II—in only one professional sport did Negroes receive an opportunity to excel. It was a sport riddled by dishonesty and misuse of human beings—but Negroes were accustomed to that. Besides, it was their only chance. The sport was boxing.

From the days of slave plantations, when one strong black man might be matched against a peer from a nearby plantation, Negroes have fought in the prize ring, usually against others of their race. The best of the earliest crop had to go to England to be recognized. Late in the nineteenth century, a champion like John L. Sullivan could conveniently invoke the color line when he wanted to avoid a difficult match. Yet many were the interracial matches.

At the turn of the twentieth century, men like the original Joe Walcott, George Dixon and Joe Gans were champions. Others, like Sam Langford and Harry Wills, might have been, had they been given the chance. And the great Jack Johnson so dominated the ranks of the heavyweights and so humiliated white men that a long search was launched for a "great white hope," not to succeed until Johnson was well past his prime.

Then, of course, came the 1930's and the appearance of two ring immortals, Joe Louis and Henry Armstrong. Louis, the Brown Bomber, the shuffling, lightning-fisted king of the heavyweights, and Armstrong, the windmill puncher known as Hammerin' Henry, the only man in ring history to hold three world championships at the same time.

Many of these men were taken advantage of by white managers, often cheated of their earnings. Many were easy touches for real and imitation friends, who took their money when it was there and ignored them when it was not. The story of these fighters is both pathetic and glorious.

Henry Armstrong

Four men in boxing history have held championships in three different classes, but only one man ever did it at the same time. His name was Henry Jackson, but he was known all over the world as Henry Armstrong.

In one ten-month period during 1937–1938, Henry Armstrong gained the featherweight, welterweight and lightweight championships. But almost as amazing as his record of success was his record of endurance. Over a fifteen-year career he is recorded as having fought 175 bouts. But he fought enough other times without any record, and enough bootleg "amateur" bouts so that the total is surely over three hundred. At the height of his career, he fought every week—and sometimes on successive nights.

His style was simple: hit the other man more often and faster than he can hit you. Henry Armstrong took just about as much punishment in the ring as any man who ever fought. But he administered much more than he received.

The punishment that "Hammerin' Henry" took was not confined to the ring. He was regularly ill-used by associates and strangers alike. Once he traveled to Mexico City and administered a fearful beating to a local favorite; he then not only lost the "home town" decision but found that the promoter had disappeared without paying him. Any number of times during his early career he was not told the true size of his purse and was cheated out of his share. He was even paid $3.00 and $4.00 for brutal bouts—sometimes two or three of them a night.

Henry Armstrong could not have known, as a young man, what the future had in store for him. He was born to a Mississippi tenant farmer; his father was Irish-Negro and his mother Cherokee Indian. The family had twelve children. To improve the situation, his mother took seven of them, all she could af-

ford, to St. Louis, where the children grew up in a ghetto. Barely in his teens, Henry was taken under the wing of Harry Armstrong, a former fighter, who gave him the ring name "Melody" Jackson at the start of his career. Later Henry resumed his real first name but in the ring used the last name of his mentor. The two traveled all over the Midwest, scrounging fights when they could, traveling in box cars as often as not.

Then they tried the West Coast, where Henry was signed by a manager with better connections, "One-Shot" Wirt Ross. Along with managing a shoeshine parlor, Henry fought when he could, losing fights when told to, getting paid a few dollars. Then his contract was sold to another manager, Eddie Mead, who had the financial backing of Al Jolson and other entertainment stars, all fans of the young Negro.

Mead wanted to get everything he could out of Henry. In 1937, Henry fought seventeen times in a seven-month period. By this time, he was weighing-in at more than 130 pounds, but he dieted to 124½ to get a crack at the featherweight title held by Petey Sarron, who had been ducking him for months. He knocked out Sarron in the sixth round and on Ocober 29, 1937, at the age of twenty-four, Henry Armstrong was the featherweight champion of the world.

Henry continued to take on all comers at a feverish pace; it was that winter that he knocked out two opponents on successive nights. But a few days later, traveling to Los Angeles by car, he had a dizzy spell and began to make strange, babbling sounds. Alarmed, manager Mead took him to a doctor, who found Henry on the verge of a breakdown. He was taken to a rest home in California for four months.

But Mead wasted little time. He pushed his champion back into action and within four months had booked another championship bout. It appeared to be a mismatch. Henry

The hands that once punched savagely at opponents in the prize ring gently turn the pages of the Holy Bible. Henry Armstrong now devotes his time and energies to working with his church and the Boys Clubs of America.

skipped completely over the lightweight class to take on the great welterweight champion, Barney Ross, spotting him 8½ pounds at 133½ to 142. The outdoor bout on Long Island drew 28,000 fans on May 31, 1938.

Ross was a great and courageous champion, but against Armstrong he made an elementary error. He tried to make a defensive fight and wait for the one big opening. He could as well have sparred with a threshing machine. Armstrong was all over him from the first bell. The pace was set by Henry—the fastest even he had moved up to that time—until the older Ross was stumbling from sheer weariness by the sixth round. Few champs ever stood up under such a sustained battering as Barney Ross took that night. Four times he was on the edge of a knockout. His face was a red mass; he had a broken nose and twenty-two stitches were later taken in his lips and eyes. There are even those who say that Armstrong could have knocked Ross out in the last two rounds, but that Henry so admired Barney's courage that he let him give up the title on his feet. After the bout, the two fighters became great friends.

Beating Ross was worth about $40,000 to Henry and Mead, their first big purse, and it led to just what might be expected of a youngster who had never had any money. Henry had his fun. He bought a wardrobe that made him a Beau Brummell in Harlem, acquired a fast car and began to take in all-night parties. Boxing experts agree that the life Henry Armstrong lived out of the ring shortened his time as champion.

Only two months after the Ross bout, Armstrong was in training again, for an effort that had the whole country excited. Lou Ambers ruled the lightweights. The Herkimer Hurricane had held off all challengers for two years. Could Armstrong pull off the unprecedented, beat Ambers, become a simultaneous triple holder of every world title between 118 and 147 pounds? Most fans thought he could, but they hadn't considered an Ambers tactic of

jumping into an opponent's punches. If the punches came too fast and without control, they might end below the belt. That almost cost Henry his third title.

In the first two rounds, Ambers hooked Henry around the face until he was swallowing his own blood. And Henry lost the 7th, 11th and 12th rounds for low blows as Ambers jumped in. Still, he came close to knocking Ambers out in the 6th round and dominated the fight as the rounds piled up. He viciously pummeled Ambers around the ring, but the lightweight champion was still slugging, too, and at the final bell both men were battered wrecks. The scoring was as close as possible: the referee scored for Henry, 7–6 with two rounds even; one judge for Henry, 8–6 with one even; the other judge for Ambers, 8–7. Armstrong had become the triple champion.

The three titles were not enough for Henry's manager. He arranged twenty more fights in the rest of 1938 and 1939. In March 1940, Henry was even booked against Ceferino Garcia, the middleweight champion, who weighed 153 pounds to Armstrong's 139. Although newspapermen covering the fight in Los Angeles thought Henry had won, officials scored it a draw.

Henry had to give up the featherweight title without a fight when he found he could no longer make the 126-pound weight limit. He lost the lightweight title to Ambers in another jarring fifteen-round bout, mainly because five rounds were taken away from him for low blows. The last of his titles to go was the welterweight, which he lost to Fritzie Zivic in October 1940.

Yet his remarkable endurance carried him on. At the age of thirty-three he was still in the ring, winning thirteen out of fourteen bouts in a 1942 comeback effort. He even fought the young Ray Robinson, but Sugar Ray, just coming into his prime, toyed with him and won easily. Henry didn't hang up his gloves until 1945.

During all those years of success, the money came in easily and went back out just as easily. He traveled, gambled, gave parties. When his career in the ring was over, he had little to show for it except memories.

Henry wandered around aimlessly for awhile, drinking more than he should have, holding no regular job. Then something new and thrilling happened to him. While managing business properties for a modest income, he was drawn to the sermons of a Baptist preacher in Pasadena, California, and a long-dormant feeling about religion was awakened in him. In 1949, at the age of thirty-six, he enrolled in a theology school and in 1951 was ordained a Baptist minister.

For a time he traveled the country, attracting large crowds because of his reputation, and exciting them with his preaching. Then he settled down in St. Louis, his boyhood home, where he became affiliated with a Baptist church. But even more important, he began to work with the Boys Clubs of America. In its first year, the club in St. Louis attracted 3,300 members, boys whom Henry Armstrong wanted to help save from a life in the streets. He did not have a great deal of money after his retirement from boxing, but this man, who had accomplished something in the ring that no other man had ever done, was richer in a different way.

Joe Louis

Joe Louis held the heavyweight boxing championship of the world longer than any other man. From the time he began his professional career until he retired as champion in March 1949, he lost only one bout, a defeat by Max Schmeling that he avenged in perhaps the most famous triumph of his career. Even after he suffered two defeats in an abortive comeback attempt, he retired with sixty-eight victories in seventy-one fights, and fifty-four knockouts.

But it was not merely for his stunning record that Joe Louis is remembered. He was a figure of national importance. There were times during his long reign when he appeared almost unique, six feet tall, 200 pounds, quick of hand, the epitome of physical strength and muscular perfection.

And he was a symbol for his race. A halo was spun over him. He was good to his mother. He bought a home for her in Detroit. He paid back to the city of Detroit $270 drawn by his family in relief during the Depression. He did not smoke. He did not drink. That was the Joe Louis the public came to know.

In truth, Louis was a happy-go-lucky guy among his friends. He could be moved to gales of laughter. He was a practical joker whose friends were never quite safe from him. He liked people around him all the time. With friends he was a soft touch for those who believed that a heavyweight champion was around only to be tapped. He did not complain because this was not his way. "It's only money," he said, "and if they didn't need it, they wouldn't grab it."

Eventually he came to owe the government so much in back taxes, assessments and interest that he could never hope to catch up. He earned $4,606,721 in purses during his career, but his income was relatively modest in later years.

What he kept were his memories—glorious memories of the years of triumph as champion, a champion who did more for boxing than any other fighter.

To see Joe Louis in perspective, it is best to go back to May 13, 1914 and a sharecropper's shack off a road running between Lafayette and Cusetta in Chambers County, Alabama. In that shack Joe Louis Barrow was born.

Joe's father was Munroe Barrow, "Mun" to everybody. He stood 6ft.-3in., and he weighed more than 200 pounds. When Joe was two years old, "Mun" Barrow was taken to Searcy State Hospital in Mt. Vernon, Alabama. He

Joe Louis, Heavyweight
Champion of the World.

His left eye nearly closed and his face swollen from Jersey Joe Walcott's
punches, Joe Louis is declared the winner in their fifteen-round 1947 title bout.

His face only slightly marked, Louis heads for his dressing room after making a successful twenty-fifth defense of his
heavyweight crown against Jersey Joe Walcott in 1948.

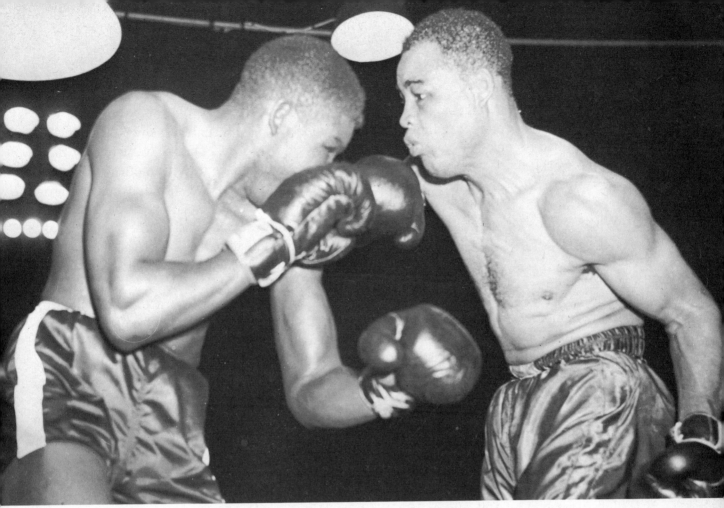

Louis gets set to deliver a left to the head of Jimmy Bivins.

Cesar Brion misses with a looping right hand as Louis deftly side-steps the blow. The plucky Argentine went the full ten rounds but lost the decision.

The "Brown Bomber," who held the world heavyweight title longer than any other man (eleven years, eight months and seven days), at his fiftieth birthday celebration in 1964.

was insane and he never came home. He died at fifty-eight without comprehending that his seventh child had become heavyweight champion of the world.

Joe's mother had been Lillie Reese before she married. She had eight children by Joe's father. When "Mun" Barrow was gone, she married Pat Brooks, who had five children of his own. In all, the cotton patch had to support fifteen persons.

When Joe was six years old, Pat Brooks moved the family to Mt. Sinai, a hamlet some miles away. Joe was a quiet lad, made self-conscious by an inability to speak distinctly. At school he refused to take part in word exercises. At home he talked little and ignored the other kids playing games. He found his own fun. He hunted snakes and fed the chickens and hogs. He skipped school in the Mt. Sinai Baptist Church when he found a favorite fishing hole, and passed many happy hours there.

Things were bad in Alabama in 1926 and Pat Brooks, hearing about the high wages being paid by Ford in Detroit, went north to find employment in an auto plant. When he was settled he brought his family to Detroit. At first the brood lived with relatives on Macomb Street. Crowded as the place was, it was like heaven. It had electric lights and inside toilets. Down in Alabama, Joe had known only kerosene lamps and outhouses.

Later, the family moved to Catherine Street and Joe went to the Duffield School. He did not improve as a student and went only as far as the sixth grade. One of his teachers suggested that he transfer to a trade school. At the Bronson Trade School, he took up woodworking. But the trade he really learned at Bronson was boxing, not cabinet-making. Joe was seventeen years old now, big and strong and awkward. He was bigger than the other boys in his class but he was still slow of speech and withdrawn. A friend who was fighting in amateur bouts told Joe about the merchandise checks he was winning.

His first fight was a lesson in pain. Joe was knocked down seven times in two rounds. His reward was a check for $7.00 worth of merchandise. He gave it to his mother. For seven months after that Joe stayed away from boxing. When the Golden Gloves came around, he entered the novice division. Joe was not a fast learner and had to work hard, but he went on to win the Golden Gloves light heavyweight title in 1933.

Shortly thereafter, Joe met Jack Blackburn, one of the most knowledgeable boxing men of the time. It has been said that Louis was a natural-born killer in the ring, but Blackburn found Joe poor in every department of boxing. Joe, however, had an aptitude for learning to box.

For his first professional fight, Joe went in against Jack Kracken in the Bacon Casino. It was July 4, 1934, and Louis knocked Kracken out in the first round with a punch on the jaw. He was paid $52.00 for the fight. The next week, he earned $54.00 for knocking out Willie Davis in three rounds. He moved to Marigold Gardens in Chicago for the next fight, July 29, and hit Larry Udell on the chin for a knockout in the second round. He was paid $101.

Now the campaign was on in earnest. Louis won three more in Chicago, and now wanted to fight in Detroit. A match was arranged with a Canadian named Alex Borchuk, at the Naval Armory. Joe knocked him out in the fourth round. Later, Joe said, "This Borchuk hit me harder than anybody. He fetched me one to the jaw that broke one of my back teeth. Nobody knew that I almost lost that fight."

In New York, Damon Runyon was touting a young heavyweight named Art Sykes. A match was arranged between Louis and Sykes in Chicago. It was a one-sided affair. Louis hit Sykes more than all his other opponents together. Sykes was taken to a hospital after the knockout in the eighth round and he never fought again. Joe said he was sorry it had happened but added, "They came to beat me up. I got to go back at them the same way."

It was decided that Louis' ballyhooed invasion of New York would be against Primo Carnera, a gigantic former heavyweight champion. The fight was set for Yankee Stadium on June 25, 1935. Louis came to New York in a sweep of glory. He was bombarded by cameramen. Sportswriters tried to pierce his seeming indifference with question after question. The twenty-year-old kid sought refuge in silence. He was unable to cope vocally with his new-found fame. Louis discovered Pompton Lakes before the Carnera fight. Dr. Joseph Bier ran the training camp, in the Jersey hills some thirty miles from New York City, and Louis even drew crowds for his workouts.

The fight with Carnera presented Louis in the best possible light. The former champion was a hulk of a man, easy to hit. He had weight on his side, but nothing else. He tried to bull Louis in the fourth round by wrestling him in the clinches. Louis asserted his own strength by actually lifting the giant and swinging him around. Louis smashed hooks to the big man's body and then, when Carnera was ready for the killing, turned his attack to the head. Louis knocked him down twice with punches to the jaw. Carnera tried to beat the count the second time, but couldn't. It was a knockout in the sixth round. The crowd of 62,000 cheered Louis and he was pleased. His purse came to $62,000 from a gross gate of $328,655. The Brown Bomber was now rich.

Less than six weeks later, Louis went against King Levinsky in Comiskey Park, Chicago. A crowd of 39,195 paid $192,906 to see the youngster, just turned 21, go after his twenty-fourth victory in a row. Louis won by a knockout in the first round without breaking into a sweat.

On June 19, 1936, Louis fought Max Schmeling, a German who thought he saw a flaw in Joe's style. But Joe was more confident than ever, and he was to suffer for his loss of humility.

Schmeling knew he could hit Louis with well-timed rights. He floored Joe in the fourth round with a straight right to the jaw. Louis was hurt. He should have taken a count of nine. Instead, he staggered up hurriedly. He thought he heard the bell. He was hearing things. Schmeling's precise right smashed against his jaw again. When the bell did ring, Louis could just about make his way to the corner. Joe was through for the night, although it was not until the 12th round that Schmeling finally knocked him out.

For Louis, it was a moment of despair. He had been aiming straight at Jimmy Braddock's title and now he was sidetracked. Only Blackburn discerned the future. "We'll be back, Chappie," his trainer told Joe. And so it was. Louis came back all the way. Within 368 days, he had won seven times and was fighting James J. Braddock for the championship, in Chicago. Boxing politics enabled him to get his shot at the title despite the fact that Schmeling, having beaten Louis, was actually supposed to fight Braddock first. Instead, Louis met Braddock at Comiskey Park, Chicago, on June 22, 1937.

At 1:10 of the 8th round, a right to the jaw demolished Braddock, and Joe was the champion at last. Inevitably, it was suggested that he was champion of all the world but Max Schmeling. He even admitted it. "I figure in my own mind, I ain't the real champ until I get that Schmeling," he said.

He was to have three other fights before the return with Schmeling. Tommy Farr surprised Joe by lasting fifteen rounds with him two months after he won the title. The next winter, Louis fought twice. He knocked out Natie Mann in three rounds and Harry Thomas in five.

By the time the Schmeling rematch came along, exactly one year after he took the title, Louis was in perfect physical and mental condition. He did not want to make a mistake in this one and he didn't. This most vicious of all championship fights ended in 2 minutes, 4 seconds of the first round. Joe Louis had hit Schmeling forty-one times in all, and Schmeling was taken in defeat from the stadium to a hospital. There was gloom in Germany—while millions of Americans rejoiced. Joe Louis had won his biggest fight.

Louis had defended the title seventeen times in four years when he went into the ring with Billy Conn for the first time. Behind in points up to round twelve, he rallied to kayo Conn. Lou Nova, who had boasted of his "cosmic punch," was the twentieth challenger to be beaten by Louis. It was a ludicrous event. Once Nova threw a right so lacking in authority that Louis simply stepped back and smiled. Joe knocked him out during the 6th round.

Three months later, America was at war. In January 1942, Louis fought Buddy Baer in a return bout at Madison Square Garden for Navy Emergency Relief. He knocked Baer out in one round and donated his entire purse to the charity. Four days later, he volunteered for service in the Army and reported to Camp Upton on Long Island. When Joe first joined the Army, he had volunteered to fight for Army Emergency Relief, just as he had for the Navy, and his offer was accepted. He took on Abe Simon in the Garden on March 27, 1942, and knocked him out in six rounds. Joe's purse of $45,882 was contributed to the Army fund.

When he came out of the Army, Louis was flat broke. But after fighting Conn in a rematch, and beating Tami Mauriello in September 1946, there was nobody left for him to fight. And he had to fight to earn money. It was then suggested that Joe fight Joe Walcott in an exhibition and Joe agreed. But when the New York Athletic Commission refused to sanction it, they agreed to fight a title fight.

The critics regarded the veteran Walcott as an unfortunate victim of circumstances. They didn't figure Jersey Joe to have a chance. But the fight turned out to be a thriller. Walcott, who was fighting as a pro three years before Louis and who had retired several times, knocked Louis down in the first and fourth rounds. Louis lacked punch and power in his record-making twenty-fourth defense. When the fight was over, the close decision went to Louis and the crowd booed. The sound was new to Louis' ears. Naturally, the sensitive champ was hurt.

Louis was so embarrassed by his showing that he hid from newspapermen. One reporter finally saw him in his Harlem apartment, bemoaning his fate, but determined to take on Walcott—then retire. He almost kept his word.

The following June he took on Walcott at Yankee Stadium. The fight drew 42,267 fans who paid $841,739. Walcott was knocked out in the 11th round. Louis had won his 25th title defense in a row; there was nowhere to go. On March 1, 1949, he formally announced his retirement as champion.

Joe was out of action through 1949 and most of 1950, although he continued to give exhibitions. Then he was prevailed upon to try a comeback against Ezzard Charles, who had become world champion by beating Walcott in an elimination contest set up by the National Boxing Association. Later, after the defeat by Charles, Louis fought eight more times, until his ultimate and crushing knockout by Rocky Marciano in Madison Square Garden on October 26, 1951. Joe was, at that time, thirty-seven years old.

He was a great heavyweight champion, together with John L. Sullivan and Jack Dempsey. Joe avoided no challenger and bragged less than any champion. He was a good-humored man who had pride in what he was. The night Marciano knocked him out, people who didn't know him wept in Madison Square Garden. They wept not for the fighter but for the man.

Jack Johnson

An expression has come into the American vernacular—"the great white hope." It generally means some hero who is called upon to gain the victory for his admirers against great odds, when all else seems lost. Something like a St. George, called upon to slay the dragon.

The man who inspired that expression was a black man—Jack Johnson, who was the first Negro heavyweight champion of the world. In recent times, more Negroes than white men have been heavyweight champions—from Joe Louis through a half-dozen more. White men challenge and occasionally win, and nothing much is thought of it. It was different in Jack Johnson's time.

That's why the expression came into use. The sports world, the "white world" it could almost be said, was looking for "a great white hope" to recapture the most coveted of all boxing titles and restore the white race's confidence in itself. Fortunately, people seldom think that way anymore in sports.

Jack Johnson was born on March 31, 1878, in Galveston, Texas. He was barely in his teens when he was hitching rides around the country on trains. He idled in New York and Boston, and returned to Galveston where he became a dock hand—and also successful with his fists. Someone offered him $25.00 for a four-round fight and he decided that this was the way to make money easily.

He traveled the country, picking up bouts and cash where he could, winning almost all the time. In 1906, he offered his first challenge to the heavyweight champion, Tommy Burns. It was met with disdain. For two years Johnson sought a bout with Burns—unsuccessfully.

Finally, Burns agreed to meet Johnson, who had followed him to Australia. The match was booked for December 26, 1908, in Sydney. Johnson wanted the match so badly that he agreed to almost incredible terms: not only did he accept a small share of the purse, but he agreed to let Burns' manager serve as referee. It didn't matter. Johnson dominated the fight and won by a knockout in the 14th round.

Johnson returned to the United States and polished off a handful of mediocre contenders. The middleweight champion, Stanley Ketchell, challenged him in 1909. Ketchell was acclaimed by many as the best fighter, pound for pound, in the world, but he weighed only 160 pounds, compared to Johnson's 209, and as another great middleweight champion—Ray Robinson—was to find in later years, a good little man cannot beat a good big man. Johnson knocked Ketchell out in the 12th round.

Then began the search for "the great white hope." There seemed to be only one. That man was Jim Jeffries, who had retired undefeated as heavyweight champion in 1904. Jeffries was thirty-five years old in 1910, the year he challenged Johnson, and had to work hard to train down to a fighting weight of 225 pounds. The fight was held under a blazing sun in Reno, Nevada, on the Fourth of July. Jeffries never had a chance. Johnson could not only hit but he had a superb defense, which the former champion never solved. In the 15th round Johnson downed Jeffries with a blazing left hook. The old champ gamely rose and Johnson did it again. The match was over.

Johnson then began to travel around the world. He invested money and lost it. He caroused. Most infuriating of all to many people, he dated white women, one of whom he married. He had brushes with the law. As a champion, though, he remained untouchable.

The life he lived eventually took its toll. In 1915, in Havana, Cuba, he fought the hulking giant, Jess Willard, on another broiling day. In the 25th round, exhausted, Johnson was knocked to the canvas by a blow to the stomach, and lay there, his left arm raised to keep the hot Havana sun out of his eyes. Rumor has it that Johnson's return to the United States

Jack Johnson in one of his many bouts with Jim Flynn.

Because of his superb defense and blazing left hook, Johnson had little trouble knocking out Jim Jeffries.

In 1931, at the age of fifty-three, Johnson returned to the ring to make a barnstorming tour around the United States. Here he poses with "Dynamite" Jackson (right) just before the beginning of their three-round bout.

had been made dependent on the outcome of this fight and that his defeat gave him the opportunity to come back.

Remarkably, Johnson continued to fight and to live high for many years. He fought exhibitions into the 1940's. By then he had no money, just skill and stamina. When he died, on January 10, 1946, it was as a result of injuries received in an automobile accident.

Peter Jackson

Toward the end of the nineteenth century there appeared on the boxing scene the "black prince" of fighters, Peter Jackson. Born in 1861, he stood 6ft.-1in. and weighed 212 pounds. Commentators of his day considered Jackson the most marvelous fighting man of his time. The Earl of Lonsdale, a British nobleman, in the foreword to *Kings of the Ring* by James Butler, wrote: "Personally, I always think that the best man—the quickest, most scientific, and the hardest hitter—that I have ever seen was Peter Jackson, whom as you know, I originally found in San Francisco, in a boxing competition, when I arrived there on my return from the Arctic. But you well know that, and a good deal of his training was done here at Barley Thorpe. The same with little George Dixon, whom I brought home at the same time. . . ."

The Earl of Lonsdale, like many other supporters of artists and celebrities, liked to claim credit for discovering those who went on to achieve fame. Although he claimed to have "found" Jackson, this sailor had won honors as the champion of Australia in 1886 by beating Tom Lees. One writer aboard a sea-going schooner, growing fanciful in describing Jackson, commented: "There was something of the lazy, indolent strength of a great cat about him. The lithe grace of his sprawling limbs, their loose suppleness, the easy way big muscles rippled and ran under the satiny skin as he moved—these things suggested it.

"But not by the wildest flight of fancy with which that Negro deck-hand whiled away the hours could he have foreseen the amazing future that a smiling destiny had already planned for him. How, indeed, could this Peter Jackson, this big and unspoiled colored seaman, guess that he was to become one of the greatest and most scientific boxers in the world, hailed everywhere as the Black Prince of the Ring"?

Peter Jackson landed in Sydney, Australia, and was taught boxing by a man named Larry Foley. Within three years after his first fight, he won the championship of Australia by defeating Tom Lees in thirty rounds. In 1888, Jackson arrived in San Francisco. At this time, nearly all American heavyweights drew the color line very conveniently when Jackson hurled challanges at them, especially John L. Sullivan.

Jackson did manage to get a fight against George Godfrey of Boston and won in nineteen rounds. The California Athletic Club then practically forced Joe McAuliffe, who was considered a coming champion, to meet Jackson, who won the purse of $3,000 in twenty-four rounds. Jackson tried hard to get matches in 1889. Finally, he was matched against Patsy Cardiff in San Francisco who had a six-round draw with John L. Sullivan to his credit. After an easy bout, Jackson knocked Cardiff out in ten rounds. Jackson then went to England and knocked out the highly publicized Jem Smith in two rounds.

On May 21, 1891, James J. Corbett—the great "Gentleman Jim" who was later to take the title away from John L. Sullivan and eventually retire as undefeated heavyweight champion—met Peter Jackson at the California Athletic Club for a purse of $10,000. Corbett at 168 was a young man of few battles; Jackson at 204 was thirty years old and had weathered the blows of a hundred fights. Corbett was beginning his career as a masterful boxer and excellent ring strategist. He skillfully managed to evade the powerful blows of the bigger man, and stayed in the ring by

PETER JACKSON

his ability to side-step, block, clinch and re-treat. After sixty rounds, both men were so exhausted they could hardly meet at the center of the ring; the referee called the fight "no contest" at the end of the sixty-first round —four hours of boxing.

In estimating the character of Peter Jackson, an English contemporary wrote: "I came to know Peter Jackson intimately. I knew him in the days of his greatness, when, sitting on top of the pugilistic world, feted and lionized, he might well have been excused some slight vanity; yet all my memories of him are of a pleasant, softly spoken, modest fellow, utterly unspoiled. . . . He was a charming rarity, unassuming, intelligent, cultured. . . ."

A year after his bout with Corbett, in May 1892, Jackson knocked out Frank Slavin in ten rounds to win the British Empire heavy-weight title. A well-known public figure now, he toured for four years as an actor in *Uncle Tom's Cabin* and other plays and fought boxing exhibitions. He fought as late as 1899 in Australia, where he spent his later years. He died on July 13, 1901 in the province of Queensland, and his grave bears an impressive monument erected by admiring friends.

Tom Molyneux

The first American Negro to fight in a major championship bout was Tom Molyneux, in December 1810, in England. Born in the Georgetown section of Washington, D.C., in 1784, he later lived with the Molyneux family in Virginia, where, of course, he received his surname.

Accounts of that day give some evidence for the belief that Molyneux's father and grandfather had been notable boxers among the plantation slaves. Rumor has it that Tom Molyneux was rewarded for his pugilistic feats by being granted his freedom.

The story of how boxing as a sport began in America is worth telling. Many of the sons of wealthy planters of the southern states were accustomed to travel and to the pursuit of education in England. There they also found time to frequent the sporting places. On their return to America, it was only natural that a plantation's Negro was matched against a fighter of some reputation of another owner as a pastime.

In 1809, Molyneux was living and working around the Catherine Markets in New York City, challenging and defeating all comers in boxing. After traveling on a merchant ship to England, where the fight game was flourishing, Molyneux was taken in tow by Bill Richmond, one of the famous fighters of his day. A squarely built, rugged young man of 5ft.-8½in. and 185 pounds, Molyneux achieved immediate success in England. He scored eight rapid victories, most of them by knockout, and earned a match with the British champion, Tom Cribb.

TOM MOLYNEUX

This was perhaps the first of the great heavyweight championship matches. The fight was held under the "London Prize Ring Rules," which meant, in those days of course, bare knuckle fighting. It was a masterful struggle, and had it not been for the trickery of Cribb's seconds, Molyneux might have been the winner. In the twenty-third round Cribb was unable to return to action within the time limit, but his seconds made a claim of "foul," whereupon the time was extended beyond the thirty seconds and Cribb was finally able to return. Although Molyneux dominated the fight, he became so weakened that at the end of the fortieth round he could not return, and Cribb was declared the victor.

Molyneux fought Cribb again in 1811, and this time lost in eleven rounds. He never really recovered from the effects of his first fight with Cribb. His last bout was in 1815, and he died in Scotland in 1818 at the age of thirty-four.

Bill Richmond

The first Negro American to develop an important reputation in boxing was Bill Richmond, born on Staten Island, now a part of New York City. He was taken as a boy to England by Lord Percy, the Duke of Northumberland, in 1777. There he worked as a cabinetmaker. Because of his physique and fighting capabilities, he became a valet to Lord Camelford, a nobleman who had great fondness for the sports of turf, pit and ring. Richmond weighed only 168 pounds, but he fought many men of different weights. In a career that spanned about a dozen years, Richmond fought fourteen major bouts, winning twelve and losing two.

His last recognized fight was in 1815, but until he died he was idolized by all classes of his day. His rooms and hotel in Whitcomb Street, Haymarket, in the heart of London, were highly patronized by the nobility and gentry of the city. That he was well known to the poet Lord Byron is attested by the references to him in the *Life and Journals of Lord Byron,* which was edited by the Irish poet Thomas Moore.

Richmond's athletic form, his civility, self-control and temperate habits made him respected by all who knew him; even a king had invited him to court, the story goes. One of the first writers of the magazine *Fistiana* said: "Richmond may be pointed to as one of the men who never lost sight of the situation in which he was placed in society. In the elevation of the moment, he always bore in mind that, however the Corinthian fancier may connect himself with milling, there are times when he has a different character to support, and must not be intruded upon. Would that many of our white-faced boxers would take a hint on this point from Bill Richmond, the Black."

There was, in those days, no way that observers of the sporting scene could avoid assessing a Negro athlete except in terms of his color. Considering that ever-present attitude, such tributes are impressive. Respected in life, Richmond was greatly mourned when he died in London in 1829 at the age of sixty-six.

John Henry Lewis

When Joe Louis defended his world championship in 1938 against John Henry Lewis, it was the first time in thirty-five years that two Negroes had fought for the heavyweight championship of the world. (The previous time was in 1913 in Paris, when Jack Johnson stopped Jim Johnson.) Lewis was one of those boxers unlucky enough to have grown into a light heavyweight, just short of the heavyweight class where lies much of the glory and much of the money in the boxing world.

John Henry, one of the great fighters of the era just preceding World War II, was also one of the finest gentlemen in the game. A man who could trace distant relationship to Tom

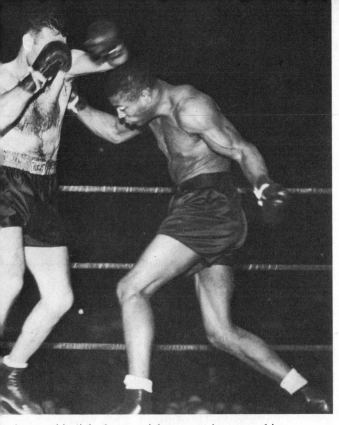

Lewis won his light heavyweight crown in a smashing fifteen-round victory over Bob Olin in 1935.

Along with being one of the finest fighters in boxing, John Henry Lewis was a true gentleman.

Al Gainer receives a short right jab from Lewis near the end of their fourteen-round bout, won by Lewis.

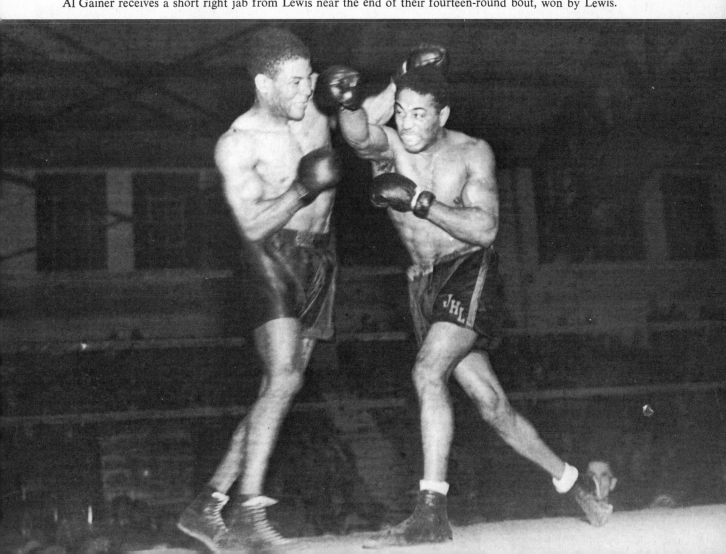

Molyneux, the first American heavyweight champion, Lewis was born on May 6, 1914 in Los Angeles, and was raised in Phoenix, Arizona. His father, also a fighter of some merit, trained John Henry.

Until John Henry met Joe Louis, he had never been knocked out in ninety-nine fights. He had won forty-eight times by knockout, thirty-nine by decision, lost seven and fought five to draws. One of those victories was over Jim Braddock, who later became heavyweight champion before losing the world title to Joe Louis.

John Henry's career extended back to 1930 and had been fought mainly as a light heavyweight. He managed to make 180 pounds for the bout against Joe Louis, while Joe scaled 200. It was generally conceded that John Henry's only hope of winning was if he could avoid Joe's lethal punches and outbox him. But Joe Louis was an experienced and able champion.

Furthermore, Joe wanted to get this bout over as quickly as possible. Against Max Schmeling he had wanted to do the same, but for a different reason. Schmeling was a hated enemy, one who should be wiped out quickly, to prove that he was an unequal foe. But facing John Henry, Joe wanted to end things fast so that he would not have to punish his friend any more than was absolutely necessary to win the match.

Early in the first round, Joe slammed a straight left into John Henry's face and followed up with a flurry of right cross punches that connected for three knockdowns. In less than a single round, the bout was stopped and recorded as a technical knockout. In his one hundredth fight, John Henry had been knocked out for the first time. The bout was good to John Henry financially, netting a purse that was big for him—$17,000. But it was the beginning of the end of his successful boxing career.

Joe Walcott

The first Negro to hold the welterweight championship of the world was a man with a name that was to live again in boxing circles almost a half-century later. The man was Joe Walcott, no relation to the fighter who was later to win the world heavyweight title—"Jersey Joe" Walcott (the later champion's real name was Arnold Cream).

The original Joe Walcott was a worthy champion whom Nat Fleischer of *Ring* magazine once called the greatest welterweight of them all. Born on April 7, 1872, Walcott was a tiny man in height, 5ft.-1½ in., but ruggedly built and he fought best at 142 pounds. He had powerful shoulders and arms, unusually strong, and was a rugged puncher. He fought men of all weights, including both middleweight and heavyweight championship contenders, and as a result often went into a fight with a significant handicap.

First a sailor and later a professional wrestler, he fought his first professional match in 1890, after winning the New England amateur lightweight and middleweight titles. On the way to the welterweight title, he beat the Australian Dan Creedon four times in the same year. In a major stepping stone, he knocked out Joe Choynski in seven rounds on February 22, 1900, in New York City.

Joe won the welterweight championship on December 18, 1901 in Toronto, Canada, when he knocked out Rube Fern in five rounds. He lost it to Dixie Kid on April 30, 1904 in San Francisco, when the fight was stopped by a foul in the 12th round. Later he and Dixie Kid fought a draw. When Kid gained weight and was no longer eligible for the welterweight class, Walcott reclaimed the title but lost it on a fifteen-round decision to Honey Mellody in 1906. He fought until 1911 before retiring. He died after an automobile accident in 1935.

Joe Gans

In an era when great Negro boxers seemed to abound, Joe Gans was an absolute standout. Born in Philadelphia November 25, 1874, Gans grew into a natural lightweight, fighting best when he weighed in the 130's. But he fought anyone at any weight.

Gans is another among a handful of fighters reputed to be the best at his weight of all time, perhaps, pound for pound, the best fighter of all time. Benny Leonard, one of the great lightweights of a later day, referred to Gans as the "Old Master." He was king of the lightweights from 1901 to 1908. (The lightweight class, first established in 1876, had a 133-pound limit until 1909, when it was changed to 135 pounds.)

In 1899, Gans defeated George McFadden in twenty-five rounds at the Broadway Athletic Club in New York. This fight brought Gans into the limelight, for McFadden had ended the fighting career of Kid Lavigne, who was a terror to lightweights. In 1901, Gans sought a chance at Frank Erne for the lightweight title. Erne tried to evade the contest, but finally, at Fort Erie, Ontario, on May 12, 1901, Gans knocked Erne out in the first round. Joe went on to knock off top contenders like Willie Fitzgerald, Jimmy Britt and a host of others. He twice outpointed Jack Sullivan, a middleweight of considerable reputation.

Two of the never-to-be-forgotten fights in the career of the Old Master were with his final conqueror, Battling Nelson. Gans does not need an alibi, yet it is a fact that when Gans met Nelson in the evening of his career his system was pretty well weakened by infection. On September 3, 1906, at Goldfield, Nevada, Nelson, the young, vigorous, rugged Dane met Gans for the first time. For many rounds the Old Master side-stepped, jabbed and countered. His blows were clean. But the tow-headed Dane kept coming in, swinging wildly and continuously. Some of the blows off

Nelson had Gans in trouble but ring strategy and the use of a lightning left kept the battler at bay. The outstanding incident of the fight that reeked of unfairness was the refusal of the referee to end the fight much earlier than he did. At least three serious fouls occurred prior to the end of the fight that justified the victory to Gans. Nelson had committed fouls in most categories.

In the 18th, 26th and 34th rounds, Gans had Nelson athwart the ropes, but in each instance the bell saved the durable Dane. Youth and vigor brought Nelson back at the beginning of each new round. Finally, in the 42nd round, Gans had Nelson in trouble. A flurry of jabs and hooks was putting an end to Nelson when he committed so palpable a foul that the referee motioned him back to his corner and awarded the fight to Gans. Observers said that Gans had won every round on points.

In 1907, Gans continued his mastery of the lightweight division by knocking out Kid Herman and Britt. Then, on the Fourth of July, 1908. Gans was matched again against Nelson, this time in San Francisco. It took the rugged, yellow-haired Danish boy but seventeen rounds to register a knockout—but against only a shell of the Gans of old. In 1910, trying to recover from a scourge of disease, Gans went to Prescott, Arizona. He returned to Baltimore, his home, when it was clear that his condition was incurable. He died August 13, 1910.

George Dixon

What Peter Jackson represented among big men in the nineteenth century, George Dixon represented among the small. Five feet, three inches tall, he fought as a bantamweight and as a featherweight—the first Negro to win championships in each class. He remained a champion for eleven years, fighting regularly.

Dixon was one of the few Americans to win in England. In 1890 he challenged the English

Joe Gans

Joe Gans (right) and Joe Walcott trade punches in their 1904 bout.

Joe Walcott (right) in one of his fights against Dixie Kidd.

featherweight champion, Nunc Wallace. The fight was for a purse of 400 pounds sterling (then, about $2,000) and took place at the Pelican Club in London on June 17, 1890. Dixon knocked out Wallace in eighteen rounds. During his stay in London, he lodged at the best hotels and trained in the beautiful countryside. There was much comment about Dixon's stylish dress and cultured manner, which led to cordial relations between Wallace and Dixon—rather unusual for fighters.

One of Dixon's finest fights was his early battle with Cal McCarthy. They met in Boston in February 1890 and for seventy rounds matched skill and strength. McCarthy was stronger but Dixon more clever and agile at defense. At the end of the 67th round, neither boxer was able to deliver a punch with sting. The referee then announced that if either lad was on his feet at the end of the 70th round, he would call it a draw, and thus it ended.

Finally, after a number of record-making fights—including the bout in England against Nunc Wallace—little George was matched again with Cal McCarthy for the championship of the featherweight division, although both were really bantamweights. They met in Troy, New York, on March 31, 1891, with McCarthy the favorite. Unlike the first, non-championship melee, this one took only twenty-two rounds to end. McCarthy had lost some of his earlier stamina, so it was said, by letting up in training, and Dixon was able to meet his wild charges and outpunch him. Only once, in the 21st round, when he was near a point of desperation, did McCarthy battle as he did in earlier fights. He swarmed all over Dixon with rights and lefts and administered real punishment. But Dixon's boxing skill and well-conditioned body staved off the dying attack. In the next round Dixon came up fresh, measured his opponent carefully, and knocked him out to gain the featherweight crown.

In his autobiography, published in 1893, when Dixon was in his prime, he wrote: "I was born in Halifax, Nova Scotia, in 1870, and when about eight years of age my parents moved to Boston, where I still reside. I received a public school education, having attended a Halifax school for two years and a Boston school for three years. When about 14 years of age I secured employment with a Boston photographer, and while there engaged, I first began to learn how to spar. I witnessed an exhibition one night at the Boston Music Hall which was given by two local athletes, and the next day I purchased a book on boxing from which I gained much valuable information.

"It would require too much space to give the name of each opponent and the result of each contest in which I have figured during my career, so I shall endeavor to give an idea of my record by stating that I have won or drawn every contest in which I have engaged with two exceptions. The first, which was to have been to a finish, was with George Wright of Canada, whom I met at Boston about six years ago, and he was declared winner on a foul. The other bout which was decided against me was with Billy Plimmer of England, who was given a decision on points in a four-round glove contest which took place at Madison Square Garden, New York City, a few nights after I defeated Eddie Pierce. . . . During my career I have won more than $100,000 in stakes, purses, and gate receipts. I have taken part in more than 500 four-round bouts and about 40 contests to a finish."

A fancy dresser and a pleasant companion, Dixon was widely popular, both in and out of the ring. Nat Fleischer, long-time editor of *Ring* magazine, wrote: "The darling of the fighters, they called him, and that is what he was to thousands of American fight fans who adored him for his fighting qualities. America has had its fistic heroes—John L. Sullivan, Jim Corbett, Bob Fitzsimmons, Jim Jeffries, Joe Gans, Jack Dempsey, and Joe Louis, among others—but I doubt that there ever was a pugilist who was as popular during his entire ca-

George Dixon

Sam Langford

Joe Jeannette

Harry Willis

reer as was 'Little Chocolate.' Even in the light of the achievements of John L. Sullivan, the critics of his day . . . referred to 'Little Chocolate' as the greatest fighter of all time."

Dixon's last great fight was with "Terrible Terry" McGovern. Despite the fact that Dixon was a relatively old man, having kept the championship for nearly eight years, he fought a memorable battle on January 9, 1900 in the old Broadway Athletic Club. McGovern had a stiff fight for eight rounds and then he dropped Dixon. George sank to the canvas, rose at the count of nine, then absorbed a crashing left and right that took away his championship forever.

Four without Glory—
Joe Jeannette, Sam McVey, Sam Langford, Harry Wills

No account of the Negro in boxing in the early years of the twentieth century would be complete without drawing upon the records of four men, as valiant as any boxers the world has ever witnessed. America's color line prevented them from basking in the spotlight of fame that many less able warriors have earned. Their names were Joe Jeannette, Sam McVey, Sam Langford and Harry Wills.

These were men whom champions feared but most of their celebrated fights were against each other. Joe Jeannette was born in 1881, stood 6ft.-1in. tall and weighed 195 pounds. Sam McVey was born in California in 1885, stood 5ft.-11in. and weighed 205 pounds. Harry Wills was born in 1892, was an impressive 6ft.-3in. and weighed 215 pounds. Sam Langford was born in 1886; he was only 5ft.-6½in., but weighed 200 pounds, a man of incredible physical strength.

They called Sam Langford the "Boston Tar Baby" and he would fight anyone, anytime,

anywhere. He fought more than 250 recorded bouts, winning about 150 of them. His spectacular career lasted from 1902 to 1923. Later he went blind and lived alone and almost penniless in a single room in Boston. Yet those who knew him in his final days found him calm, soft-spoken and gentle, never bitter about what he might have accomplished had not the color line dominated the boxing scene. He was always appreciative of anything anyone did for him.

Jeannette won seventy-four bouts in his long career, lost six and fought fifty-six to no decision—events that could not be settled without a knockout. He fought Langford ten times, Jack Johnson six times, and also fought against McVey and Wills. McVey won forty-seven fights, numbering among his victims both Langford and Jeannette. He was knocked out by Johnson, Langford and Wills as late as 1918, when he was thirty-three years old.

Harry Wills was the master boxer of his day, an especially remarkable feat for a man of his size. He fought Sam Langford the astonishing total of fourteen times. He won over Langford, McVey and Jeannette during his career and was once knocked out by Sam Langford. He is credited with thirty-one knockouts.

Wills was possessed of a remarkable windmill style, flailing punches from all angles but in a continuous and consistent flow. To someone who had not fought him his style was a puzzle. He fought everyone he could get a bout with, but there was one man who would not enter a ring with him. That man was Jack Dempsey, who found the color line a convenient excuse. There were many authorities in the boxing world convinced that Dempsey would not have been able to handle Harry Wills, but the world was never to know just how good he really was—or how good were McVey, Jeannette and the great Langford, either.

Howard P. Drew

Kenny Washington

Wilmeth Sidat-Singh

Jesse Owens

CHAPTER THREE

Race to Glory

NOT every field of athletics was closed to Negroes before the modern era. Boxing, of course, was the best example of an integrated professional sport. Its equivalent in the amateur world was track and field. Almost as long as there has been organized competition, the Negro has been at least a part of it. As usual, the Negro athlete carried a disadvantage. Only a few had the benefit of the same kind of equipment and coaching as their white opponents; they usually had to be better to succeed. Yet many did.

It took awhile for recognition to come to Negroes in track and field competition. Before World War I, Howard Drew was classed as one of the world's best sprinters. But it was not until Eddie Tolan and Ralph Metcalfe dominated the sprints in the 1932 Olympic Games at Los Angeles that Negroes reached the top of the track world. The supreme glory came four years later at the Olympics in Berlin, when Jesse Owens, the lean Ohioan, ran all over Hitler's argument for a "master race"—practically on Hitler's doorstep.

In other sports, recognition was more difficult to achieve. Few Negroes received the opportunity to attend college, which cut down their chances to compete at the outset. And even when they did, many college teams from the North withheld Negro players from their line-ups when they faced southern schools— a situation that would be unheard of today. Still, as far back as World War I, Fritz Pollard at Brown and Paul Robeson at Rutgers were All-American football players. Just before World War II, both "Brud" Holland at Cornell and Kenny Washington at UCLA achieved similar stature.

For all the difficulties, the history of the Negro in amateur sports in this country reaches well back into the nineteenth century. The first athletic director at Harvard, the nation's most prestigious school, was a Negro. A bicycle rider could achieve recognition. The story is checkered, yet often inspiring.

Jesse Owens

By the summer of 1936, the German people had become convinced that they were the "master race." They knew it because their leader, Adolf Hitler, told them so. By coincidence, the Olympic Games were scheduled in Berlin that year, the capital of this nation ready for war, and the Germans had no doubt that they were about to prove their superiority on the athletic fields. No one could beat the blond-haired, blue-eyed Aryans, so they believed.

But the Germans were wrong. Their best young men were beaten by a lot of youths from countries that did not want to conquer the world, only to live in peace and freedom. Some of these young men were Americans, and of those many were Negroes. There was no one, however, to compare with a young man named Jesse Owens.

The day the Olympics opened, before 100,000 people in Berlin's new stadium, a group of Nazi brown-shirts booed the American team. On the first day of competition, a Negro from California named Cornelius Johnson broke the Olympic record for the high jump, but Hitler, who had congratulated all the other winners, walked out of his box five minutes before Johnson was awarded his gold medal.

So Jesse Owens knew the atmosphere he was in. "I wasn't paying any attention to Hitler," he said later. "You're running against the fastest guys in the world." By the time the Olympics had ended, the whole world was paying attention not to Hitler, but to the amazing Owens.

The most dramatic event of the games was, of course, the 100-meter dash, the one that crowns its winner as the "world's fastest human." "You stand out there," Jesse remembered, "and you feel like your legs can't carry the weight of your body. Your stomach's not there."

Yet on that day in Berlin Jesse Owens, as usual, was the first man to toe the mark. "So you get down there and here's this nervous tension. But the gun serves like a dry-cell battery. When you pour water into it, you get power." Jesse, teammate Ralph Metcalfe, another great Negro sprinter, and three-time Olympian Frank Wykoff all broke perfectly to the roar of 100,000 voices.

At the halfway mark, Owens led Wykoff by a yard. Wykoff made a closing rush but Jesse stood him off. The effort sapped Wykoff, and he fell back to fourth place at the tape. Owens hit the finish line a yard in front of Metcalfe in second place. The track was not fast, but he had tied the world record at 10.3 seconds. "I considered this the greatest moment of my career," Owens said later.

The morning after that, Jesse almost ruined another of his fond Olympic dreams by lack of concentration in the trials for the broad jump. He needed to jump only 23 feet, 5½ inches to qualify, which was easy for him. But on the first of his three tries, he romped down the runway and kept on running through the pit instead of jumping; he had thought it was a practice run. That was a foul. On his second try, he went past the take-off board, fouling again. If he fouled a third time, he was eliminated in the preliminary competition—in an event that he was supposed to win without any trouble.

At this moment, a handsome young German named Luz Long walked over to him. Long was a star, a man who could beat almost anyone except Jesse, a man that Hitler considered his "white hope" against the American Negro. Long put his arm on Owens' shoulder and said:

"You should be able to qualify with your eyes closed. Why don't you draw a line a few inches in back of the board and aim at making your take-off from there? You'll be sure not to foul and you ought to be able to jump far enough to qualify."

Jesse took the advice and qualified easily. Later that day, he won the broad jump with an Olympic record leap of more than 26 feet, 5 inches. While Hitler watched with furious stare, Long warmly congratulated Owens. The two became friends during the rest of the games. But they were never to meet again. Long became a German soldier and was killed while fighting in Sicily.

The third event at the Olympics for Jesse Owens was the 200-meter dash. He won that in a new Olympic record time of 20.7 seconds. Then he ran the first leg on the American 400-meter relay team, with Metcalfe, Draper and Wykoff following. Owens gave the United States a lead it never relinquished, and the team set an Olympic and world record of 39.8 seconds. That gave Jesse Owens four gold medals.

For achievement under pressure, that sterling performance by Owens in the Berlin Olympics could be considered the greatest ever in sports. It was, of course, only part of a career that led sportswriters to vote him the greatest track-and-field athlete of all time.

Some athletes catch the public fancy and some do not. Jesse Owens did and his fame has endured. His explanation was characteristically modest: "I came along at a time when images were being formed. The Negro people needed an image and Joe Louis and I came along. It gives you a real sense of responsibility to your fellow men. It's something that you don't forget."

Jesse Owens was born into the family of an Alabama sharecropper, and he worked in the cotton fields at the age of six. His real name was James Cleveland Owens, but, in the southern style, he was called J.C.

After the family had moved to Cleveland, where his father became a laborer in a steel mill, J.C. was asked his name by his grammar school teacher. "J.C., ma'am," he replied in an Alabama drawl. "Jesse?" she asked. The boy, worried about correcting the teacher, said,

"Yes, ma'am," and from that day on, he was Jesse Owens.

It became obvious quickly that Jesse Owens could run fast. He entered his first formal competition at the age of thirteen and lost because of a bad start. But he soon was such a star that at East Technical High School in Cleveland he set a world scholastic record of 9.4 seconds for the 100-yard dash.

Jesse enrolled at Ohio State University with no athletic scholarship, merely a job promised. He was married at eighteen and by the next year had an infant daughter. His typical school day was like this: he would be up by 6:30 A.M. and at his first class by eight. Classes continued until almost three. Then he raced to the stadium to work out on the track for an hour or so. At five, he reported to his $150-a-month job as night elevator operator at the state office building. He would study every free minute while on the job, and also on the trolley taking him to and from work. By one in the morning he was home, perhaps to study or to catch five hours of rest, before starting the cycle over again.

Athletically, the most important thing that happened to Jesse at Ohio State was that he came under the tutelage of Larry Snyder, considered one of the nation's premier coaches for three decades. Snyder worked on Owens' starts, his form, his training routine. Added to Jesse's ability it was an effective partnership.

In the spring of 1933, Jesse Owens was already recognized as one of the world's best. Then one day, involved in a prank with some friends, Owens fell down a flight of stairs and injured his spine. It was the week before the Big Ten track-and-field meet at Ann Arbor, Michigan. Owens hardly practiced at all that week. On the night before the meet, he slept with chemical heating pads on his back and stomach, and spent the morning in a tubful of water as hot as he could stand. His back hurt so much that he was afraid he couldn't bend over for the start of a race.

Jesse Owens displays the form that took him to the Olympics.

At Berlin, Owens won the 100-meter dash in 10.3 seconds, equaling the world record for that distance.

After heeding advice from Germany's Luz Long, Jesse Owens sets a new Olympic record in the broad jump.

With his Olympic days behind him, Owens devotes much of his time to underprivileged youth in Chicago.

Jesse Owens takes a moment to relax in his office beside some of his most cherished awards.

But that May day, despite his injuries, Jesse Owens gave the greatest performance in a single day in the history of track athletics. First, in the broad jump, he decided to make only one try to avoid wasting his strength. He leaped 26 feet, 8¼ inches—a world record.

Then he sprinted 100 yards in 9.4 seconds, tying his own world record. Next he ran the 220-yard dash in 20.3 seconds, establishing another world record. Finally, he skimmed over the 220-yard low hurdles in 22.6 seconds, still another world record. He had set three world records and tied one in a single day. No one has come close to that performance, before or since.

From that moment on, Jesse's goal was the Berlin Olympics and, of course, the whole world believed in him after that. But almost as soon as that glory in Berlin was over, the taste turned slightly bitter. The ruling officials of American amateur sports, partly to raise funds and partly to give themselves some added vacation stops, booked the American Olympic team all over Europe. Owens, of course, was the stellar attraction. Competing day after day, traveling constantly, eating mainly sandwiches, Owens' weight fell from 138 pounds to 125. One day in London, Larry Snyder heard that the officials wanted Jesse to go to Sweden for another meet. Snyder would not let his protege go, insisting he return to the United States for a rest. So Owens was barred from amateur athletics after that.

This didn't matter much for Jesse had done everything he could do as an amateur. But track is not like football or baseball, where a star can cash in quickly. Professional races are practically non-existent. He had not much more going for him than his name.

For awhile, Jesse fronted for a touring dance band, although he didn't know a note of music. He tried a dry-cleaning business but found that dull. He went on tour with Negro baseball teams and ran exhibitions—against motorcycles and horses. "You always tried to do that with a certain amount of dignity," he said later. "You spoke to the people first and told them what you were trying to do." Given a 50-yard head start, he used to beat thoroughbred horses in the 100-yard dash.

Although these were still Depression years, Owens made money, sometimes as much as $1100 a week. He continued this periodic traveling until one day in 1949, when he was almost thirty-nine years old. "I was at the point where I hated a track suit," he said. "I didn't want to put on the shoes any more. When you get to that point, it's time to quit. I was getting tired. I had no family life."

So Owens flew home to Chicago, canceled all his exhibitions and settled down. He worked for a clothing firm, in public relations. Then he founded his own public relations firm and turned it into a success. He also became secretary of the Illinois Athletic Commission, succeeding his old friend and sprinting opponent, Ralph Metcalfe.

He and his wife raised three daughters. The oldest daughter, Gloria, was the first Negro to be elected Homecoming Queen at Ohio State University. And when her father returned to his alma mater for that Homecoming football game and shared in the roars of approval from 82,000 fans in the horseshoe stadium where he had achieved so much glory, it was a very proud moment indeed.

Howard P. Drew

The man who conquers all others in the 100-yard or 100-meter dash is traditionally known as "the world's fastest human." This title was held in the 1930's by Jesse Owens and in the 1960's by Bob Hayes, but the first Negro to be accorded this accolade was a slender youngster who competed before World War I. His name was Howard P. Drew.

Drew began his noteworthy career as an athlete at Springfield High School in Massachusetts. In both 1912 and 1913 he won the national Amateur Athletic Union championship for 100 yards. In 1913, he added the 220-yard dash title. The next year, representing the University of Southern California, Drew became co-holder with Arthur Duffey of Georgetown of the world's record for the 100-yard dash—9.6 seconds. Duffey later admitted that he had taken money for competing in track meets, and his honors were taken away. That left Drew alone as the champion runner of the world for many years.

Drew was always a consistent performer. He seldom broke prematurely from the mark. But he was a fast starter and came through in his final drive with a remarkable burst of speed.

In Drew's day newspaper reports began to take on the colorful character we know today. Wrote the *New York Tribune*: "It seems incredible that a man running without fear of life and not the slightest desire to catch a train can impel himself to such prodigious speed. The sight of Drew hurtling along inevitably suggests a concealed motor. Anybody who saw Drew run last night cannot doubt his supremacy among American sprinters."

The *New York Gazette* said: "Alvah Meyer of the Irish-American Athletic Club was once credited with running 100 yards on a board floor in Buffalo in 9.8 seconds, but no one believes he ever did it. He doesn't believe so himself. After seeing Drew perform last night, he said, 'That beat my performance all hollow. Drew is the greatest sprinter in the world. He's in a class by himself.' "

Drew competed—incredible though it may seem now—without benefit of spiked shoes, but was assured by the Amateur Athletic Union that his records would pass muster. About one of his performances, a New York paper reported: "The colored sprinter placed himself once more on the top of the athletic ladder by winning the 70-yard invitation race, which brought together four of the best sprinters in the world. So great was the crowd which wit-

nessed the sports . . . that the doors of the Garden were closed by order of the Fire Department long before nine o'clock."

Mike Murphy, who coached the United States team at the 1912 Olympic Games in Stockholm, said of Drew: "Never in all my life have I seen any sprinter with such wonderful leg action as Drew. Why, his legs fly back and forth just like pistons. He gets away as fast as any man I ever saw, and he has a wonderful finish. Trainers and experts say that he has the quickest start of any man ever seen upon the track. Yet he is so cool and collected that he never beats the gun."

That was the judgment of an Olympic coach, but Drew was never able to win in the Olympics. In 1912, he was unable to compete because of an injury, and by 1920 he had passed his prime. World War I forced the cancellation of the 1916 Olympic Games, thus depriving Drew of the opportunity to prove to everyone that he was "the world's fastest human."

Ralph Metcalfe

The career of Ralph Metcalfe is one of the most inspiring and, at the same time, unfortunate in the annals of sport. Three times he earned a place on the U.S. Olympic team. In Los Angeles, in 1932, he missed out in a dead heat for the 100-meter championship with Eddie Tolan, and the gold medal that went with it. He was again second to Tolan in the 200 meters in a finish almost as close. In 1936, at Berlin, after he had passed his prime as a sprinter, this three-time Olympian narrowly missed snatching away the 100-meter championship from Jesse Owens. Thus Ralph Metcalfe never won an individual sprint title in the Olympics, but his career was nonetheless one of the most thrilling of all time.

Metcalfe was born on May 20, 1910, in Atlanta, Georgia. As a child he moved with his mother to Chicago. He graduated from

Howard P. Drew

Ralph Metcalfe

Ralph Metcalfe (extreme right) breaks the tape to win the 100-yard dash in the 1932 Drake Relays.

Tilden Technical High School in 1930 and entered Marquette University in Milwaukee. He was an earnest student and despite his success as a runner he retained an attractive modesty in speech and manners. His popularity and ability brought him the enviable honor of captain of his track team and membership in Alpha Sigma Mu, the only all-university honor society at Marquette. His name was listed often as a record holder on the Amateur Athletic Union and the National Collegiate Athletic Association honor rolls. Upon graduation, he joined the physical education department of Xavier College in Louisiana, and discovered and developed young men who later achieved national fame.

An outstanding sports commentator, writing in 1932, said of Metcalfe: "The South Side Chicago collegian first gained note as a budding track immortal in the National Junior Championship meet held in Pittsburgh during August 1930. After two years of unbroken triumphs in school-boy competition, he came to the National Junior Championship in 1930 as a member of the Chase Athletic Club of Chicago. In his first day of competition, he won the 100-yard dash in 9.7 seconds, setting a new record. The next day, competing in the National Senior Championship 220-yard dash, he placed fourth among the cream of America's sprinting crop. From this moment on, Metcalfe's track career has been dazzling. He has run and won great races against the best competition in the world; he has carried his challenge to the enemy by going abroad and defeating the best European track stars."

In the National Collegiate meet in Chicago on June 11, 1932, two months before the Olympics, Metcalfe—in one of the most sensational individual performances in track history—shattered the world records for 220 yards, 100 and 200 meters, and tied Eddie Tolan's world's record for that year of 9.5 seconds for the 100 yards. It was the kind of day that Jesse Owens was to have for Ohio

State in 1935. But although Owens went on to Olympic triumphs after his big record-setting day, Metcalfe was to just barely miss a similar achievement in the 1932 Olympics.

Following the tremendous performances of Metcalfe and Tolan in the 1932 Olympics, there was much speculation as to which was the greatest sprinter. One commentator of the time paid tribute to Metcalfe thus: "Tolan and Metcalfe are the two greatest sprinters ever to drive spikes into cinders. It is impossible to determine which one is the better. In spite of bespectacled Eddie's two victories over Metcalfe in the Olympics, the latter is hailed by many of the experts and legions of track-lovers as Tolan's superior."

Eulace Peacock

Although he was eclipsed by his great contemporary, Jesse Owens, a young man named Eulace Peacock was a world-class sprinter in the 1930's who could handle anyone in competition—sometimes even Owens. Peacock had an unusual amount of hard luck, mostly because of an injured tendon. Except for that, he might have rivaled Owens throughout their careers.

One of the best track athletes ever to come from the East, Peacock was a product of Temple University. He was a standout in the sprints, jumps and the pentathlon. As late as 1939 he was still winning, running under the colors of the Shore Athletic Club of Elberon, New Jersey.

A contemporary description of the 1935 track season tells something about Peacock's ability: "Blinding speed set the tempo for track and field in 1935 as Jesse Owens and Eulace Peacock, sprinters extraordinary, engaged in a series of magnificent duels on straightaways and in jumping pit. After long years of dominance by the milers, track turned to the dash men for its most thrilling and startling performances.

Eulace Peacock

A familiar sight: Peacock first across the finish

Temple's Eulace Peacock wins the 100-meter race on the second day of the 1935 Penn Relays.

"On May 25, the lithe and sinewy Owens, satin smooth in his running, broke three world's records and tied another in one of the most astounding exploits in the annals of sport. Apparently there was no question about the world's fastest human after that. The 21-year-old Ohio State sophomore added to his stature in the National Collegiate Athletic Association championships. Then came the national Amateur Athletic Union title games in the sun-drenched stadium at Lincoln, Nebraska, in July.

"And another Negro sensation went rocketing right past Owens. Peacock, a sophomore at Temple University, had seen the flaming scarlet jersey of Ohio's Jesse lead him to victory all season long. This time, Peacock rode the wings of a breeze to an upset victory in the 100-meter dash, clocked in the world's record time of 10.2 seconds. (Unfortunately, the following wind caused the judges of the meet to disallow the record.)

"The spectators gasped in wonder, only to have Peacock pull them out of their seats once more by beating the 'unconquerable' Owens in the broad jump as well, with a magnificent leap of 26 feet, 3 inches, also better than accepted figures. And a few days later Peacock proved that his sprint triumph was no freak by vanquishing again the Buckeye Bullet in another race.

"There they are, then, Owens and Peacock, or Peacock and Owens, whichever is the correct order. And these two disciples of speed led the advance of America's track and field athletes into the Olympic year with the United States as well fortified as it ever was for stirring deeds at Berlin."

But the next year came, and with it the Olympics—and Peacock was not there to match talents with Owen. A tricky, troublesome tendon kept him from winning a berth on the Olympic team, and he was unable to compete for the medals and glory that might have been his.

Eddie Tolan

In August of 1932, a Negro's name made front-page headlines in newspapers around the world. Eddie Tolan, the phantom flier of Detroit, raced another Negro American, Ralph Metcalfe of Marquette University, to a photo-finish in the finals of the Olympic 100-meter dash at Los Angeles. It was the first time a Negro had won a gold medal, while also setting a new world record.

Here is a contemporary description of the circumstances and competition at Los Angeles in 1932: "The 100-meter race in the 1932 Olympics was about to be run in the Los Angeles Memorial Coliseum before 60,000 expectant lovers of track athletics. Of the six entrants in the finals of this event, three represented America: Eddie Tolan, formerly of the University of Michigan, Ralph Metcalfe of Marquette, and George Simpson, once crack dash star of Ohio State, completed the home trio. These six human rockets toed the mark; one of them was nervous, he broke, and the tension was momentarily relieved. The start was made again. The sharp bark of the gun. Six human forms catapulted toward their objective like bats from a cave. Metcalfe was last and seemingly out of it. At fifty meters, little Tolan's piston legs brought him into the lead. In the next split-second, a huge brown form, gaining momentum like a falling body, came out of the ruck. The Marquette meteor, a slower starter than Tolan, caught him at ninety meters and it seemed as though he would flash across the finish first. But the end of this epochal dash was as nice a dead heat between America's two premier track stars as was ever run. The timer's electric clock, however, caught the Michigan marvel's chest a hair's breadth ahead of Metcalfe at the end.

"In the winning of this race, Tolan not only brought the 100-meter title back to America after a lapse of twelve years, but he also established a new Olympic record of 10.3 seconds,

Eddie Tolan

Among the American sprinters for the 1932 Olympics Games were George Simpson, Ralph Metcalfe and Eddie Tolan.

Tolan breaks the tape ahead of Frank Wyckoff of Southern California to win the 100-meter dash at Vancouver.

which lowered the world mark set by Percy Williams of Canada."

That was one of the two races that make up the magic sprint double. The other was the 200-meter dash. In that one, Tolan and Metcalfe ran another thrilling struggle, again surpassing all the other sprinters of the world—and again with Eddie Tolan squeezing home first—to set another Olympic record, 21.2 seconds.

Eddie Tolan was a champion from the time he began interscholastic competition at Cass High School in Detroit. In later life the walls of one room of Tolan's home were covered with medals and trophies adorned the furniture. In more than three hundred races, Tolan was defeated only seven times. With no other amateur laurels to covet, Tolan entered the professional field and showed his flying heels to all competitors here and abroad. Not only did he contend in athletics; he battled prejudices all along the way. On a trip to Europe with white runners he was insulted repeatedly, but he never let the slights and insults keep him from training carefully and running in victory form.

He later served the city of Detroit in a variety of administrative tasks, always in an efficient, modest way. He had one chief regret. His early ambition was to become a physician, but the strenuous work of glorifying his college, his race and America made the attainment of his cherished hope impossible. However, not many men in modern times have brought more satisfaction to the hearts of Americans than did Eddie Tolan, one of the most modest and best-loved heroes of the cinder path.

A. Molineaux Hewlett

College athletics covers a relatively brief span in American life, but Negroes have been a part of it for a surprisingly long time. Prior to 1870, college athletics consisted largely of boating. There was some baseball, but little interest in track and field; the first football game was not played until 1869, and basketball was not invented until 1891.

The first important name in Negro college athletic history was not, as might be expected, a star athlete—but an official, an administrator. The first director of physical education at the oldest of all American universities, Harvard, was a Negro—A. Molineaux Hewlett.

Hewlett was employed as an instructor and director of the first Harvard gymnasium, built in 1859, and remained in charge until he died in 1871. The *Harvard Magazine* of October 1859 had this to say of him:

"Meanwhile, most fortunately, the services of Professor A. Molineaux Hewlett had been secured. He came with an experience in gymnastic training of fourteen years, the last five of which had been devoted most acceptably to the citizens of Worcester. By the fine accommodations of the new building, and under the admirable system of the new Professor, a fresh impulse was given to physical training, which, contrary to prediction, has been on the increase. The uniform courtesy of the Professor, and the personal interest which he takes in the exercises, keep alive the interest of his pupils and makes the hours spent in the Gymnasium among the pleasantest."

"Brud" Holland

As the president of Hampton Institute in Virginia, Jerome E. Holland was one of the nation's distinguished educators in the 1960's. No one who knew him when he was a very popular student at Cornell University would have doubted such a future.

But in those Cornell days, "Brud" Holland was more than a popular and outstanding student. He was one of the greatest football stars ever to wear the Big Red, and an All-American end. The first Negro to play for Cornell, he was a star on both offense and de-

Bernie Jefferson

Brud Holland

Northwestern's Bernie Jefferson drives for an 8-yard gain against Iowa in their 1936 clash.

fense, a fine pass receiver, but an especially devastating runner on the end-around play. Despite the efforts of every opponent, keyed to stop that play, Holland made it work in game after game.

Here was how this strapping, 6ft.-1in., 207-pounder was described after his final college game, the annual battle with Pennsylvania at Franklin Field in Philadelphia: "Holland's exit was a meritorious salaam. As the premature dusk settled over historic Franklin Field, and the biting mist sent its emissaries of hail, rain and snow churning the field into a quagmire, Jerome E. Holland—who by dint of superior ability, ingratiating personality and God-given courage has surmounted all barriers and gained the highest fame that can befall a college athlete—wrote the last chapter in his saga of modern-day Negro youth. He won't be forgotten."

Bernie Jefferson

At 5ft.-11in. and 185 pounds, Bernard (Bernie) Jefferson was not a giant, but he was an iron man for the Northwestern Wildcats in 1938. A triple-threat running, passing and punting star, he frequently played sixty minutes of a game in the toughest football conference in the country, the Big Ten.

The highlight of the Wildcats' 1938 season was their battle with Minnesota, which in the mid-1930's was almost a perennial champion. The final score was 6–3, and here is how the 6 came about as the *New York Times* described it: "Then Bernard Jefferson, husky halfback, took the ball on a play that used Hahnenstein for a decoy. Jefferson ripped through left tackle, was checked for an instant on the three, and with sheer running speed and form blasted over the goal line with three tacklers hanging on him. The 185-pound Negro simply would not be stopped. That furious touchdown charge crushed Minnesota's hopes. Jefferson's drive stood out in bold relief."

Northwestern, a hard-luck team all season, lost the conference championship in a rugged battle with Wisconsin, despite a 92-yard touchdown run from a kickoff by Jefferson. In a scoreless tie against Michigan, whose backfield included Tom Harmon and Forest Evashevski, Jefferson's 51-yard run after a pass completion provided the Wildcats' only scoring threat. Facing Notre Dame in the season's finale, Northwestern fell, 9–7. Jefferson, playing his final collegiate game, gained more yards than any other back, was a stalwart on defense and punted brilliantly. His selection as a conference all-star that year could surprise no one.

William H. Lewis

The most talked-about college football star of his day was a center on the Amherst College teams of the early 1890's. He was William H. Lewis, a native of Norfolk, Virginia, who first attended Virginia Normal and Collegiate Institute at Petersburg in Virginia, then transferred to Amherst. He was chosen by Walter

WILLIAM H. LEWIS

Camp as the All-American center in 1892 and 1893. A decade later, he was named to the "all-time All-American" team by the New York *Evening World*.

After graduation, Lewis became a line coach at Harvard and wrote one of the earliest books on football technique, *How to Play Football*. While coaching, he attended law school and practiced in Boston. He climaxed his career as an assistant attorney general of the United States.

"Fritz" Pollard

Perhaps the most outstanding football star ever fielded by Brown University, the Ivy League institution at Providence, Rhode Island, was Frederick Pollard, known as "Fritz." One writer had this to say about him: "No more brilliant comet ever streaked across a turfed gridiron than the flashy Fritz." He was named to Walter Camp's All-American team in 1916. That autumn Brown defeated Yale, 21–6. Here is how the *New York Times* described the game:

"Brown's clean-cut victory will stand among football critics as a victory for a superior attack, executed by a superbly coached and perfectly conditioned eleven.

"Individually, Fritz Pollard, a lithe, dusky, six-foot halfback, displayed the cleverest all-around backfield success attained on a Yale field this season. In end running, forward passing, in executing a bewildering criss-cross and delayed pass-run, which was Brown's trump card, in running back punts, in side stepping and dodging Yale tacklers in a broken field, Pollard gave a peerless performance. His headline exhibition brought the crowd of 25,000 spectators up with a roar in the opening minutes of the final playing period.

"Catching a punt hoisted aloft to midfield by the toe of Harry Legore, Pollard dexterously threw off the Yale ends, started toward the right, drawing the entire pack of the Yale tacklers in that direction, then, using a puzzling side step, switched to the left, where he outstripped every Yale pursuer in a desperate sprint for the Yale goal line, sailing across with the second touchdown for the visitors. This heartbreaking performance nailed the lid on Yale hopes and the Elis were never dangerous thereafter."

The following Saturday, unbeaten Brown tangled with Harvard, and here is a contemporary description:

"Brown realized the football ambition of years today and defeated Harvard. The score, 21–0, was the most decisive defeat that a Haughton-coached eleven ever received. . . . In view of the fact that Brown has not been defeated this year, it will have an excellent claim to the college championship, and Pollard, its star, dusky little halfback, should be unanimous choice for a position on the mythical All-American eleven.

"Besides scoring two of Brown's touchdowns, Pollard contributed largely to a third, and in addition prevented Harvard from scoring in the one flash of offensive play that the Crimson displayed during the game. From the spectacular point of view, the game was all Pollard. . . ."

When the National Football League, the nation's first major pro football league, was organized in 1919, Fritz Pollard was one of the original stars. He played for the Akron Pros from 1919 to 1921, performed for the Milwaukee Badgers in 1922, and for the Hammond Pros in 1923 and 1924. He started the next season with Hammond, then returned to Providence, the site of his college stardom, to play with the Steamrollers, before moving back to Akron, where he finished his career in 1926.

A decade later, the name Fritz Pollard lived again on the football field. Frederick Pollard, Jr., also nicknamed "Fritz," played for the University of North Dakota in 1936, 1937 and 1938. A halfback competing for a school that was not in the spotlight, the young Fritz upheld the honor of the family name by winning for himself All-American mention.

Paul Robeson

Rutgers University is well known in the sports world for two important happenings. In 1869, Rutgers and Princeton played the first football game in American history—Rutgers won, 6–4. It was also at the New Brunswick university that Paul Robeson won four sports letters and helped to build one of the finest teams in the history of his school, and was selected by Walter Camp for the All-American teams of 1917 and 1918. This is what a director of athletics at Rutgers once wrote about Robeson:

"Undoubtedly, he rates as one of the five most prominent living Rutgers alumni, and by many people connected with the university is regarded as the most distinguished alumnus now living. He is one of ten men in the university's history who won four varsity letters as an undergraduate. He was an outstanding debater while in college and was a member of Phi Beta Kappa, honorary scholastic society, and of Cap and Skull, senior honorary society. Strangely enough, he never was a member of the University Glee Club, despite the fact that it is his magnificent voice that has brought him his greatest fame."

Since Rutgers did not compete against many of the more prominent colleges, Robeson did not receive as much attention as other athletes. Also, World War I was taking its toll of athletes and fewer colleges than usual were playing in 1917, and still fewer in 1918. It was during these trying days that Robeson was performing on the athletic field. Here is a sample of the Robeson style, as described in a New York paper:

"He was a tower of strength both in the offense and defense, and it was his receiving of forward passes which shattered any hopes of glory which might have arisen in Fordham ranks during the game. Twice the big Rutgers Negro raced down the field after receiving a perfect toss from Whitehill. . . .

"Both the wings of Rutgers have been taught an excellent offense. Robeson invariably spilled two men and several times three or four were dropped to the ground, even before the play was well under way. The vicious playing of Robeson was costly to Fordham, not only in the outcome of the game but in players, since no less than three Fordham men were sent into the game at different times to take the place of those who had been battered and bruised by Robeson."

Robeson moved into the professional football ranks after graduation. He made his debut with the Hammond Pros in 1920, transferred later that season to Akron where he played through 1921, and starred for the Milwaukee Badgers in 1922.

His career after that is known to the public —as one of the great singers of all time. In his later years, unhappy with the lot of the Negro in the United States, he chose to live in the Soviet Union. But in the world of sports his career will never be dimmed.

Wilmeth Sadat-Singh

The famous sportswriter Grantland Rice wrote, in the fall of 1938: "And then a rather dull game suddenly turned into a panoramic pageant of startling episodes as Sadat-Singh, adopted son of a Hindu, turned himself into a human machine gun with a touch of the howitzer on the side."

What Rice was describing was an incredible performance, seven completed passes for two hundred yards and three touchdowns, as Syracuse University rallied to defeat Cornell. The performance was turned in by Wilmeth Sadat-Singh, a Negro boy raised in Harlem, and adopted by a man of the Hindu faith.

Sadat-Singh had to suffer the indignities of the race prejudice of those days. In 1937,

Fritz Pollard

Paul Robeson

Wilmeth Sidat-Singh

Kenny Washington

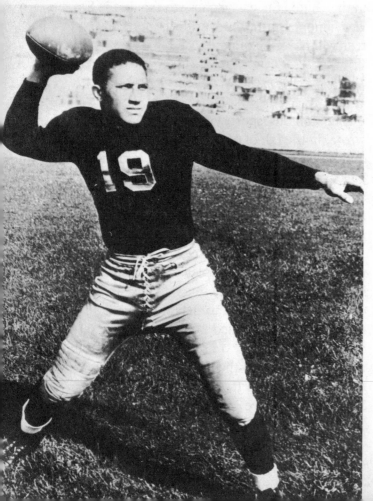

Maryland refused to let him play when it entertained Syracuse, and his school did not resist. But a year later, the tables were turned. Maryland played at Syracuse and had to face Sadat-Singh. The score: Syracuse 53, Maryland 0.

Grantland Rice compared him to Sid Luckman and Sammy Baugh, two pass-throwing immortals, and said he had "the deadly aim of Davy Crockett and Kit Carson." Performing against a Western Reserve team unbeaten in twenty-eight games, Sadat-Singh led Syracuse to a three-touchdown victory, setting up every score with his passes.

Sadat-Singh transferred those unerring arms and eyes to the basketball court. He had the "silky finesse of the born court strategist," said one sportswriter, and he led Syracuse, in the 1938–1939 season, to fourteen straight victories.

Kenny Washington

When a national magazine polled 1,600 collegiate football players in choosing its All-American team for 1939, only one player in the entire country was selected by every opponent he faced. That player was Kenny Washington, a big, fleet halfback from the University of California at Los Angeles.

Washington had been an All-Pacific Coast Conference choice the season before, as the Bruins beat Stanford for the first time in four seasons and the University of Washington for the first time in seven. In 1939, Washington, who was once called the "almost-perfect player," gained 863 yards in 141 carries and completed 32 of 76 passes for 497 yards from his tailback position. He led UCLA to what was at that time the greatest season in its history.

The segregation barrier, then World War II, prevented Washington from continuing his exploits in the professional ranks, but things had changed by the end of the war. He signed with the Los Angeles Rams in 1946, one of the first Negro players in modern pro football history, and played for three years before his retirement in 1948.

George Gregory

One day in 1925, the DeWitt Clinton High School basketball team of New York City was scrimmaging against a team representing the 135th Street YMCA in Harlem. One player sparkled all over the court. His name was George Gregory and he had already dropped out of high school. But the Clinton coach knew talent and he talked Gregory into returning to school.

The next season, DeWitt Clinton, with Gregory starring, won the New York City championship. The following season, Gregory captained Clinton to a second straight title. Gregory was an all-city selection.

Then this former high school dropout entered one of the nation's outstanding universities, Columbia, in New York. Again he became a star—and a team captain. His team was a champion for two straight years as Columbia won the Eastern title in 1930 and 1931. Gregory was named to a variety of All-American teams in both 1930 and 1931.

That wasn't the end of George Gregory's connection with athletics. He went on to become director of what was then the largest youth project for Negroes in America—the Harlem Children's Center of the Children's Aid Society.

Isaac Murphy

From early Colonial times, Negroes were involved in the work of grooming, feeding, breaking, exercising and training horses. So it was quite natural that when horses were raced, their riders should be Negroes. That was standard practice throughout the early years of competitive racing in the United States and

ISAAC MURPHY

on into the twentieth century, before Negro jockeys "disappeared" from race tracks.

Isaac Murphy was a man who, if he had been born in the twentieth century, could not have been a jockey. But, as the *Encyclopedia of Sports* says about him: "Many veterans regard Isaac Murphy, a Negro, as the greatest."

Born in the heart of the horse country, Lexington, Kentucky, on January 1, 1861, Murphy rode his first winner, Glentina, at the Crab Orchard track in Kentucky in 1875, at the age of fourteen. In 1884, he rode to victory in the most famous of American races, the Kentucky Derby, aboard Buchanan. Then in 1890 and 1891, he had successive triumphs in the Kentucky Derby, on Riley and Kingman. Only one other man ever matched his record of two straight victories in that race; only two others, Earl Sande and Eddie Arcaro, ever won as many as three Kentucky Derbies.

Murphy might never have ridden three Derby winners, however, if he had had his own

way. He was practically forced to ride Buchanan in 1884. A few weeks before the Derby, Murphy had ridden Buchanan at Nashville; the horse was so wild he nearly unseated his jockey at the post and then bolted all over the track. On Derby Day, Murphy refused to get into the saddle. The owners first flattered him, then begged him, finally threatened him with suspension. He, therefore, gave in and went on to victory with Buchanan.

Murphy won the first four runnings of the Latonia Derby in Kentucky and captured four of the first five runnings of the American Derby in Chicago. At Saratoga, New York, in 1882, his record was an incredible forty-nine victories in fifty-one starts.

Perhaps the most satisfying triumph Murphy ever achieved came on June 25, 1890 at Sheepshead Bay near New York City, in a match race between two horses named Salvator and Tenny. Murphy rode Salvator and Tenny's jockey was "Snapper" Garrison, Murphy's toughest contemporary. The match was as much between jockeys as between horses. Thousands of fans from all over the East attended. Salvator won by a head.

In the 1880's, Murphy branched out as an owner but never found a really successful horse and thus concentrated on riding. He continued to ride almost until his death, from pneumonia, in Lexington on February 13, 1896, at the age of thirty-five.

Willie Simms

Willie Simms was the first Negro jockey to earn international acclaim. Born in Augusta, Georgia, on January 16, 1870, he began riding as a teen-ager. At Sheepshead Bay in New York on June 23, 1893, he rode five winners in six months; and on August 24, 1894, at New York's Jerome Park, he matched the feat. Simms went on to win twice in the Kentucky Derby. He scored in 1896 aboard Ben Brush and repeated in 1898 with Plaudit.

Simms became one of the turf idols of his day. Two sportsmen, Richard Croker and Michael F. Dwyer, hired him to ride their horses in England. There he became the first American jockey to win an event on an English course with an American horse, owner, trainer and equipment—the first all-American victory. He continued to ride successfully in England for some time before returning to the United States, where he was welcomed as one of the reigning international stars.

Jimmy Winkfield

Only two jockeys have ever won the Kentucky Derby twice in a row. One was the racing immortal, Isaac Murphy. The other, and the last man to do it, was Jimmy Winkfield. Winkfield captured the Derby on His Eminence in 1901 and followed up with a slashing ride to victory in 1902 on Alan-a-Dale.

Winkfield had a chance the next spring to do something no one has ever accomplished— win three straight Kentucky Derbies. Riding a colt named Early, he held a commanding lead going into the stretch but misjudged the distance and almost coasted his mount home. As the field closed, Winkfield drove his horse, but the fast-finishing Judge Himes nipped Early at the wire.

Never since then, as the color barriers have been established, has a Negro jockey won the Derby. Winkfield, seeing what was happening, left the United States to compete in France, where for twenty years he was a leading jockey. As late as 1923, he won the Prix du President de la Republique du State at St. Cloud on a horse named Bahadur.

After his retirement as a jockey, Winkfield became a successful trainer in France, sending mounts all over the continent. He did not return to the United States until his retirement in 1940, after Hitler overran France.

Jimmy Winkfield riding Bahadur, winner of the 1923 Grand Prix.

"Major" Taylor

One of the greatest Negro athletes in American history is practically unknown. Born in 1878 in Indianapolis, Marshall W. Taylor was destined to win the plaudits of millions of people all over the world. They called him "Major" Taylor and he became the fastest bicycle rider the world had ever known.

Taylor won three national American sprint championships—in 1898, 1899 and 1900. Then for three seasons he invaded Europe and defeated all of its cycling champions before huge throngs. Australia offered him a royal welcome, and on three trips there he established enviable records and good comradeship.

The role of the Negro athlete in the eyes of the American public is accepted today. In Major Taylor's time, although many of his racing competitors were fair, some leading professionals sought by every trick to keep him from winning.

Major Taylor won some of his most noted victories before he was eighteen years old. He began as a trick rider. Philanthropic white friends helped him establish an early reputation as a racer, and later his prowess earned him the support of the leading sports' managements. The appearance of Taylor at a racing event, at home or abroad, assured financial success to the managers of his time.

When Taylor was ten, Walter Sanger set a mark of 2 minutes, 18 seconds for the mile at the Capital City track in Indianapolis. Taylor could not race him because of the "color" bar, but some of Taylor's friends secured him entry to the track before the crowd had gone. After a few warm-up heats, Taylor tore off a 2:11 mile, seven seconds under the much-touted Sanger mark. On the same afternoon, behind pace, he established a record of 23.6 seconds for the ⅕-mile oval, a mark that lasted as long as the Indianapolis track existed.

So bitter was the prejudice, though, that he could not enter any races with white men. On one occasion a 75-mile road race between Indianapolis and Matthews, Indiana, was scheduled. White friends secreted Major Taylor in the woods. After the start, he rode from his hiding place and followed the pack for half the distance. Then he moved to the front and rode the last twenty-five miles through a blinding rainstorm, to arrive at the finish line a full hour ahead of the nearest competing bicycle rider.

Because of the racial feeling in Indianapolis, Major Taylor and his manager, "Birdie" Munger, a staunch friend, decided to move to Worcester, Massachusetts. Munger advised Taylor that if he would train faithfully and refrain from tobacco and intoxicants, he would become the fastest bicycle rider in the world. Taylor later credited his success to his having followed that advice.

In 1898, Major Taylor determined to go after the American Sprint Championship. Although the big racing syndicates—the League of American Wheelmen and the National Racing Association—would not admit Negro riders to membership, Taylor's drawing power and the backing of white friends and the press forced managements in all of the cities except Baltimore and points south to admit him to racing. Other cities were warned that they might not be allowed to hold championship events if Taylor was barred. In that 1898 season, he defeated every one of the champions —Eddie Bald, Arthur Gardiner, Tom Butler and Owen Kimble.

Taylor continued as champion in 1899 and 1900. During his initial championship year he was first in 21 races, second 13 times and third 11 times. In the racing point system, he recorded 121 points, to 113 for the second-best competitor, Arthur Gardiner. In 1899, he was first in 23 starts, second in 3, and out of the top trio only twice. The 1900 campaign, under a revised point system, saw him double the total of the runner-up, Frank Kramer, 40 points to 20.

In the early season of 1901, Major Taylor invaded Europe and in two months rode in fifty-seven races, almost a race a day—in France, Belgium, Italy, Switzerland, Denmark and Germany. He defeated, time and again, the great national champions: Jacquelin, Quivy, Dutriew, Founeau of France; Ellegarde of Denmark; Arend and Muringer of Germany; Grognia of Belgium; Ferrai and Boxio of Italy, and scores of others who ranked in popular acclaim with champions like Willie Mays or Arnold Palmer or Jim Brown of a later day. Three times on his European jaunt Major Taylor was honored by royalty. On his return to America, he set out to retain his sprint championships but riders and, it was said, gamblers conspired to make it impossible for him to compete in enough events for his points to be counted toward the national championship.

Major Taylor finally agreed to race in Australia. Plagued with misgivings because of the reputation Australia had in its relationship to Orientals, he found streamers of welcome on entering the harbor of Sydney and throngs of Australians waiting for the arrival of the black champion from America. His racing career in Australia rivaled his successes in Europe. The only problems he had came from the other Americans who had also come to compete for the prize money—rough riding in the "pockets" and personal abuse. Despite some dangerous stunts tried against him, he defeated them all. The Australians responded to some of these tactics by suspending certain American riders from their tracks. In gratitude to the reception he received from the Aussies, Major named his only daughter, who was born on one of his Australian trips, Rita Sydney.

In 1903, Taylor suffered a physical collapse, which he blamed on his continual travels and competition. But he returned to the track in 1908 and was a championship competitor for two more years before he retired.

One of the secrets of that long and successful career was Taylor's ability to handle the constant tricks of his adversaries, and more often than not beat them at their own game. In bicycle racing, it is possible for two or more racers working in collusion to "box" a competitor, thus enabling another man to win. Rules were often not carefully enforced and locking a competitor in a "box" was common practice. But Major Taylor often overcame the tactic, thanks to his well-developed talents as a trick rider. He could make his bicycle "jump," or might suddenly move up and tap a rider in front, throwing him off balance for an instant, thus giving Taylor a chance to slip through.

A man who trained with fervor and lived a life of the highest ethical standards, he was honored around the nation. President Theodore Roosevelt paid him public tribute. Millions of Americans were thrilled by his performances, for he was a professional bicycle rider in the days when that sport was a major one in the United States. He was one of the most glorified Negro athletes in history.

A firm believer in resting between innings, Paige slumps comfortably in an overstuffed chair on the sidelines.

Cleveland ace Bob Feller poses with Satchel Paige after their teams split a two-game exhibition series in 1946.

Paige chats with ex-Dodger catcher Roy Campanella before the Negro American League's 29th all-star game in 1961.

CHAPTER FOUR

Too Good—Too Soon

THE time has finally come when the color of a man's skin does not settle the question of whether he will be allowed to compete in sports. But for a long time before World War II, a Negro athlete was almost never given the chance to prove himself equal or superior on the nation's playing fields. Despite this, many young men who loved sports and excelled in them played anyway—in the shadows of segregated diamonds and gridirons and courts. Except for a handful of whites and a relatively small number of Negroes as well, no one knew of their exploits, no matter how outstanding. If they played professionally, their earnings were small. But they played.

Some could perform long enough to have a chance later in the big time—such as the great pitcher Satchel Paige. Others could not, such as the great catcher Josh Gibson. There was not enough competition for Negro football players to prove their skills professionally. The only professional sport in which Negroes

gained real attention was basketball. There, teams like the Harlem Globetrotters and the New York Rens performed before huge crowds, whites and Negroes. In real competition, such as professional tournaments, they showed they could handle any opponent. But mainly they had to prove themselves by stunts and clowning. Men like Reese "Goose" Tatum and Marquis Haynes could have sparkled on any court; yet they were forced to earn their reputations with fancy dribbling and trick shots.

Negro colleges also produced fine teams, but hardly anyone noticed. The day when schools like Morgan State or Grambling or Florida A&M could achieve reputations in football like the major "white" colleges was far distant.

Many Negro athletes in those years were simply far ahead of their time. Their talents were recognized only by those who had eyes open wide enough to see them.

"Rube" Foster

If there may be said to be a founding father of Negro baseball in the United States, the choice would have to be Andrew Foster, born in Calvert, Texas, on September 17, 1879, the son of a Methodist minister. The name "Andrew" may sound strange even to veteran baseball fans, but they certainly would remember "Rube" Foster. One day, in 1902, Foster pitched an exhibition game for a Negro team against the Philadelphia Athletics and their great mound star, "Rube" Waddell. Foster bested Waddell and his teammates began to call him "Rube," in affectionate acknowledgement that he was as capable as any pitcher around. The name stayed with him for life.

Foster was a giant, a powerful man who could pitch almost endlessly. He knew his ability and supplemented it with an instinctive knowledge of baseball that comes to few men. He was prepared to face any club, any batting order, no matter what its reputation. In 1905, it was reported, Foster hurled fifty-one victories in fifty-five exhibition games against major and minor league white teams. In Chicago, he organized and pitched for one of the great Negro teams, the Leland Giants, who later became the Chicago American Giants.

When he retired as an active player, Foster became the manager of the Giants, operating in the aggressive way that John McGraw did with the New York Giants of the National League. In 1920, Foster helped accomplish what men had been trying to do, without real success, for three decades—form a Negro professional league. Foster won the cooperation and help of Ben Johnson, founder of the white American League. With Foster as president, the Negro league had franchises in Kansas City (the Monarchs), in Indianapolis (the ABC's), and in Chicago, Detroit and St. Louis (all called the Giants), plus the original American Giants and a team of traveling Cuban all-stars. Perhaps most remarkable of all was the fact that every team in the league, except for the Cubans who did not play "home" games, owned its own park, a rare thing for any baseball league at any time.

The formation of the National Negro Baseball League led, eventually, to the founding of others—an Eastern League, an American League. There were Negro World Series, too, and players with the reputations of Josh Gibson and Satchel Paige began to emerge. Rube Foster always ran his league the way Ben Johnson ran the white American League, as fairly as he knew how; and like Johnson, he could be tough when the occasion demanded. Organized Negro baseball, which survived the Great Depression and until the years after World War II when its stars began to play in major league baseball, was on a firm footing by 1930, so that when Rube Foster died in that year he had seen the results of his efforts.

Josh Gibson

One of the greatest baseball pitchers of all time, the "Big Train" of the Washington Senators, Walter Johnson, watched a game one spring day in Florida, and commented later:

"There is a catcher that any big league club would like to buy for $200,000. I had heard of him before. His name is Gibson. They call him 'Hoot' Gibson, and he can do everything. He hits the ball a mile. And he catches so easy he might just as well be in a rocking chair. Throws like a rifle. Bill Dickey isn't as good a catcher. Too bad this Gibson is a colored fellow."

The last sentence is the most significant. It was the fact of color—and the fact that he was born thirty years too soon—that kept that catcher named Gibson from becoming one of the greatest players baseball ever knew. His name, of course, was Josh Gibson, and he was known as the "Babe Ruth of Negro baseball." If he had had the chance that was to come later to others of his race, he might have been called

JOSH GIBSON

than his share of wild and eccentric ones. He could throw strongly and accurately. That is why Walter Johnson compared him to Bill Dickey, the smoothest catcher around in that year of 1939. (The price Walter Johnson quoted in 1939 was $200,000; it could have been $500,000 by the 1960's.)

Gibson was the great star of the Homestead Grays, and always an all-star catcher. But he played his baseball in rickety old parks of the South and on sandlots as often as not in the North, except when the major league teams would occasionally rent out their stadiums for Negro games.

Nonetheless, Gibson was one of the great baseball attractions of all time—and any color. A game involving him and Satchel Paige in the 1930's might attract 40,000 and more, often outdrawing major league teams in their own cities. Still, he commanded relatively little attention in the press.

Of all baseball players, Josh Gibson perhaps achieved the least fame for his talent. Satchel Paige made the major leagues in his twilight years and proved then what a star he would have been had he pitched there in his prime. Gibson never had the chance. He died in 1947, having lived only long enough to see Jackie Robinson break into the major leagues.

"Satchel" Paige

One clear, warm August evening in 1948, in the gigantic Municipal Stadium on the lake-front in Cleveland, the Indians were entertaining the Chicago White Sox. The Indians were drawing big crowds for most of their games, but this was something special. The attendance that night was 78,382, the biggest crowd to see a night game in American League history.

The attraction was a rookie pitcher, a right-hander named Leroy Paige. The rookie pitched a three-hit shutout that night, and in a tension-filled game the Indians won, 1–0.

instead "the new Babe Ruth." And today the batters might have been shooting at Gibson records instead of Ruth records.

Josh Gibson played professional baseball from the 1920's to the 1940's. He was a brawny man, yet quick on his feet, one of the fastest big men to play the game. He had a perfectly timed, grooved swing and could hit with power to all fields. Batting records weren't kept very well in the Negro leagues of his day, but it was reported that Gibson once hit eighty homeruns in a season. There are those who think he might have done that well in the major leagues.

As a catcher he was superb. He could handle any pitcher, and he had to handle more

The next day, Cleveland owner Bill Veeck sent a telegram to J. G. Taylor Spink, publisher of *The Sporting News,* the national baseball newspaper. Said Veeck: "Paige Pitching. White Sox No Runs, Three Hits. Should Be Candidate for *Sporting News* Rookie of the Year Award."

Bill Veeck, the clever, fun-loving owner of the Indians, was having his little joke at Spink's expense. For *The Sporting News* had not long before called Veeck's signing of this rookie pitcher a travesty on the game of baseball.

Why? The answer, of course, was that Leroy Paige—"Satchel" to everyone—was not a rookie at all, except in the technical sense that this was his first year in the major leagues. He was, by then, something over forty years old. No one really knew (except Satchel himself) how old he was, but there he was in his first season, at an age when all but a few have retired.

Taylor Spink of *The Sporting News* wasn't opposed to Paige because he was a Negro. He was opposed because, over the years, Satchel had developed quite a reputation as a jokester on the field. He had to. For most of the time when he was pitching, he was either bored, because the competition wasn't good enough, or playing an exhibition—to entertain people as well as to amaze them with his skills.

The reputation detracted somewhat from Paige's obvious ability. But even though no one, including Spink, doubted that ability, many doubted it had lasted into 1948. Perhaps it could be said also that some people feared that it had lasted that long. For Spink also objected to the fact that Satchel Paige, in his forties, could get a chance to show that he was still one of the greatest of pitchers. That would be embarrassing to baseball.

If such was the case, Spink and baseball had cause to be embarrassed. For Satchel Paige, signed in mid-season, became one of the stalwarts of the Cleveland pitching staff, even though it included such stars as Bob Feller, Bob Lemon and Gene Bearden. Paige won six games and lost one, a splendid record for any team. What made it more impressive was that he accomplished the feat in the thick of the tightest pennant race in American League history. Four teams were in contention until well into September. The Yankees were eliminated on the next-to-last day of the season. The Indians and Red Sox tied, and in the first play-off game in league history Cleveland won the pennant. Any one game would have made the difference, and Paige won six.

There are those who will argue that Paige was the greatest pitcher in baseball history. Greater than Walter Johnson or Christy Mathewson or Bob Feller or Sandy Koufax? No one will ever know. But no one doubts that he ranks in the top handful, even if he never got a chance to prove it in his prime against the best of competition.

According to the official records of baseball, Satchel Paige was born on July 7, 1906, in Mobile, Alabama. That would have made him forty-two in his first major league season, but the date could have been moved up a few years. One newspaper story written about him in 1939 said that "he retired last year at the age of 44." That, of course, would have made him fifty-four when he first pitched in the American League.

Whatever the date of his birth, Paige grew into a lanky man, 6ft.-3in., with a sinewy body, enormous arms and feet to match. The latter provided his nickname. He would wind up all in a tangle and whip a fast ball to the plate that few batters could handle. In later years, as the fast ball slowed, he mastered a precise curve, but also two things more important. One was an incredible assortment of pitches; the other was precise control.

The assortment of pitches was one of the things that was later to bother the publisher of *The Sporting News.* One of them Satchel called his "hesitation pitch." He would swing

ith grim determination, Paige delivers a strike during a game in Miami in 1958.

Despite his busy schedule, the ageless Paige always has time to show youngsters how to hold the ball for his famous curve.

A career highlight came to Paige when he was called on to relieve during the 1948 World Series.

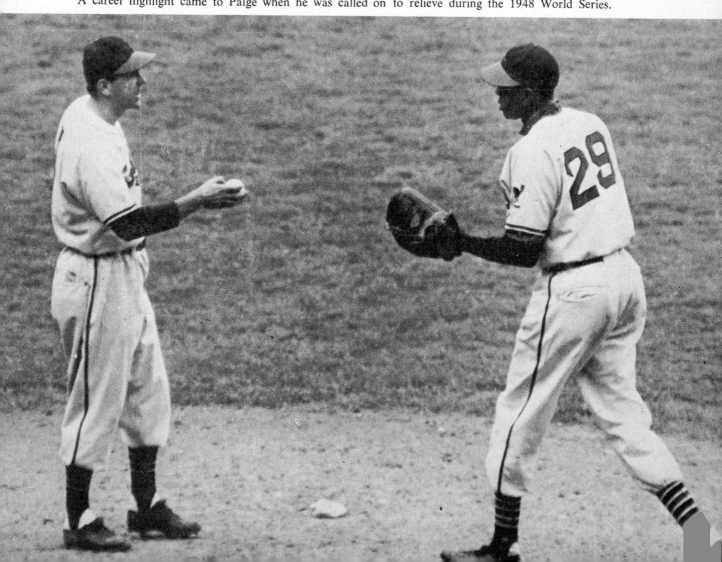

that long arm around and as he moved it toward the plate he would pause or hesitate a moment. Stopping a delivery is a balk and some opponents would cry "balk." But they were being naive. Satchel was too smart to balk, to break the rules like that. He slowed almost to a halt without halting. It was one of the most effective change-of-pace pitches ever developed. Spink thought that it looked bad for baseball but the fans disagreed.

As for control, Paige had to be near-perfect. For one thing, he was dealing with mediocre or worse umpires during most of his career. He had to be around the plate. For another, he pitched so often he would have worn out a lot sooner if he had wasted many deliveries. Paige hardly ever walked anyone. Finally, when a pitcher has many different kinds of pitches, he cannot risk not knowing how to control every one.

Satchel began his pitching career in the 1920's and by the 1930's was already a major attraction. His greatest fame came with the Kansas City Monarchs of the Negro American League, for whom he pitched sixty-four consecutive scoreless innings in 1946, but he worked for a host of other teams. In 1933 he won thirty-one games, twenty-one in succession for the Pittsburgh Crawfords. In 1936 he pitched five games in a week, winning them all, allowing a total of three runs. In South America in 1939, he won fifty-four games and lost five. Many times he pitched two games in a day. He never seemed to tire. He worked as hard on the mound as he had to. Often, of course, he was so much better than the batters that he didn't have to work hard at all.

Once in the 1930's, when Paige was in his prime, he took part in a barnstorming tour against a team of major leaguers. He won twelve games without a loss. One night, when his pitching opponents were the Cardinals' brother stars, Dizzy and Paul Dean, he threw a one-hit shutout. Another year, he fanned Rogers Hornsby, considered by many the greatest right-hand hitter ever, five times in one game. In five exhibition games against Joe DiMaggio he allowed one single. DiMaggio, who faced Bob Feller all during the regular season, called Paige the fastest pitcher he had ever seen.

It was this kind of reputation that preceded him to the major leagues. In 1948, with the Indians fighting for the pennant and needing all the extra help they could get, Bill Veeck, who had brought the first Negro into the American League (Larry Doby) the year before, thought of Paige. He discussed the matter privately with his shortstop and manager, Lou Boudreau. Boudreau was having the best season of his career. He was to hit .355 for the year, and his ability in the clutch—the crucial moment—was superb. Lou laughed at first, but Veeck insisted that Paige, at whatever age, was still capable.

So they hit on a plan. Paige would be brought to Cleveland for a secret tryout. Boudreau himself would bat against him. If Satchel could stop him, he could stop anyone. That is what they did one day inside an empty stadium—empty, that is, except for Veeck and some other Cleveland officials. And Paige baffled Boudreau—with an assortment of pitches the player-manager had never seen before. That convinced him. Paige was signed.

After that first thrilling season in Cleveland, Paige slipped to a 4–7 record for the Indians in 1949. He dropped out of the majors the next season and everyone assumed that was the end of his career. But when Bill Veeck took over the sad St. Louis Browns in 1951, he called on Satchel again.

Working only part of the 1951 season, he won three games. Then in 1952, with next to no batting support from the Browns, Satchel appeared in forty-six games, won twelve, lost ten and had an earned-run-average of 3.07—all that at the age of forty-six or fifty-six. The most memorable moment of that season came when another "old-timer" of baseball, Casey

Stengel, who was managing the American League all-star team, chose Paige as an all-star pitcher. When he worked in that game, Satchel had achieved the third of three major ambitions—to pitch in the major leagues, in the World Series, and in an all-star game.

After the 1953 season, when he won three games for the Browns, Satchel retired, finally, from the major leagues. But he continued to pitch in exhibition games and to thrill crowds. His marvelous style of strolling to the mound as if he didn't have a care in the world never ceased to delight the fans. After he left baseball entirely, he lived in Missouri, near Kansas City, becoming active in politics.

It seemed logical to assume that by now Satchel Paige had placed his active athletic career behind him. But this astonishing man had not finished astonishing people. In mid-season of 1968, the Atlanta Braves startled the sports world by announcing that they had signed Satchel Paige to a contract. The pitcher's age was at least sixty-two, and possibly seventy-two.

The reason given for the signing was to make Paige eligible for the major league baseball pension plan. His career had left him part of a season short of the required five years. He needed the remainder of 1968 and part of 1969 to qualify. Atlanta said it would keep him that long.

Naturally, everyone wanted to know if Paige would actually pitch. Even the man himself was not sure this time "I'll have to unwind first," he said. But he seemed confident he could still get the ball over the plate and even get batters out.

By now no one was complaining about this elderly man in a uniform. People were past the point of surprise. They agreed he deserved the pension. They were in awe of his ability. Throughout his career, Satchel Paige was one of the marvels of baseball, and one of the great, and sad, examples of a man who, because of racial discrimination, never

had a real chance to prove his superlative ability.

Xavier College

During the years before World War II, playing competitive basketball was not easy for Negroes. As professionals they were limited almost entirely to traveling teams like the Harlem Globetrotters or the New York Rens. Only a handful managed to go to college and play with collegiate teams in the North. The majority who did play competed for segregated Negro colleges in the South.

Perhaps the greatest of all these Negro college fives was the club that represented Xavier of New Orleans in the years 1934–1938. In four seasons, the Xavier Ambassadors won sixty-seven games and lost two. Both defeats, by LeMoyne in 1935 and by Clark in 1937, were by a single point. At the close of their college careers, these young men competed twice in exhibition games against the world championship professional team, the New York Rens. The Rens won both times—but by a mere four points and one point.

The ball-handling skill and teamwork that made Xavier so strong were not due entirely to ability but in large part also to long experience. The whole regular line-up—Bray, Rhodes, Colege, Gant and McQuitter—had played together as a unit at Wendell Phillips High School in Chicago and had matriculated en masse to Xavier. After eight remarkable years together, each knew exactly where the other would be at any instant on the court, and it showed in their record achievements.

The Harlem Globetrotters

When Abe Saperstein gathered five basketball players together in 1927 and called them the "Harlem Globetrotters," not one of them was from Harlem and they certainly were not world travelers; in fact, except for Saperstein

Abe Saperstein, founder of the Harlem Globetrotters.

In typical Trotter style, "Sweetwater" Clifton holds the ball beyond the reach of All-Star Ed Dahler.

Using facial expressions as well as deft ball-handling, Trotter Ermer Robinson brings the ball down the court as his team defeats the All-Americans 70-62.

Posing before their four-month European tour in 1951 are (from left to right) Ermer Robinson, Reece "Goose" Tatum, Bill Brown, Bill "Pop" Gates and Marquis Haynes.

Meadowlark Lemon clowns behind All-Star Jerry Lucas during a game in Helsinki in 1961.

Trotter Bob Hall goes into his clowning act after snatching a felt hat from one of the fans.

himself, who was born in London and moved to Chicago when he was eight, none of the original members of the Harlem Globetrotters had ever even been outside the United States.

Today, things are different. In the more than forty years since Saperstein, then a social worker in the slums of Chicago's North Side, piled his players into a model-T Ford and drove them to Hinckley, Illinois, for a game with the local high school team, Globetrotter teams have traveled over five million miles to almost one hundred countries and have played before over sixty million spectators. Combining extraordinary basketball talent with slapstick comedy routines worthy of the old Mack Sennett silent films, the Trotters produce a unique spectacle that many consider the most popular sports show in the world.

Before 1927, the Globetrotters went by the name of the Savoy Big Five, in honor of their home court, the Savoy Ball Room in Chicago. When the Savoy evicted them in favor of roller skating, Saperstein decided to take his team on the road and felt they needed a new name: " 'Harlem,' " Abe later explained, "because I wanted people to know the team was Negro, and 'Globetrotters' because I wanted people to think we'd been around."

During those early years, Abe drove the car, coached the team, was manager, trainer and physician. And because there were only five players, he also served as the team's only substitute. Some of those early games provided memorable moments in Globetrotter history. Near Miles City, Montana, one winter, the model-T ran into a blinding snowstorm. Coming upon a sheepherder's shack, Saperstein and his players sought refuge and spent the next forty-eight hours cooped up inside with the herder—and his sheep. When the blizzard had subsided, the Trotters went on to Shelby, Montana, where local bettors threatened to shoot them if they won and the local sheriff threatened to shoot them if they lost. They solved the problem by winning

easily, then leaving town with their street clothes under their arms.

Once, while playing a game on the second floor of a barn in Wheatland, Iowa, Trotter Willie Oliver was gently nudged out of bounds by a 200-pound opponent. Oliver ricocheted off the barn wall and out an open door, falling to the ground below. A worried Saperstein raced down the stairs to assist his injured player, only to find that Oliver had landed softly, and unhurt, in a pile of manure. From that day on, he was known to his teammates as "Sweet Willie."

Saperstein's team had phenomenal success from the start, usually walloping every opponent. In fact the Trotters were so good that they had trouble drawing anyone to the games; Abe settled for a $2.50 profit after one game. Traveling all day and playing every night began to drain the players' energies, so Saperstein suggested that they play hard the first ten minutes of each game, then slow things down, clown around, do anything as long as it didn't run up the score. This would keep the fans interested and the Trotters from getting tired. With natural-born comedians like Al "Runt" Pullins and Inman Jackson on those early teams, the Trotters had no trouble following Saperstein's suggestion. They began running less and passing the ball more, usually in a razzle-dazzle style that confused opponents but entertained the fans. They shot the ball behind their backs, spun it on their fingers, did everything but eat it. (In later years, they even did *that,* when Saperstein had a special pumpernickel ball made.) People began to talk about the show that the Globetrotters put on, and the crowds began to grow.

Their big break came in 1940, when the promoters of a world basketball championship tournament in Chicago invited the Globetrotters to play, in order to fill out the opening round. When Saperstein's men walked off with the championship, both fans and promoters throughout the country heard about it and the Globetrotters were on their way. Saperstein himself was an excellent promoter, and adding half-time exhibitions of juggling, table tennis and other attractions, he began a worldwide tour that soon became an annual event. The Globetrotters became international favorites and have played in the cowfields of Morocco and before white-tie audiences in London's Wimbledon Stadium. They played before Pope Pius XII and attracted the largest basketball crowd in history—75,000 in Berlin's Olympic Stadium.

The Globetrotters' top attraction has been a 6ft.-3in. basketball wizard named Reese "Goose" Tatum. Tatum combined his gawky appearance (size 14 shoes and an 86-inch arm spread) with a natural comic sense, to earn the nickname "The Clown Prince of Basketball." Ever since he had been a small boy in El-dorado, Arkansas, Tatum had wanted to be a Globetrotter. He eventually signed a base-ball contract with the Birmingham Black Barons of the old Negro American League, but when the Globetrotters' business mana-ger saw him shooting baskets in a gym one day and offered him a contract, Goose jumped at it. From 1942 to 1955, he was the center of attraction in the Globetrotter at-tack, whether scoring on thirty-foot hook shots or simply dangling from the rim. One of his favorite tricks was to go into the crowd under one basket and sit in a spectator's lap while play was at the other end. A Globe-trotter would get the ball and fire it the length of the court and, suddenly, there Goose would be to catch it and lay it in, while wearing some fan's felt hat.

From 1946 to 1952, Tatum was joined by diminutive Marquis Haynes, who was billed as "The World's Greatest Dribbler." Haynes had fantastic fingertip control of the ball, and one of the fans' favorite sights was four Globetrotters talking to each other or reading newspapers while Haynes dribbled around,

through and under the entire opposing team.

One might think that with all of the show-manship going on, the Globetrotters wouldn't have time to develop their talents, but their overall record of over 9,200 victories in 9,600 games is a tribute to the excellence of their play. In 1948 and 1949, they defeated George Mikan's Minneapolis Lakers, then considered the best team in basketball. Over the years, they have played hundreds of games with various college all-star teams and have seldom lost. (Their record in 1962, the last year they toured with the college all-stars, was 14-1.)

In 1952, Marques Haynes left the Globe-trotters and formed his own team, the Fabu-lous Magicians, which still tours the country successfully. For a while, Haynes was joined by his old teammate Goose Tatum, who quit the Globetrotters in 1955. Tatum died in 1967, one year after Abe Saperstein's death.

The excellence and the joy that the Harlem Globetrotters bring to basketball goes on. Most of the clowning now is done by "Mea-dowlark" Lemon and the dribbling by "Curly" Neal. Perhaps some of the younger players will eventually go on to successful careers in the major pro basketball leagues, as did former Globetrotters like Nat "Sweetwater" Clifton, Wilt Chamberlain and Connie Hawkins. But if the names change, the idea that once belonged to Abe Saperstein remains, and the Harlem Globetrotters continue to bring joy to millions as goodwill ambassadors the world over.

The New York Rens

The year 1923 saw the founding of what many people believe was the greatest basket-ball team of its time—in a class with the Harlem Globetrotters. This was the New York Renaissance, one of the earliest of organized professional basketball teams. So uneven was the competition, that few people saw the team perform at its best. Players were instructed not to run up a large score against weak opponents. Frequently, the Rens turned to an exhibition of fancy and trick passing that for machine-like precision beggared description.

In this same period, the great and more famous all-white team was known as the Original Celtics of New York, led by lanky Joe Lapchick and Nat Holman. But when they clashed in 1928, the Rens won. During the 1930's the Rens drew what were for those times almost unheard-of crowds, 11,000 and 15,000, for example, on successive days for weekend games in Cleveland in 1932; more than 15,000 in Kansas City; and more than 25,000 for two battles with the Celtics in 1938.

Over a period of nearly two decades, the Rens won 1,588 games and lost 239. In the 1938–1939 season, they won 112 games and lost 7. For fourteen straight years they won at least one hundred games a season. In March 1939, in the first professional world championship basketball tournament, the Rens swept to victory. That merely confirmed what many basketball followers already knew: no team could even think about being called a champion until it took on and defeated the New York Rens.

That world championship victory was a particular pleasure to a well-known and genial resident of Harlem, Robert J. Douglas. It was a dream he had cherished ever since he sent the first Ren team on the floor in 1923. The victory in Chicago marked not only concrete realization of the honors that the team had long deserved but vindication of the unswerving faith that Douglas had so long placed in it.

It was in October 1923 that Douglas organized the Rens. An ardent follower of the game that he had played himself for more than a dozen years, he watched the amateur game sink lower and lower during 1921 and 1922 and decided that backing a professional team might prove a worthwhile enterprise. For that first team, Douglas recruited such stars as Hilton Slocum, Frank Forbes, Leon Monde, Hy Monte, Zack Anderson and Harold Mayers. Slocum captained the squad from the first game until he left the club in 1932.

The naming of the team—officially the Renaissance Big Five—was purely accidental, or perhaps it would be better to call it a result of circumstances. Douglas said later that he did not care for the name at all; he had intended to call the team the Spartans after his old amateur club. But in seeking to procure as a home court the Renaissance Casino, which had just been built, Douglas offered to use that name for the team and thus give the Casino itself additional publicity when the basketball squad played elsewhere. The proposition was accepted and the name stuck. Outside of Harlem, though, the team was seldom if ever known by its full name. To the thousands

THE N.Y. RENS

From left to right are William "Willie" Smith, Charles "Tarzan" Cooper, John Isaacs, William "Pop" Gates, Clarence "Puggy" Bell, Eyrie Saitch, Zack Clayton and Clarence "Fats" Jenkins.

of fans all over the country who awaited their annual visits, the crack New Yorkers were known as the Rens or Rennies.

The second season the team played saw the addition to its roster of the perennial star "Fats" Jenkins, the revered George Fiall, "Clix" Garcia and the one and only "Pappy" Ricks. Forbes, Monde, Monte, Anderson, Wardell and Harold Jenkins dropped out. The replacement of Garcia by Walter Saunders in 1925 and the addition the next year of Eyre "Bruiser" Saitch were the only changes until 1930, when Fiall was replaced by Charles "Tarzan" Cooper. Bill Yancey took Saunders' spot on the team in 1930, and in 1932 Johnny "Casey" Holt replaced Harold Mayers and William "Wee Willie" Smith replaced Slocum. That squad, which remained intact through the 1934–1935 season, was viewed by Douglas as perhaps the cream of the Rens.

It was the team of Cooper, Smith, Saitch, Yancey, Holt, Jenkins and Ricks that doubled the 1925 Celtics' professional record of forty-four straight victories by gaining an amazing eighty-eight triumphs in a row. The Rens capped their performance by whipping the Celtics seven out of eight times. This marked the second season that the Rens could claim the world title; in 1929, they had defeated the Celtics and every other major American professional club in a number of series.

In 1935, Ricks and the Rens parted. Johnny Isaacs, another recruit, succeeded Jackie Bethards and Al Johnson took over for Yancey in 1936. When the team assembled in October 1939, Johnny Holt, who had become a police officer, Al Johnson and Lou Badger were among the missing. In their places were William "Pop" Gates, who had made high school basketball history at Benjamin Franklin High School in New York City; Clarence "Puggy" Bell, whose name was uttered in reverence by fans at the Harlem YMCA; and Jack Clayton, a crack defensive player and alumnus of Central High School in Philadelphia. These three,

along with Jenkins, Isaacs, Cooper, Smith and Saitch, comprised the team that won the world tournament.

Jenkins, who assumed the captaincy after Slocum's departure in 1932 and held it into the war years, was the best known. A former star athlete at Commerce High of New York City, he set longevity records for the Rens and was an inspirational floor leader throughout his career.

Next in point of service came Saitch. Admired by feminine fans as the most handsome man on the team, "Bruiser" was also a New York native, a DeWitt Clinton High School product, and the crack floor man. "Tarzan" Cooper, a veteran of more than a decade, was regarded as one of the game's top centers. He was the pivot man on all the Rens' set patterns. Smith, a 6ft.-5in. tower of power from Cleveland, had been seen by Douglas playing in a preliminary to one of the Rens' games and was signed immediately. He was voted the team's top player for the 1937–1938 season. Isaacs, from Textile High School, was a unanimous All-New York City selection at center during the 1936–1937 season; he was signed after one workout with the Rens.

The Rens' fame attracted a couple of dozen ambitious young players to New York City for tryouts every October. Douglas, eager to encourage every youngster, paid the round-trip fare and expenses in New York for every boy, even those who didn't make the club, an unusual custom in those days for there were no rules to require it.

In one typical season in the late 1930's, when the Rens were at the peak of their drawing power, the team traveled on its own bus more than 38,000 miles, including trips to Louisiana, Wyoming and Iowa. The club's publicity office estimated that it sent out more than 200,000 posters advertising the team's appearances. But that might be expected of a club that could claim ten world championships.

CHAPTER FIVE

The Milestone—Jackie Robinson

No one in the history of major league baseball ever entered the game with more impact than Jack Roosevelt Robinson. In this one individual was wrapped all the dreams and aspirations not only of Negro people but of all Americans of whatever color who knew that segregation was wrong. And at the same time, all the fears of those who, deep in their hearts, knew that when Negroes were given a chance they would prove themselves every bit the equal of whites. The biggest challenge was Jackie's. But there were risks for others, too, notably the president of the Brooklyn Dodgers, Branch Rickey, who had signed him. Rickey, however, had chosen carefully—in the player and in the man.

Jackie has always seemed to be in the middle of the action—whether on the ball field or off it. Looking back at the statistics of what he accomplished as a player, fans might question whether he was as sensational as his contemporaries said he was. After all, he finished his career with a lifetime batting average of .311, outstanding, but below the marks of men like Stan Musial and Ted Williams.

Never, however, have records meant so little in discussing a player's value as they do in the case of Jackie Robinson. His presence alone was enough to light a fire under his own team and unsettle his opponents. There was never—as Manager Leo Durocher often pointed out—a player who could beat you in as many different ways as Jackie could. Most experts thought Jackie should have been a better hitter than his record indicated. It is possible, though, that it was because hitting didn't mean as much to Robinson as it does to most players that he became the greatest all-round ball player of his time.

"I like hitting only because it's a challenge," he once said. "I always like to meet a challenge. But I don't especially care for the batting part of baseball. I like the running and the fielding better."

Jackie didn't spend as much time in the batting cage as the other regulars. It certainly had nothing to do with the fact that he was thrown at so often. Nobody ever played the game more fearlessly than Jackie did. He hung right over the plate and was always in danger of being struck by a close pitch. Only his great reflexes kept him from being hit more often than he was. He boasted early in his career that, though he might be hit often, he would never be beaned. He never was.

What probably kept Robinson from being among the great hitters, oddly enough, was that he had the most marvelous pair of legs any player ever had. He liked to run the bases and race after ground balls and pop flies. He had pride in those legs and he loved to use them. Racing through the enemy secondary on a football field, dribbling up the floor on a basketball court, out-sprinting opponents on the running track or stealing home on the diamond—these were all chances for Robinson to show off those legs. An athlete is only exciting when he takes such pleasure in his skills that he can transmit that pleasure to his audience. You know Willie Mays is having fun when you see him roaming center field, and you certainly knew that Robinson was in his glory taunting enemy pitchers on the basepaths and disturbing enemy defenses with daring dashes for the extra base.

He meant more to the Dodgers than just the fact that he would pick up an extra run for them now and then. There was his tremendous exhibition on aging legs during the 1955 season. The Dodgers had pulled off to an early lead that year, but after mid-season they began to bog down. They seemed to have lost their grip on the race. Then Robinson, who had been out of the lineup with injuries, went back in and immediately put on one of the most electrifying displays of his career. Day after day he stole bases, took the extra base on hits and infield outs, and taunted enemy pitchers into wild pick-off throws.

After one such display of daring base-running, a writer asked Jackie what had spurred him to this extraordinary effort on legs that obviously were hurting him. "This is a dead ball club," Jackie said. "We're frittering away our lead. Nobody has been able to put much life into us since that spurt in the early spring and I thought that if I took some chances it might stir things up a little. Half the time when I take the chance now I don't even care if I make it. It's just a way to stir up the boys."

Not only did Jackie run into very few "outs" during that stretch, but his brilliant display gave the Dodgers that little extra nudge they needed. They began to roll again and they won the pennant easily. Jackie's work wasn't finished, however. The Dodgers found themselves in the World Series against their arch-tormentors, the Yankees; and though some of the experts gave them a good chance in this series, it quickly began to look as if they would be frustrated again in their bid for their first world championship. The Yankees knocked them off in the first two games.

Then the Series moved from Yankee Stadium to Ebbets Field and Jackie went into action. He had given the fans a thrill in the first game by stealing home, but he didn't get much help. Now, in the third game, he brought the Brooks back to life. He belted a single and a double, scored two runs and played inspired ball at third base. He was at his most spectacular on the bases, however. No fan who saw it will ever forget his exhibition in the seventh inning. He lined a double to left and, taking a big turn at second, lured leftfielder Elston Howard into trying to pick him off the base. Feinting beautifully, Jackie drew the throw to second and then, when the unfortunate Howard had committed himself, he took off for third and made it. A moment later he scored on a single through the drawn-in infield.

That was the turning point. The Dodgers came roaring back to win their first World Series. The records show that Jackie batted only .256 during the regular season and .182 in the Series that year. The records do not show the tremendous spiritual contributions he made to the victories in the pennant race and in the Series. They were immeasurable.

Many criticized his aggressiveness when it spilled over into heated arguments with opponents and umpires. But Jackie's frequent pop-offs were as much a part of his winning spirit as his daring on the bases and his ability to dodge a bean ball and come back with a game-winning hit. He had kept most of his intense feelings bottled up through his first major league season in 1947—when he was named the National League's rookie of the year. But gradually, purposefully, he began to express his emotions the way his fellow players did.

By 1949, for example—when he batted .342, stole thirty-seven bases, and was named the league's most valuable player—he had wrangled with the umpires and been forced by Commissioner A. B. Chandler to tender an apology to umpire Cal Hubbard during the World Series. In 1950, he took the brakes off his feud with Leo Durocher and it burst forth into the open. He accused certain National League umpires of having formed a heckling cabal against him and charged they were attempting to provoke him. He invited an investigation by National League President Ford Frick. Another time, in an exhibition game at Asheville, North Carolina, he stood on the diamond chin to chin and argued heatedly with umpire Frank Dascoli for several minutes.

He resented bean balls being thrown at his head and the heads of his teammates in their interborough scraps with the Giants. In one game, he laid down a bunt to force pitcher Sal Maglie to field the ball on the first-base line, where he could bump him.

"I did it deliberately," Jackie admitted, "to force the league to step in and stop this bean balling before somebody gets hurt. I'll take the fine, the suspension or anything else that goes with it, but this throwing at a man's head has got to be stopped. If the umpires haven't the courage to stop it, then Mr. Frick should step in himself."

That night, watching the game from her usual seat at Ebbets Field, Jackie's charming wife, Rachel, who had made priceless contributions to her husband's pioneering job in baseball, became aware of a new kind of tension. A man seated near to her said, "There's a guy getting big-headed." It was a comment repeated many times over in many places, as Robinson served notice that he was as free to express himself as any other player in the game.

To appreciate Robinson's situation, one must understand what it was like for him at the start to play baseball, "in a mask." Jackie expected crank notes, abuse, roughhousing, segregation in certain hotels, animosity from the opposition and even from some of the players on his own team. But at first Jackie could not respond. In tight pennant races, in slumps, in spurts, on bad plays and close decisions by umpires, there are times a man must let off steam or burst. But for Robinson there was no release permitted.

Rachel Robinson recalls the torment of Jackie's early days in baseball: "At the end of his first season in baseball," she said, "I became extremely worried about Jack. I knew nobody could go along day after day, week after week, and month after month bottling up his emotion. I knew what Mr. Rickey had advised and, like Jack, I agreed. Yet I expected my husband to break loose at home, even if he couldn't do it on the field. Understanding his problem, which was mine as well, I would have welcomed an outburst at home. I asked him to speak his piece when we were alone together. Every man needs to talk himself out when he has a problem, but instead Jack became less talkative. He couldn't eat, and at night he'd toss constantly in his sleep. Finally, I insisted that Jack consult a doctor, who warned him if he didn't stay away from the ball park he would surely suffer a nervous breakdown. But Jack wouldn't give it up. In two days, he was back, playing as well as he ever did before and carrying the same problems around within him."

There have been stages in Jackie's life as he advanced from being a hungry little boy in a fatherless family of five children to the dominating personality he is today. There was the kid who sold papers, did odd jobs, searched for lost golf balls and junk and peddled them in and around Pasadena, California, to bring money into the house and help put food on the table.

There was the young college student pushing a broom to stay in school, while he also played football, baseball, basketball and starred for the track team. There was the Army lieutenant, in uniform as millions of other Americans were, railroaded into a court martial, charged with serious military infractions because he refused to abide by Jim Crow laws while riding a bus on an Army reservation in the South. There was the ball player, the first of his kind but one who had to subordinate his natural inclinations and personality because he knew he would not be allowed to disassociate himself from the color of his skin.

A point in each stage must be examined before the full significance of what Mrs. Robinson said can be realized. For only by examining the boy and the circumstances under which he lived can one come to know the man.

Jackie's grandmother was a Georgia slave, and his mother was a sharecropper on a big plantation. As she later was to tell her five children after their father deserted them, "It was all right. If you tend to your own business, nobody bothers you."

But Jackie never got to know about that. When he was barely over a year old, Mallie Robinson moved her family to Pasadena. A woman who would work, doing domestic chores for others, could raise a family there. They were the only Negroes on their street, but the Robinsons got along. He played with white boys, Japanese and Mexicans and even a little white girl, who, at ten, was Jackie's own age when they had their first argument.

The two kids had the same chore. Each morning, they were assigned to sweep the sidewalk in front of the house in which they lived. Jackie doesn't remember who started the

name-calling, but as all kids do he said, "You're a this," and she accepted the challenge by shouting, "You're a that." It was strictly kid stuff, the kind of spats that are all but forgotten ten minutes later. But when the girl shouted, "You little black nigger," Robinson grabbed a stone and threw it at her. The girl, in tears, called for her father, and as he came from his house, she shouted what had happened. The adult called Jackie the same name and tossed a stone at him.

Tears streaming down his face, Jackie threw some debris at the father. It started a rock fight which lasted well over an hour. The neighbors, locked behind their doors, watched the pitched battle. Mallie Robinson tried to stop it, but each time she would open her door, a stone would force her to bang it shut. Jackie's brothers, Edgar, Frank and Mack, loved it. They formed an ammunition train for their youngest brother, running from tree to tree carrying armfuls of stones.

The shame of the spectacle finally forced the man's wife to dare the barrage and drag her husband off the street and into their home. The last words Jackie heard as he and his brothers stood triumphant in the street was the woman shouting to her husband, "You ought to be ashamed of yourself out there fighting with that little boy."

It may have been there that Jackie first learned he could not run and hide from the basic hatreds which surrounded him, or perhaps it was in high school and college where he found he could give free rein to his competitive spirit and an aggressiveness which was to make him one of UCLA's all-time greats.

In Muir Tech, Jackie weighed only 143 pounds, but light as he was he could not be persuaded to stay away from varsity tryouts. He made the football team, as well as basketball, baseball and track, but his first public notice came on the gridiron. He was most spectacular in that sport. Pasadena Junior College wanted him, and after two years there it was the big

Jackie Robinson had an outstanding athletic career at UCLA, starring in track, basketball and football.

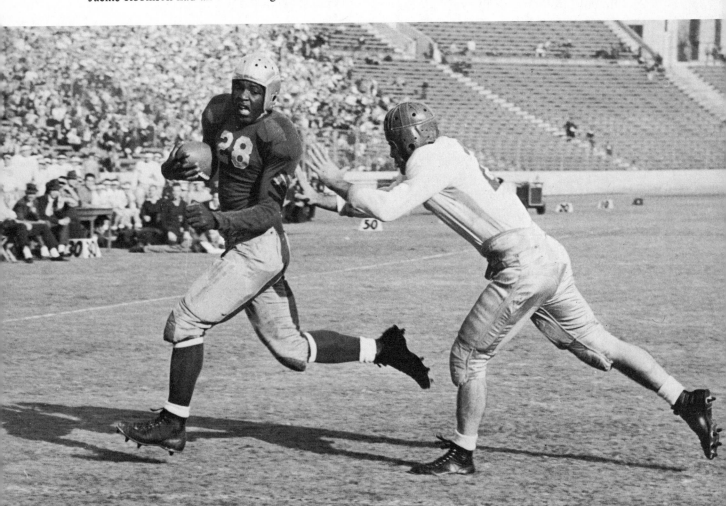

time, with Robinson running beside Kenny Washington at UCLA.

In the years to come, as Rickey narrowed his search for a Negro player down to Robinson, there was more to be considered than what sort of an athlete Jackie had been in his college days and how good a baseball player he had become. He dipped deeply into the athletic record, of course, but went beyond Jackie's 12-yard ball-carrying average in 1939. Rickey was a man with friends and contacts in every big city and little hamlet in the nation, and it was from them that he obtained information about Robinson that never appeared in the headlines or found its place in the box scores.

He learned, for example, that in high school and college Robinson had not been the kind of person other students, players, officials and coaches took to their bosoms. They cheered his performances on the athletic field if they were on his side and tried to knock him out if they were against him, but most of them disliked him. The sum-up came in the remark that as an athlete Jackie had been "over-assertive."

As Rickey searched in the remote corners of Jackie's personal life, he came across one instance that should have made it clear that Robinson was not a man who would knuckle under to intolerance, or that if he did, the result would be a backwash of emotion in him which would have to burst its dam one way or another.

In April 1942, Robinson entered the Army as a cavalry private. By 1943, he had won a commission. An old football injury had left bone chips in one ankle, however, and Army medics soon discovered these and placed him on limited service. For the next few months, Robinson shuttled between the hospital in Waco, Texas, and Camp Hood while he underwent re-examination. On one such night, Robby decided to visit the officers' club. To reach the club from the hospital sometimes took the better part of an hour. It was many miles from Waco to the post, a change of busses and another ride on Army property. When Jackie reached his destination, he learned the friends he wished to see were out on maneuvers.

Jackie started back to the hospital almost immediately, accompanied by the wife of one of his fellow officers, who was going into Waco. She was a light-skinned Negro, whose fair color was emphasized by Jackie's dark skin. As the pair took seats midway in the bus, other occupants stared at the two. But Jackie didn't notice. He was exasperated by the Army's indecision over his status and was explaining it to his companion.

In the midst of his explanation, Jackie became aware that his companion was no longer listening. She was looking to the front of the bus and as Robinson followed her gaze he heard, for the first time, the bus driver shouting at him.

"You hear me?" he called. "I said go back and sit in the rear of this bus." The driver rose from his seat and came toward Robinson. Standing above Jackie in the aisle, his face set in rage, he snarled, "Get in the back where you belong or there'll be trouble."

For a moment, Robinson said nothing. The driver was a civilian, but he must have known there was no segregation on the post. Jackie restrained his companion as she started to rise. "I'm not moving any place," he said. "You better drive this bus and leave me alone."

He couldn't cow the lieutenant, the driver knew. He returned to his seat, but still he did not throw the vehicle into gear. "When this bus gets to the front gate you better be in the rear or there's going to be trouble," he warned.

Robinson was resolute. "The directive said there's no segregation. Now just drive this bus and let me alone." The bus moved toward the gate. When it got there, the driver jumped off before his passengers. As Robinson and his companion stepped down, the driver was there. He thrust a finger at Jackie. "This is the nigger's been giving me a hard time," he said, talking to a dispatcher. Jackie wanted no trouble. He had broken no rules. He led the girl across the street where the bus to Waco would come in. As they waited, a jeep stopped at the curb. An M.P. said to Jackie, "Excuse me, sir, but the bus driver and dispatcher have complained to me there's been some trouble. They've put in a complaint about you."

Robinson explained what had happened. The M.P. said, "Would it be all right with you to come over to the Provost Marshal and get this thing cleared up? I've got to carry it through because of the complaint." Jackie entered the M.P. jeep and told his companion it shouldn't take long for the matter to be straightened. She wanted to come with him, but he assured her he would not need her testimony.

As Robinson recalls the incident now, there is understandable bitterness in his recollection and voice. To this day, he has never taken a drink of whiskey, but before that day was over, Jackie was charged with drunkenness, conduct unbecoming an officer, willful disobedience of an order and disrespect to a commanding officer.

His fellow Negro officers at Camp Hood were dismayed by what had happened. They protested the action and appealed for assistance to the National Association for the Advancement of Colored People. Before the unpleasantness was done, Jackie was forced to stand a court-martial. It was under reduced charges, and Robinson was completely exonerated.

These were some of the experiences and reactions of Jackie Robinson, the man chosen to break the color line in baseball. His baseball life had to be as unnatural, and he had to learn to live with a clearly drawn line of conduct. Plans were made by others, by friends especially, about how to deal with him.

His own conduct, on and off the field, had to be almost flawless. He could not, of course, endorse products, thus swelling his income, as other players did. He had to avoid adulation as

much as possible. Jackie was obviously a symbol, and the less time he remained one, and the sooner he became "just another ball player," the better for everyone.

How long could a man be expected to take this? Indefinitely, if what was once said by Rickey can be accepted as the real meaning of his plans. It was a bitter, wintry night on February 5, 1947. Robinson had made good at Montreal the season before. The fact was indicated by the announcement that the Dodgers had shifted their base of spring training operations from Florida, where they were threatened with locked ball parks because of Robinson, to Havana and Panama. Herbert T. Miller, Executive Secretary of the Carlton YMCA, had invited thirty distinguished Brooklyn Negroes as Rickey's guests at a dinner. They expected that Branch would announce Robinson's historic promotion to the Dodgers.

The only white people in the room, as Rickey started to speak, were Judge Edward Lazansky, Rickey's friend, and a stenographer, who had been brought to transcribe the minutes of the meeting. Though an accomplished speaker, Branch seemed to have difficulty beginning his talk. Few in the audience realized that the Brooklyn Mahatma had written three speeches for this occasion and had discarded them all.

When he did talk, Rickey talked extemporaneously. "You good people who have come here on a bitter night such as this," he said slowly and with great pause, "sort of embarrass me. The pleasant smiles on your faces are not entirely due to the fine chicken dinner. Well, I'm not going to tell you what you expect, what you want to hear."

With these words the atmosphere of the room changed suddenly. There was a tenseness, a chill, as though a cold draft of wind had somehow come through the windows into the warm room. "I was told by someone close to me that I couldn't tell you what I wanted to

The fact that Jackie was a star for Montreal made his entry into the majors a little easier.

Brooklyn Dodger Manager Leo Durocher talks things over with Robinson during an exhibition game in 1947.

Robinson's first major league game was an exhibition against the New York Yankees. Here he is shown in the first inning of that game, reaching for a high throw that arrived too late to get Phil Rizzuto at first.

The ability to beat out a bunt made Robinson one of the most feared hitters in the National League.

...use of his speed and agility, Robinson was one of the best base-runners of his time.

Robinson was not one to let a close decision go against him without a complete explanation from the umpire.

say. That I didn't have the courage to give it and that you people won't be able to take it. Well, I don't believe that. I think all of us here tonight have courage enough to give or take anything. I have a ball player named Jackie Robinson. He is on the Montreal team. He may stay there. He may be brought up to Brooklyn. I don't know at this point exactly when or if at all. But I want to say that if it happens, if Jackie Robinson does come up to the Dodgers as a major leaguer, the biggest threat to his success—the one enemy most likely to ruin that success—is the Negro people themselves.

Rickey had anticipated the effect of his words on his audience. Through the room there were exclamations of shock, amazement, even anger. "I mean it and I'll repeat it as cruelly as I can, to make you all realize and appreciate the weight of responsibility that is not only on me and my associates but on Negroes everywhere. Every step of racial progress you have made has been won by suffering and often bloodshed. This step is being taken for you by a single person whose wounds you cannot see or share. You haven't fought a single lick for this victory, if it is one. And yet, on the day that Robinson enters the big league, if he does, every one of you will go out and form parades and welcoming committees. You'll hold Jackie Robinson Days and Jackie Robinson Nights. You'll get drunk. You'll fight. You'll be arrested. You'll wine and dine the player until he is fat and futile. You'll symbolize his importance into a national comedy and an ultimate tragedy—yes, tragedy. For let me tell you this," Rickey shouted, his voice brimming with the full measure of emotion within him: "If any individual group or segment of Negro society uses the advancement of Jackie Robinson in baseball as a symbol of a social 'ism' or schism, I will curse the day I ever signed him to a contract, and I will personally see that baseball is never so abused and misrepresented again."

As a result of this extraordinary meeting and speech, further committees were formed dedicated to one purpose: "Don't spoil Jackie's chances." From Negro church pulpits throughout the territory in which baseball is played, sermons were preached on the subject. In cafes and saloons patronized by Negroes, waiters and bartenders advised their patrons against doing anything that would jeopardize Jackie's standing.

On the whole, it was an admirable campaign, and for the most part it served a tremendous purpose. Yet here was an attempt to stifle unnaturally the enthusiasm of the millions who saw in self-identification with Robinson their own step toward 100 per cent citizenship.

Rickey's detractors still say that when he opened the door for Negroes in baseball, his eye was on the ticket gate rather than on any humanitarian possibilities. Rickey himself has insisted, and those who were close to him all during the period leading up to the great experiment agree, that the motivating force behind the challenging action was pennants for the Dodgers.

This may be correct, but surely of considerably more enduring significance were the sociological aspects of Robinson's pioneering. Anyone watching Robinson entering or leaving the parks around the league would have recognized immediately his tremendous influence on a whole race of people. Thousands would wait for the Brooklyn Dodger bus to pull up in front of the stadium. They would mob Jackie on his way in and they would be there after the game to catch another glimpse of him as he left the park with his teammates. They called his name, shook his hand, touched his clothes. Jackie had a smile for them—and pleasant, friendly conversation.

Despite his pioneering, Robinson never wanted a role of reformer. All he asked, once he had proved himself to Rickey, was to be accepted as a player among other players. He didn't once whimper when the restrictions were placed upon him and the opposition began to test his courage and temper. He took everything anybody had to give. He began his career in organized baseball under a manager reared in Mississippi and was faced in his first season with the Dodgers with the threat of two strikes against him, both literally and figuratively.

Robinson may never have heard what Clay Hopper, his Montreal manager, said about him, but Jackie surely knew how the pilot felt. This was during his first spring training at Daytona Beach in 1946, when Robinson played in an intra-squad game. Jackie was splendid in the field and Rickey, who sat next to Hopper, raved about Robinson's performances. Jackie ranged far toward second base, scooped a hard-hit ground ball from the dirt, wheeled and threw to first base for a spectacular out.

"No other human being could have made that play," Rickey exclaimed to Hopper. The Mississippi man, who had remained completely uncommunicative in the previous days that must have constituted the most tumultuous period of his life, turned to Rickey. "Mr. Rickey," he said, "do you really think he *is* a human being?"

Before Robinson, whose performances that year sparked Montreal into a play-off victory, and Hopper parted company as Jackie moved up to the Dodgers, the man from Mississippi came to Rickey and said: "You don't have to worry about that man. He's the greatest competitor I ever saw. And what's more, he's a gentleman."

This was what Rickey wanted to hear, but it took more than Hopper's okay to convince some of the men with whom and against whom Jackie was destined to play in 1947.

The seeds of dissent were sown months before the announcement of Jackie's actual promotion to the Dodgers. Rickey knew Robby would be moved up, but many considera-

tions prompted a delay until the propitious moment. The Dodgers had definite weaknesses at first base and third base. Robby's arm was not fit for the long throw from third. The shift of Robinson to the position at which he had never played before seemed indicated. Rickey also had in mind the series of exhibition games between the Dodgers and Royals in which he felt sure Robinson would impress himself on the minds of the Brooklyn players as the man who could help them win the pennant.

The first step in this complicated plan was put into effect while the Dodgers were off for three weeks of side trips to Venezuela and Panama. Left behind was the Montreal club, with Robby ostensibly still a second baseman. One morning, Mel Jones, the Royals' general manager, handed Jackie a first-baseman's glove.

"What's this all about?" Jackie asked. "It's Mr. Rickey's idea," Jones explained. "He wants to give you a chance to make his club. He says there's no other place for you to play. He thinks you can learn to play first base in no time."

Robinson was definitely against the switch. He had been a shortstop with the Kansas City Monarchs and had spent a full year mastering second base. Now he was being asked to break in at a new position. Hopper, the Montreal manager, was equally enraged. He was beginning to get the idea that Rickey was using Montreal merely as the proving ground for Robinson. By so doing, Branch was keeping Howie Schultz and Ed Stevens from competing for the Royals' first-base job.

Rickey was adamant. Robinson began to work at his unfamiliar job and the strange sight, when the Dodgers returned to Havana, erased any doubts in their minds about Jackie's status. At first, the plan seemed to be proceeding in the way Rickey had hoped. But Branch soon learned that all was not well. Certain players were surreptitiously stirring up sentiment against Jackie's promotion. The grapevine reported a petition was being pre-

Robinson's smile indicates satisfaction with his contract from Dodger President Branch Rickey.

With wrists cocked and muscles tense, Jackie waits for the right moment to meet the ball.

Robinson poses with National League President Warren Giles and other members of the All-Star Team, Curt Simmons, Bob Rush and Ed Sauer.

ter a great career on the ball field, Robinson
epted an executive position with the Chock Full
O' Nuts Company in New York.

Along with the Rev. Martin Luther King, Jr., Robinson
was awarded an honorary Doctor of Laws degree from
Howard University in 1959.

Jackie Robinson poses with his wife Rachel after being the first Negro voted into Baseball's Hall of Fame.

pared. Harold Parrott, the Dodgers' traveling secretary, was the first member of the front-office staff to learn of the underground dissension, although not to this day has anybody uncovered the initiator of the revolt.

He rushed to Rickey with his information. Branch was astounded. He had not figured such a turn, but he was up to it. Whatever steps Branch took at this point are still uncertain. Some people say he enlisted the help of Eddie Stanky, who initiated counter-propaganda that had the effect of lessening interest in the petition. Others insist that Branch called in every member of this group and told them he was aware what they were doing and offered to trade them if they felt they could not be on the same side with a Negro.

Most of the players backed down when Rickey confronted them with the knowledge of their plot. Two men, reared in the tradition of the South, gradually emerged as particularly obstinate. One was Bobby Bragan; the other was Dixie Walker, who, in his years of playing with Brooklyn, had become the most popular performer at Ebbets Field.

Rickey's interview with Bragan was one of the most heated, but Bobby, a third-string catcher, remained firm in his conviction against Robinson. "Would you like your contract transferred to another club?" Rickey asked. "Yes, sir, I would," Bragan said. "But I don't want to be made the goat of a mess I didn't create." "Then I may accommodate you, sir!" Rickey replied. "Good night."

On March 26, 1947, Rickey received a letter from Walker, which Dixie later sought to have returned to him. In it Walker spoke feelingly of his years in Brooklyn but said it would be best for all concerned if a trade to another team could be arranged for him. Branch quickly attempted to effect such a deal.

But a contemplated deal with Pittsburgh never came off, and so it was that Bragan and Walker played through a season with Robinson. The trouble they had anticipated from within did not arise, but as Jackie's teammates, they had front row seats in observing how he reacted to the hostility from the opposition, if not from his own teammates.

When the season was over, Bragan came to Rickey and said that while his attitude about Negroes in general had not changed, he felt it only fair to say he had begun to like Robinson and playing on the same team with him. Rickey could not have asked Bobby to say more. When a managerial opening developed at Fort Worth, Rickey gave the job to Bragan. Walker, of course, was eventually sent to Pittsburgh, but not until he had spurned an offer from Rickey to manage the Dodgers' St. Paul farm.

In their one season together on the team, Robinson and Dixie were particularly circumspect in their relations with each other. Robby knew and appreciated the torment that the season must have been for Dixie, and when it was over and Robinson was asked about their relationship, he said: "I think Dixie had accepted me on the ball club so far as the playing end of it went. Socially, no. But that was perfectly all right with me. I understood and it wasn't embarrassing except once or twice when he hit a home run while I was on base. Normally, you wait at the plate to shake hands with the man who hits the home run. With Dixie, I wasn't sure what he expected me to do but I thought it would be the smart thing to get out of there. I would just go to the dugout without waiting for him to reach the plate."

In the sum total of incidents that have surrounded Jackie's days in baseball, this now becomes a minor one. Difficulty was avoided by walking around the corner, so to speak. But there were others that would have to be met bluntly, with a head-on attack, if necessary.

A short while after the Phillies, under Ben Chapman's direction, worked Jackie over profanely, he appeared in the Dodgers' office. It was thought at the time that he had come to ask for some sort of assistance against such attacks. One club official asked Jackie if he wanted an emissary to go to Chapman or Robert Carpenter, the Philly boss.

"I do not," Jackie said bluntly. "They'll either stop it by themselves or they won't stop it at all. Either I can take it or I can't. I didn't come for that anyway." Jackie took a letter from his pocket. "This came in the mail for me today. It may be nothing but a crank. It may be serious."

The letter did, without any doubt, call for action because it was the first of many such threatening notes Jackie was to receive. The letter, threatening physical harm to Jackie and his family, was turned over to New York's police commissioner. The authorities learned the name signed to it was fictitious and so was the address.

Hardly had this crisis been discovered to be a very minor affair when one arose that had repercussions all through the nation. It was learned that the St. Louis Cardinals intended to strike in protest against Robinson on May 16. The disclosure was all that was needed to prevent what could have become the seamiest incident in the history of baseball. To this day, Jackie himself expresses uncertainty that any strike was contemplated. Yet despite denials by the Cardinal players, president Sam Breadon, their owner, as well as Branch Rickey and Ford Frick, president of the National League, admitted that such a movement had gained headway in the Red Bird locker room. Quick action had rendered it stillborn.

Frick sent an ultimatum to the Cardinals. In it he said, "If you do this, you will be suspended from the league. You will find that the friends you have in the press box will not support you, that you will be outcasts. I do not care if half the league strikes. Those who do will encounter quick retribution."

There was no strike and as the season progressed the opposition, which had contended that the idea of playing a Negro in the majors could not possibly work and would only breed trouble, noted soon enough that Robinson's presence on the diamond was good for baseball instead of being bad for it.

Wherever the Dodgers played, great crowds came to see Jackie. Not just Negroes, although Jackie's presence on the field increased their numbers in the stands immeasurably, but there were more whites, too, and like all others, they soon discovered Robinson was a big leaguer in every way.

It is almost impossible to make an accurate evaluation of what Robinson has meant to baseball and, indeed, to the American way of life. The record book supplies the evidence that he was one of the great players since World War II, and it notes that he was elected to baseball's Hall of Fame in 1962. Everyone knows about his batting, his stolen bases, and his versatility in playing first, second, third and left field. But where is there written proof of the inspirational lift he gave his teammates time and again? Where does it say that Robinson found more ways to beat the other side? Where does it say, in the records, as Birdie Tebbetts once said, "In one spot, in one ball game, where I need the one big base hit, I'd rather have Jackie Robinson up there for me than any other man in baseball?" Or, as Leo Durocher said, "When it came to the key spot of winning or losing a ball game, Robinson was the one man I feared most." Jack dominated this sport in his time.

Now he works for New York's Governor Nelson Rockefeller as special assistant for community affairs, is chairman of the board of the Freedom National Bank, and serves as vice president of a new enterprise, the Proteus Company, designed to provide business opportunities through the establishment of a chain of seafood stands. He speaks out on civil rights, politics and issues of public concern. He goes at life with the same unrelenting drive he had for excellence in baseball. And he notes, characteristically, "I think I've been much more aggressive since I left baseball."

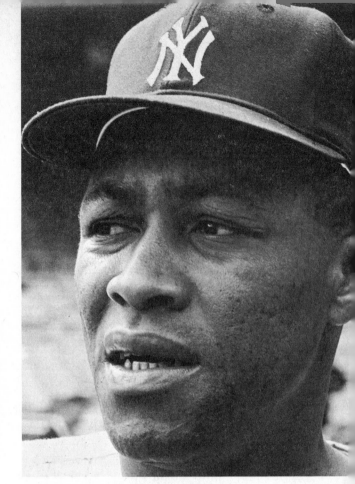

Willie Mays

Elston Howard

Frank Robinson

Maury Wills

CHAPTER SIX

Stars on the Diamond

Baseball is often called "The National Pastime." Whether or not that claim is accurate, baseball is the oldest established professional sport in the nation, which made it particularly significant when Jackie Robinson broke its racial barrier in 1946. But Robinson's appearance, even though closely followed by other performers, such as Roy Campanella and Don Newcombe of the Dodgers and Larry Doby of the Indians, didn't bring an immediate rush of Negro stars. Some teams, such as the New York Yankees, the Boston Red Sox, and the Washington Senators, held out a long time—or until they knew they could not continue to compete without tapping the Negro market. Not merely the Negro player market, it might be added, but the Negro fan market as well, for the appearance of the players brought Negro fans to the ball park in unprecedented numbers.

Over the past decade, much has changed. Now Negro players are a significant factor in the major and minor leagues of baseball. The 1960 Census recorded an 11-per-cent Negro population for the country. Yet for the 1967 season, of the eighty players (not counting pitchers) who could be rated regulars on the ten National League teams, twenty-seven were Negroes, or just over one-third. In the American League, the number was twenty-one, or better than one-quarter. For the same season, five of the top ten batters in the National League were Negroes, and three in the American. Even more striking is this fact: of the nineteen National League most valuable players from 1949, when Jackie Robinson became the first Negro so honored, until 1967, twelve were Negroes; two of the past five in the American League have been Negroes.

The story began with Robinson. But it has continued with stars of equal magnitude— Willie Mays, Henry Aaron, Frank Robinson, Maury Wills, to name a few. A new coterie appears, like Bob Gibson and Richie Allen, to continue the Negro's rise to glory in professional baseball.

Roy Campanella

"Of all the men playing baseball today," said baseball immortal Ty Cobb in 1953, "the one they will talk about the most twenty or thirty years from now will be Campanella." Cobb's remark came at the crest of Roy Campanella's career with the Brooklyn Dodgers, and Cobb was talking about a man who would win three most valuable player awards in the National League—a stocky catcher who could put together a season of a .312 batting average, 142 runs-batted-in, and 41 home runs—as Roy did in 1953.

There was a special excitement to his play. Though he appeared fat, he could pounce with deadly swiftness on a slow-rolling ball in front of the plate and throw his man out. At the plate in his widespread stance, bat cocked high, he could launch into a powerful swing that had somewhat the same effect on crowds that Babe Ruth's swing had in another era. Connecting solidly, he would send the ball on a high arc deep into the left-field seats. Missing cleanly, he would spin completely around, going almost to his knees and drawing long "oohs" and "aahs" from the crowd. No one could deny his substantial contributions to the Dodger pennants in 1949, 1952, 1953, 1955 and 1956.

He caught with all kinds of injuries and had a love for the game that was unequalled. One day late in 1956, when he wasn't doing so well and everyone was suddenly aware that he was thirty-five years old, Roy repeated a question: "What am I gonna do when I'm through? I'm not gonna be through. They may be ready to take me, but I'm not going."

He was taken two years later, about 3 A.M. on January 28, 1958. He had closed his Harlem liquor store at midnight and then spent another busy hour and a half tidying up and checking receipts. He left the store, got into his rented sedan and headed for his beautiful home on Long Island, where he had great kids, a $35,000 yacht, and a beautiful wife, Ruthe, who was one of the most popular women in the country club the Campanellas belonged to.

Roy was on an S curve, about a mile from his house, when he hit ice. The sedan went into a skid. The right fender hit a telephone pole, the sedan whipped into a spin, turned over and for a moment the night was rent by the awful noise of shattering glass and tearing metal. It took crowbars and thirty minutes to get Campy out from under the dashboard. His body was wreckage.

His 18½-inch neck was broken. The surgeons drilled holes on each side of his skull, then clamped in hooks to hold his head steady. But that wasn't the worst of it. Campy's spinal cord had been severed at the fourth cervical vertebra. The only muscle life and sensation remaining below Campy's neck was in his shoulders and arms. He could raise his elbows almost to the level of his shoulders but his hands were lifeless.

Yet he was alive. He refused to die and he fought back against the odds. In a wheelchair but out of the hospital in the early 1960's, he rebuilt his life. He got himself radio and television shows and his liquor store was making good money. Then his new life was shattered.

Ruthe's boy, David, whom Campy had raised from the age of two, was in trouble with the law. Campy was bewildered. He himself always walked a straight line. In three thousand games he never even called an umpire a dirty name.

In January of 1963, Ruthe died of a heart attack. Six months later Campy remarried. He was going to put the pieces together again but his troubles weren't over. When CBS bought the Yankees, Campy's radio and television shows were cancelled. When New York State changed its liquor laws, taking off price controls, a lot of small liquor dealers, including Campy, were badly hurt. Still, through it all, Roy Campanella endured.

Campy had always taken things as they came. He left school at sixteen in 1936 and knocked around in the Negro leagues for ten

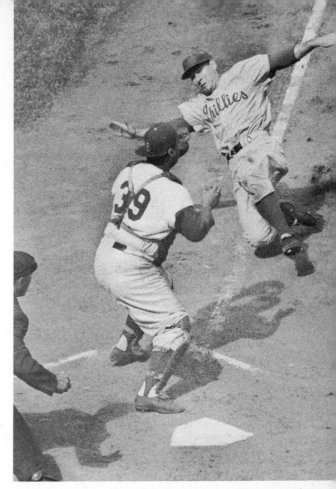

With his bat, his glove and his dugout wisdom, Roy Campanella was truly a "100% ballplayer." Although the crippling auto accident slowed him down, he could visit the ball park to see old friends, like Johnny Podres (below).

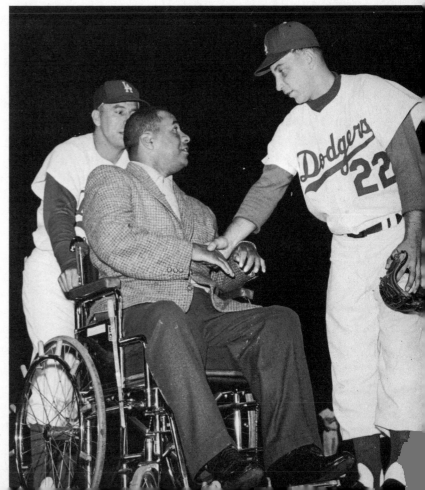

years without really hoping to make the major leagues. But then in 1946 he was signed by the Dodgers and sent to their class B farm team in Nashua, New Hampshire. He subsequently advanced to AAA St. Paul and, midway through the 1948 season, the Brooklyn Dodgers sent out a call for Campanella. They felt he was ready. They were right. He caught his usual superb game from the start and socked nine hits in his first twelve times up, including two homers.

The next year he won the Yankees' admiration for his play against them in the World Series. Though the Dodgers lost four games to one, Campy picked off such smart baserunners as Phil Rizzuto and Tommy Henrich. "As long as I've been playing," marveled Rizzuto, "that's the first time I was ever picked off third by a catcher. What an arm that guy has."

In 1951, he batted .325, hit 33 homers, drove in 108 runs and won his first MVP award. Now he was an established star. Thereafter came glory days mixed with seasons marked by injury, and then, finally, his tragic accident.

Roy himself probably best summed up his career in a conversation he had with a reporter after a ball game with the Cardinals. He had hit home runs in five straight games and would have tied the record for homers in consecutive games if he could have belted another in this one. But he didn't, although on his last trip he hit a fly that was only about fifteen feet short of the left-field stands. The crowd, keenly aware of the record-tying possibility, whooped loudly as the ball flew off Campy's bat, and groaned in disappointment when the fly was caught.

"You missed a chance at a record," the writer said to Roy afterward. "Never mind the record," Roy said. "We won, didn't we?" He stopped to light up a big cigar. He took a long puff of the aromatic blue smoke and grinned contentedly, patting his substantial stomach. He looked around the locker room at the other Dodgers.

"I don't have anything to kick about," he said softly. "I've had some pretty good days."

Elston Howard

Elston Howard had always excelled in sports. He was exceptional in high school athletics, starring in football (at end), track (shot put), and basketball (forward) and compiling a .500 batting average in baseball. His mother wanted him to study medicine in college, but that was forgotten when he accepted an offer from the Kansas City Monarchs for $600 a month. "I wanted to try baseball," he said, "and we all had in the back of our minds the major leagues. Jackie Robinson had been signed by the Dodgers and that is all Negro players talked about."

The one-year tour with the Monarchs taught Howard a valuable lesson. He realized he didn't want to play baseball in the Negro leagues. "We would start out at 6 o'clock after a doubleheader in one town, bounce along for ten or twelve hours and arrive in the next town in time for two more games. We would eat cold hamburgers in the bus. Sometimes we would drive an awful long distance to find a garage which would allow Negroes in the bathroom."

The Yankees paid the Monarchs $30,000 for his contract in 1950 and assigned the twenty-year-old catcher-outfielder to Muskegon, Michigan, in the Central League. The following year Howard was drafted into the Army and spent two years playing baseball. In 1953, he reported to his first Florida camp with the Yankees' Binghamton, New York, club. It was decided he'd be a catcher exclusively, which seemed to be a bad move for Howard. Yogi Berra was at the height of his game as a twenty-eight-year-old catcher who played every day.

A reporter told Howard: "The Yankees are giving you the runaround. They have Berra for catching. If they wanted you on the team it would be as an outfielder."

With a sure glove, a fiery competitive spirit and a strong bat, Elston Howard fit the pattern of a typical New York Yankee. But his greatest achievement was being the first Negro to be chosen as the American League's most valuable player.

"I don't think so," said Howard, "let's wait and see." To Casey Stengel, who was about to win his fifth straight pennant and World Series as Yankee manager, it was the logical move. "I saw him run," said Casey, "and I knew he wouldn't play the outfield real good. I also saw him bat and he had power. Why wouldn't you have him catching against left-handed pitchers and playing the outfield when you needed him?"

Howard showed enough in camp to be promoted to Kansas City, then a minor league team, where he hit .286. The next season, at Toronto, he batted .330, won the International League's most valuable player award and was brought up to the Yankees.

In 1955, his rookie season, Howard played the outfield, caught, played first base and hit .290 as a one-man right-handed hitting platoon. He got into ninety-seven games and the other subs called him "Casey's bo-bo." "I was second string to a man (Berra) who was going to be in the Hall of Fame, so thank God I could play other positions. That kept me going," said Howard.

With Berra going strong, Howard played 98 games in 1956, 110 in 1957, 103 in 1958 and 125 in 1959. Most of the time he was in the outfield. His fielding did not entitle him to much notice, but he made up for it with one catch in the 1958 World Series against the Braves. Howard earned the Babe Ruth Award as the hero of that series (the first Negro to be so honored), and it was mostly on the strength of that one catch.

The Braves, who had beaten the Yankees in 1957, were leading the Series three games to one. The Braves were at bat in the sixth inning of the fifth game with the Yankees leading, 1–0. Bruton singled. Then Red Schoendienst dropped a short fly ball into left field. Howard, playing the difficult sun field, raced in for the looper, slid on his knees, stuck out his glove, lost his hat and caught the ball in the webbing of his glove. Bruton was doubled at first, and

when Eddie Mathews followed with a single it was a meaningless hit. The Yankees scored six times in the bottom half of the inning and eventually won the Series, four games to three.

Berra began to slip the next season and by 1960, Stengel's last year with New York, Howard was No. 1 catcher. Under manager Ralph Houk in 1961, Howard had his best season. He hit .348. The trouble was, hardly anybody noticed. Norm Cash hit .361 but not many people noticed that either. It was 1961 and the year of Roger Maris' sixty-one homers.

"I have the best year of my life," said Howard, "and I have to pick that season." Elston reached the pinnacle of his career in 1963. Maris and Mantle were both injured much of the season and Howard caught 135 games, held the Yankees together, batted .287 and nursed along the young Yankee pitching staff.

A couple of months later it was official— Howard had become the first American League Negro to win the most valuable player award. What did that mean to Howard and his family?

"It meant so much," his wife said, "because of the American Negro revolution. It makes me proud, him being the first. I tried to explain it to Elston, Jr. (age seven at the time) what it meant to have his father get the award. The older boys in school made it sound very big to him. He asked me. 'What's the MVP?' I told him, 'It's like winning the Nobel Prize, Elston. Only it's the Nobel Prize of baseball.'"

Bob Gibson

The best summation of Bob Gibson's pitching style comes from Bob himself: "I never save myself—never!" From the moment the St. Louis Cardinal right-hander first steps on the pitching rubber, Bob Gibson is a hard-throwing, tough-minded pitcher who expends all the strength in his body to attain victory for his team.

The Boston Red Sox found this out in the

The fireballing motion of Bob Gibson.

1967 World Series. Gibson went against them three times and came out with three complete-game victories. He gave up just fourteen hits in the twenty-seven innings he pitched, tying Christy Mathewson's sixty-two-year-old Series record. For his three overpowering victories Gibson was voted the World Series' outstanding performer.

The triumphs were really a comeback for Gibson. On July 15, he had suffered a fractured right shinbone when he was hit by a line drive off the bat of Roberto Clemente. He missed eight weeks of the season and didn't start another game until September. The injury had kept Gibson's record to 13–7, but he had already established himself as a big winner with eighteen victories in 1963, nineteen in 1964, twenty in 1965 and twenty-one in 1963. Hitters respected his lively pitching arm, but there were whispers as late as 1964 that Bob Gibson was a seven-inning pitcher. "Stay near him into the late innings," some said, "and you can beat him." The Philadelphia Phillies, in particular, felt Gibson deserved that reputation.

Gibson's reputation suggested he could not win nine of eleven games during the 1964 pennant stretch as he did, including a 5–1 victory over the Phillies in the opener of a crucial series that last week of the season. The reputation suggested he couldn't pitch thirty-nine innings in the last two weeks of the season, then strike out thirty-one batters in the World Series (a record). The reputation certainly suggested he could not win two Series games, including the last one. Yet all those feats became part of Gibson's 1964 record.

"I always thought he was the kind of man you could depend on," said his manager at the time, Johnny Keane. "I set him up to open important series, to get us off right." Keane admitted that the reputation had its basis, although not the basis the whispers suggested. "He did have a problem," Keane said. "He gave so much of himself on every pitch that we had to watch him in the late innings."

"I never pace myself," Gibson admitted. "I just go out there and give all I've got as long as I can."

"He'd be exhausted at the end of a game," Keane said. "But I wanted to leave him in every game. I felt that he would do better for me, as tired as he was, than anybody in the bullpen. I had the feeling that he'd reach back and find one more pitch. There was no holding back with him. Another pitcher, you might not be sure he could reach back. You knew it with Gibson."

Gibson had every opportunity to disappoint Keane and validate the whispers, even in the last game of the 1964 World Series. With a 6–0 lead in the sixth inning, Gibson gave up a three-run homer to Mickey Mantle. Keane visited the mound.

"I went out there to see how he looked," Keane recalled. "I wanted to see if he was upset by the home run. I wasn't going to take him out. I had a commitment to his heart."

Gibson wasn't coming out. "I'll go get 'em," he told Keane. He struggled with a weary arm and a weary body and held off the Yankees to gain a 7–5 victory and the Cardinals' first World Series Championship in eighteen years.

Bob's determination has always been apparent. He overcame more than his share of childhood illnesses and grew up tall (6ft.-1in.) and strong (190 pounds) and athletic. He was the star athlete at Omaha's Tech High; the St. Louis Cardinals and Creighton University were paying close attention. His brother, Josh, had studied for his master's degree at Creighton, which is in Omaha. Josh persuaded Bob to try Creighton for a year. Bob stayed four years. He became the outstanding basketball player there (21-point average) and the star outfielder (.368), as well as an occasional pitcher. He also attended classes and that was college for him. "I didn't do much else," he said. "Sports and homework. I was living at home so I wasn't on campus very much."

He left Creighton after four years but he didn't leave Omaha. Bill Bergesch, general manager of the Cardinal farm team there, had been supplying Josh Gibson's city recreation department with bats and balls for years; there was a lot of goodwill built up. Josh brought Bob to the ball park one day, introduced him to Bergesch and Johnny Keane, who was the manager there—and Gibson was a Cardinal. Gibson had a 2–1 record in ten games for Keane. "He had been mostly an outfielder in college," Keane recalled. "He needed a lot of work."

When the baseball season was over, Gibson made a tour of the country with the Harlem Globetrotters. "Don't give me a lot of publicity about it," he once said. "I only played one winter." He had not been drafted by any of the National Basketball Association teams and he may have wanted to prove something to himself. But the Cardinals forbade him to play after that winter.

"I think he did it for the money," Keane has said. "He was a fine basketball player but I don't think he felt like a Globetrotter. He plays a different brand of ball than they do. I don't think of him as being a Globetrotter type."

Gibson did some trotting of his own the next three years: Omaha, Rochester and St. Louis —back and forth. But by 1961, the Cardinals were the old home team. He's been there ever since, giving his all—which is considerable.

Don Newcombe

The high fastball thrown to the inside corner is a classic pitch, provided it is both fast and live. In Don Newcombe's best years he often used his fastball, then mixed in a sharp curve at the knees outside, with excellent results. Leo Durocher once remarked about Newcombe, "When those two pitches are working right, there's no way to hit him."

As a rookie in 1949, those pitches had to be pretty good because Newcombe won seventeen

games. In succeeding seasons he won nineteen and then twenty, before going into military service. He came out in 1954 and won only eight games, but then took twenty and twenty-seven the next two years. That 1956 season was a marvelous one for him—a 27–7 record, a pennant for the Brooklyn Dodgers, the most valuable player award for him—but it ended with a bitterness he was never really able to shake off.

Despite all the games he won for a team that was almost always in the pressure of a pennant race, Newcombe had been accused throughout his career of never being able to take the big game. His critics pointed out how Tommy Henrich's homer had beaten him 1–0 in a Series game in 1949, how Dick Sisler's homer had defeated him in the tenth inning of a game with Philadelphia that decided the 1950 pennant, and so on.

Then in his first start against the Yankees in the 1956 Series—and still looking for his first Series victory—Don Newcombe was knocked out in the second inning when Yogi Berra hit a homer with the bases full. When a parking lot attendant taunted him after the game, Newcombe allegedly punched him.

Newk got a chance to redeem himself. The Series went to the decisive seventh game and the Dodgers called on their twenty-seven-game winner. By the fifth inning, he had yielded two homers to Berra and one to Elston Howard, and he left the game, losing 5–0. The Dodgers couldn't make up the deficit.

What followed was cruel torment for a pitcher who had contributed so much to those powerful Dodger teams of that era. Two years after that twenty-seven-victory season, Newcombe was an ineffective pitcher, and retired. What effect his World Series problems had had could only be guessed.

Newk had entered organized baseball in 1946 after an unhappy boyhood in Elizabeth, New Jersey, and a brief, bright career pitching for the Negro Newark Eagles, from which

Don Newcombe set records both as a pitcher and as a hitter. Here he is shown with two of his most prized awards, the Cy Young Memorial Award and the National League's Most Valuable Player (MVP) Award.

Larry Doby moved to the major leagues. About his childhood he later said: "I was kind of a bad kid in school. Not like some kids now, guns or things. But it seems like I was always talking back to a teacher or getting called down to the principal's office or something like that. If my father hadn't worked for a man on the board of education, I probably would have been kicked out of school."

Don got through junior high school (where he failed to make the baseball team) and one year of high school. By then he was playing semi-pro baseball, and soon it was year-round, in his home area during the summer and in South America in the winter. One evening in 1946, Don and his wife were coming home from a movie when he bought a newspaper and saw the headline: "Robinson, First Negro, Signed by Montreal."

A short time later, Branch Rickey signed Newcombe for the Dodgers. At first, though, Brooklyn had trouble finding another minor-league team that would take a Negro player. Finally, the club in Nashua, New Hampshire, agreed. There, at the age of twenty, Newk won fourteen games and lost four; the next year he won nineteen for Nashua and moved up to Montreal. Then, of course, he went to Brooklyn.

After he left baseball, without being offered any job within the game, Newcombe went into business in Newark, New Jersey. He was successful awhile, but then the business failed. He moved to Los Angeles, where he became an executive with a natural gas producing company, specializing in ways of training the hard-core unemployed. "Baseball kept me out of trouble," he has told the young men he works with, and he wants to do the same for others.

Richie Allen

One day early in his rookie year in 1964, Richie Allen hit a homer, a triple and two singles to lead the Philadelphia Phillies to victory

over Cincinnati. Afterwards, Philadelphia manager Gene Mauch commented, "He's so strong he'll hit a ball some day and split it in half. He'll get a single to right and a single to left!"

By season's end, Allen had twenty-nine homers, ninety-one runs-batted-in and a .318 batting average. He was the rookie of the year and ever since that time players, managers and fans have marveled over his strength and ability with the bat. Though he has had trouble with his fielding (at third base and in the outfield), getting along with his teammates and bosses, and remaining healthy (he seriously damaged two tendons and a nerve in his right hand as a result of an accident in August 1967), Allen has already reached superstar status. There are very few ball players around who can put together a season of forty homers, 110 runs-batted-in, and a .317 average the way Richie did in 1966.

During his short career, ever since leaving his hometown of Wampum, Pennsylvania, Allen has had more trouble fighting down his own temper than with any of the mechanics of baseball. Richie's manager during his first two years of minor league ball ran a strict ship, refusing him permission to steal bases at his own discretion and otherwise holding a tight rein on him. "I like to play ball like I'm playing in an alley somewhere," says Richie. "But under that man I was playing *not* to do something wrong."

The manager changed Richie's batting stance, Richie says, and his average plunged. "I said, 'Let me hit my own way,' and he said, 'Okay, you'll hit .200.' Then he said a few more things and I packed my clothes and bought a ticket and called my mom to tell her I was coming home. But she said, 'It's time you grow up now. You're out in the world on your own. Be a man.'"

Richie hit .281 and .317 those first two years in the minors. But the Phillies, experimenting with him at shortstop and then second

One of the National League's newest superstars is the Phillies' Richie Allen. A power-hitter with good speed on the base paths, Allen has improved his fielding in his desire "to be known as the best."

base, were so dissatisfied with his fielding that they offered him to the National League's two new franchises, Houston and New York. Neither wanted him.

The Phillies in 1963 assigned him to their top farm club, Little Rock, although no Negro had ever played there. The city's violent 1957 stand for school segregation remained fresh in Richie's mind, and at first he rejected the promotion. He was ready once more to pack his bags and go home, but Pat Corrales persuaded him to report. "I was scared to death," says Richie.

He remembers the difficulties of Little Rock—his first day in town when a restaurant counterman told him, "Go in the kitchen and tell the cook what you want" . . . the stuffy Negro movie house . . . shouting fans, whom he assumed were abusive drunks. He says he was miserable. "I used to pray at night, 'God, just give me the strength to go out there and play good ball.' I wanted to do good for my race— for the Negroes who would have to play in Little Rock in the future."

Richie hit only .289 at Little Rock but his thirty-three home runs—many of them produced in a home park not suited to right-handed power hitters—led the triple-A International League. Even though Richie had never played third base, manager Gene Mauch told the front office: "Let me have that fellow. I can make a third baseman out of him."

Richie was finally in the majors and off on a successful, if stormy, career. Some criticized his fielding—he made forty-one errors that first year—and others began to find fault with his not showing up on time at the ball park and, later, for his lack of interest in spring training. In 1965, there was his on-field brawl with teammate Frank Thomas. In 1968, when Gene Mauch was fired, many people said the reason was his inability to get along with Allen.

But through all the controversy, Allen kept up his power hitting. The boos, the cheers, even the healing hand injury didn't impede his success at the plate. "I'd just like to be known as the best," he says, and no one seemed willing to bet against him.

Ernie Banks

In his time, Ernie Banks didn't merely play the game of baseball—he almost revolutionized it. He was the first great slugger of the "Era of the Lively Bat" and he introduced the era by going to a lighter, snappier bat.

The result: he became the hardest-hitting shortstop in the history of the major leagues. In one six-season span—1955 to 1960—he hit more home runs than any other player in the majors. He hit 248 homers; Mickey Mantle, 236; Willie Mays, 214. He won the MVP award in 1958 (47 homers and 129 runs-batted-in) and 1959 (45 homers and 143 runs-batted-in), and became the first National Leaguer to win it two years in a row.

But more than that, the entire style of slugging changed. All over major league baseball, the batters began following Banks' precedent. The light-but-lively bat became the style for sluggers in the big leagues. As it happened, the lively-bat era that Banks introduced was ideally tailored to his own physical dimensions. He looked as burly as a broomstick and his weight was as carefully disguised as a CIA agent. "I carry it in my toes," he said wryly. "I've got very muscular toes." A small-boned man with delicate features, in his batting helmet he looked a trifle like "little boy lost." But he got his power into the swing by the snapping of the wrists, not by a big powerful sweep of his arms. In effect, he lashed his bat at the ball, a little like snapping a whip. The effect had the beauty and brevity of great art. "Ernie Banks swings a bat the way Joe Louis used to punch, short and sweet," said Clyde McCullough, long a major league catcher. The result is that the ball leaps off the bat. "Ernie hits line drives, not fly balls," said Sheffing. "And

Ernie Banks of the Chicago Cubs demonstrates the long stride and powerful wrist action that have made him one of the most feared sluggers in the National League.

Despite a busy schedule, Banks takes time out to visit with members of the Long Island City Boy's Club.

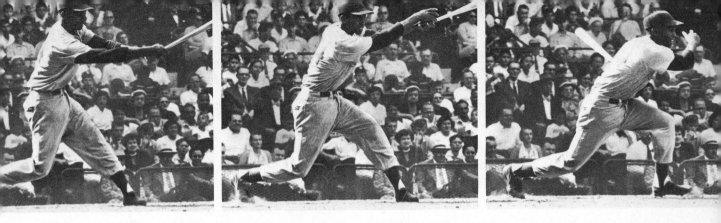

Ernie Banks became the first National League player to be named MVP in two successive years. Here he is shown receiving the award from National League President Warren Giles.

they get off his bat so fast and hit the wall so fast that he frequently gets only singles instead of doubles."

Ernie had joined the Cubs in 1953. He and Gene Baker came in together, the first Negroes to play for the team. Baker was 5½ years older than Banks, played shortstop in the minors and played it ably. But when the two men reached the Cubs—Ernie's only experience being with the Negro League Kansas City Monarchs—Baker shifted to second and Banks was sent in at shortstop. "They felt that Gene had more experience and could make the change more easily than I could," said Ernie.

Banks did very well at shortstop. He was never a great fielder because he had only an average throwing arm, but he was good enough. In 1959, he handled more chances than any other shortstop in baseball—and he set a record for fielding by shortstops that still stands: .985 in 154 games.

Then he injured a leg and that made it more difficult to cover ground at shortstop. In 1961, the Cubs shifted him to left field, but that was not the ideal position for a man with a bad leg and a throwing arm that was never powerful. So the next year, the Cubs moved him to first base—and there he performed ably and occasionally brilliantly. In 1966, for instance, only one first baseman in the National League committed fewer errors than Banks—Bill White of Philadelphia, who had nine errors to ten by Banks. And only one first baseman in the National League handled more chances than Banks—White again, who appeared in twenty-eight games more than Banks.

It wasn't easy, but he always had the determination; the positive thinking developed in all the years of frustration (for his team, not himself). It took determination—and a superb, if muffled, talent—to make it to the big leagues.

Ernie grew up in the shadow of the Depression. Born on January 31, 1931, he was the second of twelve children sired by Eddie Banks, a one-time semi-pro catcher who later became a wholesale grocer in Dallas, Texas. Young Ernie played football and basketball and softball and ran track—but never baseball. "My dad, he bought me a glove for about $2.98 when I was a kid but he had to bribe me with nickels and dimes to play catch," Ernie once said.

But his natural athletic talent was so obvious that it had to lead to the big leagues. The route was devious: he played softball so well that when he was seventeen, he got a chance to play with a semi-pro team, the Amarillo Colts, that barnstormed the south and the middle-west. That, in turn, led to a summer swing with the Kansas City Monarchs baseball team. He spent two years in the Army, then returned to the Monarchs to bat .386 and hit 20 home runs. It was an active life but hardly an affluent one: "Five, ten, maybe 15,000 miles a year and our biggest payday was in Lincoln, Nebraska—$20 for the night." But the Cubs bought him from the Monarchs in 1953—and that led him to affluence.

Ernie's one big disappointment was never getting to play in a World Series, but the even-tempered superstar always played on, hitting his homers and dreaming of pennants. "If not this year," he would say, "then next year." Ernie learned to live, though, with the fact that he might never make it to the Series. "I was taught," he said, "that whatever I have, to be happy with it." With a record like his, Ernie Banks has plenty to be happy about.

Maury Wills

In baseball, where statistics are worshiped, two records, each set by a god of the game, were long recognized as supreme. The first, Babe Ruth's record of sixty home runs in a season, inevitably had to be broken. The second, Ty Cobb's record of 96 stolen bases in a season, seemed unlikely ever to be broken. The reason was simple: baseball, built upon speed when Cobb set his record, had been rebuilt upon slugging after Ruth set his record.

In 1962, Maury Wills brought speed back to baseball with a significance it had not known for five decades. He stole 104 bases, and made speed the major weapon of a Los Angeles Dodger offense that came within an inning of winning a pennant. He intimidated opponents, inspired teammates, induced fans to uninhibited delight.

The little shortstop played his heart out for the Dodgers that year, batting .299 and scoring 130 runs, in addition to his base-stealing. He was named the league's most valuable player. Typical of his fierce play was a game against Houston that went into the thirteenth inning, tied 3–3. Wills drew a walk. Then he stole second and third and scored the winning run after the catch of a pop fly to shallow right field. The pennant chase came down to a final play-off game against the Giants, and Wills got four singles, stole three bases and scored a run. Yet it wasn't enough as the Giants scored four runs in the ninth to win, 6–4.

Wills played eight years with the Dodgers and during that time led the league in stolen bases six straight years. Since the Dodgers had little power at bat, Wills' slaphitting and his running were the main ingredients of the Los Angeles attack. Los Angeles won four pennants while Maury was there, proving that good pitching (supplied by Sandy Koufax and Don Drysdale, primarily) and a lot of intelligent hustle can predominate. Traded to Pittsburgh in 1967, Maury kept right on harassing the opposition despite advancing age and injury. He batted .302 and stole twenty-nine bases.

Actually, success had never really come easily for Maury. His baseball career has been a struggle—against disbelief, doubt, the hardened traditions that a "little man" can't make it in major league baseball. He spent 8½ years in the minor leagues in his struggle against them—and eighteen years of childhood before that simply to prepare for the struggle. He was born in Washington, D.C., on October 2, 1932, one of thirteen children of a machinist at the Naval Gun Factory. At Cardozo High School, he was a pitcher on the baseball team but his swiftness and agility in football and basketball—mostly football—earned him scholarship bids from nine colleges, including Ohio State and Syracuse. But he turned them down to play baseball—or to *try* to play.

His first attempt came in a tryout camp for the Giants—then of New York—at nearby Havre de Grace, Maryland. The Giants told him he was too small to be a big league pitcher, even after he struck out eighteen batters in a pair of three-inning pitching stints on two different days. Not long afterward the Dodgers—then of Brooklyn—held a tryout camp and Maury, somewhat depressed, went through the motions. But the Dodgers elected to sign him to a Class D contract and sent him to Horlen, New York, in the Pony League.

In the years that followed he played all around the infield and all around the Dodger farm system—Pueblo, Miami, Fort Worth, Seattle, Spokane. But the Dodgers had Pee Wee Reese at short and Don Zimmer waiting in the wings. At twenty-six Maury Wills felt the years closing in on him. It wasn't that he didn't think he could make the team; it was that the Dodgers apparently didn't think so. In spring training of 1959, they sent him to the Detroit Tigers on a tryout, but the Tigers sent him back to the Dodgers, who, in turn, returned him to Spokane.

Before long came the day that Maury says he "will always bless." Bobby Bragan, whom the Cleveland Indians had just let go, became the Spokane manager. Almost instantly Maury felt something different about Bragan's kind of ball game. Bragan hollered for teamwork, for speed, for glovework, base-stealing, clutch plays. Maury felt more *team,* less striving to prove himself. In turn, Bragan was impressed

A healthy lead off first, a quick break toward second and a hooking slide into the bag have made Maury Wills the greatest base-stealer since the days of Ty Cobb.

by the little shortstop. "His base-running and glovework sparkled," Bobby said. "He used his brain. When told to steal, he almost psyched pitchers. His poor bat was what hurt him.

"I couldn't shake the strong hunch that he was like Eddie Stanky and many others who had stayed in the minors long after they could do a major league job."

That hunch took hold of Maury's career one morning while he was horsing around in the batting cage. He jumped from his usual right side and swung from the left. Bragan was out in the field, but his attention became riveted as Maury kept it up. Maury's left-handed swing was fluid and strong. Bragan knew the valuable potentials of a native versatility. He quickly trotted in to the batting cage. "C'mere," he said to Maury. "You ever think about switch-hitting?"

The next three weeks, with his manager pitching, Maury practiced batting from the left side. Finally Bragan said, "Pretty soon, you switch in games." But he withheld the go-ahead until the club went on the road, away from the home fans. In Sacramento, Maury hit left-handed for five straight singles.

His batting average quickly climbed with the switch-hitting advantage. Bragan, encouraged, went all out for his hunch about Maury's skills. "Now I want you to sharpen up the base-stealing," Bobby said. "You've got all the speed you need. But study the pitchers more. Get their moves down pat."

For Bragan, Maury slaved in practice as he never had before. In the 1959 season, he was batting .313. Almost routinely, he smacked safe liners, ran singles into doubles, stole bases with a boldness that frequently turned pitchers almost apoplectic. When he came to bat, Spokane's fans gave Maury a hero's hand.

In June, the Dodgers called him up and he batted .260 and helped them to the pennant. Maury hit .250 and fielded well as Los Angeles took the World Series, too. When his hitting faltered in 1960 and he got less and less play-

ing time, Wills became discouraged. But coach Pete Reiser came to the rescue. He forced Maury to come out for extra hitting practice every day for a month and taught him how to bunt, hit to the opposite field, and hit the kind of infield bouncers he could beat out. Wills responded to the coaching and ended up at .295 for the season. He was on his way, and no one ever learned how to slow him down after that.

Hank Aaron

"The funny thing about Henry Aaron," said Bill Bruton, the one-time Braves' centerfielder, "is you're not going to be impressed with him at first sight. I know I wasn't. He's just that way." To a man, Hank Aaron's Atlanta Brave teammates say the same thing: "You have to see him every day to really appreciate him."

Hank Aaron has hit more than five hundred homers since he joined the Braves in 1954. He has averaged nearly .320 over that period, has won awards for his fielding, and has even stolen thirty-one bases in a season when his team needed such a performance. And yet it is true: Hank Aaron of the Milwaukee-turned-Atlanta Braves has done all this with a quiet efficiency that seems dull next to the flashy way a Willie Mays does many of the same things.

Aaron is certainly not an electrifying batter at the plate. A pitcher once said of him, "Aaron's the only man I know who can go to sleep between pitches and wake up in time to hit the next one out of the park."

A right-handed batter, he does relax at the plate, but he is always ready to hit. His powerful wrists and quick reflexes enable him to wait until the last second before bringing the bat around.

His hitting has been heroic. By Labor Day of 1956 he was in a slump, and Cincinnati pitchers were advertising that they'd found the secret to stopping him. In a doubleheader on that day he reached them for three home runs, three doubles, a single and nine runs. A year later the Braves needed an 11th-inning extra-base hit in September to clinch the pennant and, on the first pitch from the Cardinals' Billy Muffett, Aaron hit a home run into the center-field stands. In the World Series that year, Hank hit three homers and had a .393 batting average. One day the Giants' pitcher, Johnny Antonelli, snarled at Aaron, who'd doubled off him earlier: "You can afford to lose some teeth . . ." "But can you?" said Henry, easily. Johnny threw a fastball head high and Aaron hit it 450 feet into the top deck. For the nine innings Henry had three homers and seven RBI and the Giants lost, 13–3.

"Forget statistics. It's just the conviction of most managers that Aaron wins more games than any guy since maybe Hornsby in his prime," said Dodger manager Walter Alston. "One night, for example, we concentrated on stopping him. I mean we gave it the *works*. We gave him nothing but very bad pitches. We jammed him and dusted him. We worked every trick to pick him off base. We got rough on him when he slid. So he winds up with two singles and a home run, stole a base, robbed us of a triple with a great catch, accounted for four runs and beat us from here to Toledo. More times than anyone else he's made me wish I wasn't a manager."

Aaron's life has always been baseball. That is what sustained him back in his childhood, growing up in the streets of Mobile, Alabama. Henry helped out the family economically when he was old enough by delivering ice around town. (He thinks that might have had something to do with the development of his strong and quick wrists, which give him his hitting power.) When he wasn't delivering ice he was playing ball, and when he wasn't playing ball, he was watching his elders play ball.

In his grammar school days he was a catcher for one of the teams in the Louisiana Recreation League. When he went to high school he switched to shortstop. But at Central High, it was softball, not baseball; the school couldn't afford the equipment needed for baseball. It made no difference to Hank, though. He was the star of his high school's ball club (he starred in football, too—a 150-pound guard), and when he was graduated from Central High in 1952, he began to play with the Mobile Bears, a Negro baseball team. After an exhibition game against the Indianapolis Clowns, in which he got three hits, he was signed by the Clowns.

It didn't take long for major league scouts to draw a bead on Hank. He was playing a lot of shortstop for the Clowns and hitting over .450, and Yankee, Phillie, Giant and Brave scouts all flocked around Sid Pollet, the owner of the Clowns, to inquire as to Hank's availability. It was the New York Giants, not the Braves, who almost nabbed Henry that year.

Pollet had just about completed a deal for Hank to report to the Giants farm at Sioux City, Iowa, but at the last minute the deal fell through. "What it boiled down to," Hank says, "was that the Giants wanted to give me an A contract and a C salary. With the Braves I played C ball and got a B salary." Scout Dewey Griggs had the honor of signing up the young Mobile athlete for the Braves. Henry reported to Eau Claire in the Northern League for the latter part of the season, long enough to: (1) hit .336; (2) be named the all-star shortstop; and (3) be voted rookie of the year.

In 1953, Henry moved up to the Jacksonville Tars of the class A Sally League, and he proceeded to break everything up. When the dust had cleared it was found that he had led the league in hits, 208; runs, 115; runs-batted-in, 125; batting average, .362; putouts and assists (and errors, too—he led in everything). He also hit twenty-two home runs and was second in the league in triples. Naturally, he was voted the league's most valuable player.

Ben Geraghty, who managed Jacksonville to its first pennant in forty-one years in 1953, still shakes his head when he thinks back to that performance. "I don't know when one player

Although he is best known for his hitting, Hank Aaron is a complete ballplayer. He has quickness and cunning on the base paths and great range in the outfield. His strong arm prevents long singles from becoming easy doubles.

When Aaron is at the plate, he is extremely relaxed but always ready to hit. His powerful wrists and quick reflexes enable him to wait until the last second before swinging.

so thoroughly dominated all the offensive departments in the league before. Henry just stood up there flicking those great wrists of his and simply overpowered the pitching."

Under the Braves' long-range scheme of things, it was expected that Henry would devote one more year to minor league seasoning; then he would be ready. So he was signed to a Toledo class AAA contract. As sort of a sop to his record at Jacksonville, he was invited to work out with the Braves at Bradenton, Florida.

He had played ball that winter in Puerto Rico and he reported to spring training camp at peak hitting form. The Braves immediately put him in the outfield. He managed to keep from getting maimed out there, but it was his hitting that interested everybody. He wasted no time proving that his phenomenal year at Jacksonville was no fluke. Then came a lucky break for Aaron, and a bad one for Bobby Thomson, who had just been acquired from the Giants in the deal that sent Johnny Antonelli to New York. Playing against the Yankees in St. Petersburg, Thomson suffered a triple fracture of his right ankle sliding into second base. The way Aaron had been hitting the ball, Charley Grimm had to put him in Thomson's place.

It proved to be anything but a rash move. Until he broke his ankle himself in September, Hank was one of the brightest stars on the club, batting .280, driving in 69 runs and hitting 13 home runs, and everyone could see that there was only one place for the twenty-year-old youngster to go—up.

That's exactly where Aaron went. He led Milwaukee to two pennants; he won the MVP award in 1957 with 44 homers, 132 runs-batted-in and a .322 average; he topped the league in batting, home runs and runs-batted-in at various times. And he did it all in a business-like way that never really generated high excitement. How does Hank Aaron feel about being baseball's neglected superstar? "I get a

kick out of the trophies," he says, "but it's pride that counts. My record speaks for itself."

Larry Doby

It has been said by some that Larry Doby never fully developed his considerable baseball talents because he fought too hard, mostly with himself. A boyhood in Paterson, New Jersey, did not prepare Larry for the handicaps of the color line. Confronted with them in 1947, when he became the first Negro to play in the American League, he brooded hard and thought hard and fought hard.

"To play baseball is one thing," he said. "To live with the problems you have, knowing you're not getting equality, it has a tendency to affect your baseball if you're the sensitive kind. I was. I had a lot of sleepless nights."

Doby averaged about .280 for his career and hit about twenty homers a season, both fine marks. In the outfield the fleet Doby had excellent range and a strong arm. He was a good professional baseball player. But Larry —along with most who have evaluated his career—thinks he should have done better. "With the exception of Willie Mays," Doby said, "I had as much God-given talent as anybody I've seen in my time." With his talent, Larry tried to prove himself and his race. If he did well, he insisted, he might silence the bigots and make it easier for other Negroes to succeed. But he pressed too hard, overestimated the burden he was carrying. It proved him a man of considerable stature, but it hurt his baseball.

There were great moments, though. In 1948, for example, he led the Cleveland Indians down the stretch with some heavy hitting that propelled them into the World Series. He topped off a strong year (.301 average, 14 homers, 64 runs-batted-in) by batting .318 in the Series, best on the club. The Indians took the Series from the Braves. There were other successful Doby years, like 1950 when he

As a home-run hitting member of the Newark Eagles (above) and a neighborhood star (below), Larry Doby displays the form that led the Cleveland Indians to make him the first Negro to play in the American League.

collected 25 home runs and 102 runs-batted-in while hitting .326, and 1954 when his league-leading totals of 32 homers and 126 runs-batted-in sparked Cleveland to another pennant.

The Doby story really began on July 5, 1947, when Larry, a .400-plus batter with the Newark Eagles of the Negro National League, signed a Cleveland contract. Elevation to the majors alone has been enough to butterfly the stomachs of the most confident of minor league stars. The air is pretty rarefied up there —only the best players in the land can make the grade. What, then, of a fellow just twenty-two who was to be loaded with more burdens than any other player, except Jackie Robinson of the Dodgers? It didn't matter that Bill Veeck of the Indians announced, "I am not interested in the color of his skin—I'm looking for good ball players." Larry was squarely on the spot.

The beginning was an ordeal the like of which no ball player before him had ever undergone. The way had been paved for Jackie Robinson's advent, a few months earlier, into the National League. Branch Rickey had made elaborate preparations, had eased Robinson into full membership in the Dodgers by way of a season at Montreal. Long before he donned a Brooklyn uniform, most of his future teammates knew him and respected him for his professional attainments.

Doby had no such advantages. Younger than Robinson by four years and lacking Jackie's maturing experience as a college athlete, he had been yanked out of obscurity and, denied even the chance to think out the problem in his own mind, he had been thrown into a "white" major league on less than a week's notice. The Indians, many of them from the Deep South, didn't know him and didn't want to know him.

Within a few weeks, most of them had changed their minds. Within a year, they embraced Larry as one of them and congratulated themselves on having him on their side. For without his notable contributions, there would have been no pennant and world championship in 1948.

But it remained difficult for Doby. There was the pressure of being the league's first Negro—the abuse from fans and rivals, the segregation in certain places. Many baseball people believe that Larry never really felt he was accepted. His moodiness became almost as legendary as the talk about his unlimited—and unrealized—potential. Al Lopez once said of him: "The guy's fighting himself all the time, and this game should be easy for him. He has every physical attribute to become one of the great players of the game. But somebody comes up to Larry and tries to help him and you can see him going on the defensive. His reaction to assistance seems to be, 'What are you picking on me for?'"

Doby was finally traded to the Chicago White Sox and later moved on to Baltimore to finish his career. He hoped for a chance to coach in major league baseball but received no offer. He knew, and said, that the white man could count on a good job when he finished his playing career, but a Negro could not. So Larry returned to New Jersey and set out to make a business career for himself. Within a few years, he had become a successful insurance salesman.

Larry Doby holds a permanent place in baseball history for his pioneer roles. But that is not all: he had proved himself as a talented player. And there will never be any way to know how good he might have been had he not been subjected to the pressures of breaking the American League color line.

Willie Mays

The story of Willie Mays is, on the face of it, the satisfying saga of an American youth struggling out of difficult conditions to a position of heroic eminence. Mays is paid a salary of more than $100,000 for a year's work. In his first season in the major leagues, he was a vital member of a pennant-winning club. In his first full season, 1954, he was baseball's most valuable player, and he was the leader of a World Series winner. Mays' deeds, are written into the record books: the four home runs in one game in 1961, the three triples in one game in 1960 (no player in the history of baseball has ever put together this twin accomplishment), the seven home runs in six consecutive games, his leadership in runs scored in all-star games, his triples in all-star games, his major league home-run leadership, his slugging titles. Willie Mays has fulfilled his own dream: he has reached the top of his pyramid, and it is the very pyramid he chose to climb. He accepted no substitutes.

Mays was born in Fairfield, Alabama, in 1931, the son of a steel-mill hand who never earned more than $2,000 a year in those days. William Howard Mays, his father, was a ball player himself, and his grandfather, Walter Mays, had been a player at the turn of the century. There is the story of Willie's dad rolling a ball across the carpet of the living room when Willie was fourteen months old, Willie rolling it back and crying when his father got tired of the game. Willie and his dad used to play catch when the boy was three, and when Willie was six he used to grab a fungo bat, hit himself fly balls and chase them down.

Willie attended Fairfield Industrial High, where he was an outstanding athlete. He led all the county basketball players in scoring, regularly running up between twenty and twenty-five points a game. He was the school's varsity quarterback and occasional fullback; he did all the passing, all the punting, but not too much ball carrying. One day he threw for five touchdowns in a 55–0 rout; he used to get off occasional fifty- and even sixty-yard punts.

Football was so much his sport that once he shinnied up a tree to watch a game and fell off and broke a leg. That broken leg and a hairline fracture of an ankle during his Army stay are the only two serious ailments Mays has ever suffered.

But baseball was the sport his dad was nursing him along in, and Willie was swinging a semi-pro bat, pitching and playing a little outfield when he was fourteen years old. One day William Howard Mays took his son to see Lorenzo (Piper) Davis, manager of the Birmingham Barons in the Negro National League, and Davis liked what he saw.

When Willie was seventeen, he broke into the Barons' lineup, getting three hits in seven trips in a doubleheader, and playing center and left field. Piper Davis did not like everything he saw. He tinkered with Mays' stance, to open him up a little. "Trouble was," Davis said, "he stood a little too close and stuck that left shoulder around in front of him like he was peekin' at the pitcher. I made him aim, not peek."

Mays had other loves besides baseball. One of them was playing pool. While with the Barons, where he labored for $300 a season and once hit against Satch Paige, Mays got so involved in a pool game one day that the Barons' bus left without him for the next town. Miles later, the bus driver saw a cab pull alongside, flagging him down, and an irate Mays screaming at Piper Davis: "What you gonna do? You gonna leave me? I'm a pro ball player, hear! You can't leave me!"

Willie was definitely a pro and the Giants spotted him and signed him. They assigned him to their AAA team in Minneapolis and Willie hit the ball from the start. Giant manager Leo Durocher saw no reason to waste any time. He called Willie up to the majors in 1951.

The day the Giants decided to bring up Willie, Leo called him personally. "Willie," Leo roared over the long-distance wires, "pick up your ticket, hop a plane and I'll see you here tomorrow." Willie didn't want to go. "You're making a mistake," he said. "You don't want

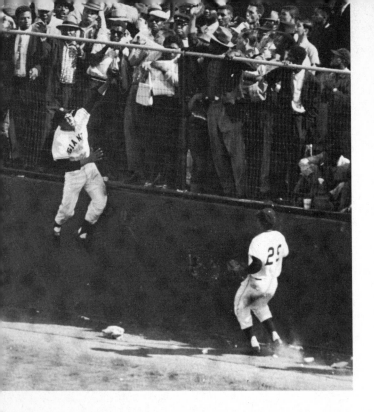

Willie Mays is sheer excitement. He climbs fences to capture line drives, belts home runs at a pace second only to Babe Ruth and has developed a style for catching fly balls that is truly distinctive.

Nowhere can the excitement of Mays be better felt than on the base paths. Whether he is diving across home plate or just leading off first, there is a tension that few others can generate. There is little wonder why Mays has joined the select ranks of National League Most Valuable Players.

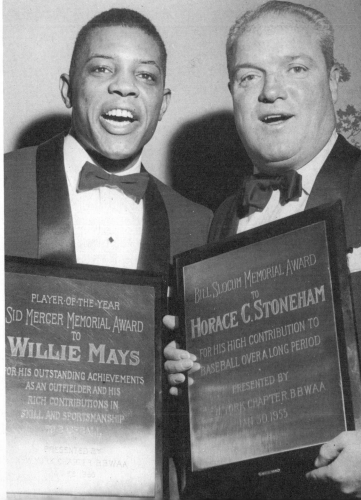

me." "Course I want you," Leo said. "You're just the man I want, Willie." "No," Willie said. "You're making a mistake." "What do you mean?" Leo said. "I'm not good enough." "Willie," Leo said, "what are you hitting?" "I'm hitting .477." "So you pick up your ticket," Leo said, "hop a plane and I'll see you here tomorrow." It began like that.

In Mays' early years in the majors few denied his diverse talents. He could, as Durocher often pointed out, run, throw and hit with power. But Willie had never been known primarily as a home-run hitter, even though his lifetime home-run total should place him second only to Ruth.

His greatest home-run day came on a cool Sunday in April 1961. It came at a strange time, too, because Willie had gone hitless two days in a row. Willie is "swinging badly," remarked Warren Spahn. But on this afternoon Willie was swinging fine. In the first inning he hit a home run off Lou Burdette. In the third he did it again, this time with a man on. In the sixth he homered once more, off Seth Moorehead, with two on. In the eighth, he hit his fourth homer of the game, off Don MacMahon, with one on. Four home runs, eight RBI. "The greatest day I've ever had," Willie said later.

Willie's exploits in center field became just as legendary as his strong and timely hitting. Ask anyone close to baseball to recreate some defensive play by Mays that sticks in memory and there is never any hesitation. Broadcaster Russ Hodges says instantly that it was a play Mays made on Roberto Clemente in Forbes Field; the ball was heading for the light tower when Mays made the catch. Hodges says it was the greatest catch Mays ever made; he says it was the greatest catch any human being ever made.

Charles Einstein, who wrote Willie's "autobiography," says Mays' greatest play was on a sinking line drive hit by Ed Bouchee in Candlestick Park in 1960; Einstein also recalls that in the second game of that day's doubleheader Mays scored from first on a single by Willie McCovey. Some remember best the catch Willie made on Vic Wertz in the first game of the 1954 World Series. Others vouch for the catch and throw Mays made on a line drive hit by Brooklyn's Carl Furillo in 1951, one-handing the ball after a tremendous run into right-center field, and then pivoting to his left and firing to Wes Westrum to get the sliding Billy Cox at the plate. Mays himself says that was his best throw.

Mays says the finest catch he ever pulled off was against Brooklyn's Bobby Morgan, Mays running far to his right, into left-center field, leaping through the air so that his body was stretched full out and parallel to the ground, catching the ball with the tip of his glove and then falling so heavily that his right elbow caved in his solar plexus, knocking him unconscious. But somehow, as he collapsed, he had brought the gloved hand and the ball up under his body, tucking it against his chest, so that at no time had the ball touched the ground. And when Leo Durocher ran to the outfield and turned Mays over, there was the ball cradled against the letter on Willie's chest.

Willie's playing inspired his team. He had hit .274 as a rookie in 1951, then had gone into the Army for most of 1952 and all of 1953. Coming out in 1954, he batted .345, with 41 homers, and led the New York Giants to the pennant and a sweep of the Cleveland Indians in the World Series. He won the league's MVP award—and years later, after the franchise moved to San Francisco—he won it again (in 1965). He did it with such deeds as his fifty-two homers during that year.

Early in his career, Mays' unbridled enthusiasm for baseball and the way he played the game provided a kind of unspoken leadership. As he matured, however, he took on more responsibility for the functioning of the team. He encouraged the rookies and advised his fellow outfielders about playing the hitters.

And always he does the little things, as well as the hitting and fielding. He will take the extra base when it is the right time to do it. He can steal and, for example, led both leagues with forty stolen bases in 1956. After watching Mays' baserunning spark the National League to a 5–3 victory in the 1963 all-star game, NL manager Al Dark said, "That Willie always finds a way to win for you. If you were stuck somewhere in China, he'd come up with a rickshaw."

Frank Robinson

In the spring of 1966, Frank Robinson reported eight days late to his new team, the Baltimore Orioles, and, immediately, the Robinson doubters were put on guard. "Maybe he *is* a troublemaker," they said, "maybe he is a malingerer, maybe that's why Bill DeWitt [of the Cincinnati Reds] got rid of him." DeWitt hadn't put it quite that way; his argument for the astounding trade was that Frank was "an old 30." So here he was, reporting eight days late—he had had car trouble—and people had begun to wonder.

His first day of batting practice as an Oriole, Frank stepped in and hit a high infield pop-up. Luis Aparicio grabbed it, looked toward the batter, and hollered loud enough for everyone to hear: "Bring back Pappas." Everyone laughed at that one, even Frank, and everyone laughed when in his first exhibition game appearance, as a pinch-hitter, he singled. And when he homered in his first starting game as an Oriole, everyone laughed again and it was all loose and cool among the Orioles. And it was that way all season, the Orioles laughing their way to the bank as Frank Robinson, the dispossessed, drove, led, hustled and needled his team to a pennant and a World Series victory. He did it all. He led the league in batting, .316; he led the league in home runs, 49; he led the league in runs-batted-in, 122. He became the first man in the majors since

1956 to win the triple crown. He became the first man ever to win the most valuable player award in both leagues (he did it for the Reds in 1961). And he continued his onslaught in the World Series, starting the rout of the Dodgers with a first-game, first-inning home run, and ending it in the fourth game with the home run that gave the Orioles a 1–0 victory and a sweep of the Series. Said teammate Brooks Robinson: "I've never played with a better hitter, a better all-round player and a better competitor than Frank Robinson."

Brooks Robinson had more to say about the way Frank goes at his profession: "He can't be bothered. He can't be scared. If you're gonna hit up here, you need talent but you also need, well, I don't like the word guts but you can't let that guy on the mound scare you. If you like the ball in here," he said, gesturing close to his body, "then you just have to stand up there tight and when some guy throws seventy or eighty miles an hour at you, you can't back off."

Frank Robinson had never been the type to back off. He came out of high school, signed with the Reds for $3,500, and at seventeen hit .348 in seventy-two games for the Reds' farm club in Ogden, Utah. The next year they sent him to Columbia, South Carolina, in the South Atlantic League. He was there in 1954 and again in 1955, before they brought him up to Cincinnati. Columbia played in cities like Macon and Columbus, Georgia, and there were times he had to eat a sandwich on the bus while the rest of the team went into the restaurant; when he wanted to see a movie, he could go to two of the three theaters as long as he sat in the balcony. Once he started to pack up and go home. But Frank just isn't the type to quit.

"The South," he once said, looking back with candor, "really made me a better ballplayer. I was just determined to get out of there and the only way I could think to do it was to

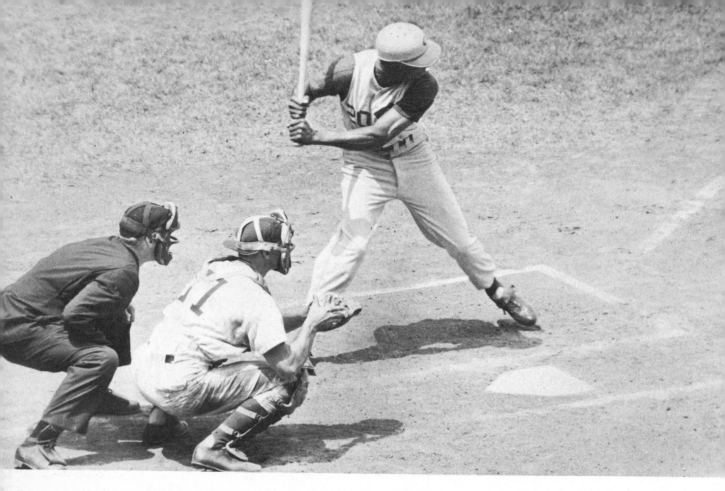

Frank Robinson, with Cincinnati (above) and with Baltimore (below), became the first man to be named Most Valuable Player in both major leagues.

get all the way to Cincinnati—or at least to a higher classification. It never occurred to me," he laughed in the self-deprecating manner that is more defense than modesty, "that they might have sent me to another Southern city."

In the spring of 1956, the Reds took him to camp and kept him. We hit .290, and tied a record for rookies with thirty-eight home runs. His ten years with the club established him as a great star. In 1961, for example, the Reds won the pennant and Frank Robinson, who hit .323, drove in 124 runs and hit 37 homers, winning the MVP award. The following year, he hit .342, drove in 136 runs and hit 39 homers. He played in six all-star games for the Reds. And he played a kind of tough baseball that didn't exactly endear him to his rivals. He wanted to win and he went all-out. His teammate and friend on the Reds, Vada Pinson, describes Robinson's approach: "You take a routine force play. When Frank is on first, then it's not going to be routine. He'll come down there and he'll knock you on your tail because he wants to let you know that he isn't going to be easy. He wants you to know and, more important, he wants you to remember it."

He was tough on the field and he was equally firm in expressing himself off the field about management-employee relations. He admits this and explains that as a veteran in Cincinnati he was in a position—because of his salary range—to voice beefs that far less affluent members of the team could not. Many people think that this is the reason he was traded to Baltimore.

At any rate, the Orioles got a very determined ball player in 1966. "He's a swinger," said teammate Curt Blefary. "He starts swinging the minute he leaves the dugout. You look at him real close. Look at his upper torso and those shoulders. He can hit the ball farther with one hand to the opposite field than anybody has a right to hit one."

Robby used that bat well and did his usual competent job in the outfield, and all of Baltimore cheered him on as he led the team to pennant and World Series triumphs. The following year, 1967, was not so fortunate for the team, but it showed the kind of ball player Robinson is. Following his great triple-crown season of 1966, he desperately wanted another good year, for himself and his world-champion Orioles. But it wasn't to be. By June 25, the Orioles were in sixth place. Robinson himself was doing fine. He was leading the league in batting with .336, in home runs with twenty-one and he had fifty-one runs-batted-in. And then, in a game against the league-leading Chicago White Sox, Robinson went into second to break up a double play. He went in, as he always does, "like the Marines storming Inchon," said one writer. Only this time his head made connection with Al Weis' knee and he came out of it with a concussion and double vision. Frank missed twenty-eight games, then played the rest of the season without perfect vision. He finished with a .311 mark, 30 home runs and 94 runs-batted-in.

The point is that Frank Robinson played—where another player would have quit for the season—and he played with superlative skill. The test of a ball player is ability to produce no matter what the pain or pressure, and as his first Oriole manager Hank Bauer said, "In a close ball game, you know Frank Robinson is going to do it for you."

CHAPTER SEVEN

Modern Basketball—
The Negro Domination

THE game of basketball is played by men with superb physical coordination, speed, agility and endurance. It is played magnificently by many Negroes; of all the major team sports, the Negro has come to dominate basketball more than any other.

Of the 139 men who played in the major professional league, the National Basketball Association (NBA), during the 1967–1968 season, an astonishing seventy-one, or better than half, were Negroes. Eight of the ten starters in the all-star game of that year and sixteen of the twenty-four who played in the game were Negroes. Negroes made up the entire first college All-American team for the 1966–1967 basketball season and three of the top five the next season.

Yet no Negroes were playing professional basketball less than two decades ago, and only a few were on college teams. Professional basketball was even slower than baseball and football to knock down its racial barrier. It

was not until 1951 that Chuck Cooper was signed by the Boston Celtics, the first Negro in the NBA. But basketball has made quick strides. The first Negro to coach a major league sports team was Bill Russell, the brilliant center of the Celtics, and he led his team to the world championship as a coach just as he had as a player. It is probably not coincidental that the same man signed Cooper and later gave Russell his chance to coach— Arnold (Red) Auerbach, the eminently successful, long-time coach and general manager of the Celtics.

In the college world, the ultimate moment, perhaps, was reached in the national championship game of the 1965-1966 season. The University of Kentucky, ranked first in the polls all season and with not one Negro on the squad, faced little Texas Western College, which did not use a single white player in the entire contest. Underdog Texas Western won the title.

Lew Alcindor

Lew Alcindor was probably the most publicized player ever to play high school basketball. He started out at Power Memorial High School in New York City, the center of the communications industry. When New York has a 7ft.-1in. ball player, the whole world soon knows about it. People wondered what college Lew would attend, knowing that this school would have to be favored for the national championship ever year that Lew was eligible.

Throughout his high school career, Lew was sheltered from the press by his coach, Jack Donohue, who was fearful that the publicity would hurt him. Donohue meant well, but probably complicated Alcindor's problems. The lack of publicity made people even more curious about him. When Alcindor finally decided to enter the University of California at Los Angeles, the athletic department there adopted the same policy, and throughout his freshman year Lew was incommunicado to the press.

There was no hiding his debut as a varsity basketball player, though. On December 3, 1966, Lew Alcindor took the court against Southern California, scored fifty-six points, and let it be known that no one man was going to stop him. USC tried to play Lew man-to-man, but Alcindor's mates simply lobbed the ball into him and his superior height enabled Lew simply to dunk the ball straight in or lay it up softly. UCLA went on to an undefeated season and a national championship.

After the season was over, many coaches were asked if there was any way to beat Alcindor. Here are some of the replies: Johnny Dee, Notre Dame: "The only way to beat Alcindor is to hope for the three F's—foreign court, friendly officials and foul out Alcindor." Guy Lewis, Houston: "Nothing worked on Alcindor. He peeled us like bananas." Vic Bubas, Duke: "Alcindor is so tough he is capable of

scoring as many as eighty points in a game." Marv Harshman, Washington State: "He can hold you off with one hand and stuff the ball with the other."

What was especially dangerous about Alcindor was the number of ways he could hurt the opposition. As a sophomore in 1966–1967, he averaged 29 points a game and 15.5 rebounds, and shot 66.7 per cent from the floor, a major-college record. When he was covered, he passed off beautifully. When he wanted to score, he did: sixty-one points against Washington State, fifty-six against Southern California. On defense he blocked shots left and right and center. Often on defense his greatest weapon was the same one used by the Celtics' Bill Russell—intimidation.

Whenever coaches gather, they talk about possible ways to stop Alcindor. Most of the time the scheming is useless. But the NCAA rules committee came up with a way of limiting Alcindor's offensive effectiveness. It passed a no-dunk rule for 1967–1968 which was viewed as a plot against Lew in particular. Alcindor himself saw it as a wider plot against Negroes in general, insisting that "most of the people who dunk are black athletes."

More orthodox among the stop-Alcindor attempts were the various on-court strategies. Southern Cal almost pulled it off once with a stall, only to lose in overtime, 40–35. In the 1967–1968 opener, Purdue went into a free-floating defense that bottled up Lew relatively well (17 points), but still they lost, 73–71.

It wasn't until Lew suffered an injury that the Bruins finally lost a varsity game. It was during Lew's junior year, when UCLA went to play Houston in the Astrodome. Lew had suffered a scratched eyeball the previous week in a game against California. The injury was a serious one and if the Houston game hadn't been nationally publicized, Lew probably would have sat it out. As it was, he might have been better off. He was thoroughly hampered by the

Alcindor goes high to block a shot by North Carolina's Larry Miller in last year's NCAA Championship game.

When Alcindor makes up his mind to score, there is practically no way to stop him.

One of the reasons for his high scoring is his ability to hit from the foul line—a rare talent for a big man.

bad eyesight. Still, he gave it a try. And what he got for it was a back seat. Elvin Hayes, who scored thirty-nine points that night as Houston upset UCLA 71–69, was voted player of the year largely from that performance.

Big Lew had to wait until the end of the year before he could get his revenge. Both Houston and UCLA continued through the season without losing another game. Houston wound up the year as the No. 1 team in the land. UCLA had that one blot against it and had to settle for No. 2. The two teams swept through the NCAA regional play-offs until the meeting in the semifinals at Los Angeles. Now Lew was back on home grounds and fully recovered.

The stage was set for the showdown. UCLA had beaten Houston a year earlier in the NCAA semifinals and Houston had come back with that victory in the Astrodome. This game would decide which team was superior. It was the most important game of Lew's career. The big game was anything but that, thanks to Alcindor. He led an incredibly capable UCLA team to a rout. Houston was helpless against the seven-footer. At about the ten-minute mark, the game was still fairly close; UCLA led by four points. Alcindor was his usual effective self in the middle, both offensively and defensively. Hayes wasn't hitting at all. As soon as Elvin started, most folks felt, there would be a real battle. But a strange thing happened. UCLA just kept playing better and better. All of sudden, the Bruins broke loose to build up a 51–29 half-time lead.

Houston never did recover; if anything, things got worse for the Cougars. Alcindor continued to dominate both backboards—he picked off eighteen rebounds—and wound up with nineteen points to share high-scoring honors with two other Bruins. The final score was 101–69. Houston and Elvin Hayes had truly been beaten. Hayes wound up with only ten points. When the game was nearly over, Alcindor walked off the court signaling everyone that UCLA was No. 1. The next night UCLA went out and destroyed North Carolina in the finals, 78–55, as Lew scored thirty-four points. And for the second straight year, he was voted best individual in the tournament.

Walt Bellamy

The story of 6ft.-11in. Walt Bellamy is a remarkable one. He is loaded with talent and plays good basketball, yet he never seems fully to satisfy the critics.

Walt is really a hard worker. When he was a freshman in college, he was awkward, timid and bewildered. One visiting coach to the Indiana University campus said to the Hoosiers' coach, Branch McCracken: "You know, Branch, that center of yours, Walt Bellamy, would do better in a sideshow than in a gym. How do you ever expect to teach him to play college basketball?"

McCracken smiled. "Walt's got a long way to go," he said. "But I hope he develops." McCracken did more than just hope in the next two seasons. He worked hard with Bellamy, teaching him to rebound, run and shoot. By the time Walt finished college, he was rated one of the outstanding pro prospects in the country, and played on the U.S. Olympic team in 1960.

"I'd take him right now," said one pro coach while Bellamy was still a senior. "He's great. He has all the moves, and if he goes with a fast-breaking team, he'll be terrific."

In his first pro season Walt was terrific. Playing for an expansion team, the Chicago Packers (now the Baltimore Bullets), Walt set what was then a record for the National Basketball Association with a field-goal percentage of .513. His 2,495 points left him only five short of becoming the second man in NBA history to score 2,500 points in one season.

When he left Indiana in 1961, Walt Bellamy hardly seemed prepared for professional basketball. He was a lanky youth who wore a

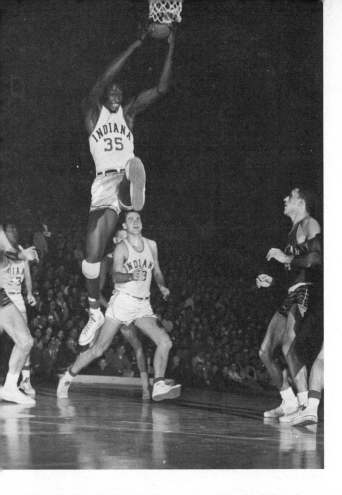

When Indiana's Walt Bellamy came into the NBA, he was selected by an expansion team, the Chicago Packers (now the Baltimore Bullets). Having no established stars on their roster, the Bullets tried to develop them quickly—and Bellamy was equal to the challenge. Here he is seen driving around Boston's Bill Russell (top right) and battling Russell for rebounding position (bottom left).

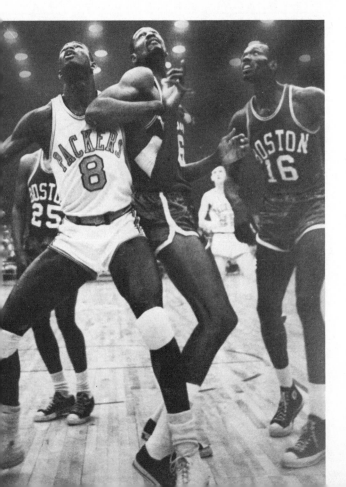

quizzical look on his face. "He doesn't like to show his emotion," said his first pro coach, Jim Pollard. "He doesn't want people to know that he's shook up, that he's scared."

He had reason for his fright. He couldn't play defense and his college offense hadn't prepared him for the pros. "Indiana played fast-break basketball. He'd rebound, pass out and the guards would be down the court shooting before he could get into position," recalled one of his former Big Ten rivals. When he did get into position, Walt needed only a narrow range of shots to be effective. He was big and strong and took advantage of his size to pile up relatively easy points and an all-American rating.

But he had the potential to do more—to shoot from farther back, to learn to rebound the rough way, the pro way—and he had the good fortune to join a pro team that could afford the luxury of letting him develop the potential immediately. Chicago was a new team, put together with NBA discards. The club had to develop new stars quickly, not let men of potential ease into the lineup. So Walt had to play and he had to learn as he played. "I learned more in twelve games as a pro," he said, "than I did in three years in college."

Bellamy's career in the NBA is full of outstanding achievements. In his first season he averaged 31.7 points per game. The next two years he had averages of 27.9 and 27.0. He has always been among the leaders in rebounding and shooting percentage, though in the past few seasons he has seen less and less playing time because he didn't have to play a full forty-eight minutes a game.

Walt Bellamy, despite the criticism of some experts, is a valuable man. It's just that lately he has not needed to be the dominant figure on the floor every minute of every game. But a good indication of how he can do what is needed can be found when he faces the Celtics or the 76ers. Invariably, whenever Big Walt goes up against either Bill Russell or Wilt

Chamberlain, he comes out of the game with what the sportswriters call an inspired performance. That is the important thing about Walt Bellamy: he thrives on competition.

Wilt Chamberlain

Wilt Chamberlain is generally regarded as the greatest offensive threat in the history of basketball. Pro basketball's all-time scoring leader, he averaged a record 50.4 points per game in 1961–1962 and holds the individual professional single-game scoring mark of 100 points in a contest in that same season. Besides being the greatest scorer in pro basketball history, he is also the best rebounder. Experts feel that Chamberlain is almost the equal of rival Bill Russell at pulling down rebounds on the defensive board. But on the offensive Wilt is in a class by himself. Time and again he uses his immense height of 7ft.-2in. and strength to follow up either his or a teammate's missed shot, and many of Wilt's points have come from this maneuver.

The 265-pound Chamberlain, who disproved the idea that a seven-footer must necessarily be clumsy and limited in his movements, is one of the country's finest natural athletes. Extremely fast, powerful, and agile for a man of any size, Wilt ran the 100-yard dash and the 440, and threw the shot as an outstanding all-around athlete at Philadelphia's Overbrook High School. He has been approached by pro football scouts who feel he would make a great receiver, and by boxing trainers and promoters who view him as a potential heavyweight champion. It is not just his awesome size and strength that make Wilt Chamberlain the top basketball star that he is—other seven-footers have failed to achieve even a modicum of his success. It is Wilt's quickness and coordination that stamp him as an athlete who could have succeeded in any sport.

Perhaps the impact that Chamberlain has had upon the game can best be determined by looking at the rules changes made because of him. While at the University of Kansas, his play forced a change in out-of-bounds procedures. Kansas had developed a play in its offensive end of the court in which the in-bounds toss would be looped over the basket to a leaping Wilt. He would catch it as it cleared the top of the backboard and ram it through the hoop. Few teams could cope with this maneuver and the rules committee subsequently barred it.

In Chamberlain's freshman year in professional basketball, he averaged 37.6 points per game and again the rules-makers were worried. So the three-second violation area (the area from the foul line to the end line in which an offensive player is not permitted to remain for more than three seconds) was widened from twelve to sixteen feet to keep Wilt further away from the goal. Other rules changes, too, have been enacted to cut down on Wilt's natural advantages. One of his favorite scoring weapons, the "guide-in" shot, in which Wilt would leap high into the air and guide a teammate's slightly off-line shot attempt into the basket, was barred after he became too proficient at the practice. And yet another of his weapons, the tap-in, has been restricted in direct proportion to the proficiency he has achieved with it. Offensive players are no longer permitted to tip in balls hanging on the rim of the basket and the tap-in of a free throw counts one point (credited to the free-throw shooter), if the tipping rebounder does not return to the floor with the ball before scoring.

Chamberlain, who is outstanding at almost all phases of the game, had his best scoring year in 1961–1962. He knew he had to make a lot of points because he was playing with a weak Philadelphia Warrior team. With his accurate fadeaway jump shot and an assortment of lay-ups, tip-ins and turn-in shots, Wilt averaged 50.4 points per game. It was during that season that Wilt recorded his 100-point game as the Warriors topped the New York Knickerbockers, 169–147, at Hershey, Pennsylvania. In that historic contest, Chamberlain connected on thirty-six of sixty-three field-goal attempts and twenty-eight of thirty-two free throws.

Impressive as Chamberlain had been, leading the NBA in scoring for six straight seasons and in rebounding for four, there remained a blight on his record as far as some experts were concerned. During his first seven seasons as a pro and in his two collegiate seasons, Chamberlain was unable to lead his team to a championship. In his sophomore season in college, Wilt's Kansas team was beaten out of the Big Eight championship by a powerful Kansas State team led by Bob Boozer. In Wilt's junior year Kansas did win its conference title and reached the finals of the NCAA tournament. But Kansas was defeated, 58–57, in triple overtime by North Carolina's sticky defense that often hemmed Wilt in with four defenders. Wilt left Kansas after his junior year to play professionally with the Harlem Globetrotters.

In 1959–1960, Wilt joined the talent-poor Philadelphia Warriors of the NBA and his scoring totals rose as his team dropped in the standings. In 1963–1964, the team moved to San Francisco. When the team's fortunes failed to improve in new surroundings, Wilt was traded to the talent-rich Philadelphia 76ers (formerly the Syracuse Nationals), joining Hal Greer, Chet Walker, Lucius Jackson and a host of other fine ball players to form the nucleus of a new championship dynasty. The losing years seemed over for Wilt. He adapted his style to his new team—the 76ers needed his defense and rebounding more than his scoring —and the 76ers started winning a string of Eastern Division titles. Chamberlain finally got to play with his first NBA championship team in the 1966–1967 season.

The persisting criticism of Chamberlain's play, a supposed inability to subordinate his talents for the benefit of his team, was laid to

From his high school days at Overbrook in Philadelphia, Wilt Chamberlain became the most talked-about basketball player in history. He went on to stardom at Kansas, both on the court and off. Along with being Kansas' greatest cage star, Chamberlain was a good high jumper, and his 6 ft.-6 in. jump placed him second in the 1957 Kansas Relays.

Before entering the NBA, Chamberlain spent a year with the Harlem Globetrotters. He became a living legend when he entered the NBA and set scoring records no one had previously believed possible. In 1966-67, scorer-Chamberlain turned playmaker-Chamberlain and led Philadelphia to the NBA Championship.

rest with Wilt's success with the 76ers. His phenomenal point totals, contrasted with the mediocrity of his teams' records, had suggested the criticism.

However, his coaches, Frank McGuire in Philadelphia and Alex Hannum in San Francisco and Philadelphia, never accepted that. They felt that when Wilt played with the Warriors his job was to score and he did it well. When he joined the 76ers, he re-tooled his style to complement his teammates' play. In 1966–1967, his second full year with the 76ers, he relinquished his league scoring title to Rick Barry because he was passing off more, blocking more shots, and working harder off both backboards. Wilt led the 76ers to the Eastern Division title and league championship in the playoffs, unseating the great Boston Celtics. In 1967–1968, Wilt outdid himself as a "team player," becoming the first center to lead the league in assists.

Then, because he wanted to play again on the West Coast, he was traded to the Los Angeles Lakers in the summer of 1968. He said he wanted to finish his career there.

Wilt has proved that he can do everything on the basketball court. There is just one phase of his game still open to criticism. Chamberlain is a poor foul-shooter, with a lifetime percentage of less than .500. He has shot them underhanded and one-handed, and has found that no amount of practice will improve his accuracy. Wilt feels it is a mental block that he will never overcome. It may not leave his critics much to shoot at, but it does make him seem more human to the average fan.

Bill Russell

Long after the major leagues in professional sports had dropped the color barrier to players, and when Negroes made up nearly half the rosters on some teams, the barrier remained intact at one point—no Negroes managed or coached a major team. The wall cracked, however, in 1966, and the man who stepped through into new territory was Bill Russell.

The team that offered this opportunity was perhaps the most consistently successful in all of organized professional sports—the Boston Celtics of the National Basketball Association. They were to basketball what the New York Yankees had been to baseball or the Cleveland Browns to football in their era. The single man most responsible for putting the Celtics there had been Bill Russell, who, most authorities agree, has been the most valuable player any basketball team ever had.

Once a fact, the step seemed most logical. The man who offered Russell the job was Arnold "Red" Auerbach, who had long been both coach and general manager of the Celtics. Auerbach was seldom wrong about any player and he knew Russell and Russell's standing among his teammates; he had years before appointed him floor captain of the Celtics. Russell was a star player, an astute basketball strategist and a leader of men, whatever their color. He had proven his ability and his courage by speaking frankly on the issues of civil rights. He had displayed his business judgment by turning his basketball earnings into a business empire that includes holdings in both the United States and Africa.

Until the 6ft.-10in. Californian joined the Celtics, they had never won a championship. With him as a player, they began their incredible dynasty. He joined early in the season of 1956–1957, after the Olympics, and they went on to their first NBA title. The next year, with Russ injured in the play-offs, they were beaten in the final round. They then proceeded to win the world championship of basketball for eight consecutive years. In Russell's first season as coach, with an aging team, the Celtics slipped to second in their division. But the next year, Russ rallied his club for another world title— and he had reached still another pinnacle in his glorious career.

Russell first splashed on the national sports scene with the University of San Francisco basketball team. In both his junior and senior years, 1954–1955 and 1955–1956, he led the Dons to perfect records and two consecutive National Collegiate Athletic Association championships. San Francisco, with Russell and K. C. Jones, who was to be his Celtic teammate, leading the way, scored sixty consecutive victories—a college record. As a senior, Russell was voted college player of the year.

The next winter he was faced with a choice. Named to the U.S. Olympic team, Russell had to decide whether to compete for his country or immediately enter professional ranks. The Olympics were scheduled for December 1956 in Australia (summer on that continent), and to play meant that Russ had to fall far behind in training for his first professional season. He chose to play for the United States and led the American team to a gold medal.

When he returned Russ reported to the Boston Celtics. Everyone expected him to be good, but Auerbach had made a more astute estimation than any of his competitors. Because they had finished too high in the standings the season before, the Celtics had no chance to draft Russell, who was picked by the last-place St. Louis Hawks. But Auerbach wanted him. So he traded a proven star, Ed Macauley, and another potential star, Cliff Hagen, for Russell. Auerbach believed that Russell would make the Celtics into a championship team—and he could not have been more accurate.

Russell was never the scorer that his contemporary, Wilt Chamberlain, was. But he is acknowledged as the finest rebounder the game has ever seen and the finest defensive player of all big men. His timing is flawless, his leaping ability tremendous, his hands quick. He not only blocked shots but directed them to his teammates. That made possible the Celtics' fast-break offense that crushed opposing basketball clubs.

It took only a year or two for the league to realize Russell's domination. That was the period when Chamberlain was playing in college and everyone who followed basketball waited for his emergence into the pro ranks to give Russ his supreme test. In that first season, their respective importance to their teams was clearly shown. The competition against each other was relatively even during the regular season, but the Celtics breezed to first place over Chamberlain's Philadelphia club by ten games. In the play-off series, best-of-seven, when no one could relax for a minute, Russell displayed his skill under pressure. He outplayed Chamberlain, who was three inches taller, stopping his offensive moves and dominating the rebounds. Russell was not nearly so dramatic on the court or in the box score; he simply made sure his team won. That is the story of their rivalry over the years.

In 1966–1967 came the ultimate challenge. When Russell was offered the coaching job, he had, of course, no formal experience—just the skills and tactics he had picked up on the court and from talking at length to Auerbach. The team he took over was not as good as the ones he had played on. Many stars had either retired, like Bob Cousy, or were getting older, like Russell, and he himself could not be as good if he had to divide his attention between playing and coaching.

When the season started, Russell and the Celtics had their troubles. The older players were having off seasons and Russell couldn't get them to respond as the experienced Auerbach had. Russ himself wasn't playing as well, with so many things on his mind. And this was the year that Wilt Chamberlain picked to stop scoring points so fast and concentrate more on being a team player—something he had learned from Russell. Philadelphia moved ahead of the Celtics early and stayed there; in the play-offs, Boston was beaten four games to one by the 76ers, who went on to win the title.

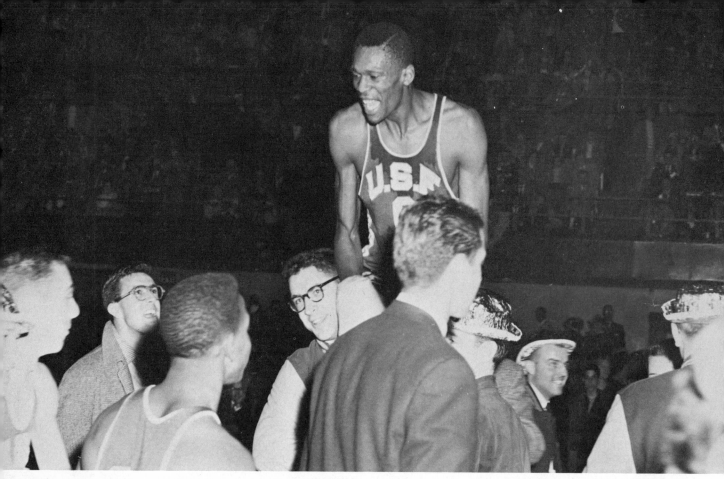

Bill Russell is carried off by his teammates after leading them to the NCAA Championship over La Salle.

Because of his brilliant all-round play, Russell was the 1966 recipient of the Podoloff Cup, awarded to the winner of the Newspaper Enterprise Association (NEA) Players' Poll conducted at the conclusion of each season. Murray Olderman of the NEA presents the award to Russell.

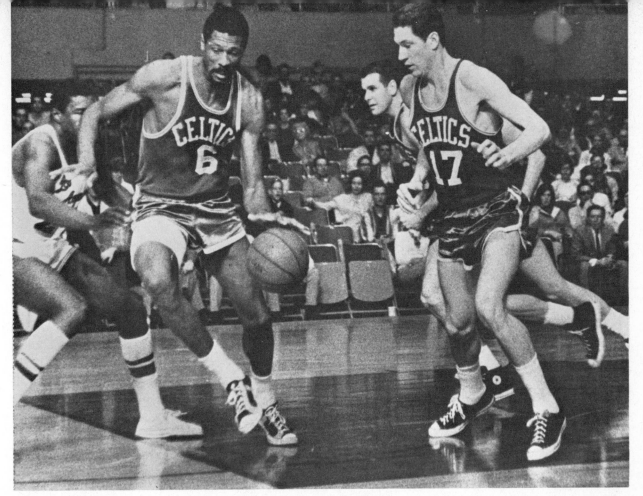

Normally limited to working under the basket, Russell demonstrates that he can move with the ball when necessary.

In his first season as coach of the Celtics, Russell helps Art Heyman during a team workout.

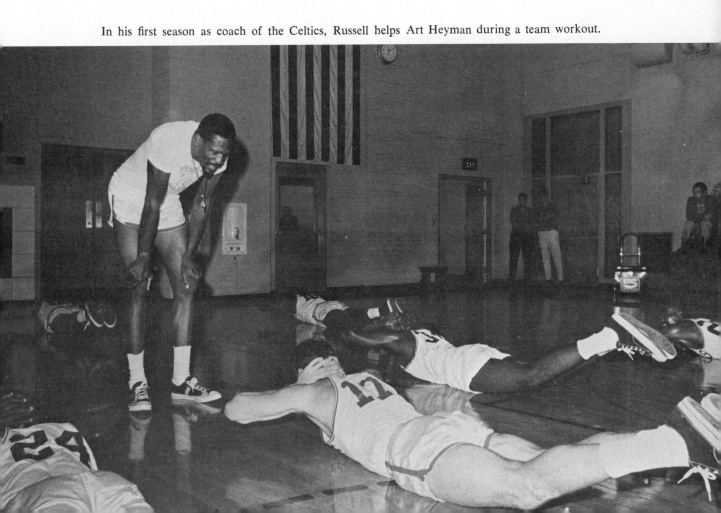

But the next year, Boston was again functioning as it had for so many years. Russell played more minutes than any other player, was second on the team in assists, and led in rebounds as he had for twelve straight years. In the regular season Boston again finished second to Philadelphia, but in a closer fight.

Then came the play-offs. Boston and Philadelphia met in the Eastern finals, the Celtics a decided underdog. They won the first game, then lost three in a row, and all seemed ended, especially with two of the next three games at Philadelphia. But in a magnificent display of stamina, ability and pure inspiration, Russ coaxed the best out of himself and his teammates for three straight victories and the Eastern title. The finals were almost an anti-climax, despite the fact that Boston had to stop the strong Los Angeles Lakers with Elgin Baylor and Jerry West. This time it was four games to two and the Celtics were again champions.

Nate Thurmond

The San Francisco Warriors' Nate Thurmond is an unusual ball player, better defensively than Wilt Chamberlain and better offensively than Bill Russell, and considerably younger than either one. He is not quite as good as either in the individual's specialty but he could become better. He is perhaps the best all-round center in the National Basketball Association, and still learning. Handicapped by a bad back, he has been only half a player, but even then he is still twice the man most of his opponents are.

Wilt Chamberlain once said of Thurmond: "He's the toughest center I have to play. He can rebound, play defense and you've got to worry about him scoring, too. He's terrific and I don't think he gets the recognition he deserves."

Without realizing it, Wilt had summed up the career of Nate Thurmond. Take the pro all-star game of 1965–1966. Nate, playing more minutes than anyone else on either team, scored sixteen points and pulled down eighteen rebounds, against the combined talents of Russell and Chamberlain. His 12-point first quarter got the West team off to a 39–33 lead, paving the way to a 135–120 upset victory.

Player sentiment was unanimous after the game. Jerry West said, "We controlled the boards and you can give Nate the credit. To me, he's the finest all-round center in the league." Elgin Baylor chimed in: "I haven't seen Thurmond play a bad game yet. I don't think most people have any idea how valuable he is."

But who was the game's most valuable player? Rick Barry, who scored thirty-eight points. And even Barry said Thurmond was more deserving of the MVP award. Second billing is nothing new to Thurmond. When he first came to the Warriors, he was moved into a forward spot. Why would a 6ft.-11in. center be asked to play forward? The Warriors had a 7ft.-1in. center named Chamberlain at the time. As soon as Nate became accustomed to his forward spot, Wilt was traded and Nate returned to his natural position, center. At last he would become the big man. But along came Rick Barry a year later and back into the shadows retreated Thurmond. Not too far in the shadows, though.

In 1966–1967 Nate averaged nineteen points and twenty-one rebounds per game. Though it was Barry who led the league in scoring, it was Thurmond's rebounding and defensive play that helped the Warriors win. Despite a broken hand and chronic back trouble, he brought the Warriors into the NBA championship finals against Chamberlain and the 76ers. And after that performance, Nate finally began to get some of the recognition he deserved.

There are some people who believe that Nate is the best big man in the game. He does not score as well as Chamberlain, when Wilt wants to score. He does not defend as well as

To be praised by one's peers is the highest form of flattery that an athlete can receive. San Francisco's great center Nate Thurmond received just such acclaim when Wilt Chamberlain commented on his ability: "He's the toughest center I have to play. He can rebound, play defense and you've got to worry about him scoring, too. He's terrific and I don't think he gets the recognition he deserves."

Russell, when Russell is up on his game. But somehow Nate manages to put together a total game that is often better than either Chamberlain's or Russell's. And when he goes head-to-head with Chamberlain or Russell, as often as not he outplays his man. On November 4, 1967, he shut out Chamberlain from the floor. Nobody had ever done this before, not even Russell. Former Los Angeles coach Fred Schaus calls Nate a "complete ball player."

Yet during his second season in pro basketball, Nate's career seemed headed for trouble. He began to experience back pain. No one could figure out why until Nate went to see Dr. Robert Kerlan, who had treated baseball's Sandy Koufax. The doctor found that Nate had one leg shorter than the other and this was putting too much pressure on his back. Nate has had to wear an elevated sneaker since then.

He still experiences some pain, but the sneaker has helped him to play as ruggedly as ever. Before he was injured again in the 1967–1968 season, the Warriors were once more near the top in the West, but with Nate out of the lineup, San Francisco had to struggle, and wound up third. That illustrates just how valuable Nate Thurmond is.

Elgin Baylor

Elgin Baylor does practically everything for the Los Angeles Lakers that can be done on a basketball court. He is their top scorer, best rebounder, and frequently leads the team in assists. But Elgin is more than just a ball player. He is an inspiration to his teammates and to all the players in the National Basketball Association.

The reason that Baylor is thought of so highly is that he is not only a great ball player but he is also one who has overcome severe problems. During the 1964–1965 play-offs, Elgin suffered a knee injury that was supposed to end his career. He had gone up for a rebound and when he came down, part of his kneecap had been ripped away. The doctors who operated on him agreed that there was only a 1-to-99 chance that Elgin would ever play basketball again.

But Elgin beat those odds with sheer determination. He did exercises every day for five months to help strengthen the knee, but his complete recovery took a lot longer than those five months. He tried to play the next season but was hampered by the lack of mobility. He suffered through a whole season, averaging only 16.6 points per game, far below his usual 24 or 25 points. Slowly the knee improved and then one night Baylor decided to forsake the caution with which he had been playing. The result was a 45-minute performance in which he scored 28 points. A month later he scored 46 points against the New York Knickerbockers, while pulling down seventeen rebounds. But by this time the season was drawing to a close and fans everywhere had to wait until the next season to see if Elgin had truly recovered.

The next year Elgin proved that he had. He finished the season with a 26.6 average and wound up as the fifth-leading scorer in the league. But his struggles still were not over.

On October 28, 1966, Elgin again suffered an injury which could have ended the career of a lesser man. The Lakers were playing the New York Knicks, and with a little less than two minutes left in the first half there was a scramble for the ball and Elgin dived for it. Unfortunately, Dick Van Arsdale of the Knicks did too and he came down on Elgin's knee. Baylor rolled on the floor in agony and a hush fell over the crowd. Again a cast would be required to correct the knee. Again Elgin Baylor was forced to suffer.

But he overcame this setback, too, and in 1967–1968 he led the Lakers into the finals of the NBA championship play-offs. He averaged 26.0 points per game while pulling down 941 rebounds, the eleventh-best total in the league. It is performances like these that make Baylor such an asset to basketball.

Los Angeles' Elgin Baylor is one of the superstars of the NBA. Drafted off the Seattle campus (upper left), Baylor soon showed the NBA why he was everybody's All-American. Able to drive and shoot (above right) or feed off (below) as well as rebound, he has been called the perfect forward.

Baylor executes his favorite move for two points against the St. Louis Hawks. From near the side of the free throw circle he fakes, steps, jumps, twists and shoots—in one continuous motion that leaves his opponent, Don Ohl, flat-footed.

Baylor played college ball at Seattle University. There the 6ft.-5in., 220-pound player kept his coach, John Castellani, in a state of rhapsody by single-handedly keeping Seattle among the top ten teams in the country. Elgin transformed an ordinary team into one that closed out its 1958 season with a 23–4 record, including a period in which Seattle won eighteen straight. Said Castellani, "Once you see him in action, you are converted to Baylorism. He has the grace of a gymnast and the accuracy of an adding machine." He led Seattle to the national title game, before it lost to Kentucky.

Baylor has a curious characteristic. He seems almost to defy the law of gravity. He has tremendous body control and the ability to jump and hang in mid-air, then twist his body in two or three directions at once. He finally releases the ball from an impossible angle, with impossible spin, and makes the shot.

Considering that Elgin has suffered from many injuries that would hamper this type of movement, it is easier to understand what a great ball player he is. Next to Wilt Chamberlain, who is nearly nine inches taller, Baylor holds the highest scoring total for one game in NBA history. Against New York in 1960, Elgin scored seventy-one points. His versatile inside-outside skill had never been more brilliantly displayed. He had scored fifteen, nineteen and thirteen points in the first three periods for a total of forty-seven. Then the old Madison Square Garden crowd had started to clamor, "Give it to Elgin."

The Lakers complied and fed Baylor. For a moment he lost his shooting control. The forced feeding conflicted with his style. Baylor had been, and always will be, a team player. Now he was being forced to shoot by his own teammates. He was missing the shots but just as quickly as he turned cold, he turned hot. He added twenty-four points in that final quarter to give him what was then a scoring record.

Baylor is the complete offensive player—the perfect forward. He is equally effective from the outside as he is from underneath. He is a scorer and a feeder, in addition to being a strong rebounder. When he throws up a shot, he follows it to the basket. That second effort in rebounding his own misses has paid off time and again in baskets.

In addition to his aggressiveness, Elgin has another characteristic that is exclusively his. When he is playing, he will frequently twitch his head. His head repeatedly thrusts toward his shoulder, but the twitch only manifests itself when Elgin is in a competitive situation, underscoring the intensity with which he strives to beat his opponent—whether it be on a basketball court or in a friendly card game.

Dave Bing

During the 1965–1966 NBA season, the Detroit Pistons lost fifty-one games. At the end of the season they also lost a flip of the coin and wound up with the 1966–1967 rookie-of-the-year. It all began just before the annual collegiate draft. The two last-place teams in each division the year before, the Pistons and the New York Knicks, were going to decide who would get first crack at the top college prospect in the country by tossing a coin. Both clubs were after the same player—Cazzie Russell.

The Knicks won the toss and Russell packed for Madison Square Garden. The Pistons, despite losing the toss, solved most of their problems. "After we lost Russell," says owner Fred Zollner, "we went ahead and drafted to our weakness—a take-charge guard."

The take-charge guy was Syracuse University's "Mr. Terrific," Dave Bing. The 6ft.-3in. guard had led the Orangemen in scoring (28.4 points per game), rebounding (eleven per game) and assists (seven a game). Still, he was rated well below Cazzie Russell on pro potential. He had something to prove.

And prove he did. While Russell had trouble getting untracked with the Knicks, Dave

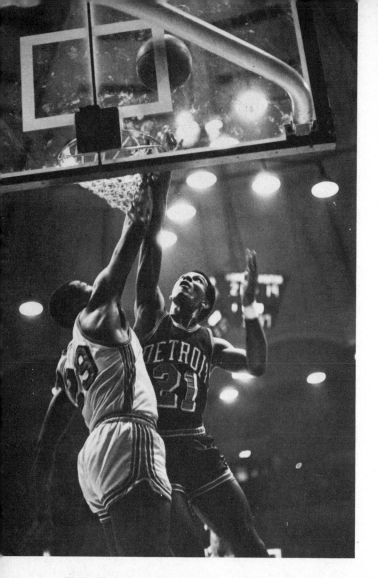

Dave Bing, Detroit's newest star, demonstrates the form that enabled him to become the NBA's 1966-67 Rookie-of-the-Year. Whether battling under the boards (above left), hitting with his fade-away jumper (above right) or setting up a play (below), Bing shows that he has all the tools necessary to become one of the NBA greats.

began a little slowly and then improved throughout the season. He finished up his first season tenth in scoring, becoming the sixth rookie in NBA history to score more than 1,600 points (the others were Elgin Baylor, Wilt Chamberlain, Oscar Robertson, Walt Bellamy and Rick Barry, select company indeed). He led the Pistons in scoring with a 20-point average, pulled down 359 rebounds and added 330 assists. He topped off the season by being named NBA rookie-of-the-year in the annual poll of sportswriters and broadcasters, receiving seventy-four of ninety votes.

And he put new life into the Pistons. Detroit improved its season record by seven and a half games, and there was improvement at the box office. Since Bing was the only significant new face on the losing team, he got most of the credit.

In his second year Dave really came into his own. He led the NBA in scoring 2,142 points for a 27.1 points-per-game average. He also finished fourth in assists, with 6.4 per game. A starter in the mid-season all-star game, Bing was eventually named to the All-NBA five.

"I hate to think of him getting any better," said Boston player-coach Bill Russell, after Dave had scored forty-four points against the Celtics in a play-off game last season. "No one in the league can stop him when he gets hot," said Donnis Butcher, the Detroit coach. "He's the best shooter with a hand in his face in the league."

Dave always was a good shooter. In his first varsity season at Syracuse University, he shot and passed the Orangemen to a respectable 17–8 record. Most observers felt that this would be the team to beat in the East the following season. But Dave's teammates got the idea that if Dave could score 22 points a game, so could they and everybody began bombing away; Syracuse tumbled to a 13–10 mark. It took a whole season for the rest of the team to realize that they weren't going anyplace unless they let Dave Bing guide them there. In his

final season Dave took Syracuse to the quarter-finals of the NCAA championships. They wound up the season with a 22–6 mark and were the highest-scoring team in the history of major-college basketball, averaging 99.0 points per game.

If Dave was a take-charge guy in college, he did the same things for Detroit. In the pros, too, he was surrounded by people who are capable of appreciating his talents and making good use of them. Throughout the 1967–1968 season, Dave was the leading scorer in the league as well as being close to the top in assists, the mark of a team man. The result was that Detroit made the NBA play-offs for the first time in six years and began to look like a team that would have to be reckoned with.

After being drafted by the Pistons, Dave had actually had some misgivings. "I was worried in the beginning," he once said. "I felt I wanted to go to an eastern team. After reading different articles, I wondered if I would be accepted in Detroit."

He was accepted all right, but he was not fully happy with his own performance that first season. "I had a good season," he said, "but I would have been happier if our team did better and made the play-offs." He figured Detroit could make the play-offs his second year if he could improve his rookie performance, especially on defense. He worked all summer, and when he was ready to report he said, "I hope it shows."

It certainly did. Not only did Dave improve his defense, but he improved every phase of his game after his rookie year. And the result was a play-off berth for the Pistons and more awards for him.

Elvin Hayes

The biggest story in college basketball during the 1967–1968 season was the emergence of Elvin Hayes as the top player in the country, despite the fact that Lew Alcindor was playing for UCLA at the same time. It was the "Big E" who captured people's imagination. What the experts think of Elvin Hayes is demonstrated by the lavish way two shaky professional teams bid for his services after his final game for the University of Houston.

The Houston Mavericks of the American Basketball Association reportedly offered the "Big E" $500,000 and the San Diego Rockets of the National Basketball Association countered with a reported $440,000. Hayes, responding to what he considered the finer competition in the NBA, signed with the Rockets, even though the Mavericks, protesting that they had just begun to bid, came back with a reported $750,000 offer.

Hayes, a 6ft.-9in. forward and the first Negro to play for the University of Houston, scored 1,214 points in his senior year, breaking by five the single-season, major-college record total scored by Frank Selvy at Furman fourteen years before. (Elvin's 2,884 career points placed him second on the major-college list, behind the great Oscar Robertson.) He led Houston to a 31–0 regular-season record as a senior, and even though a loss to UCLA in the semi-finals of the NCAA championship tournament ended the Hayes era on a somewhat disappointing note, the Big E will not be soon forgotten in Houston.

Elvin Hayes was not a great player all his life. He worked hard to get where he was in 1967–1968: player of the year in college basketball. Pride helped make Elvin a star; pride has been spurring him ever since he was a 6ft.-3in. high school freshman who couldn't make the varsity. The coach appreciated his size, but he couldn't untangle Elvin's hands and feet. He advised Elvin to practice.

"Did I work!" Elvin once recalled. "I practiced from 9 A.M. until noon, took a half hour off and went back to practicing. I'd usually end up about 10 P.M. I practiced six days a week." Convinced that he was ready, Elvin went out in his sophomore year and promptly was

dropped again. He ended up in the school band.

Finally, when Hayes was a junior and had grown to 6ft.-5in., the basketball coach relented. As a senior, Elvin was 6ft.-7in. and 210 pounds and nobody could touch him.

Hayes was an instant sensation as a University of Houston freshman, smashing every record in the book. "I've been around basketball players for 22 years," said freshman coach Harvey Pate, "and I've never seen anything like him. He's big, powerful and springy. On defense he's like Bill Russell. He just hangs around the basket and stuffs shots back into the shooter's face."

At first, Pate was accused of being a trifle extravagant. Later on, folks began wondering if he had been too cautious. After Hayes broke the freshman records, he knocked out most of the varsity ones as a sophomore. As a junior, he broke the ones he missed as a soph while extending his old ones. He scored 789 points for a 27.2 average as a sophomore. He had 881 points for a 28.4 average in his junior year.

Despite these figures, Elvin Hayes will be remembered primarily for his showdown battle with Lew Alcindor of UCLA in the college basketball regular-season game of the decade. Texas is famous for showdowns, but few have been as exciting or as well publicized as the January 1968 meeting between Alcindor and Hayes. UCLA, the defending national champion, went into the game with forty-seven consecutive victories. Houston had a streak of its own—seventeen straight.

The Cougars' last loss had been to UCLA in the semifinals of the 1967 NCAA tournament. After that game Hayes had said, "Wait'll we get them in the Astrodome next year." When the time came, the largest paying crowd in college basketball history, 52,693, packed the famous Houston Astrodome.

Hayes was ready. In a performance that Houston coach Guy Lewis later called "the greatest I've ever seen in college basketball,"

Houston's All-American Elvin Hayes.

Elvin blocked Alcindor's shots, hit on long, arching jump shots and continually beat the seven-footer down court for easy shots. When Hayes picked up his fourth foul early in the second half, Alcindor had an opportunity to score heavily on the cautious defense. But hampered by an eye injury, big Lew was unable to score consistently.

UCLA was still in the game, however, and with only 28 seconds left, the score was tied when Hayes was fouled. Normally a mediocre foul shooter, Elvin did what he had to do. He calmly dropped in both shots to give the Cougars a stunning 71–69 upset victory. It was also a personal triumph for Hayes, who outscored Alcindor 39–15 and outrebounded him 15–12. Alcindor and UCLA got the better of Hayes and Houston in the NCAA semi-finals later in the year, but nothing could take away from the Big E's clutch performance in stopping UCLA's winning streak.

Earl Monroe

Earl Monroe was the National Basketball Association rookie-of-the-year for 1967–1968. He was the most exciting player the Baltimore Bullets have ever had, one of the most exciting any team ever had.

In his first season as a pro, Monroe scored 1,991 points—only Dave Bing, Wilt Chamberlain and Elgin Baylor scored more in 1968— an average of 24.3 points per game. But that was only part of his value. He is glamorous on a court. He "turns people on," not just in Baltimore, but in cities all around the league. He plays with a flair—the behind-the-back dribble, the Globetrotter pass and move, the body control that makes lies of the laws of natural science.

He's called "Earl the Pearl." It fits. It has just the right show-business ring to it because on the court Monroe is the consummate showman. Even the most devoted "Pearl watchers," including his own teammates, miss parts of the

show. Driving for a lay-up, Earl will suddenly pass the ball quickly behind his back. And what starts out as a right-handed shot often will become a left-handed one. It all happens so fast people aren't quite sure how it happens. The crowd gasps at the speed of the move and the sheer audacity of it.

There is a communication, a rapport between Earl Monroe and the NBA crowds. "A crowd turns me on," says the 6ft.-3in., 190-pounder. The crowd itself is turned on by the nonchalance, the gleaming teeth, the pipestem legs, the glistening body of the Pearl.

Earl has worked hard to become the ball player that he is today. "I can remember as kids," says a life-long friend, "we'd play basketball in the morning and then come home to eat at about two or three. Then we'd see Earl heading back to the playground with a ball. We'd say, 'Hey man, where you going? You're not going to get any better.' I have a feeling he must have known even then that he had the potential. Later I knew he did. I can remember we were driving back to college for our senior year when he said he was going to lead the country in scoring. [He did—averaging 41.7 points per game for Winston-Salem State College.] The next year, he told me he was going to be the rookie-of-the-year in the pros. [He was.] But it hasn't changed him. You still never know what to expect."

"You just pray when you're playing a guy like that," said "Butch" Komives of the New York Knicks. "Nothing helps. He can shoot falling down."

The quotes were similar around the league. But opponents also spoke, in much less flattering terms, about Monroe's defensive abilities. "It's impossible to give it everything you've got at both ends of the court," Earl says. "You have to decide which is more important." This is not a tough decision for Monroe.

"There is no doubt in my mind that he should be first-team all-pro for what he's done for this club," said teammate Bob Ferry. "He

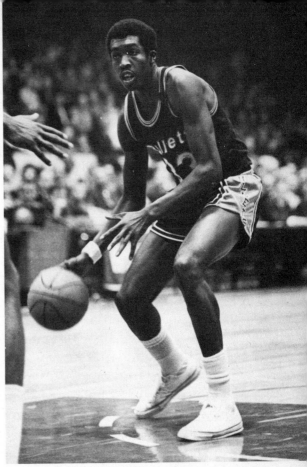

Earl Monroe is surrounded (from left to right) by Baltimore Bullets co-owner Arnold Heft, Bullets coach Gene Shue and co-owner Abe Pollin after being made the Bullets top draft choice for 1967.

Muscles tense and ready to spring, Monroe sizes up the defender before planning his next move. His cat-like quickness makes him a tough man to cover.

In action against Los Angeles, Monroe moves across the foul line, looking for an opening.

can carry us on a slow night." Making all-pro is an ambition of Monroe's. So was making rookie-of-the-year and scoring fifty points in one game, both already accomplished. His greatest ambition, though, is to play on a championship Baltimore team, but that will have to wait for some rebuilding.

Still, a player like Monroe is a good start for any team. Pearl was not very brilliant during the first half of his first season, and the Baltimore management wondered if it had made a monstrous mistake in taking on a small college All-American. It hadn't. Just after the all-star break, the Pearl emerged from his shell. Suddenly he was unstoppable. During one stretch, he scored thirty or more points in eleven of twelve games, and he reached a season high of fifty-six points against the Los Angeles Lakers. He dominated the Bullets' floor game the way Oscar Robertson took over for the Cincinnati club.

"Pro basketball needs players who can excite fans," says the Pearl. Baltimore certainly has one.

Maurice Stokes

Maurice Stokes' story is probably the most poignant in recent basketball history. Tragedy struck the night of March 15, 1958. That afternoon the Cincinnati Royals had lost to the Detroit Pistons in the play-off series. Stokes hadn't been his usual self before the game. It was to be televised and usually, on such occasions, Mo would kid his teammates about how he was going to star for the national audience. This time, however, there was no joking.

His teammates hadn't thought much of Stokes' subdued behavior. Three days earlier, against the Minneapolis Lakers, he had been struck in the head during some furious action on court. And he was suffering from a boil on his neck. It was understandable, they figured, that he didn't feel in a joking mood.

Stokes played thirty-nine of the forty-eight minutes of the game against the Pistons. He scored twelve points and grabbed fifteen rebounds. It wasn't quite par for him, but neither was his physical condition. "After the game," recalled teammate Dave Piontek, "Mo said he didn't feel well. Still, none of us thought too much about it."

Stokes had a snack across the street from the Sheraton-Cadillac Hotel in Detroit. On the bus ride to the airport, though, he again complained of feeling ill. "We opened the window for him so he could get some air," Piontek recalled. It was on the trip to the airport that Stokes vomited for the first time. At the airport he became violently ill. "Get a doctor," he pleaded. "I feel like I'm going to die."

"The time for departure for our plane had been announced, though," said Piontek, "and we didn't have time to do anything. Richie Reagan and Dave Ricketts and I carried Mo onto the plane." Stokes was settled in a seat in the rear of the plane. "Some of the fellows thought maybe he'd had too much beer," Piontek said. "You know, the last game of the season and all that. And they were staying away from him so he wouldn't be too conspicuous. You know, the owners of the team were on the plane. So was Maurice Podoloff, the president of the league."

It wasn't long after takeoff that Stokes again became ill. His breathing became labored and that is when a stewardess gave him some oxygen, which probably saved his life. By now he had lapsed into a coma, and the pilot called ahead to request that an ambulance meet the plane.

The blow that he had received in the Lakers game ended the basketball career of Maurice Stokes. Two years before, he had been named rookie-of-the-year and was headed for stardom. His illness was diagnosed as brain damage of the motor-control center, caused by a blow on the head. He was left immobile and speechless.

With a delicate touch and a great instinct for the game, Maurice Stokes was on his way to stardom in the NBA when a tragic court accident left him speechless and immobile. For a lesser man, this would have been the end, but for Stokes, it was only a new beginning. With the help of former teammate Jack Twyman, Stokes has learned to move and speak again and has become an inspiration in courage to all those about him.

Stokes will never be normal again, but sheer willpower has enabled him to make some progress. He rarely leaves the Good Samaritan Hospital in Cincinnati. He sits in a specially constructed wheelchair. He finds it difficult to feed himself and can't hold a spoon in his hand. He can take only a few steps and has to lean against parallel bars when he does. Unless you listen carefully, it is very difficult to understand what he is saying.

He endures partly because of the efforts of his friend Jack Twyman. Twyman is a successful insurance executive and a television sports commentator. In 1958, he was a teammate of Stokes' but just a casual friend. After the 1958 season all the players returned to their homes, confident that Mo would be completely well in a week or so. Only Twyman, who lives in Cincinnati, remained.

"About two weeks later," Twyman has recalled, "I could see how sick Maury was and realized then how much money he would need. He was still in a coma and the prediction was that he would be for a very long time. His family lived in Pittsburgh, but the doctors advised strongly against moving him. Since I was the only one available, I became his legal guardian."

In 1959, Kutsher's Country Club in Monticello, New York, offered to run an annual benefit game for Mo if enough players would volunteer their services. The athletes were very willing and through the years since its inception, all the great players have participated. About $75,000 has been raised from the Kutsher's game.

Twyman would relate to Mo each year in great detail everything that had happened at the benefit game. Mo would listen and ask questions. "I could see how much he wanted to be there," says Twyman.

He talked to the doctors and it was decided that Mo would attend the 1967 game. A private plane was hired for the occasion and a nurse went along. Mo was delighted to see all

his old friends there. He acted like a little boy at his first party.

So all is not hopeless for Maurice Stokes. A nurse in the hospital sums it up: "After such a tragedy, most people lie in bed, become vegetables and quietly fade away. Not so with Maurice. He's glad to be alive and makes you feel the same way."

Sam and K.C. Jones

For many years the Boston Celtics were led by the slick back-court combination of Bob Cousy and Bill Sharman. Those were good years for the Celtics but not too many of them were championship ones. The championships came when center Bill Russell arrived with his defense and rebounding, and by then the Celtics had to start finding replacements for those two extraordinary back-court operators. The men who took over for Cousy and Sharman were the Jones Boys, Sam and K.C. (no relation to each other)—and they turned out pretty well in their own right.

The Celtics took a long chance when they drafted Sam Jones in 1957. An unknown athlete from a small college, he came on the recommendation of a man who had never met him and had seen him play only once. The Celtics didn't have that much choice anyway. The college crop was skimpy that year and Boston had last pick. The coach, Red Auerbach, took Jones strictly on speculation. Sam hadn't won All-American ranking and hadn't even made sectional honors. Still, he has proved to be one of the most important acquisitions the Celtics ever made. Sam started out as a replacement for Bill Sharman. He fitted perfectly into the Celtics' fast-breaking offense.

Sam's ultimate success is something of a miracle for he is to pro basketball what Johnny Unitas is to football. Like Unitas, Jones was older than the average rookie, and like Unitas he came up from nowhere. Sam was a graduate of North Carolina College in Durham.

It isn't often that a college player who fails to get even sectional honors as an All-American can rise to stardom in the NBA. But if you have great speed and a deadly scoring touch, then the job becomes much easier. Sam Jones, the sharpshooting guard for the Boston Celtics, combined these qualities with a lot of hard work to become a major factor in the Celtics' dominance of the NBA.

Many men make it to the NBA as ball-handlers and sharpshooters, but K. C. Jones was the only man to achieve cage stardom as a result of defensive ability. He did have the ability to score (below) but was better known, and feared, for his ability to stop others from scoring.

Originally, the Lakers had bid for Sam after he got out of the service in 1956. They had heard about him through Bob Leonard, who had played against Jones in the Army. But Sam turned down the offer; he wanted to return to college to take the few courses he needed to get a degree. The next year, when the Lakers had first choice in the draft, they took Hot Rod Hundley. Nobody else had ever heard of Sam, and the Celtics wouldn't have either except for Bones McKinney, the former Wake Forest coach.

McKinney, a close friend of Auerbach's, received a call from Red just before the 1957 draft. Red wanted to know if McKinney knew of any players the Celtics should draft. "I saw a boy named Sam Jones play in a game here in Winston-Salem this winter," McKinney said. "He's a great shot and the fastest man I've ever watched on a basketball court. If I were you, I'd grab him."

Grab him they did, and regret it they did not. When he first reported, he amazed everyone with his shooting. In his first practice session he sank shot after shot. Bob Cousy, who had been watching Sam, noticed that Jones always threw from an angle, never from in front of the basket, and that he banked shot after shot off the same spot on the backboard.

"Where did you learn to shoot like that?" Cousy asked. "In school," Sam replied. Before going to college, Sam had prepped for five years at Laurinburg Institute in North Carolina. His coach, Frank McDuffie, had put a strip of tape on the backboard at the point from which the ball would always carom into the basket. Sam had spent so many years aiming for that spot that he knew it by heart.

Sam has been "banking" his way through the NBA ever since that first practice session. His career is filled with outstanding games and his record testifies to his accomplishments. He is high on the career list of NBA scorers with an average of 17.5 points per game. In the play-offs, he has done even better and has been on the all-star team eight times. Not bad for a man with an obscure sports background.

K.C. Jones had just the opposite career in college. He was on the same team as Bill Russell, at the University of San Francisco, and starred on the U.S. Olympic team, again with Russell. But just like Sam, K.C.'s emergence as a star is surprising. K.C. was not a good shooter. His highest season average was 9.1 points per game in 1961–1962, and he scored just 4,999 points in his ten-year career, a total exceeded by Wilt Chamberlain in his first two seasons.

But the value of K.C. to the Celtics was best put by his ex-coach, Red Auerbach, during K.C.'s days as back-up man for Bob Cousy: "When Jones goes into a game and we're behind," said Red, "we begin to catch up. When we're ahead, Jones puts us further ahead." As a substitute for Cousy, K.C. was the most highly respected second-stringer in the league. When Cousy's retirement in 1963 elevated Jones to a starting position, he lost no time in establishing himself as one of the toughest defensive players in pro basketball.

About K.C., Auerbach once said: "He is the only player ever to win a job in the NBA solely on the basis of his defensive ability." What Jones did better than anyone else was to force his opponents into crucial mistakes, taking a hurried shot or making an off-target pass. Jones led the Celtics' hustling, harassing defensive style that set up their fast breaks and made them the terrors of the league.

Although he was shorter than most guards, quick and strong K.C. was generally assigned to the best outside shooter the opponents had, men like Oscar Robertson and Jerry West. No one stops players like those, but K.C. made them work extra hard and helped choke up opponents' offenses. The Celtics won the title year after year and basketball experts agreed it was their defense that made the difference, thanks largely to K.C. and his old San Francisco partner, Bill Russell.

The NBA careers of the two Joneses were separated by two years at the end, but still they had something important in common. Both could play their final seasons with the knowledge that there was a college coaching job waiting for them. K.C. retired after the 1966-1967 season to become head basketball coach at Brandeis University in Waltham, Massachusetts, one of the first Negroes chosen to coach at a predominantly white university. Sam went into his last campaign, 1968–1969, having already signed as head basketball coach and athletic director at the Federal City College, a brand-new school in Washington, D.C.

Hal Greer

Hal Greer is a lean, long-legged guard who epitomizes the run-and-shoot school of basketball that has become so prevalent in the National Basketball Association. No one in basketball is more effective than Hal Greer at sprinting down the middle of the court on a fast break, stopping just beyond the keyhole and scoring on a jump shot. "Hal," said one NBA coach, "has the finest middle-distance shot in the game. From fifteen to eighteen feet, Greer is more deadly than the Big O."

At 6ft.-3in. and 178 pounds, Greer frequently gives away 40 pounds and 6 inches to NBA adversaries assigned to shutting off the middle. The key to Greer's success, therefore, is maneuverability and speed. Particularly speed. "I must be quick," says Greer. "The day I slow down I'm finished."

One February evening in 1965, Hal proved his point. The instep of his left foot was bruised and his right ankle was badly sprained. Playing against the Los Angeles Lakers, Greer obviously had no speed. As a result, his split-second moves behind those split-second picks vanished and Greer floundered. He scored only four of eighteen shots, hardly the accuracy of a man who generally scores more than twenty points a game. Frustrated, he lost his poise and started complaining to and about the referees. That's how things affect Greer. He is a tough competitor and cannot stand to play below par.

Hal's college career at Marshall University had a dramatic impact on West Virginia college athletics because he was the first Negro to make a major-college varsity in the state. Greer had a successful college career, leading Marshall into the era of the 100-point game.

His last coach there was Jules Rivlin. Rivlin had once coached a youngster named Paul Seymour and in 1958 Seymour was the coach of the Syracuse Nationals of the NBA. Greer became Syracuse's second draft choice. "I've always had a high regard for Jules' opinion," said Seymour.

The transition period from college to pro ball taxed Hal's patience. "He was just a little boy from a little coal-mining town," said Dolph Schayes, who was a Syracuse superstar at the time. Greer had talent and exceptional speed, and he couldn't understand why he was sitting on the bench. He just needed time to adjust to pro ball.

Hal remembers Seymour "easing me in." Seymour would play him for a quarter and then take him out. By the end of his first season, Hal had moved into the starting lineup. He scored forty-five points in one game in his second season. After that he was on his way.

Year in and year out, Greer has been chosen to play in the annual all-star game. In the 1968 game he was voted the MVP after scoring nineteen points in one quarter to set a record. Hal has always been one of the outstanding scorers in the NBA.

When Wilt Chamberlain joined Hal on the 76ers, Greer became even more effective. There is no better man in the league than Wilt in setting up a pick. Greer would come down the middle and shuffle the ball off to Chamberlain. While Hal cut by him, Wilt sometimes shot. More likely, though, Chamberlain would

It was a proud moment for high-stepping Hal Greer and his wife, Mamie, when he was named the Most Valuable Player in the 18th annual NBA mid-season All-Star East-West classic in 1968. It was Hal Greer's eighth consecutive All-Star game.

fake the shot while defenders swarmed to him and deftly pass off to Greer for an easy lay-up or a five-foot jump shot. And Hal didn't miss many of those.

Oscar Robertson

High School basketball is a favorite pastime for sports fans all over the country, but in the state of Indiana it is a passion—almost an obsession. They call it "Hoosier Hysteria." Not surprisingly, Indiana has produced some of the greatest teams, greatest players and greatest coaches basketball has ever seen. Indiana stars populate college teams all over the nation every season.

Thus, when anyone says that a player is the best Indiana high school basketball has ever seen, the statement should not be taken lightly. That is what the fans and sportswriters were saying in the mid-1950's about a youngster from Indianapolis—Oscar Robertson.

Oscar played basketball for Crispus Attucks High School. As the name implies, it was an all-Negro school, even though the city's schools had been "officially" desegregated in the late 1940's. Oscar was tall and slender but, most important, blessed with a quickness and a shooting eye that no one could match. In the 1954–1955 season, as a junior, he led Attucks to the state championship, a coveted and hard-won honor in any season. The following year, Oscar and the Crispus Attucks Tigers went unbeaten and were again the state champions. "The best ever," people said about Robertson.

Colleges all over the country offered him scholarships, and finally Oscar chose the University of Cincinnati, which had a top coach, George Smith, but had never been an outstanding basketball power. The presence of Oscar Robertson took care of that almost immediately—or rather, by his sophomore season, when he first became eligible.

In his sophomore season he led the UC Bearcats to a 25–3 record, the Missouri Valley Conference championship and a berth in the national Collegiate Athletic Association tournament. The next season, UC won another conference title and advanced to the NCAA semi-finals before losing to the eventual champion, California, closing with a 26–4 record. In Oscar's senior season he again sparked Cincinnati to the Missouri Valley crown, and again to the national semi-finals before a loss to California, UC's second defeat in thirty games, ended his college career. In the three years before Oscar played varsity basketball, the Bearcats' record was fifty-two victories and twenty-two losses. For his three campaigns, it was seventy-nine victories and nine defeats.

That was his effect on the team. His achievements as an individual are unequaled in college basketball history. During three seasons he scored a total of 2,973 points, a record for a college player, and averaged 33.8 points per game. He set fifteen school and thirteen conference records. He set scoring records in arenas around the country, a sixty-two at North Texas State, for example, and a fifty-six at Madison Square Garden in New York. He played at the Garden for three seasons and each year he was voted the outstanding college player to appear on that court.

He packed gymnasiums. UC had drawn 185,244 fans at home and 377,007 overall for the three years before he competed. In his seasons the Bearcats attracted 333,548 at home and 805,159 overall. In a sense he became a national figure. At the time he was playing college basketball a new cigarette was introduced on the market with an advertising campaign selling "the Big O." Soon everyone was calling Oscar "the Big O." Before too many years had passed, the cigarette had disappeared, and when "the Big O" was mentioned, people knew it meant Oscar Robertson. When the University of Cincinnati built its gymnasium, a bronze plaque was placed at the entrance as a tribute to Oscar Robertson.

The summer after he graduated, he starred for the U.S. Olympic team which swept to the gold medal at Rome. In the team's crucial game, against the Soviet Union, Oscar led a spectacular fast-break attack that outscored the Russians 17–1 at one point in the second half to turn a close game into a rout.

His impact on basketball at the University of Cincinnati was not confined to his playing career. He made UC a power and his presence helped attract other stars. The year after he graduated, a matured UC team won the national championship, followed by a second straight crown the next year. It lost in overtime in a bid for an unprecedented third straight championship in 1963. It had all begun with Robertson.

But he was not finished with Cincinnati basketball. The city's professional team, the Cincinnati Royals, drafted him and now this player who had been the very best in both high school and college had to prove himself in the professional ranks. He was 6ft.-5in., not big for a basketball star, and certainly not big for a scorer in the National Basketball Association. But it wasn't long before the experts were agreeing: skill for skill, Oscar Robertson was perhaps the greatest all-around basketball player who had ever competed.

Not only should his individual talents be noted, but his effect on a team. It was clear at Crispus Attucks and at the University of Cincinnati. With the Royals, he was joining a team that almost never made the play-offs, one of the losers of the NBA. His rookie season they still did not. Then he led them to the play-offs for six straight seasons; the string was not broken until 1967–1968, a season in which Robertson was hurt and out of the lineup much of the time.

In that "sub-par" season of 1967–1968, Oscar simply led the league in scoring average, 29.2 points per game, in assists, 9.7, and in free-throw percentage, .873. For most of the season, when he played, it was with a thigh muscle injury that would have kept less determined men out of action.

Ex-Celtic coach Red Auerbach summed up Robertson's talents this way: "Oscar is different from most superstars. Others usually hurt you in one way—scoring, rebounding, or play-making. But Oscar hurts you all ways. He's the complete ball player."

Oscar can do everything with a basketball, and he has a unique knack of controlling the tempo of every game he plays. Ex-teammate Jack Twyman said: "The thing that expresses [Oscar] best is that you can't stereotype him. Whatever is needed at the time, against the particular opposition, comes out, because he has complete physical control of his body. It's not any one thing, it's his completeness that amazes you. It would be hard to say that he still improves with every game because he's so good to begin with, but on a given night, he can always show you something different, something new."

On the floor Oscar, who seems so mild and easy-going, begins to crackle with intensity. He has the kind of boyish features and big, soft eyes that will make him look young at forty. He has an upturned nose which would give him a clown's face except that he is not a laugher. Once the game starts, though, the dominant feature becomes his moving, inquisitive eyes which seem to be taking in everything that is happening everywhere around him.

He seems to start slowly, getting the feel of the game, feeding his players in turn, as if he's trying to find out who might be in for a good night. He seems to be under a tight rein until, suddenly, there is a loose ball and Oscar is sprinting in, picking it up and driving in on the basket.

What is most impressive about Oscar is the ease and rhythm with which he moves. His style is to change speeds, to fake and feint, to move in bursts. He never seems to be rushed, never seems to hurry, never seems at all ruffled. He starts to drive in, finds himself in a pack of

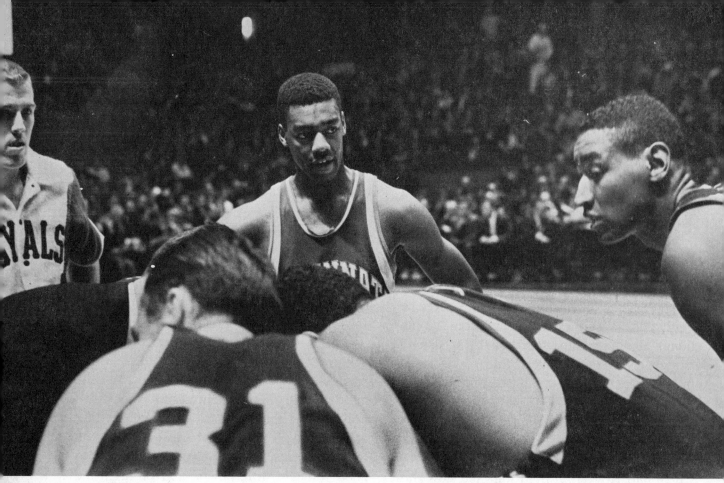

Moments before play is resumed, Robertson joins his teammates for a strategy session on the sidelines.

In a 1967 game against Boston, Robertson suffered a mouth injury requiring six stitches. Never one to complain or miss any playing time, he played nonetheless—using a protective faceguard.

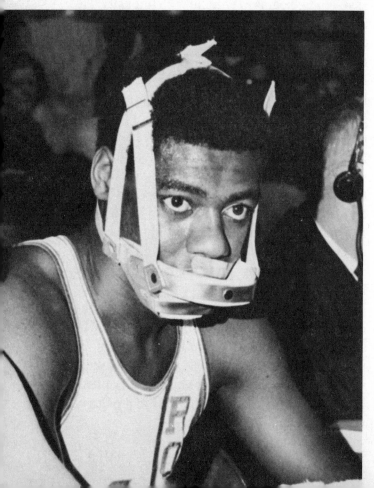

In leading the Cincinnati Royals to a victory over the New York Knicks, Oscar Robertson demonstrates why he has been a superstar for so many years in the NBA. His ability to bring the ball up court (above), score from any point (below left) and battle for rebounds under the board has been a major factor in Cincinnati's success in the 1960's.

three opposing players and, without seeming to blink his eyes, amidst all that arm waving, he just bends his head way over and bounces the ball through all those legs to a teammate for the basket. Or he might pull up short and work his own way through for an easy jump shot. If he's given the ten-foot shot, he'll work his way in for the eight-footer, and when he is given that, he'll try to work his way in for the six-footer. He does this all the time until he has frustrated his defensive man so much that the defender will often give him the lay-up.

This kind of effort has been acknowledged with Robertson's selection to the NBA all-star team every year he has been in the league, and his choice as the most valuable player one season, an honor almost never won, as his was, by a member of a non-championship team. There is, by common agreement, nothing that he cannot do superbly on a basketball court.

Cazzie Russell

During Cazzie Lee Russell's collegiate career at Michigan, he was three players. On defense he played the corner, and often became the third forward on offense by driving to the baseline. Forty per cent of Michigan's offense was geared toward Russell playing as a center in the low-post position, while teammate Bill Buntin, the official center, came out to play the high post. So there were two positions, center and forward. Cazzie played both well.

But it was as a big all-round guard that Russell earned his collegiate success. Many people thought he reminded them of another outstanding collegiate guard, Oscar Robertson. About the only person who didn't think that was Oscar himself. He once said, "Cazzie has got a style all his own." Robertson was kind, but not truly accurate. Russell pleaded guilty to plagiarism: "I find myself copying Oscar when the game is close."

There is nothing wrong in being an imitator —if one choses the right model and can emu-

late him well. Russell cannot be faulted there, and he added flourishes of his own. Once in a game during the 1964 season, he dribbled down court with just one defender to beat. Cazzie, a right-hander, whipped the ball behind his back with his left hand. The opponent was faked out of position, and in one sweeping motion Cazzie pulled the ball back and dunked it into the basket.

Even with all his showmanship, Russell is definitely not a candidate for the Harlem Globetrotters. He is very sensitive about being considered a clown. Once, in a freshman intra-squad game, he broke away. When he reached the basket he gave a little hesitation jig in mid-air and then stuffed the ball. Soon after, he broke away again and just then a spectator yelled "Showboat!" "That bothered me," Russell said later, "so I just laid it up. That's the thing about the public—they have to realize we're human too. This thing about them having paid to get in so they say what they want—that's for the birds."

Russell is a refreshing, candid person who says exactly what he thinks, always has a reason—right or wrong—for saying it and is not afraid to reveal himself. He was probably the most popular player ever to play basketball at Michigan. When he graduated, the NBA's Detroit Pistons were anxious to sign him. But the New York Knicks won a coin flip to determine who would get the first crack at the draft. And New York wanted Cazzie, too.

Russell signed a contract with the Knicks calling for a reported $250,000. But he wasn't quite the immediate success that he had been in college. As a guard, Russell, who stands 6ft.-5in. and weighs 220 pounds, found that he could no longer overpower the opposition guards because of superior height or weight. There were some NBA guards who were just as big, just as strong, and a lot of the guards were quicker than he was. He had serious problems trying to stay with his man on defense. It looked as if the Knicks had made a bad choice. Cazzie suffered through a whole season in the pros, playing a position that did not suit him.

Then in 1967–1968, the Knicks decided to take a chance. If Caz wasn't quite quick enough at guard, then why not try him against slightly bigger, slower men at forward? After all, there were some 6ft.-5in. forwards in the league. So the Knicks made Russell a forward, and he responded to the switch. It took him a little while to get adjusted to playing a corner and his defense needed some brushing up, but it was better than playing guard. Cazzie now had the speed advantage. He worked at his new position through the exhibition season and when it came time to start the regular games he was ready. Gradually, his shooting touch returned to what it had been at Michigan. Cazzie was hitting the jump shot and he worked, too, on his moves to the basket.

The Knicks made it a little easier for Cazzie. In 1967–1968, they switched to a pressure defense, sometimes employing a full-court press. During such a press, the forwards must be able to move quickly in order to force the opposition into mistakes. This was easy for Cazzie. He had "arrived" by a combination of circumstances—a coin flip, a change of position and a new defense. His ability to adapt proved he was truly an outstanding player.

Despite a full court press by the St. Louis Hawks, Russell moves the ball past Paul Silas on his way up court.

Virgil Akins

Muhammed Ali

Floyd Patterson

Sandy Saddler

CHAPTER EIGHT

Kings of the Ring

WHETHER it's one of the little men, like featherweight champions Davey Moore and Sandy Saddler, the average-size men, like Ray Robinson, or the big men, like Joe Louis and Muhammed Ali, the Negro has risen to the top in boxing.

Boxing is the only major professional sport that never officially barred Negroes from participation. This is not to say that Negroes have always been treated equally, given the same opportunities for important fights, given the same financial terms, or the like. But they could receive a chance to compete and to win. Thus, there is not the sharp break with the past in boxing, as in baseball or football, both of which can be separated into eras by World War II.

If there is any major connecting link through those war years in boxing, it is personified by "Sugar Ray" Robinson, whom many consider, pound for pound, the best fighter ever. He started his career in 1940, in time to fight and beat the triple champion, Henry Armstrong, and was still at it two dec-ades later. He himself won the welterweight crown and the middleweight crown and narrowly missed the light heavyweight title, collapsing from the heat with victory in his grasp.

Not since Robinson has there been an American Negro middleweight champion. But three of the last five heavyweight champions have been Negroes, three of the last five light heavyweights, two in the welterweight class, three among the lightweights, two among the featherweights.

And in the 1960's has come one of the most striking figures in ring history—Muhammed Ali, born Cassius Marcellus Clay. At first, fans and experts alike were skeptical of his skills and amused by his antics. Then they had to accept his superior skills, but as Ali spoke ever more strongly of his Black Nationalist beliefs, many whites were turned away by his attitude. It was as if they sought a new "white hope," just as they had when Jack Johnson reigned. The Negroes, however, understood.

Muhammed Ali (Cassius Clay)

Superb champions come along in every sport periodically. They run faster, or throw more accurately, or kick farther, or hit harder than others do. But what happens seldom in the world of sports is the appearance of a champion who excels not only with ability, but with charm. Such a rarity is Cassius Marcellus Clay, who, after he had captured the heavyweight boxing championship of the world, changed his religion from Christian to Muslim and took the new name of Muhammed Ali.

As a child, Cassius Clay was strongly encouraged by his mother, Odessa Clay, who inspired the kind of family life in which a child wanted to do the right thing. Her love nurtured self-confidence in all her children. And her husband, Cass Clay, showed through his easygoing attitude that a person could be aggressive, could stand up for himself and his rights, without deliberately offending others.

When young Cassius was twelve, his bicycle was stolen. A police officer found him in a fit of rage, ready to take on the world. The boy was strong, and to channel these pent-up feelings into something positive, the officer encouraged Cassius to learn to box. Cassius was an apt pupil and dedicated to his new sport. He refused to ride to school, preferring to run, so that he could increase his speed. After school, he would have his brother Rudy throw rocks at him to improve his reflexes.

Young Cassius fought his way through a succession of local tournaments in his native city of Louisville, Kentucky. He entered the Golden Gloves tournament and the national Amateur Athletic Union tournament, where he became the light heavyweight champion. His speed, furious combinations and disarming low-guard style were too much for his amateur foes. Then he qualified for the U.S. Olympic team in 1960. In the Olympics at Rome he knocked off all opposition easily, to win the light heavyweight gold medal.

There was by then no doubt that Cassius would turn pro. The only thing standing in the way of a major career was his weight. He was a light heavyweight and special glory is reserved for the heavyweights. But Cassius was only eighteen, still a growing boy. It seemed he would get bigger—and he did.

Cassius was also a local hero in Louisville. Because of his achievements and his natural personality, many of the citizens there did not want him to become involved with the rougher elements of the boxing world. A group of ten men, successful professional and businessmen in Louisville, got together to form a syndicate. They would handle Clay's contract, pay for his trainer, give him a weekly allowance, take a managerial cut and invest the rest for him. Thus, when his career was over, if he had made big money, Cassius would not have to worry about financial security. Cassius signed an agreement with the men.

His new managers and his outstanding trainer, Angelo Dundee, brought him along slowly. His first, carefully selected opponents were men like Tunney Hunsacker, Herb Siler and Tony Esperti, all nonentities in the boxing world. He won easily. Then Cassius was tested against some better but over-the-hill fighters, like Alexander Miteff and Will Besmanoff. He disposed of them just as easily.

Now the Clay image began to develop. He began calling the rounds for knocking out his opponents and was usually right. He gave vent to his natural instinct for poetry; some of his doggerel proved charming. It was a good time for a young fighter like him. Floyd Patterson had been the previous Olympic hero to become heavyweight champion, and Patterson took everything seriously. The public loved this outspoken new slugger.

The major test of Cassius' early career came in November 1962, about two years after he had won at Rome, when he fought Archie Moore. Here was a perfect match for Clay in at least one respect—box-office appeal. Working hard to build the gate, Archie began to hurl insults at young Cassius and, of course, the Kentucky belter responded. Their name-calling, more in fun than anger, lasted for weeks. Clay at first predicted that Moore would be taken out in eight, then shifted to six, and finally when Moore's insults grew more pointed he said Archie would fall in four. And although Moore was a tough, ring-wise, take-care-of-himself champion, Cassius did, in fact, knock him out in the fourth round.

The public was warming to Clay now, but still was not sure of his skill. He was matched in March 1963 against a top foe, Doug Jones. In the weeks preceding the fight, Cassius read poetry in a Greenwich Village coffee shop, went on major television shows and gave frequent interviews. But he was also setting aside time to train. Finally, the night came and 18,732 fans crowded into Madison Square Garden to see the bout.

Jones, still young but a ring veteran, made Clay look bad at times, worse than he had ever looked. But Cassius always avoided the other man's big punch. The fight was close and before it was over the game underdog, Jones, had won the crowd's sympathy over Cassius who had bragged about his prowess. The officials split 2–1, for Clay. Many in the unruly crowd roared their disapproval of the decision. But Clay's winning streak was intact.

Now past that milestone, Clay's tutors booked him against one of Britain's top heavyweights, Henry Cooper. The Britisher surprised Cassius by knocking him down early in the bout, but Clay responded by cutting Cooper badly. Cassius had said the fight would end in five, and in the fifth round he scored a technical knockout over the bleeding Cooper.

Now Cassius was unbeaten in nineteen professional bouts and ready for the biggest game of all. He traveled to Las Vegas, Nevada, where Sonny Liston was to defend his heavyweight crown in a return bout against Floyd Patterson, and stole the show. Entering the ring before the fight, he shook hands with Patterson, stared across the ring at Liston and, in mock terror, fled outside the ropes. No one was fooled. Cassius Clay wasn't afraid of Sonny Liston or anyone else. After Liston had knocked Patterson out in the first round for the second time, Cassius was the logical contender.

Clay knew he would get the title bout and he began to build up the attraction as much as to perfect his talents for Liston. He greeted Liston at the airport in Miami when the champion arrived, hired a bus to heckle him at home, and told everyone who would listen that he was the greatest. Since no one had yet proved otherwise, people had trouble disputing that. But Liston was big and tough and mean and most experts thought he would be too much for the relatively inexperienced Clay. Of forty-six boxing writers polled before the bout, three picked Clay to win.

At the weigh-in on fight day Cassius moved around yelling, "Float like a butterfly, sting like a bee." He screamed insults at Liston who, as usual, simply stood there silently. Cassius was fined $2,500 for his tactics by a Florida boxing commission that didn't know what to make of him, but that was only small change to him.

At the fight, though, Cassius was calm. He did, indeed, float like a butterfly and sting like a bee. Liston shuffled after him and hit hard, but Clay seemed untroubled. In the 4th round, though, Cassius got in real trouble when something entered his eyes and blinded him. He gamely held on to weather the round. He fought through the 5th and in the 6th turned the tables on a stunned Liston. He battered the champion all over the ring. Before the 7th round started, Liston said that he had dislocated his shoulder and did not come out. No one knew whether it was true or that he was simply afraid to do battle with this young tiger.

Fighting as a light heavyweight, Cassius Clay (or Muhammed Ali as he now prefers to be called) jolts Russian boxer Shatkov to advance in the Olympic Tourney.

Ali lived up to pre-fight predictions as he kayoed Charlie Powell in the 3rd—the round he designated.

Floyd Patterson receives a hard right to the jaw in an unsuccessful attempt to defeat the champion.

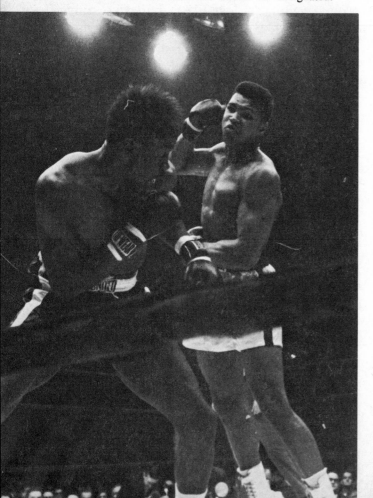

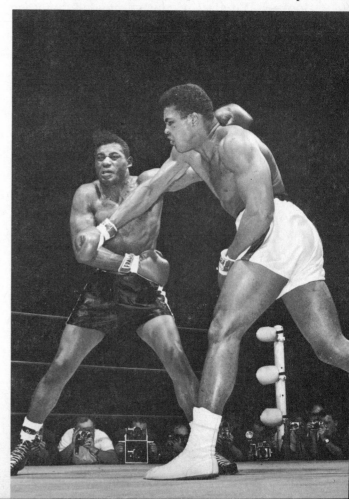

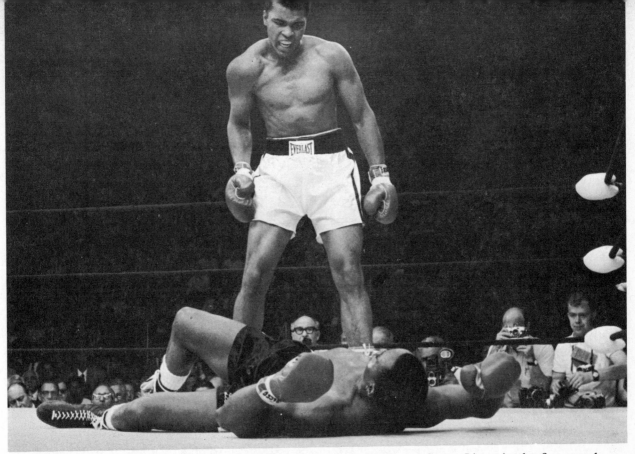

In one of the most controversial fights in history, Muhammed Ali floored Sonny Liston in the first round.

Striking a familiar pose, the champion waits for Zora Folley to rise from the canvas after a fourth-round knockdown in their 1967 title bout.

Now involuntarily "retired" from the ring, Muhammed Ali spends most of his time preaching and studying in the Muslim faith.

Cassius Clay had fooled the world. He was the heavyweight champion and those who didn't believe in him were tasting sour grapes. Some said he couldn't punch, but he knocked men out. Some said he didn't have a good defense, but no opponent hit him much. No one could doubt his speed—with his feet or his fists. At 6ft.-3in. and 220 pounds, he was a classic size, big enough to hit, rangy enough to move.

But there were doubters. Liston got another shot at him and many believed that Sonny wouldn't take a beating again. Incredibly, Cassius fetched Liston one good punch and the ex-champion was down in the 1st round.

Some still refused to believe and, of course, these would never be convinced. All Clay could do was defeat everybody in sight. He left the Canadian George Chuvalo a swollen red lump. He looked at Cooper again for six rounds. Another canny Britisher, Brian London, fell in three. The German Karl Mildenberger, the heavyweight champion of Europe, did better, lasting until the 12th round. Cleveland Williams and Zora Folley went next.

Now Cassius began to have real troubles. What one one could do to him in the ring, officials tried to do outside it. Cassius had changed his religion, had become a Black Muslim. He represented a new kind of Negro —one who stood up to everyone. Many in the white establishment of the country couldn't stand that.

Cassius took a new name, Muhammed Ali, but many sportswriters refused to call him that. They weren't offended when Arnold Cream called himself Jersey Joe Walcott or when Walker Smith used the name Sugar Ray Robinson. But they refused to accept Muhammed Ali.

He began to spend more and more time preaching his Black Muslim religion. When he began to associate almost exclusively with Muslims, some of his old friends were offended. He dropped the Louisville men who

had helped him, even Angelo Dundee, the trainer who had taught him everything.

But Ali's biggest troubles were to be with the law. He had been called for induction into military service and twice failed the mental test. Then he was given it again and passed. But he claimed exemption as a Black Muslim minister. The Army didn't agree and said he was primarily a fighter. Ali refused to report to the Army and was indicted for draft evasion.

This gave the boxing overlords an excuse. First the National Boxing Association took his title and gave it to Eddie Machen. Ali fought Machen and stopped him. Then the NBA and the New York commission took the title away again, when he was convicted of draft evasion. There wasn't any rule that said they should; they simply did.

Right or wrong, Muhammed Ali stood for what he believed. He didn't fight anymore, so he preached. He appealed his conviction and lost. He faced the prospect of jail. If he had to serve a sentence, he would almost surely emerge too old and too out of shape to regain his heavyweight title. But Muhammed Ali knew, and even his worst detractors knew as well, that this was the only way to keep him from remaining the heavyweight champion. He had said that in the ring he was "the greatest," and in his era that was something no one could deny.

Ezzard Charles

Ezzard Charles became a professional boxer in 1940, after fighting as an amateur while he was still in school. His career was not really successful until September 27, 1950, when he beat Joe Louis and became the heavyweight champion of the world. The years in between were very long.

Charles was a poor boy from Cincinnati who had to battle for every break he ever got. He had to survive the discouragement of being refused a shot at the light heavyweight title

Harry Wills (right), boxing star of the 1920's, gives a few pointers to former heavyweight champ Ezzard Charles.

Charles apparently learned his lessons well as he knocks out Bob Satterfield in the second round of their bout.

when everyone knew he was the logical challenger. He had to shake off the legacy that became his the night his thudding gloves killed a man. He had to overcome the handicap of being a natural 175-pounder competing in the unlimited class. Above all else, he had to fight his way out of the ominous shadow of Joe Louis, who was the enduring favorite of the American public and Ezzard's own boyhood idol.

Charles was not a colorful personality in the tradition of Sullivan or Dempsey, and he wasn't a paralyzing puncher the way Louis was. He did have, though, the determination and courage to give everything he had every time he entered the ring. He had a magnificent body, broad-shouldered, narrow-waisted, deep-chested, with long and muscular arms to go with his height of six feet. And he had the desire to stay on the path to the heavyweight title.

If anything would have turned the amiable, soft-spoken Charles away from his quest, it would have been the events of the night of February 20, 1948, when Sam Baroudi died. Matched with Charles in a ten-rounder at Chicago Stadium, Baroudi fought a losing battle. Though badly beaten, Baroudi tried to finish out the last round, to protect his record of never having been knocked out. It was the last round of Sam Baroudi's life.

Ezzard, always plagued by the public's concept of him as a classy boxer with no punch, wanted a knockout. He swarmed all over his stubborn opponent. With a flurry of fast, crisp punches, he rocked Baroudi noticeably. Then, with a smashing combination, he blasted him to the floor. Baroudi lay there motionless. The defeated boxer could not be revived in the ring and died in the hospital without having regained his senses.

Charles, an emotional man, considered never fighting again. But gradually Ezzard realized that the death was an accident, a sudden, unforeseen tragedy for which he should

not be asked to take the blame. He did what he could. He took a bout with Elmer Ray in Chicago on the condition that the promoters match his own donation of $5,000 to the Baroudi family. When Ezzard turned over the $5,000 after the fight, he didn't even have enough to cover his own expenses.

The Ray fight was the turning point in his career. To keep his feet moving in the right direction, he had to win. To lose meant that the weight of the death was too much for him to carry, and retirement would have been the next step. In the 9th round Ezzard hit Ray with a wicked right and Elmer pitched forward on his face; he couldn't get up. All of a sudden, all the joy left Charles as he saw his opponent writhing on the floor. "Oh, God," he muttered, "not him, too!" But Ray wasn't dead. He was just temporarily indisposed.

Ezzard had now advanced a step closer to the light heavyweight championship, but he was not able to get a title fight. He switched to the heavies and on December 10, 1948 he met Joe Baksi, an ex-coal miner from Pennsylvania. Baksi had a considerable weight advantage over Charles but it wasn't enough. After absorbing a lot of punishment, Joe asked that the fight be stopped in the 11th.

After that, nobody complained that Charles was too small to tangle with the big boys. Certainly Joe Louis didn't. The champ, in fact, pointed the finger at Charles as the one most likely to take over the throne that he was ready to renounce. Since the skeptics wanted more proof, Ezzard fought and beat Joey Maxim. Not enough.

The day after, Joe Louis announced his retirement and promoted a bout between Jersey Joe Walcott and Charles for the championship. The battle was approved by the National Boxing Association but not by the New York State Athletic Commission. Ezzard was the winner, but people were not so quick to look on him as the new champion. Although the NBA governed in forty-seven of the forty-eight states, the one that wouldn't conform was the biggest of them all. New York still listed Louis as the heavyweight champion.

So a fight was arranged between the two to see which one would wear the whole crown. Even though Joe was past his prime and somewhat out of condition, many liked his chances. Part of this feeling was sentimental, and part was based on his devastating left hook.

Charles knew he could dance around the ring and tire the older man, but he chose to slug it out against the wishes of his trainers. There were no knockdowns in the fight. During the 14th round, Charles almost had the great ex-champion out on his feet, but Louis managed to hang on and finish upright.

After the fight, Ezzard again showed the kind of man he was. The announcer handed him the microphone and asked him to tell the people how it felt to be champion of the world. Ezzard said: "I only hope and pray that I will some day be as much of a credit to boxing as the man who is leaving the ring."

Charles was champion from 1949–1951, then fell before Walcott, the man he had beaten to get the NBA title. There were no dramatics, no tears when Ezzard went out. It was all businesslike—the way it had always been for him.

Jimmy Ellis

No matter where they were, protocol was the same. He might arrive with the champion, but always he would be walking behind him. No matter what the champion did, he wasn't seen because the people were watching Muhammed Ali.

Jimmy Ellis came a long way after Ali left, but Jimmy's burden is that Ali didn't leave because he was beaten; other circumstances forced him out. So even though Ellis has achieved fame and fortune, he is still looked upon as a man who perhaps didn't deserve to succeed the other champion.

Yet should Ali return to the ring someday, Ellis, the new world heavyweight champion, would not abdicate. He remembers earning a three-round decision by "beating him all the way," when he and Cassius Clay (Muhammed Ali was the Muslim name he took later) were teen-agers together in Louisville, Kentucky, and he remembers a sparring session in Toronto when Clay "moved to his left to slip my jab and I came straight down the middle with a good right hand" that flattened the champion.

"He always said he was 'the greatest,' " Jimmy says with a smile, "but I never thought he was that much better. He just had an opportunity to show what he could do. I had to struggle."

With six kids to feed and clothe, Ellis never had enough money to pay all the bills. When Clay was training, Jimmy earned a living as a sparring partner. But when Clay wasn't training, Jimmy returned to working as a cement-finisher.

Then times changed financially, but the struggle for identity went on. Jimmy wants to make people forget that he was second fiddle to Ali. There is also the added confusion of Jimmy's being recognized as heavyweight champion in some states and Joe Frazier's being considered the champion in others. To the general public, of course, neither is the champion until he beats Ali in the ring.

But Jimmy must keep trying. He used to be a middleweight who had surrendered to frustration in 1965. But his manager, Angelo Dundee, the same man who trained Ali, worked with Jimmy and helped him over some of the rough spots. Finally, in April 1968, Ellis beat Jerry Quarry for the World Boxing Association title.

He was now a champion, but he could never be the kind of showman Ali was. It just isn't in his nature. Ellis is more of a craftsman, and this no doubt comes from his upbringing. He was born on February 24, 1940, the middle

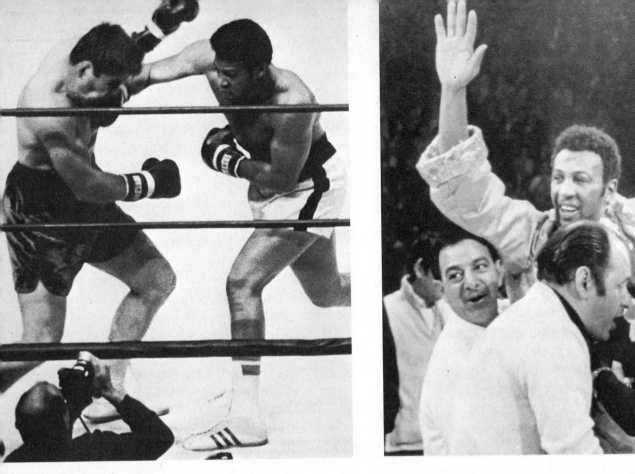

Jimmy Ellis gained the heavyweight championship by a decision over Jerry Quarry. Here he is seen delivering a hard right to Quarry's chin, being declared the winner and receiving a well-earned kiss from his wife.

child of nine. His father worked as a cement-finisher, but also concerned himself with religion, being a lay Baptist minister.

During his years with Ali, Ellis remained true to his Baptist teaching despite the influence of the Black Muslims who surrounded him. "I never tried to convert him," Jimmy says, "and he never tried to convert me. He knew that I had my faith."

As a boy, Jimmy developed that faith in a household dominated by soft spiritual music and his father's dignity. But Jimmy had his battles outside of the house. In 1957, he was matched with Clay in an amateur bout. Ellis was outweighed and outmatched in experience. He remembers: "I won the first round and half of the second, but I wasn't used to fighting and he outfought me at the end" to get the three-round decision.

About a year later, they had a return bout. "I stayed on Clay the second time," he recalls, "and beat him to everything he did. I banged him hard. There wasn't no doubt about the decision. I'd been beating him all the way."

After that, their careers separated. Clay grew into the light heavyweight Olympic champion in 1960 and, soon after, into a heavyweight contender. Ellis remained a middleweight. Later, Ellis' career dimmed and he decided to work with Clay. He kept up his boxing but with little success. He fought on the nights Clay battled for the title. The night Clay knocked out Liston in the 1st round, Ellis also had a 1st-round knockout against Joe Blackwood. Jimmy defeated Charles Leslie a few days before Clay stopped Patterson. Of his five bouts in 1966, all but one were on Clay's title cards. Ellis won them all.

The night Ali fought Zora Folley in Madison Square Garden, Ellis had a bout with Johnny Persol. Shortly after the opening bell, Ellis uncorked a left hook that flattened Persol and blurred the vision in his right eye. Persol was squinting when he arose and Ellis, sensing his opportunity, let go a lunging left hook and a short right, flooring Persol again. Moments later, the referee stopped the fight, and Ellis had achieved his third consecutive 1st-round knockout.

After that, Ali beat Folley and, in a post-fight interview, said: "It's beginning to look to me like James Ellis is the only man around to give me a good battle." Ellis doesn't think it would be a bad idea since that may be the only way he'll be able to achieve his own identity.

Joe Frazier

Down in Beaufort, South Carolina, Joe Frazier was the youngest of seven brothers in a family of thirteen children. He was born into poverty, with little future other than to work on the family farm. Joe was suspended from school in the tenth grade for thrashing a boy who called his mother names. That's when he decided to go north to Philadelphia, where he moved in with an aunt.

His first job in Philadelphia was as a meat cutter in a slaughterhouse. After trimming sides of beef one day, the seventeen-year-old Frazier showed up at the 23rd Police Athletic League gymnasium to lose some weight. "My legs were so fat," he remembered, "that I couldn't get my pants on." He got interested in boxing and showed a flair for it. Soon people were calling him "The Slaughterhouse Kid," and they talked about his lethal left hook.

Frazier trained hard and learned quickly. Of forty amateur fights, he lost only two. He won the Golden Gloves in 1962, 1963 and 1964. Later, in 1964, he entered the Olympic trials and scored six knockouts before losing a disputed decision to Buster Mathis. Frazier went to Tokyo as an alternate. Then, big Buster injured a knuckle during training and Joe was back in business. Using his left hook to its greatest advantage, Frazier punished his opponents. His big victory came against Russia's Yemelyanov in 1 minute, 59 seconds of the 2nd round, but it almost put him out of

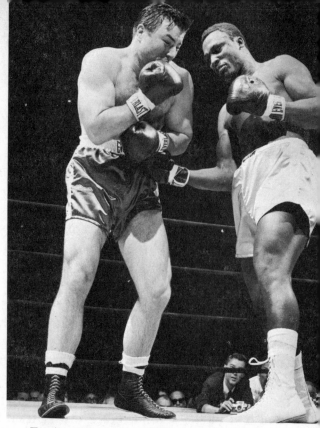

Frazier delivers a solid right into the midsection of Canada's George Chuvalo en route to an easy victory.

Joe Frazier sends his opponent, Russia's Yemel Yanov, down for an eight-count on the way to an Olympic victory.

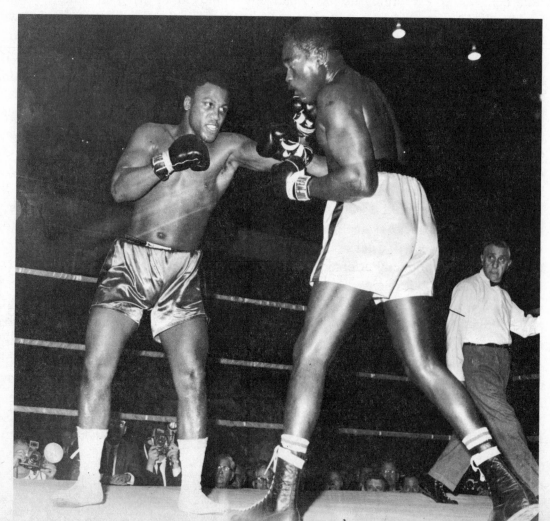

Frazier lands a solid left to Doug Jones' chin, one of the many bruising punches he landed before the fight was stopped by a Frazier left hook in the 6th round.

the tournament. He dislocated his left thumb. Keeping the injury a secret, Frazier won the Olympic heavyweight crown by outpointing Germany's Hans Huber, almost with one hand.

When the Olympic heavyweight champion arrived home in Philadelphia, he could not return to the slaughterhouse because his injured hand made it impossible for him to work for almost a year. To make matters worse, it was just before Christmas and Frazier, then the father of two children and with almost no bank account, faced a bleak holiday and an uncertain future.

Yank Durham, the man who had trained Joe since the beginning, initiated the formation of a syndicate. Forty people put up $250 each and gave Joe a three-year contract, at $100 a week, and loaned him the money to buy a house for his family.

Joe was on his way. He won every fight and soon was in the ring with the big names of the business. He was on his way to the heavyweight championship.

His first "name" fight was against Doug Jones. Jones was the man many thought had beaten Cassius Clay, although the decision went to Clay. Joe was the favorite, but Doug in assessing his opponent had stated, "He keeps coming in and I can keep putting it to him."

Jones was wrong. He did not put it to Frazier. He was too busy protecting himself from Frazier's aggressive attack. After the second round, when Joe connected with a vicious right to the midsection, it was only a question of how much punishment Jones could take. He took it longer than the crowd expected and tried to fight back. At the beginning of the fifth round, the crowd called for the referee to stop the fight. He didn't and Frazier stopped it in the 6th. He hit Doug with a smashing left hook and the referee could have counted to one hundred.

In November 1967, Joe was matched with his old friend, Buster Mathis, in a Madison Square Garden bout to crown a New York version of the heavyweight champion. Buster was 6ft.-3in. and weighed 243½ pounds, while Joe was only 6 feet, 204 pounds. In the 11th round, Frazier landed a short right to the chin, and followed with a thudding left hook to the temple. Buster crashed to the canvas. "I heard that man counting '9, 10' and I said to myself, '11, 12'," Frazier said later.

Joe's ambition has always been to do well enough so that it won't be necessary for his kids to fight. "My kids can become lawyers, or doctors, or something like that. I don't want them to get their heads banged around like their father."

Joe doesn't love a life in the ring. He doesn't like to hurt people, but it is the only way he knows to earn good money. "I'm not the kind of guy who enjoys knocking people down. I'd rather help them up."

Floyd Patterson

It is a compliment, not a criticism, to say that Floyd Patterson could be hurt more easily than any other heavyweight champion in history. For this tough man was sensitive and this humble man was proud, and these are admirable traits. However, it is also possible that these traits made Floyd less of a champion than he should have been. He brought immense natural skill and complete dedication to the ring. Yet perhaps Floyd Patterson was not destined to be a fighter.

Floyd was one of eleven children and lived in the poverty-stricken area in Brooklyn called Bedford-Stuyvesant. He was very shy and reserved yet big for his age. In the fifth grade he became a consistent truant and, after a while, his mother heard from the school authorities.

Although punishments were levied, Floyd continued to skip school. The threatened blow fell. With the approval of his mother, he was committed to the Wiltwyck School for Boys, an institution for the emotionally disturbed. Wiltwyck is located in the foothills of the Cat-

Floyd Patterson throws a hard left to the head of Archie Moore in the first round of their title bout. Patterson knocked out Moore in the 5th round to become the youngest heavyweight ever to win the title.

Patterson, in his first defense, sends a hard right to the head of challenger Tommy "Hurricane" Jackson. Jackson was decked three times before the fight was stopped in the 10th round.

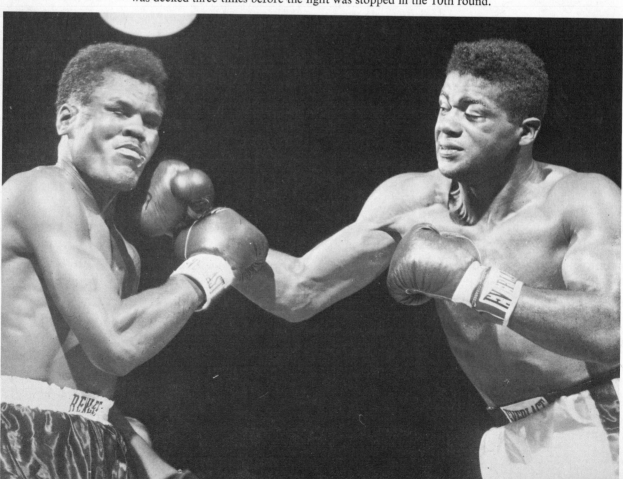

skills, near the small resort town of Esopus, New York, ninety miles from New York City.

"While I was on the way there," Floyd has said, "I thought I was going to be cooped up because of what I'd done, like somebody in a prison. When we came in sight of the place, I saw boys playing with a football, others running up and down a hill, all having fun, and I said to myself, 'They must be in a different group, I won't be allowed to go free like that.' "

Floyd was delighted to learn that the program was the same for everyone at Wiltwyck. And it was there that he first put on boxing gloves. He boxed in a tournament and he was matched against a much bigger boy. But Floyd had his speed and hitting power even then, and he came out the winner.

Floyd left Wiltwyck and eventually completed one year at Alexander Hamilton High School in Brooklyn. He then decided to follow in the footsteps of his older brothers and become a fighter. It was at this point in his life that Floyd met Cus D'Amato, the man who was to play such a dominant role in his later development as a fighter and as a man.

In 1950, Patterson became an amateur champion for the first time. In 1951, he took the New York open class 160-pound title and the All-Eastern crown. In 1952, Patterson won a gold medal at the Olympics in Helsinki. When Floyd returned from the Olympics, Cus D'Amato announced that Patterson's amateur career was over.

Floyd had twelve straight victories as a professional, then lost to Joey Maxim. Many observers thought it was a bad decision. Second-guessers said it was a bad match because Floyd had nothing to gain. Floyd said it was good to lose because he was getting too cocky and it was good to know he could lose.

The Maxim fight was in 1954. His first big victory and the one that led to his title shot was over Tommy "Hurricane" Jackson in a title elimination bout on June 8, 1956. He couldn't put the granite-chinned "Hurricane" away, but he gave him a methodical and artistic shellacking in twelve brutal rounds. And then came his big chance when Marciano retired and Floyd was matched against the formidable Archie Moore for the vacant title.

The Moore fight was the closest thing to a planned fight that Floyd ever fought. He studied the movies of the Marciano-Moore fight and noticed that Moore's right hand, rather than his left jab, was his instinctive punch.

In Chicago on Friday, November 30, 1956, Patterson knocked out Moore in five rounds and became the heavyweight champion of the world. He was the youngest man ever to hold the prized title.

With the championship came the vulnerability to public criticism, and Patterson was not always able to accept the comments of writers who refused to recognize his talents as a fighter. No matter whom he fought—Archie Moore, Hurricane Jackson, Pete Rademacher, Roy Harris, Brian London—the reports all read: "Patterson Beats Another Bum." When Ingemar Johansson signed to fight Patterson, most people said the Swede was "another bum." Then Ingemar unloaded a knockout punch, and he immediately was compared to Louis and Dempsey.

The period following that loss was one of the most depressing for the ex-champion. Floyd saw Johansson flaunting the new title and he got mad. It is said that the second fight was the only time Patterson became angry in the ring. He bashed the Swede about and finally separated Johansson from his senses for better than five minutes. Patterson became the first fighter in ring history to regain the world heavyweight championship. He could now live with himself again. The bitterness and self-doubts that had plagued him were gone.

Then he signed to fight Sonny Liston, a man with a twenty-five-pound weight edge and a thirteen-inch advantage in reach. Liston was depicted as being a dangerous, evil-tempered fighter who had trouble reading and writing. It is unfortunate that a man with Patterson's basic insecurities should have been put in the position of playing the part of the good guy, but he became the unwitting symbol of good in a clash against evil. It hurt him in the fight.

Floyd determined that the way to beat Liston was to keep moving until the big man got tired, then attack. He didn't move at all and was knocked out in 2 minutes and 6 seconds of the 1st round, after a right uppercut and a series of lefts.

But their second fight was to be different, thought Patterson. This time he would follow the plan and bob and weave. But just as suddenly in the second fight, he stopped moving. This time Liston knocked him down three times and when Patterson couldn't make it to his feet after the third, the rematch was over —at 2 minutes and 10 seconds of the 1st round—a four-second improvement over the first fight.

Fortunately, Patterson suffered no greater physical damage than a temporarily loosened tooth in these fights. But it severely damaged his ego. To any follower of boxing it was obvious that Patterson's poor performances as champion far outnumbered his good ones. He always could hit but seemed so easy to hit and hurt in return. With the exceptions of the night he won the championship from Moore and the night when he regained it from Johannson, he fell short of the promise he first showed in winning the Olympic title in 1952. From the third Johansson fight, when he was knocked down in the 1st round before going on to win, through an agonizing four-round match with totally inexperienced Tom McNeeley, the two Liston fights, and a loss to Cassius Clay, Patterson's talents seemed to decline. And the more he was criticized, the more he withdrew.

He always interpreted criticism of the fighter as criticism of the man. He felt he was admired in a way, but never respected. Other champions lost their titles and could laugh about it, but Floyd Patterson, in both victory and defeat, always remained something of a stranger.

Jersey Joe Walcott

At the age of thirty-seven, in Pittsburgh, Pennsylvania, Jersey Joe Walcott beat Ezzard Charles and became the heavyweight champion of the world. The reward of such a victory would be a bonanza for any heavyweight. For Jersey Joe the fact that he was in the ring that night at all was a miracle.

One of the patterns of Walcott's life started at birth—the pattern of hunger. He was born Arnold Raymond Cream on January 31, 1914, one of the ten children of a consistently destitute road worker. The boy's father, who came from the West Indies, had settled in Merchantville, New Jersey, a few miles from Camden.

At age seventeen, Arnold Cream went to Philadelphia to become a fighter. He impressed the ring-wise Jack Blackburn, who took over as his trainer. The youngster, then a welterweight, took the name of Joe Walcott, a favorite of his father's and one of the great Negro fighters of a previous era.

Although Joe came along fast, a fighter named Joe Louis had been brought to Blackburn's attention. Blackburn decided to concentrate on Louis, and Walcott was left by the wayside for the first time.

He had other managers, many other managers, some of whom took Joe for what they could get and left him. He was winning almost every fight, but he wasn't making enough money to eat on. He had odd jobs, working as a stevedore, on an ice truck and a garbage truck, in the shipyards, on a road gang, and anywhere else he could earn a few dollars.

He still fought on the side, with most of his bouts around Camden. Travel costs money so he stayed close to home. When Louis trained for the Schmeling fight in New Jersey, he hired Jersey Joe as a sparring mate. But this job didn't last long. Nobody knows why Walcott was let go, except for the fact that Louis was dropped three times in two days by the unknown.

The years dragged on and Walcott's family grew. In 1936, he fought just once. He had four bouts in 1937, six in 1938, two in 1940 and one in 1941. His family was always hungry. Finally, in 1941, Walcott announced he was through with fighting for good.

Early in 1945, seventeen years after he had started, Joe went back to fighting, although he didn't actively seek a return. He was working in a shipyard, eating well enough, and didn't really want to go back to the life of the old days. But he was talked into fighting and he joined up with Felix Bocchicchio and Joe Webster.

On August 2, 1945, he met Joe Baksi, the second-ranked heavyweight, in Camden. His managers made sure he was trained properly for the first time in his life. Joe won the decision although the pre-fight odds were 5–1 against him. Many thought it was a freak win, but Walcott, now with good support, started beating everyone he faced.

On February 25, 1946, Walcott squared off against Jimmy Bivins, who had won twenty-five out of his last twenty-six fights and was rated the finest heavyweight since Joe Louis. Jersey Joe made it twenty-five out of twenty-seven.

Sportswriters were beginning to notice Walcott but Louis refused to fight him. After this disappointment, Jersey Joe began to sag again, but a fight was promoted with Joey Maxim that guaranteed Walcott his largest take in nineteen years in the ring. Joe won and was back in the spotlight. Joe Louis saw the fight. He climbed into the ring and the two men had their pictures taken together. Nothing was said in the ring, but a short time later Louis gave Jersey Joe a title fight.

Walcott lost the fight on a disputed decision, but he had made it at last. When Louis retired, he was impressed enough with Jersey Joe to promote a Walcott-Ezzard Charles bout to fill the vacant championship. The time still wasn't right for Walcott—he lost to Charles—but he kept on fighting and hoping for another chance.

Finally, it came—in 1951 in Pittsburgh. He had a shot at Charles and the crown, and this time he didn't miss. When Walcott clobbered Charles with a single left hook to the chin in the seventh round, the ring became a wild demonstration by Walcott handlers and friends. He became the champion too late to last long, but it was almost a miracle that he was there at all.

Harold Johnson

One of the most skilled boxers to enter the ring in modern times was a slab-jawed, doe-eyed, steel-muscled Philadelphian named Harold Johnson. At 175 pounds, Johnson was a powerful middleweight who enjoyed the challenge of taking on the bigger fellows in the heavyweight division.

With all this skill and power, Johnson lacked one thing that kept him from becoming a financial success—fan appeal. Why was he cut off from the adulation and the roar of the mob? The answer is that Harold Johnson was one of the most mechanical, colorless fighters around. In fact, the controversy over his actual ability probably caused more fights among patrons than Johnson caused in the ring.

A considerable portion of the caution in Johnson's style was forced upon him by the twists his career had taken. He fought on the fringe of success for more than a decade, falling down the boxing ladder almost every time he seemed set to climb to the top. He was overshadowed and outdone by Archie Moore. In fact, in March 1961, when finally he won the light heavyweight title at the age of thirty-two

Harold Johnson is shown on the canvas after collapsing in the 3rd round of his scheduled ten-round bout with Jersey Joe Walcott. This was the same round in which Walcott had kayoed Johnson's father fourteen years earlier. It marked the first time in modern boxing annals that a fighter met one opponent and later fought his son.

Jersey Joe Walcott winces under a hard right by heavyweight champion Joe Louis in the first round of their fifteen-round title bout. Walcott lost on a disputed decision but later came back to kayo Ezzard Charles for the title.

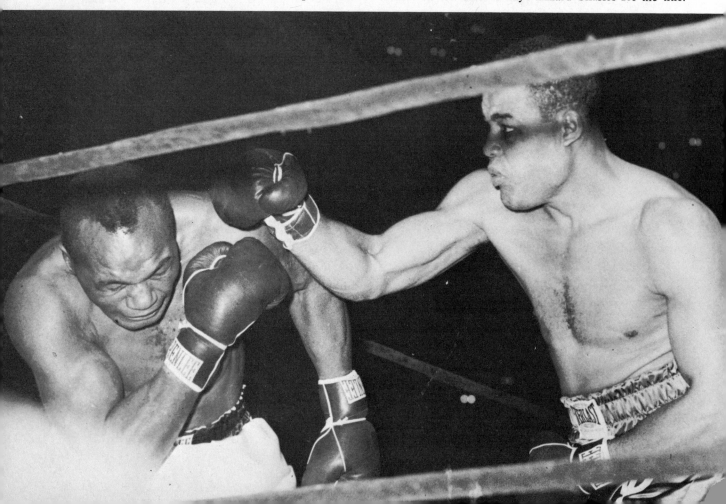

it was only a piece of the title, the slice that the NBA owned and had stripped from Moore.

Johnson trained in Champ's Gym in Philadelphia, a dusty, photo-lined, abandoned cafe with a ring, small bleachers, and a two-bit admission price. Into this tawdry corner came Sonny Liston and many others. But when Johnson worked out, the clan stopped shuffling on the scarred floor and watched, very much the way the hitters used to watch Ted Williams in the batting cage.

"Johnson is quality," said Joe Gramby, a fight manager. "When Johnson comes here, the fighters watch his every move. A master, that boy. Sometimes I think only the fighters know how good Johnson is." He may have been right because none of the promoters broke down Harold's door to arrange fights. The television people paid $150,000 to screen Archie Moore against the Italian, Guilio Rinaldi, but would not risk $15,000 for Johnson's title fight against Von Clay.

Rumors had spread that the reason for his tedious style was not that he was overly cautious, but that he lacked the courage to match his superb physical equipment. Not the type to explode with anger over these kinds of taunts, Johnson did feel moved to defend his ability.

"Those people that want to see me swing wild for a knockout all the time, those people just want blood," he said. "They're gonna yell and get excited and go home and get up next morning and go to work. If I bleed, they don't bleed. If I get beat up, they don't hurt."

The most famous part of his career concerns his series of battles with Moore. The legend lives that all five of these fights were close. The legend is wrong. In the first ten-rounder in 1949, Johnson was knocked down twice, and he was wobbling and barely able to survive the last bell. In the second fight, Archie did not warm up until the 6th round, but at the end Johnson was masked with blood, and not consoled by the fact that one judge called the fight even in rounds.

By then, 1951, Johnson was getting the knack of fighting Moore. In their third fight, three months later, he boxed adroitly and only lost when Archie outbombed him over the last three rounds. In the fourth fight, Johnson won at a tranquil pace, although Moore staggered him in the last rounds. The last of the series was the championship bout in New York in 1954, when Johnson was leading on points until Moore knocked him out in the 14th round.

His series of career ups and downs continued until the National Boxing Association stripped the light heavy title from Moore and declared an open tournament to find the successor. At long last Harold had the chance to be champion. And he made every use of that advantage by beating Jesse Bowdry in Miami before only 4,017 fans.

But Archie was old and refused to get into the ring with Harold to give him the chance to get the world title. Old Archie couldn't hold the title forever, though; on May 12, 1962, Johnson beat Doug Jones in Philadelphia and the championship, unscathed, was his. Was Johnson an underrated artist or an overrated bore? Whatever the answer, he did finally make it as light heavyweight champion of the world.

Archie Moore

Archie Moore, author, actor, raconteur, philosopher and fighter, may be the only man who could fool all the people all the time. His age was once said to be "43 going on 54" and his weight as being "175 to 210 pounds." He was described as a "fair to excellent" fighter with a "cynical to saccharine" disposition.

Archie's career began either on the streets of Benoit, Mississippi, or St. Louis, on either December 13, 1913 or December 13, 1916. As a youngster he went to live with an aunt, Mrs. Willie Moore, in South St. Louis, when his parents separated. Life wasn't easy and at fourteen or fifteen he began running with a bad

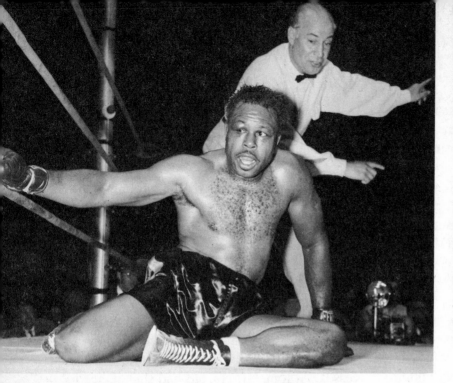

Archie Moore goes down for the last time in the 9th round in his fight with Rocky Marciano.

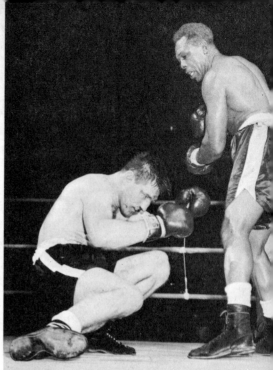

Champion Archie Moore drops Canadian Yvon D‍ in the 11th round of their 1958 title fight.

Floyd Patterson is driven back by a hard right from Archie Moore in the 4th round of their title fight.

crowd. Three times he was caught stealing, and finally he was sent to the Missouri State Reformatory when he was sixteen. He spent twenty-two months there and came out knowing he wanted to be a fighter. He joined the Civilian Conservation Corps, the Depression project created by the Roosevelt administration to get idle youngsters off the streets and out into the country. It wasn't a reform school, but it wasn't freedom either.

Many years later, Archie was asked if, with his background, he had ever done anything to help end juvenile delinquency. "Sure," he said. "What?" "I grew up."

At one time Archie stated that his first pro fight was April 3, 1935. On another occasion he said his first was in 1934 when he weighed only 147 pounds. All through the 1930's and 1940's, he was a gypsy, going from town to town, from country to country, from continent to continent, taking on anybody for a decent purse.

Only the dumb or desperate would tackle Archie in those days. Blessed with the barrel chest and power of a heavyweight, and the slim legs and speedy footwork of a middleweight, he was just too tough. He was a shrewd and calculating strategist, an excellent fighter who eyed an opponent's weaknesses and took advantage of them with a flurry of deadly combinations which he called a "succession of successes."

But Archie was making only a poor living for all his battles. He was the light heavyweight champion for so long that most people forgot how long he had to wait for his chance at the crown. It took Archie sixteen years to get a bout in Madison Square Garden, ten years to get a title fight.

Moore finally coaxed Joey Maxim into the ring in December 1952, in St. Louis. Archie won the fifteen-round decision handily and he was the light heavyweight champ. Maxim was holding a $100,000 guarantee so there wasn't much left for Arch. In fact, he didn't earn a dollar and had to borrow $10,000 to pay for his training expenses.

After that, Archie lived expansively. He met and beat every light heavyweight contender and then decided to go after the heavyweight title. He started a campaign to get Rocky Marciano to fight with a classic case of stunt-thinking that supposedly cost Moore $45,000 for publicity. Once, when Rocky was refereeing a benefit bout in Washington, Archie flew there, got himself introduced, and issued a challenge from the ring. He then printed press releases and FBI posters that read: "Wanted. Reward for capture and delivery of Rocky Marciano to any ring in the world. . . .Advise Sheriff Archie Moore."

Finally he got the fight. Archie decided to make Rocky nervous by showing the heavyweight how much bigger he was. While the referee was talking to them, Rocky looked down and saw Archie standing on tiptoes. Marciano knocked out Moore in the 9th round.

After that beating, people thought it was the end of the line for Archie. But, in classic fashion, he responded: "A fighter can take two kinds of beatings. One of them is a physical beating, and I've taken one or two of them. The other kind is the hard one. That's the psychological beating. I never took one of them."

Two years later, Arch challenged Floyd Patterson and took another beating. Finally, in the winter of 1959, Archie had the fight of his life. He fought a French Canadian named Yvon Durelle. It was scheduled as a weekly television bout, but it ended up a lot more for the viewers. Before he knocked out his man in 49 seconds of the 11th round, Archie had been down four times. It was the 127th KO in his long career, a new boxing record. This was Archie at his valiant best and he was named fighter-of-the-year at the age of forty-two, or forty-five or forty-nine.

Archie is famed not only as a great fighter but as a great talker. One of his most widely spread theories concerned his magical formulas for losing weight. His real secret, he said, came from an Australian aborigine in exchange for a red turtle-neck sweater. "I never saw a fat aborigine," said Archie. While losing all this weight, Archie had another secret potion in liquid form that he sipped to increase his strength. He claimed it was an "extract from goose juice" from Brazil or Argentina. Actually, he was sipping chicken soup. His secret formula was really no secret at all: he worked hard, chopped wood, did plenty of roadwork and cut down on calories and liquids.

In the last days of his career he promoted a fight with Cassius Clay. The two quipsters used all their powers to promote the fight to the public, and sell it they did. It is rare that a fight could have such tremendous preliminary coverage with little mention as to their pugilistic abilities. Clay was in the middle of his forecasts and predicted that Moore would go down in eight. Moore retorted by saying that "section three, page 17, lines 13–15" of their contract provided that the loser would have to keep a thirty-day silence. Clay then changed his prediction and said that Archie would "fall in four." The old Mongoose, as Archie called himself, told Clay that "I'll guarantee you'll do the St. Vitus dance—flat on your back."

Archie then added the clincher, that he had designed a special punch for Clay that was called the "lip-buttoner." Clay responded: "I had to invent myself a new punch, too. I call it the old-age pension punch." Cassius was right. Archie fell in the fourth round. Moore was a nimble-minded and ambitious, astute and sophisticated, shrewd and sensible fighter-humorist. He was a charmer and a faker and a fearless battler. His success is attributable to ability and enthusiasm, and he used these assets for more than twenty-five years in a sport where the average participant's tenure is only a fraction of that. Said Archie: "It's not fighting that makes you old. It's getting hit that

does." Before Archie retired from boxing, he had already started on a movie career and other enterprises. He could take care of himself.

Sugar Ray Robinson

Sugar Ray Robinson was called by many the greatest fighter who ever lived. He fought 202 bouts, starting in 1940 and covering a quarter of a century.

Walker Smith (his real name) was born on May 3, 1920, in Detroit. He had two sisters, Marie and Elizabeth, and a father and mother who didn't get along. The family was poor, and Ray doesn't remember his earliest years as being anything except a lot of misery and very little fun. The most fun was going down to the Brewster Center Gymnasium in Paradise Valley. There they let him hang around and watch the fighters train, exacting payment by running him all over the neighborhood on errands and odd jobs. The skinny kid with the happy grin and the hungry eyes could run like the wind. He could handle two errands while another kid was running one. And handle them right, too.

The Smith kid quickly developed his own personal idol, an amateur heavyweight who worked out at the Ford plant, Joe Louis. He was a slick boxer for a big fellow, but it was what he could do to a man when he hit him that impressed wide-eyed Walker Smith. His boyish admiration of the Joe Louis knockout punch was to exert a heavy influence on his ultimate ring style.

When Walker was twelve, his mother and father separated. Left with three children, Mrs. Smith pulled up stakes and moved to New York, settling in a Harlem tenement. Counting his meeting with Joe Louis as the first, young Walker had his second brush with fate when he bumped into the great tap dancer, Bill Robinson. The happy-go-lucky "Bojangles" used to stop at the famous "Wishing Tree" in Harlem at least once a week, kiss his fingertips and touch the tree with them for luck. After that little ritual was concluded, the magnificent dancer would hoof a few steps and wait while the gang of kids around the tree tried to copy them. Then he would give them a few more, always waiting patiently while they struggled to imitate him, pointing out their mistakes, patting them on the back, and distributing pieces of candy and coins. One of the urchins who was always on hand for Bill's informal dancing class was Walker Smith, the newcomer from Detroit who kept talking about what a great fighter his friend Joe Louis was.

Smith was the crown prince of Bojangles' little group. He seemed a natural-born tap dancer. His legs were as limber and pliant as birch rods, his body full of rhythm. It wasn't long before he had organized a troupe of kid dancers and began roaming the bright-light district of midtown New York, dancing on the sidewalks for whatever coins the passersby felt like throwing at his busy feet. On a fair night, Smith and his gang took in anywhere from $5.00 to $10.00, and on holidays they did better.

It has been said that Sugar Ray was obsessed by a desire to become a professional dancer, that he didn't have any stomach for the fight racket and had to be virtually dragged into it. This isn't so. Ray loved to dance, but he also had a hunger for the beckoning excitement and big money of the prize ring. He kept on dancing for nickels and dimes, but he also began to hang around the Salem-Crescent Athletic Club in Harlem. There fate gave him his third push—into the arms of big George Gainford, the Salem-Crescent boxing coach, a former professional who had campaigned with a good deal of success in the middleweight division and who knew the sport of boxing well.

At first Gainford was inclined to doubt that the skinny, undernourished kid would ever be strong enough to make a fighter. He brushed him off. Later, though, he saw Walker in a couple of street fights and was impressed by the tigerish ferocity with which he tore into his opponents. The kid wasn't weighted down with muscles but he was loaded with guts.

George talked to him in the gym and decided to do something with him. As a starter he bought the boy a complete boxing outfit. Then, for a couple of days, he didn't see him around. Puzzled, the coach went out and hunted him up. Walker had sold the whole outfit and spent the money. He was afraid to go near Gainford. But big George didn't give up so easily. He dragged the boy into the gym and put him to work in his underwear. He could go without the equipment.

It was hard work, but Gainford made Ray keep at it. The street dancing was okay at night, but in the daytime it was punching the bag, skipping rope, shadow-boxing, sparring, learning the ABC's of boxing the hard way. Oddly enough, the dance-happy kid who loved to play also got a bang out of the routine of training. He was faithful and he learned fast. Gainford began to look at him with a new thoughtfulness.

Like most managers, Gainford made a habit of taking the boy to the fights whenever he could. A beginner can often learn as much by watching a good match as he can by spending hours in a gym. One night, they were at an amateur show when the promoter found himself stuck for a substitute in one of the preliminary bouts. George was willing to let Smith go on, but the kid didn't have an AAU registration card. The harassed promoter scouted through the house and came up with a recently retired Negro boxer named Ray Robinson, who happened to have his AAU card with him. Robinson had no objection to making Walker Smith a present of the card.

So Walker Smith became Ray Robinson, fought, won—and that is how a world champion was born. The name "Sugar Ray" was picked up on the amateur circuit. Ray was

Sugar Ray Robinson delivers a volley of head and body punches to Gene Fullmer during one of their middleweight title bouts in 1957. Robinson lost the first fight but won the rematch on a knockout in the 5th round.

Sugar Ray stands victorious after knocking Bob Young to the canvas for the fourth time in the 2nd round of their fight. The referee stopped the fight after the fifth knockdown.

Sugar Ray drives a left to the midsection of Denny Moyer on his way to a unanimous decision.

Sugar Ray, who retired in 1965, takes his final bow in Madison Square Garden.

fighting in Watertown, New York—a watch to the winner and a money order and a pair of pants to the loser. A local sportswriter called out to Gainford, in Robinson's corner: "You got a mighty sweet boy there." "Sweet as sugar," Gainford agreed. In his story the next day, the writer referred to Ray Robinson as Sugar Ray. The nickname stuck.

Ray's amateur record lists 89 bouts, of which he won 69 by knockouts, 44 of them in the first round. Actually, he fought almost 125 amateur bouts, many of them unlisted. He fought all over the eastern seaboard, for any kind of prize.

He made his first splash in the boxing world when he won the Golden Gloves lightweight championship in 1939. When the New York and Chicago teams tangled in the Inter-City championships, Ray won again.

A year later, Robinson moved up to the welterweight class and repeated his 1939 Golden Gloves victories. By now, he was a prime target for the cold-eyed talent hunters who were constantly on the prowl for good professional fighters. But Gainford had a tight hold on the boy and George wasn't letting any Johnny-come-lately touch Ray.

After Robinson won his second Golden Gloves championship, a wealthy young white man named Kurt Horrman, one of the heirs to a beer-brewing fortune, began to hang around the Salem-Crescent gym. Horrman was scouting a big heavyweight named Buddy Moor, who greatly resembled Robinson's idol Joe Louis.

Horrman stayed around and finally made an open offer to take over the managership of Robinson. George Gainford calmly handed his valuable property over to the strange white man with the big car and all the money. Not without getting a few things straight first. Ray was to get a weekly allowance whether he fought or not, and his mother was to be taken care of. Gainford was to continue as the boy's trainer.

Under Horrman's sponsorship, Robinson made his professional debut—in Madison Square Garden on October 4, 1940. He was given a four-round preliminary bout against Joe Echeverria on the Henry Armstrong-Fritzie Zivic card. Ray picked up $100 for knocking out Echeverria in the 2nd round. Four days later, in Savannah, Georgia, he kayoed Silent Stefford in two. Then he took a rest for two weeks before going back to work in New York in a six-rounder against Mitsos Grispos.

A rugged young Greek with a good punch, Grispos gave Robinson his first tough pro fight. In the 5th round he had Ray on the canvas, in real trouble, and it took a slashing last-round rally by Robinson to earn the decision.

After that fight, Ray went on to win thirty-seven in a row, twenty-seven by knockouts. Then he lost to Jake LaMotta in a rough ten-rounder in Detroit. But after that fight, Ray went on an incredible string of ninety-six bouts in which he was never the loser. Included in the fights was a fifteen-round decision over Tommy Bell for the world welterweight title, five defenses of that title, a fifteen-round decision over Robert Villemain for the Pennsylvania middleweight title, one defense of that title against Bobo Olson (Robinson knocked him out in the 12th round), and finally, on February 14, 1949, a 13th-round knockout of Jake LaMotta, the last man to have beaten Ray, for the world middleweight title.

After that, Ray's career was studded with title fights. He lost the middleweight crown to Randy Turpin of England in July 1951, but regained it in September when he kayoed Turpin in the 10th round. In 1952, he had two middleweight title bouts. In the first he won a decision from Bobo Olson and then knocked out Rocky Graziano in the 3rd round in his second defense of that year. After the Graziano fight, Ray went after Joey Maxim's light heavyweight title, but was knocked out by Maxim in the fourteenth round. Actually, it was the heat that got to Ray more than the punches of

Maxim. After that fight, Ray announced his retirement.

He sat out the year 1953, then made a comeback in 1954. He fought for the middleweight crown in 1955 against the new titleholder Olson. Ray knocked him out in the 2nd round and in a return bout in 1956 he kayoed Olson again.

Then in 1957, he lost his title to Gene Fullmer. Again he won a return bout, knocking out Gene in the 5th round. In September, he went through the same lost-won cycle with Carmen Basilio. Finally, in January of 1960, he lost the title to Paul Pender. This time, Ray wasn't going to get it back. He lost to Pender in a return bout and then drew with Gene Fullmer for the NBA middleweight title. In a return with Fullmer, he lost a fifteen-round decision. It was the last time Sugar Ray fought for the title.

He kept boxing, though, for five more years and finally, after a 10th-round loss to Joey Archer in 1965, he retired from boxing. There was a big farewell party for Sugar Ray when he announced his retirement on December 10, 1965, after twenty-six years in the professional ring. He was as good as fighters come.

Virgil Akins

Veteran boxing men who visited Virgil Akins' training camp just before his championship fight with Vince Martinez in St. Louis in June of 1958 came away shaking their heads —not so much at what they saw as at what they heard. Akins was working every bit as hard as one might expect a thirty-year-old fighter in peak condition to work, but his cocky predictions of victory raised eyebrows and knowing winks.

"I'm not only going to beat Martinez, I'm going to knock him out," Akins said forthrightly, and his co-managers, Eddie Yawitz and Bernie Glickman, beamed in approval. "I figure to get him by the tenth." He was talking about one of the cleverest boxers in the welterweight division, a fancy dan who had never been so much as knocked off his feet in sixty-five professional fights. But it didn't bother Akins a bit. With each passing day he grew more optimistic.

There were two surprising circumstances connected with the Akins bravado. The first was that these bold words were being uttered by a fighter who had the dubious distinction of having been beaten seventeen times in an in-and-out career dating back to 1948, a fighter with a reputation as a $100-a-fight trial horse, a fighter who at one time had gone for two years without winning once.

The second surprising circumstance, and almost an anticlimactic one, was that Akins did to Martinez almost exactly what he had predicted he would, dropping the Paterson, New Jersey, star eight times before the referee stopped the slaughter in the opening seconds of the fourth round. Virgil Akins, who had gone into the fight as the welterweight champion of Massachusetts, added the rest of the world to his crown in less than fifteen minutes.

He had once been so discouraged because of the small purses he was earning and the way he was being passed from one manager to another that he was ready to quit. How then did this trial horse suddenly become a cocky tiger and the welterweight champion of the world? Eddie Yawitz, the St. Louis pharmacist who managed fighters as a sideline, gave most of the credit to loving care and a large dose of psychology, both rare items in the fight racket.

Bernie Glickman, who co-managed Virgil, was more succinct. "He was a lazy, temperamental sort of guy who wouldn't put out if he didn't feel like it." It had to be drummed into his head that he could be great if he really wanted to be.

But a champion cannot be made overnight; he has to be born with some ability. Even during his first seven years of mismanagement, overmatching and pitiful purses, Akins had

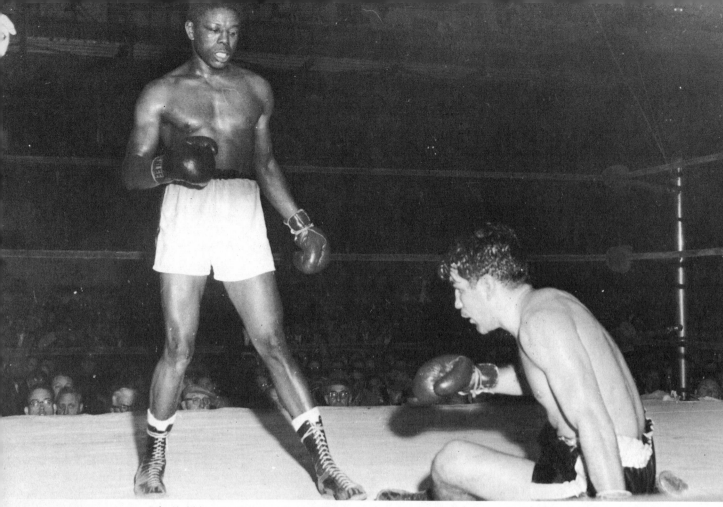

Virgil Akins stands over Tony DeMarco after flooring DeMarco early in their fight.

In his quest for the welterweight title, Virgil Akins (right) scores an upset, a 6th-round TKO over Isaac Logart.

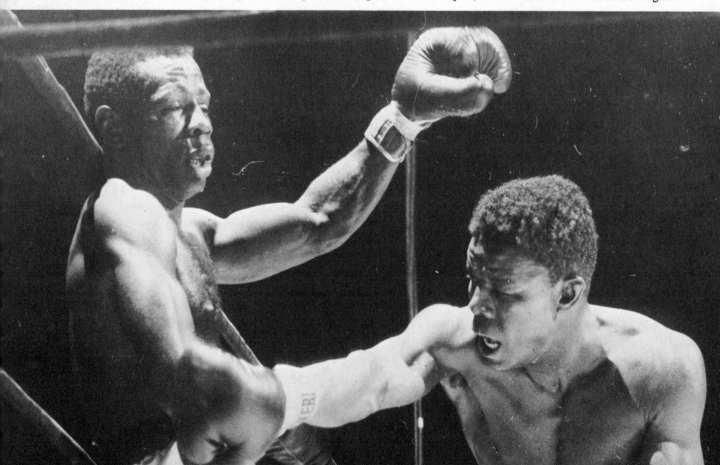

always had a champion's equipment. He was a fine boxer who punched well with both hands.

Akins really had no choice; he had to be tough. One of a family of ten children, left fatherless at the age of nine, he was working hard along the docks of the Mississippi from the time he was ten, a runty little scrapper whose big sister sometimes had to come to his rescue when the odds were too heavily stacked against him in the frequent fistfights. For a while he thought about becoming a jockey, but instead went to work for the railroad, developing his bulging shoulder and neck muscles by chopping ties. At sixteen, he forged his mother's name to an application blank for an amateur boxing tournament. By 1946, when he was eighteen, he had won his first Golden Gloves title, and he repeated the following year before turning professional in 1948.

He was a likable guy who was happy to fight anybody for just about any amount in order to get to the top. As a result, he was overmatched and knocked out in his second fight, and by 1951 he had already been tabbed as an ideal trial horse, heavy enough for ambitious lightweights and light enough for promising welterweight newcomers.

His transformation started on May 2, 1955, when Akins was called to New York to substitute against Ron Delaney, a highly regarded welterweight. The odds were 8–1 against Virgil, but he surprised everyone when he won by a knockout in the 8th. Three weeks later they matched him with Joe Miceli, the left-hooker who had beaten him three years before, and Akins flattened Miceli in the 1st round. Suddenly the ranking welterweights refused to have anything to do with their old playmate.

In desperation, Yawitz took whatever fights and purses he could get for Akins. Virgil was twenty-eight years old, with a wife and two children in St. Louis, making $100–$150 for a fight, and he was ready to quit. It was then that Yawitz sent for Glickman and the soft-sell job on Akins began.

After a while, Akins got a lucky break. Welterweight champ Carmen Basilio challenged middleweight champ Ray Robinson and won, leaving the welterweight crown open. In a tournament devised to fill the vacancy, Akins and Martinez came out on top, setting up the big championship fight.

The showdown came on June 7, in the suffocating heat of St. Louis Arena. Akins later said he noticed that Martinez looked tense before the fight. Virgil peeled off his colorful robe with the leopard-skin lapels, looked at the sleepy-eyed features of Martinez and decided to bring the fight to him. Akins feinted, threw a slow left lead and smashed a right over it, hit Martinez on the chin and he went down. This was to be the routine for the entire next three rounds, until the 52-second mark of the 4th round when the fight ended. At that time, all the memories of overmatches and $100 fights faded out of the life of Virgil Akins.

Joe Brown

Joe Brown, like Archie Moore, had to wait until the twilight years of his boxing career before becoming a champion, and didn't bloom into full glory as a fighter until he had reached that pinnacle. Brown was thirty-two years old when he won the lightweight title from Wallace "Bud" Smith in 1956. That triumph came after years of ups and downs that might have discouraged a less ambitious man.

Brown's ring style was always distinguished by his savvy and mature patience. He would stalk an opponent round after round, probing for flaws in the other man's approach. Then Joe closed in and applied his noted power to best advantage. That is why so many of Brown's knockouts came in the late rounds.

Joe began his boxing career in the Navy. He won sixteen bouts while serving in the Pacific theater during World War II, including an all-service lightweight title. After the war, he began fighting professionally—and successfully

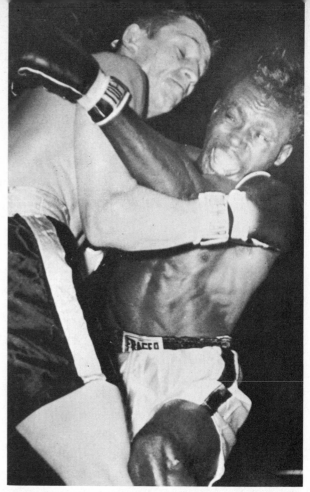

Joe Brown smiles in the dressing room after successfully defending his lightweight title against challenger Kenny Lane. The match, which featured a lot of close-in fighting, went the full fifteen rounds.

Lightweight champ Joe Brown pounds his left into the face of Ernie Williams in the 5th and final round of their scheduled ten-round non-title fight.

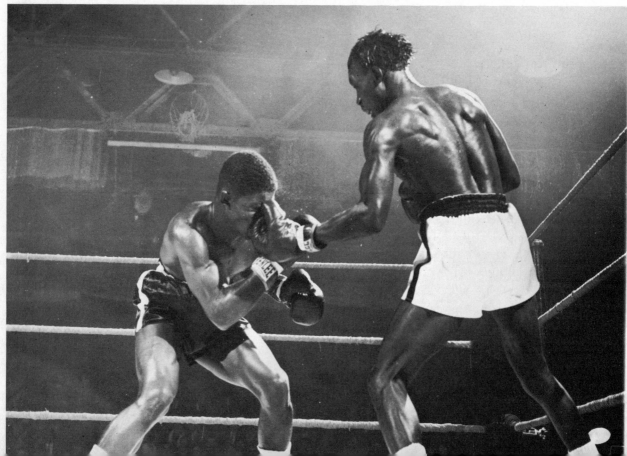

—around his native New Orleans. But the first downturn in his career came when he was overmatched with the experienced Sandy Saddler, who cut him up badly and knocked him out in the third round.

By 1949, Joe had a reputation largely as a club fighter. His biggest payday that year was $187 against Luther Rawlings, whom he whipped in ten rounds. So he went to Australia to fight, then came back and stirred up some attention by beating a highly ranked lightweight, Tommy Campbell. It was at that point that Lou Viscusi, a shrewd, experienced fight manager with solid connections, got hold of Joe. For a time it looked as if Viscusi had been wrong. He put Brown in the ring against George Araujo, and Araujo won easily. This so discouraged Brown that he quit boxing and began a succession of jobs as carpenter, cement worker and truck driver. He was far from through, however.

Brown returned to the fight wars in 1955 and Viscusi sent him to Panama to sharpen him up. When Joe returned, he had recaptured his former skills and he was hungry. In 1956, after a big knockout victory over Arthur Persley, a ranking contender, Joe was on his way at last. Six months later, he won the lightweight championship.

Brown owed Smith a return bout and this time disposed of him with an eleventh-round knockout. He promptly dropped Orlando Zulueta and Joey Lopes and on May 7, 1958 engaged in what may have been the most satisfying event of his career.

He was booked against Ralph Dupas, twenty-two years old and a fellow Louisianan. Although the fight was a natural for New Orleans and was originally scheduled there, the Louisiana boxing commission would not sanction it; the state still would not allow a Negro and a white to compete in the same athletic event. So the bout was moved to Houston where, thanks to an influx of Louisiana fans, it drew the largest gate for a fight in Texas up to

that time. For five rounds Dupas moved all around Brown's superior power, but gradually Joe began to solve him. During the 8th, he smashed Dupas down three times, and when the plucky youngster refused to stay down, the referee stopped the bout.

Brown continued to defend his title busily until 1962. Then at the age of thirty-eight, well past the retirement age of most fighters, Joe Brown finally gave up the crown in a gruelling fifteen-round bout with Carlos Ortiz. Joe Brown's reign over the lightweights may have been belated, but it was noteworthy.

Jimmy Carter

Jimmy Carter was probably the most erratic champion ever to hold the lightweight title. He made a habit of winning, losing and winning again in fights that meant the championship. Only a few times did Jimmy ever beat an opponent in a bout, with no return match.

Carter, despite all the losses, was a good fighter. He came into the game at a time when television was just beginning to rise in popularity and, as a consequence, the attendance at fights was beginning to dwindle. It was difficult to make money from a single fight, and in order to make a good living it seemed as if Jimmy would lose on purpose in order to build up the gate for the return bout—not unlike wrestling.

The series of ups and downs started with a fight with the then-lightweight champion, Ike Williams. Carter had begun pro fighting when he got out of the service in 1946. During his Army years he had fought a number of bouts with good success, regularly sending clips back home to a friend. The friend had saved every one of them and when Jimmy returned home, the friend advised that he turn professional. Jimmy arranged for Willie Ketchum to be his manager.

Jimmy fought around the world for five years, until finally a fight with Ike Williams

Jimmy Carter (white trunks) slashes his way to the lightweight championship of the world with a stunning, upset TKO over Ike Williams at 2:49 of the 14th round.

Carter pounds lightweight champ Paddy DeMarco to win the crown for the third time.

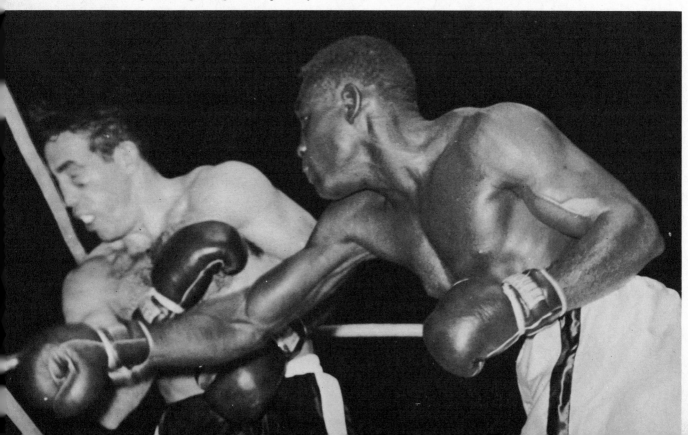

was arranged. Williams was the champion at the time, and the press had been complaining that he wasn't defending his title properly. He had been ducking stronger contenders in favor of lesser fighters. Carter was rated only twelfth when he fought Williams and the newspapers took a dim view of a challenger who had a so-so record of only forty-five wins in sixty-two fights. Moreover, Jimmy had suffered two losses in his last three fights.

Williams, despite being a lightweight, had ballooned out to 151 pounds some three weeks before the fight, then starved himself to get down to the 135-pound weight limit. With skin taut and ribs protruding, he weighed in at noon only to find he still was twelve ounces over. Ninety minutes of callisthenics and a vigorous rubdown finally got him down to the proper weight and the odds favoring Ike dropped from 3–1 to 2–1. It was obvious that Williams was not in good condition, but still the public refused to believe in an unknown like Carter. But Jimmy floored Ike four times and referee Petey Scalzo stopped the bout at 2 minutes, 49 seconds of the 14th round. Carter was the new champion.

That was the last New York saw of Jimmy for some time. He lost to Art Aragon in Los Angeles, but then beat him in a title defense that drew a gross gate of $109,000 and gave Jimmy his biggest purse, $32,000. Next Jimmy met up with Lauro Salas, winning two of the three meetings and winding up in 1952 as champion—although Salas had had custody of the crown for five months.

There followed two bouts with Canada's Armand Savoie. He beat Jimmy in a non-title bout, but in their title fight in November 1953 Carter caught Savoie with a left to the body and a right to the chin and knocked him out in the 5th round.

Jimmy then defeated Tommy Collins and went on to a fight with George Araujo. After knocking Araujo out during the 13th round, Carter signed up for what probably were his two biggest fights—with Paddy DeMarco. Apparently, no man Carter ever lost to was happier to have the loan of the world championship than DeMarco. Not that Paddy approached their first fight in a spirit of "Please, mister, can I hold your title for a while?" DeMarco thought he could beat Carter on merit, and there is no doubt that when he won the championship he glowed with pride—and determined to keep it. Many who saw the fight were convinced that Carter couldn't win his title back from DeMarco. They had seen Jimmy bulled and punched round after round. They had seen him set himself and then be beaten to the punch, time after time. It looked like one of those questions of style: DeMarco was, and could remain, the wrong man for Carter. DeMarco had the title for eight months and then came November and the rematch in San Francisco. He used the same style—and Jimmy read it like a telegram. He handled the rushes with ease. He belted DeMarco in the body for a while, and then belted him on the eyes, ears, nose and throat. At the start of the 15th round, he took his championship back and went home.

Jimmy could take a punch. He could hit with both hands, and he was smart, cool and patient. He could beat speed by precision, as he proved against Araujo—and his great chest and shoulders, small hips and waist, gave him the capacity to hurt his opponents efficiently and everywhere. That's what made him a champion.

Beau Jack

The story of Beau Jack begins with two bootblacks. Jack was bootblack No. 2. Bootblack No. 1, both in chronology and shoe shining skill, was Bowman Mulligan, who was the fighter's friend, guardian, de facto manager and father confessor. Without Bowman Mulligan, there would have been no lightweight champion named Beau Jack.

Beau Jack puts Frank Vigeant on the ropes with a hard left before gaining a decision in their ten-round fight.

Beau Jack sends Sammy Angott through the ropes before gaining his well-earned victory.

Other than bringing him into the world on April 1, 1921 and naming him Sidney Walker, his parents seem to have done him few other favors. His life was rough-and-tumble from the start. He had no real home, no education, no opportunities except the privilege of scrapping with other urchins for favorable shoe-shine locations.

Beau Jack did get a couple of breaks, though. First, Bowman gave him a locker-room shoe-shining job at the Augusta National Golf Club in Georgia. Second, when the National closed its winter season in 1940, Bowman departed for Springfield, Massachusetts, and he took Beau Jack with him. In nearby Holyoke is the Valley Arena Club where Bowman was able to open the door for Beau's first real ring experience.

Certain members of the Augusta National were well aware that their steward and their shoe-shine boy were cutting a swath through western Massachusetts, and they beamed with pride. One of these members was the general manager of the New York *Herald-Tribune,* who told a sportswriter for the paper about it. The writer scented a good yarn, a story about a bootblack with wealthy benefactors, a climb from rags to riches. He thus, unwittingly, laid the foundation for the story that was to become the Beau Jack legend.

To help get Beau Jack started, the writer, Richard Vidmer, approached twenty men, the majority of them members of the Augusta National and all of them prominent in professional circles, and asked them to contribute $25 each to finance Beau Jack's first fight in the big city. One of those responding to the plea was the great golfer, Bobby Jones, who, like the others, had never seen Beau Jack fight but sent a check as a compliment to Bowman. The Beau Jack Fund soon reached $500.

At the bugle-blowing introduction of Beau in New York, Vidmer created colorful newspaper descriptions of the "Twenty Millionaires" who had acted as Beau Jack's sponsors. The publicity was quite a surprise to the conservative businessmen. But they were even more surprised when their money was returned to them. Bowman paid back every cent out of Beau Jack's first lucrative fight, the one he had with Allie Stolz at the Garden on November 13, 1942.

He beat Stolz that night, knocking him out in the 7th round. A month later, he beat Tippy Larkin in the 3rd round and was awarded the then-vacant New York lightweight title. Unfortunately, he couldn't cash in on his fame or skill because the United States was at war at the time and Beau Jack's income was severely taxed. He was earning from both his ring encounters and outside investments an average of about $16,000 a year, after taxes, during his best years.

Beau retired at the end of 1951 and attempted a brief comeback in 1955, but was stopped by Ike Williams. That ended his boxing career.

Ike Williams

Ike Williams was called boxing's businessman. He was a cold, calculating fighter, and after a fight, in the dressing room, he would have few words for the press. But away from the ring he was a warm person, laughing, smiling, enjoying life.

Williams was a superb boxer. He boxed smoothly, lashed out with one-two combinations, a left and a right, and stood up to an opponent. And he did it with the detachment of a bored mannequin.

Only once did he explode in a victory speech. That was the night in 1947 that he gained worldwide control of the lightweight division by knocking out Bob Montgomery in six rounds in Philadelphia's Municipal Stadium. Three years earlier, Montgomery had almost beheaded Williams in the last seconds of a twelve-round bout, and Ike, ashamed, had promised himself that he would even things up.

Ike Williams displays awesome power with both hands as he drives Lester Felton back with a terrific right cross (above) and stuns Fitzie Pruden's already bloody face with a hard left jab (below).

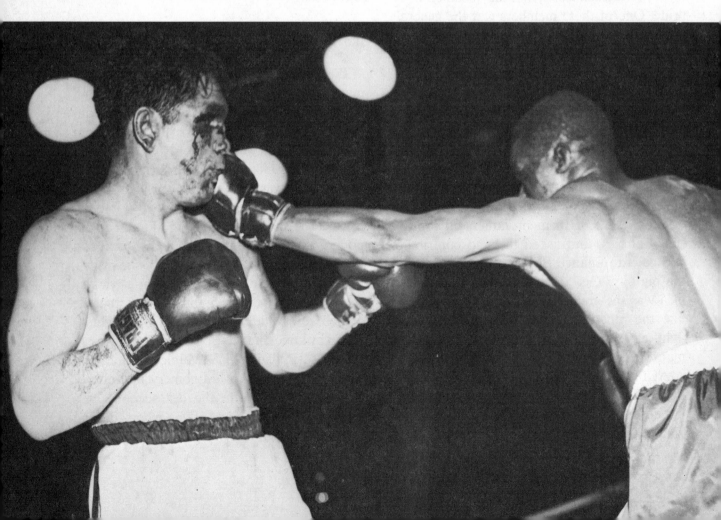

In their title meeting, Williams was clearly superior. Aggressively, he went after Montgomery, who was recognized in New York State as champion. Ike pinned him in a corner and smashed him to the floor. When Montgomery arose, Ike smashed him again. Montgomery was finished. It was sweet revenge.

He rushed back to his dressing room and once there, deep in the Stadium catacombs, the words swirled forth, hot in their indignation, poisonous in their intent. "I didn't get him as good as I wanted to," Williams spat. "I wanted to murder him. He's no good. He's dirty and I'll get him better the next time." There was no third meeting, for the pasting by Williams had planted Montgomery as a boxing wallflower. He was finished.

Williams played for keeps—hard and without compassion. He had come a long way from the days of great poverty in Trenton, and he had found financial security. But security became a preoccupation with him; he seemed to live only for money.

"The main thing," he would say, "is security. I want to give my kids the kind of things I didn't have, an education and a home. I want them to go to some real nice school and be something."

Ike had had a tough beginning. He quit school when he was sixteen and still in the eighth grade. "We were poor, real poor," he recalled. He went to work as a waterboy on the Pennsylvania Railroad and his wages were $45 semi-monthly. This helped but when he became an amateur in 1939 and then a professional fighter in 1940, he stopped other work.

Ike turned pro under the direction of a Trenton gym owner, Jesse Gross, and he had immediate success. But Ike was not impressed by the four dollars he was paid for fighting Patsy Gall in Hazleton, Pennsylvania, and he decided to seek out a big-time manager.

It was a cold day in 1942 when he left Trenton for New York in search of a new agent. His hero of the time, Henry Armstrong, was through as a premier performer and Ike thought perhaps Henry's manager—Eddie Mead—could work with him, too. But Williams found out that Mead had died a few months before, so he signed with Joe Woodman and Connie McCarthy.

After thirty-four straight Williams victories, pressure began to mount for a fight against Montgomery, and the match was finally made for Philadelphia's Convention Hall in January 1944. It was a packed house and Williams was eager for conquest. Montgomery had promised to knock Ike out because earlier Williams had stopped Bob's pal, Johnny Hutchinson, in three rounds. Montgomery was relentless in the torment he heaped on Ike that night. He slashed him and pummeled him. He battered his body and smashed his head, and just seconds before the end of the final round, the 12th, he did knock Williams out. Ike was blasted through the ropes and his head hung over the apron, as though it had been separated from his body.

Fighters rarely come back from such beatings. Ordinary fighters never do. Ike brooded, quietly, alone, inwardly tormented. But he trained and fought and this time ran up fifteen straight victories before losing to Willie Joyce in 1944. Beating Joyce in a return bout set him up for a fight against Juan Zurita, who was recognized as the National Boxing Association lightweight champion. But in the shadowy dealings that permeated the boxing world one requirement was that Ike's manager, McCarthy, give up one-eighth of Ike's contract to other parties.

Williams won the title, but that was the beginning of a new and trying period for him. He and McCarthy became embroiled in continual financial disputes. A court ordered Williams to pay a portion of his purses to McCarthy; Ike refused to fight so that McCarthy wouldn't get anything. The stalemate didn't end until early 1947 when "Blinky" Palermo, an influential figure in Philadelphia boxing circles and, some said, an underworld figure of importance, took over Williams' contract.

Ike suddenly got that return bout with Montgomery he had been seeking. Coldly, purposefully, he finished his man off. Then Ike Williams was undisputed lightweight champion. He was not often a happy man but that, at least, was a happy moment.

Davey Moore

Davey Moore is one of the recent tragedies of boxing, dying as a result of injuries he received in a fight with Sugar Ramos. The fight took place in March of 1963 and was a championship bout for the featherweight title, which Moore had won three years before.

Davey Moore was born in Lexington, Kentucky, in 1933, and raised in Springfield, Ohio. He was one of seven children. The father was a minister who also worked in a construction gang. The father and mother were both strict with their children, who went to church daily.

One of Davey's brothers grew up to be a minister and one of his sisters married a minister. There was no smoking, drinking, or cursing in the Moore house. Davey never smoked or drank, even later, though he kept cigarettes and whiskey in his own home for visitors.

As a boy, perhaps in rebellion to strict religious upbringing, Davey was hard to handle away from home. He was small and others often tried to push him around. He fought back and fought well, and soon became what he proudly called "the head leader" of his gang. The gang got into various troubles, breaking windows, stealing small things.

Once, when challenged to a fight with gloves, Davey went to the gym—and that began his boxing career. Some of his friends got hooked on narcotics and crime, and some wound up in jail. Later, when Davey would go home, he would see them all, the good and the bad. "But they couldn't make me go bad," he said.

He had never gone hungry as a child, but he did later on. He quit school in the ninth grade to get married, and, after fighting in the 1952 Olympics, began raising his family. He turned pro in 1953, but couldn't get a good manager or regular fights. When he did fight, he wasn't ready. He didn't lose often, but he wasn't getting anywhere.

Moore felt the turning point in his life came when he met Willie Ketchum, who believed in him as a boxer and would work for him. At the time Davey was living with his parents; his wife and their first two children were with her parents. Ketchum bought his contract for $500, staked him and put him in a gym, trained him and got him regular fights. Moore began to rise and won 120 of 125 amateur bouts.

He won the featherweight title from Hogan "Kid" Bassey in 1959. Going into his final fight, he had won fifty-seven of sixty-five professional bouts. He had defended his title five times. Unfortunately, American promoters and television matchmakers had always been interested only in the bigger fighters. Davey had to become a boxing gypsy. He fought in Mexico, Spain, France, Italy, England, Finland and Japan, where little fighters are usually more appreciated.

It was a hard life. Foreign fans threw chairs, cushions, rocks, broken glass, bottles and even live snakes at him. But he was stoic and won and his popularity overseas grew. He was unhappy because his own people didn't know him. He hated the long, lonely tours away from home and family.

The Ramos fight was part of a tripleheader at Dodger Stadium in Los Angeles. Emile Griffith was matched against Luis Rodriguez for the welterweight title, and Roberto Cruz was fighting Battling Torres for the junior welterweight crown. A crowd of 26,142 turned out that Thursday night. Moore was a great all-around fighter. Ramos, the underdog, was good, too. It was a good fight, savage and hard.

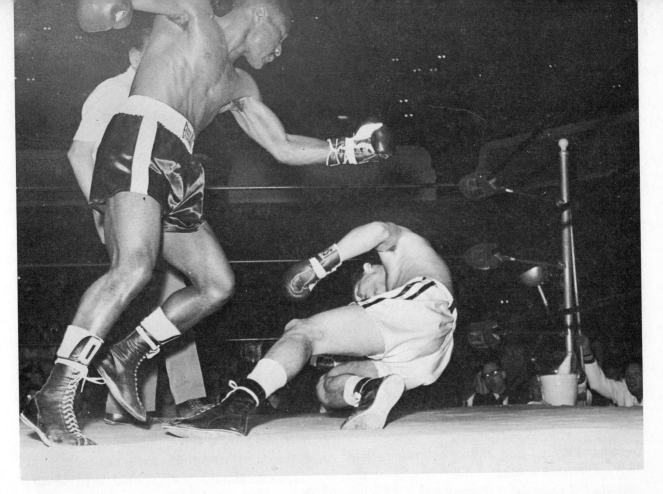

Davey Moore is declared the winner by announcer Jimmy Lennon after flooring Danny Veldez in their title bout.

Moore went ahead early, but without his usual conviction. In the 5th round Ramos began to come on. He pumped hard left jabs, he threw hard right crosses. He knocked out Moore's mouthpiece. Moore began to bleed from the mouth but he rallied in the 7th round. He hit Ramos with seven straight right-hand smashes but Ramos did not go down.

In the 8th, Ramos hurt Moore badly. In the 10th, he draped Davey over the ropes twice and knocked him down twice. After the 10th round, Ketchum threw in the towel and Davey Moore had had it. In his dressing room, Davey complained of his head hurting and then fell into unconsciousness. An ambulance took him to the hospital. All night he lay in a coma and finally, in the early morning hours, he passed away.

When Davey's gold coffin was flown back to Columbus, his brother Phillip met it at the airport. "If Davey could speak today," Phillip said, "he would say: 'don't let my death be the end of boxing.' "

Sandy Saddler

Sandy Saddler was the featherweight champion of the world for most of the decade of the 1950's. He was tough and fearless and he fought all over the world—in South America, Asia, the Pacific Islands and Europe. When he had finished, his record was one of the most impressive ever. In 162 bouts he scored 103 knockouts, a mark bettered by fewer than a half-dozen men in professional boxing history.

It took Sandy five years and ninety-five fights to win the featherweight title from Willie Pep. And it took less than three months for him to lose the title back to Pep. After that fight, he went on an eighteen-month round of small fights (he met and defeated twenty-three boxers) before he was able to get Pep back in the ring.

Sandy was always an active fighter. Already the champion, he fought thirteen times in 1951, once in defense of his title, and he traveled from Buffalo to Los Angeles to Santiago to Buenos Aires for matches. Or take 1945, his record year as a pro. He fought twenty-four times that year, or almost once every two weeks. And he won every fight, including seventeen by knockout.

But Sandy is perhaps best remembered for his four fights with Willie Pep. The first—the fight which made Saddler and gave him the title—was in February 1949. Willie, a prohibitive favorite, was rocked by a good left in the early seconds of the 1st round. In the 4th round, Sandy dropped him for the full count.

The second match showed Pep's greatness, on display for the last time. Willie fought for his life that night and fought as only he could at the time. He whirled, danced and jabbed his way to a fifteen-round decision.

"I never thought a man could do to me what Willie did that night," Sandy said. "He stepped on my toes, spun me around, then hit me five, six times with a right hand or a left hook. He butted me, he did everything to me. After that fight, I was sure no man would do those things to me again."

Sandy showed that he meant it. In their third fight, the men mixed it up in a rough-and-tumble battle that was anything but polite. After the 8th round, Willie, sitting in his corner, said his shoulder was dislocated and he couldn't go on.

The final rematch came a year later and it was a donnybrook. Willie and Sandy tugged and wrestled and cartwheeled each other around the ring. They tumbled to the floor in each other's not-so-fond arms. When Pep quit after the 9th round, one of his eyes looked as if it had been massaged with a scalpel. Sandy was still the world champion. After the bout, the New York state boxing commissioners suspended Saddler for three months and hit Pep with a lifetime suspension.

Except for the Pep fights, Sandy didn't get involved in such rough stuff. No one else gave him that tough a time in the ring. He was simply too good. He was unusually potent with either hand. Although a natural right-hander, with knockout power in the right fist, he did most of his damage with the left. He used the left most of the time, shuffling after an opponent, digging the hand to the body, then, when his opponent was in trouble, firing a series of thumping left hooks and jabs.

Sandy reigned as undisputed king of the featherweights until 1957, when an eye injury suffered in an automobile accident forced his retirement. They called him the Harlem Scotsman—his real name was Sandy and he had relatives in Scotland—and they also called him one of the best and most durable featherweights ever, a winner in the prize ring a total of 144 times.

Ernie Davis, the 1961 winner of the Heisman Trophy.

CHAPTER NINE

Football—The New Success

On September 3, 1946, a new major league of professional football, the All-America Conference, made its debut. The Cleveland Browns took part in that first game, beginning a dynasty that was to last through the lifetime of the All-America Conference, until its merger with the National Football League (NFL) in 1950. And in the Cleveland lineup that evening were two young men who were to become pro stars of the first order: Bill Willis and Marion Motley, both Negroes.

Thus in a season when Jackie Robinson was still playing minor league baseball, Coach Paul Brown of Cleveland had brought Negro players to major league football. Nothing like the attention that was focused on Robinson, or Branch Rickey, who had made the decision for the Dodgers, ever came to Willis and Motley or Paul Brown. They simply did the job. Now Motley is in the Professional Football Hall of Fame. And dozens of Negroes dot the rosters of both professional football leagues and colleges large and small.

Willis and Motley were not the first Negroes to play pro football; Paul Robeson and Fritz Pollard, among others, had played in the NFL in its infancy in the early 1920's. But the color line had grown up; it had to be shattered again. By the year 1967, nearly one-quarter of all players in the National Football League were Negroes, and nearly one-third in the American League. Two-fifths of the NFL all-star team selections were Negroes. Nearly all the statistical categories in both leagues are dominated by Negroes. And when the great stars are mentioned, names like Jim Brown, Deacon Jones and Willie Davis are heard most often.

Through the years when Negroes did not play professional football, a handful performed on college teams. Now they are regulars and stars at dozens of colleges and are named to all-star teams of every description.

In the 1960's, football began to replace baseball as the nation's most glamorous sport. This occurred as the Negro began to make his full contribution.

Jim Brown

Jim Brown was, simply, the greatest runner in football history. He led the National Football League in rushing in eight of his nine seasons. He carried the ball for a record 12,312 yards and averaged 5.2 yards every time he ran. He made believers of players and coaches alike. Washington linebacker Sam Huff called Brown "the strongest man I have ever tackled." New York coach Allie Sherman said that Jim is "the greatest runner I have ever seen."

Brown had the power (at 6 ft.–2 in., 228 pounds) and exceptional speed, but he was also a superbly coordinated man who could play basketball, golf or lacrosse with surpassing skill. He carried the football with a flair, cutting instinctively, breaking tackles, always gaining yardage. He played with a title team in 1964 and retired gracefully.

He left the game because it was becoming a grind, and because he wanted to begin his new career of acting and spend more time promoting civil rights causes. "You should get out at the top," Brown said. He did. And there may never be another like him.

Brown had several emotional problems to conquer before he became a superathlete. He was born on Saint Simon's Island, Georgia, and his parents split up a while later. He was raised by his great-grandmother for seven years until he went to live with his mother, a domestic in the high-income town of Manhasset, New York. Jimmy was a shy, lonely, nearly homeless boy who desperately tried to gain a measure of independence. He found he could do it best by excelling in sports. Studying only enough to remain eligible to play ball, he won thirteen letters at Manhasset High School and attracted the scholarship attention of nearly forty-five colleges.

Although Syracuse did not offer him a scholarship, he went there with the understanding that he could get one if he did well in freshman sports. A group of friends and ad-

mirers in Manhasset paid Jimmy's first-year expenses, but his failure to star in athletics discouraged him to the point of wanting to quit school. Ken Molloy, a Manhasset lawyer and a former Syracuse lacrosse player, talked him into trying again, and the only people who ever regretted that pep talk were Jimmy's opponents. He worked hard, starred in every sport he tried and made a few Syracuse coaches moan because he didn't have enough time to try every sport.

Jimmy concentrated on lacrosse, football and basketball and received varying All-American ratings in all. As a football halfback, he scored 106 points in his senior year and set a Syracuse rushing record of 986 yards, finishing third highest in the country. He scored 43 points (six touchdowns and seven conversions) in his final regular-season game against Colgate, and then closed out his college career with twenty-one points (three touchdowns and three conversions) in Syracuse's loss to Texas Christian University in the Cotton Bowl.

Watching Jimmy spar with a member of the school's boxing team one day, the Syracuse boxing coach shook his head and sighed. "What talent going to waste," he said. "I am convinced that Jimmy could have been the national intercollegiate heavyweight champion if he had put his mind to it and fought competitively."

Jimmy chose to make football his career and in his nine years scored 126 touchdowns, set eleven NFL records and established himself as the greatest ball carrier ever. There were some who criticized Jim for not being an enthusiastic blocker, but Brown's admirers point out that he had enough to do carrying the ball as often as he did. He had some legendary Sunday afternoons that fans still talk about. One came on November 24, 1957 —his rookie year—against the Los Angeles Rams. The Browns were trying to hang on to a half-game lead in the Eastern Conference, when, early in the first quarter, starting quar-

Jimmy Brown of the Cleveland Browns.

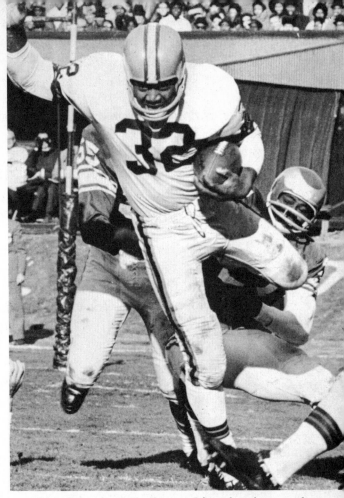

Using brute strength, Brown drives for short yardage.

Besides being the greatest runner in football history, Brown was a fine receiver, as he demonstrates here.

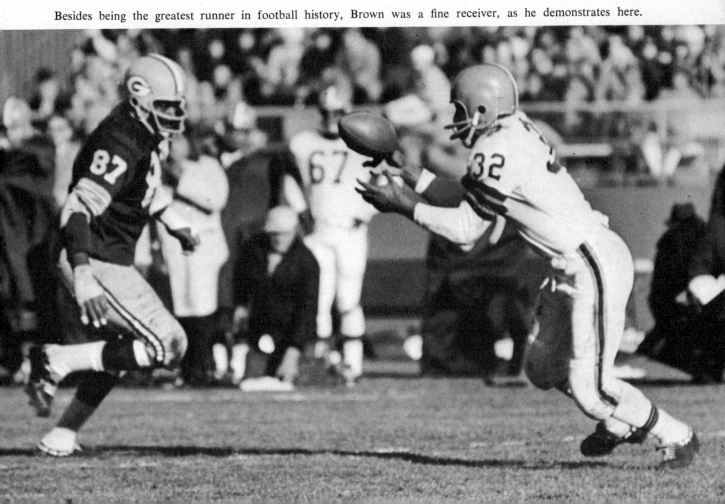

terback Tommy O'Connell got knocked out of the game. Jim Brown realized he would have to make a super effort that day. So by game's end, he had scored four touchdowns, set up two others and a field goal, and picked up a record 237 yards on 31 carries. Cleveland won, 45–31.

There was another Jim Brown classic in 1959 against the Baltimore Colts, who had won the NFL title the year before and were to win again that season. When Jim had finished with the Colts that day, Cleveland had won the game, 38–31, and he had scored all five Browns touchdowns.

The listing of Jim Brown's achievements could go on endlessly. Almost everyone who ever saw him play has a favorite story of this run or that run. He was so good that opposing players held him in awe. Cleveland Brown coaches, in studying films of the team's games, discovered over and over again that tacklers would come up to him and slide off without hitting him hard or avoid a direct tackle to take a side shot at him. High school players often do that against opponents they fear, but rarely do pros. The reason was that Brown hit so hard that they unconsciously avoided contact. When he hit, his legs never stopped moving, and he used his forearm as a straight arm with stunning effect.

In Jim's rookie season, 1957, the Browns had won their division championship before losing the league title to Detroit. The next year, they lost a play-off to the Giants for division honors. Each season the Browns would challenge for the championship and barely miss. It began to discourage Jim.

After the 1962 season, when he was hurt in several games and failed to win the rushing crown for the only time in his career, he complained that he was being misused by the team's coach, Paul Brown. Arthur Modell, the Browns' new owner, wanted to take over active control from Paul Brown, who had run the team as coach and general manager from its

founding. Modell and Jim Brown, along with some other players, cooperated, and Paul Brown was ousted. Blanton Collier, who had been the top assistant, took over. He was a gentler man and more to Jim Brown's liking.

The Browns again finished second in 1963 but 1964 was another story. They swept to their first Eastern division title in seven seasons and clashed with the Baltimore Colts for the NFL crown before a sell-out crowd of nearly 80,000 at Municipal Stadium in Cleveland. A driving wind from Lake Erie swept the field this biting cold day.

Baltimore, which had ended Green Bay's championship reign, was a solid favorite. But neither team could get a consistent offense moving for the entire scoreless first half. Jim Brown's dashes to the outside and plunges inside were Cleveland's entire attack. As the second half opened, a short Baltimore punt gave the Browns a break and Lou Groza kicked a field goal for a 3–0 Cleveland lead. The next time the Browns got the ball, Jim Brown shot around left end for forty-six yards to Baltimore's 18. The Browns scored on the next play and they were in complete command. The final score was an amazing 27–0. Jim Brown said later that he now felt fulfilled. He had not only won individual championships but he had led his team to the championship. It was almost automatic when he was voted the National Football League's most valuable player for 1964.

Jim Brown sparked his team to the division title the next year, too, although Cleveland lost the championship game to Green Bay. By this time he had already acted in a motion picture, receiving favorable reviews. In the summer of 1966, the film he was making in England was delayed by bad weather. He told owner Modell that he would have to report late, but Modell refused to allow that. Jim Brown felt his contributions to the team deserved better treatment. He also knew that he was going to have to start a new career soon and he didn't want to ruin his movie chances. So he suddenly announced that he was through with football.

By then in nine seasons, Jim Brown owned almost every record—game, season and career —a player could have. And he had earned from old-timers and younger fans alike the supreme accolade: the greatest runner football had ever seen.

Ernie Davis

It all started so beautifully for Ernie Davis. During the 1959 football season, Ernie, a Syracuse University sophomore, was the No. 1 back on the nation's No. 1 team. While mighty Syracuse steamrollered to its first undefeated season in 71 years, halfback Davis gained 686 yards in 98 carries, a 7-yard average, and scored 10 touchdowns. "That's not bad," some cynics said, "but before we start calling him an all-time great, let's wait and see what he does next year without that powerful line in front of him."

Of the top eleven players that Syracuse lost from that national championship team, nine, including two All-Americans, were linemen. Thus depleted, Syracuse had to settle for a 7–2 record and a low national ranking in 1960. Davis? He merely gained 877 yards in 112 carries, a brillant 7.8-yard average, and scored ten touchdowns. The cynics said nothing, but many of the college coaches who elected Ernie to their All-American first team did. "We consider Davis as fine a running back as there is," said Jack Mitchell of Kansas. "He could play for any pro team," said Steve Sinko of Boston University. "Stopping Davis is like trying to stop a runaway express," said Eddie Anderson of Holy Cross.

Again, in his senior year, Ernie shredded rival defenses with his power and speed. He became the first Negro to win the Heisman Trophy, awarded annually to the nation's best college player, and enthusiastically looked forward to testing himself against the pros. It would be a special thrill for Ernie because he would get to play alongside superstar Jim Brown, himself a former Syracuse great and the guy who had helped recruit Ernie for Syracuse. The Cleveland Browns had given up a top draft choice and superb halfback—shifty, speedy Bobby Mitchell—to obtain Ernie Davis. Cleveland coach Paul Brown drooled over the size and speed he would have in his backfield.

He knew all about Ernie Davis' accomplishments. He knew how Ernie had won eleven varsity letters at Elmira Free Academy in New York and that he had made schoolboy All-American three times, once in basketball and twice in football. The Academy never lost a game in either sport while Ernie was in school there.

And Paul Brown knew about the highlights of Ernie's career at Syracuse, during which he broke all of Jim Brown's records. One of the early highlights had come in the Cotton Bowl in Dallas, during Ernie's sophomore year. A crowd of 75,000 watched the post-season game, waiting to see if undefeated Syracuse and heralded Ernie Davis were really that good.

After the opening kickoff, on the first play from scrimmage, quarterback Dave Sarette pitched out to Syracuse's captain, halfback Gerhard Schwedes. Schwedes, on the option, chose to pass. He threw the ball forty yards; Davis caught it at midfield. Ernie flashed between two defenders, faked out the safetyman and sprinted into the end zone. The play covered eighty-seven yards—the longest major-bowl pass play on record. Later, Ernie scored another touchdown and a pair of two-point conversions. Furthermore, he set up Syracuse's third touchdown by running sixteen yards with an intercepted pass and smashing twenty-two more yards from scrimmage. Davis won the Cotton Bowl's most valuable player award, and Syracuse took the game, 23–14. Ernie Davis was that good.

Both the NFL and AFL made him their first draft pick, and Paul Brown—trading his top choice and Mitchell for Washington's number one draft choice—was happily able to sign Ernie up.

Prior to the 1962 season, Ernie reported to advance summer camp with Cleveland and then left for Chicago to play with the college all-stars against the Green Bay Packers. A few days before the game, doctors sent Ernie to the hospital for tests. The diagnosis: leukemia.

Ernie Davis never got to fulfill his greatest dream. He never played a minute of football for the Cleveland Browns. He worked out with the Browns through the 1962 season and did his homework. When they told him his illness was terminal, he did not complain. He lived the way he always had—as a cheerful, gentle human being. Then, during the o:-season, Ernie Davis, age twenty-three, died. No one knows how great a football player he might have been as a pro. But John Brown, a teammate of Ernie's at both Syracuse and Cleveland, can testify to his greatness as a man. "When I feel low," said John Brown, "I think of how Ernie stood up under his burden and it gives me strength. He's an inspiration to me. I'm a better man because I knew Ernie Davis."

Leroy Kelly

In July of 1966, Leroy Kelly was in his parents' home in Philadelphia when he heard the radio broadcaster: "Jim Brown today announced his retirement from football. . ." Kelly's reaction was a loud, "Great." For until then, Leroy hadn't seen much action with the Cleveland Browns. Superstar Jim Brown had been the fullback and Ernie Green had been the halfback, and that made Leroy a spare part. He had earned his keep primarily as a hard-nosed player on the specialty teams. On the kicking unit, he would run down under punts and make jarring tackles. On kickoffs

and punt returns, he was a "long-ball" threat. In his second pro season, 1965, Kelly had been the NFL's punt-return champion, with a 15.6-yard average. Against Dallas he had run one back for a sixty-seven-yard touchdown, and the following week he zigged and zagged through Pittsburgh for a fifty-six-yard score.

Now, in 1966, Leroy Kelly was stepping into the Cleveland backfield as a starter and naturally everyone would compare him to Jim Brown, the best runner who ever played the game. The 6-ft., 200-pounder did just fine. He scored fifteen touchdowns to lead the league and finished second to Gale Sayers in rushing, with 1,141 yards. Leroy's 5.5 yards-per-carry average was tops in the league.

Said Ernie Green, who had moved over to fullback: "Leroy is like a cat. So was Jim, only a bigger cat. It's difficult to knock a cat off his feet. He's agile and has balance. The same is true of Jim and Leroy. And they both have tremendous attitudes about their play. In so many ways he reminds me of Jim. Of course, since he doesn't have Jim's strength he has to compensate in other areas. Jim broke tackles; Leroy has to move about more, give a head-and-shoulders fake and side-step to get around tacklers."

Kelly, by season's end, had established himself as one of the NFL's premier ball carriers and he came back in 1967 to lead the NFL in rushing yardage (1,205 yards), rushing average (5.1 yards a carry), and touchdowns scored (rushing) eleven. He had arrived.

Leroy had grown up in Philadelphia and was actually a quarterback while playing for Simon Graetz High School. In school, Leroy was the highest scorer in the Public League and received the most votes for the all-public team.

When graduation time approached, Leroy's coach, Louis De Vicaris, sent letters to several Negro colleges extolling Leroy's ability. Leroy, a fine shortstop, had considered baseball as a career but wanted to get a college

Leroy Kelly gained his chance for stardom upon the retirement of Jim Brown. With Brown gone, Kelly had the opportunity to show his ability and he really came through. He is an all-purpose back with the ability to go over a tackler, follow a blocker (such as #77 Dick Schafrath) or use his speed and agility to work free of a defender and haul in a pass for a TD.

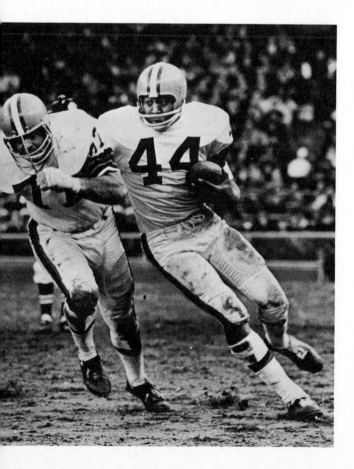

education. Kelly had a trade preparatory background and this made it difficult for him to follow up feelers from Temple and Michigan State. But Morgan State suited Leroy fine, for Baltimore is close to Philadelphia and he never had been away from home before.

Like De Vicaris at Graetz, coach Howard Banks at Morgan Staate discovered Leroy could do everything on offense: block, run, catch passes. He was a star on Morgan's perennial powerhouses.

Cleveland drafted Kelly in the eighth round and outbid the New York Jets to sign him. "I recommended him because I thought he was good," said Paul Bixler, who scouted Kelly. "But he's much better than I judged him. I didn't think he'd be this great." Kelly may never make Cleveland forget the incomparable Jim Brown, but Leroy has proved that he can keep the attack moving with some pretty fancy stepping of his own.

Ollie Matson

Ollie Matson was a dramatic figure, a gifted athlete, and yet he always seemed a step away from the greatness people had continually predicted for him.

Consider his track career. Muscular and swift at 6ft.-2in., 203 pounds, Ollie decided that he wanted to run the quarter mile in the 1952 Olympic Games. So, after completing the 1951 football season at the University of San Francisco, he started his first serious track training in three years. Dink Templeton, the old Stanford coach, observed that "if Matson had been running quarter miles for three years, there would be nobody near him today." Matson gave a good account of himself in Helsinki. He won a silver medal for third place in 46.8 seconds. Ollie also ran a leg on the 1,600-meter relay team that finished second to the speedy Jamaicans.

Matson had done well, when you consider his belated efforts at training for his event.

Next he decided to try professional football. The Chicago Cardinals had made him their first draft choice and had high hopes for him. After all, in 1949 he had romped for touchdowns of sixty and fifty-three yards within three minutes to spearhead USF's 27–12 victory over Loyola of Los Angeles. The same year he broke a 13–13 tie with San Jose State College on an eighty-yard run. In 1951, he ran for three scores against Fordham, two for ninety-four and ninety yards, respectively, and rolled up 302 yards rushing. Other runs that year went for distances of 68, 67, 54, 46 and 45 yards.

In his first pro game, against the Bears, he ran back a kickoff one hundred yards and stole the ball another time to run thirty-four yards for a touchdown. "I was a defensive back then," he says. "I didn't become an offensive back until later in the season when I broke my wrist." That year he was clearly the NFL's best rookie. The following year, 1953, Ollie was in the Army but he returned to the Cardinals in time for the third game in 1954, and immediately ripped off two long touchdown runs to help the Cards beat Pittsburgh, 17–14.

Ollie had speed and power. "No arm tackle will pull him down," said one rival coach. "He's too strong. He'll bust right through you unless you hit him hard with a head-on tackle." In 1958, Matson led the pros in kickoff returns. He averaged 35.5 yards per return—a figure that was 10 yards better than the runner-up's. Throughout his career, he was spectacular in the open field and had kickoff returns of 105 and 100 yards to his credit.

Still, by the end of the 1958 season, Ollie Matson had never rushed for 1,000 yards or more for a season and had never led the NFL in that department. His best effort was 924 yards in 1956. The problem was that he played with a generally weak team. "If we had had a real good quarterback or another real good halfback," said one of his teammates years later, "it would have been different for Ollie.

Ollie Matson, displaying the quickness and agility that made him one of the top runners in the NFL. Using deft body moves and bursts of speed, Matson threatened to go "all the way" each time he carried the ball.

As it was, he was all we had. The defense could set itself for him—nobody else, just him."

Then, in 1959, the Chicago Cardinals made one of the most spectacular trades in sports history. They sent Matson to the Los Angeles Rams for eight players and a draft choice. The Rams had the passing of Bill Wade and the running of nimble halfback Jon Arnett, and now they had added the speedy Matson.

But Los Angeles never won any titles with Matson. He had a good season in 1959—863 yards rushing—5.3 yards per carry—but skidded downhill dramatically until the Rams sent him off to Detroit in 1963. Many people thought LA had given up too much to the Chicago Cardinals to get Ollie and would need years to rebuild.

Ollie went from Detroit to Philadelphia in 1964 and by then age had slowed him up. There were occasional flashes of brilliance, but Ollie's career was substantially behind him. He had been good, very good—a stunning blend of muscle and swiftness.

Lenny Moore

As a pro, Lenny Moore has actually had two careers. In the first, he was Lenny Moore, the pass-catching halfback, the guy with the quick feet and all those pretty moves. The second career came harder. There had been injuries and a slump and then he was mostly a running halfback who had to make his way through heavy traffic.

Moore came to the Colts as a first draft choice in 1956. He had been a splendid halfback at Penn State and it had all come so easily that he never really took the game seriously. As a rookie, he romped for 649 yards—averaging 7.5 yards a carry—and scored nine touchdowns. He was rookie of the year and it was a lark. But 1957 brought a turning point in Lenny Moore's attitude about football. He made a disastrous fumble against Detroit that helped the Colts lose the conference title, and

suddenly Lenny realized that he needed to work much harder to excel as a pro.

"I stopped loafing and started learning the game's finer points," he said. And it seemed to pay off. He was All-NFL flanker four years in a row after that. In 1958, his fourteen touchdowns helped Baltimore gain its first conference championship. Then he scored a crucial touchdown in the famous overtime play-off victory over the Giants. That victory made the Colts world champions and the Baltimore club repeated in 1959. On the first offensive series in the 1959 title game against New York, Moore took a flat pass from John Unitas and sped 60 yards for the score. Baltimore won it, 34–16, and afterwards the Giants quarterback Charlie Conerly shook his head and said, "Moore is so quick and shifty it's almost impossible to defend against him."

"If the defender watches my legs and feet, he's lost," Lenny has said, "because I can make my legs do a million and one things. If he tries to follow my hips, I can fake him right into the stands."

Those were the good times—career No. 1. Then in 1961 the Colts traded for Jimmy Orr, a fine receiver, and career No. 2 started for Lenny Moore. Orr was put at flanker and Baltimore made Moore into a running back. Lenny did not prosper there. He didn't pick up good yardage on the ground and his pass-receiving slipped, too, for he had trouble running his patterns through the big linemen.

Then came a series of injuries. Late in 1961 it was a head injury. In a 1962 exhibition game he cracked a kneecap and missed half the season. Just before the 1963 season, he underwent an emergency appendectomy and then a head injury sidelined him for the last five games of the year. Many people in Baltimore felt that Moore—though legitimately hurt at times—didn't really want to play football any longer.

Lenny showed them in 1964. In the second game of the season against the Packers, Moore

Lenny Moore, voted by the AP as the comeback player of the year in 1964, poses with two other Baltimore greats, Johnny Unitas, the league's MVP, and Don Shula, the best coach. Moore shows why he won the award (below) as it takes two Packers to haul him down from behind.

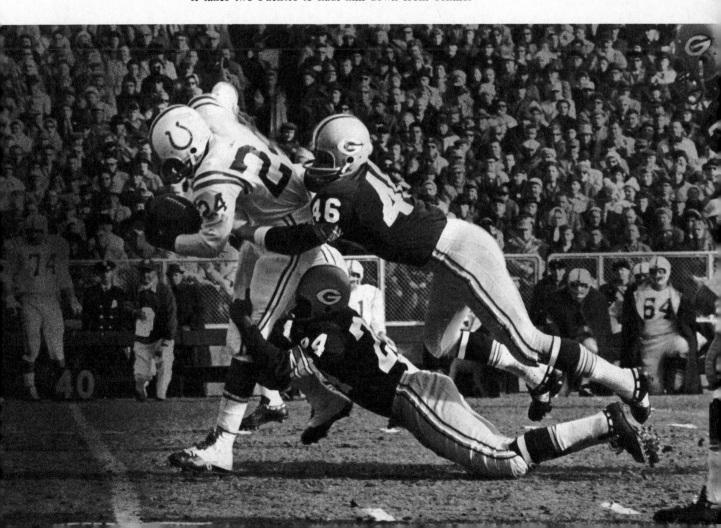

started out by taking a Unitas pass and streaking for a score. Later, he plowed four yards for another touchdown, blasting through tough linebacker Ray Nitschke at the goal line. "He really ran like he wanted it," Nitschke said afterwards. The Colts won, 21–20, and began their drive for the title.

Four weeks later came a crucial showdown game with Green Bay again. Moore scored a touchdown on a twenty-one-yard run and broke three tackles to do it. But with a minute to go, the Colts were losing, 21–17, and had the ball on Green Bay's five. Moore got the call and rammed through left guard. As he had been four weeks earlier, Ray Nitschke was waiting for him. Lenny just smashed straight ahead and carried Nitschke into the end zone with him. It was Baltimore's game, 24–21, and the Colts went on to the conference title.

By season's end, Lenny Moore had scored a record twenty touchdowns, had picked up 584 yards rushing on 157 carries, and had caught twenty-one passes for 472 yards. Lenny Moore had come back.

Moore showed them in this year that he still had those natural gifts that had made him one of the game's greats. As a teammate said of him, "Lenny Moore always had the ability to do anything he wants on a football field. Run. Catch the ball. Block. Tackle if he has to. Anything." Even after 1964, as age limited his playing, Lenny Moore carried on with a grace distinctively his own.

Marion Motley

Paul Brown, one of the most successful football coaches of all time, does not hesitate when asked to name the finest back who ever played for him. His answer: Marion Motley.

Dozens of fine backs have played for Paul Brown during his successes in high school, college and professional football, and one of them was the great Jim Brown. What made Motley superior, in the eyes of Paul Brown and

many others, was his all-round talent. Motley was an outstanding runner, with as much power if not the speed of Jim Brown. But he was a rugged blocker as well. He even helped the Browns by playing linebacker in tough situations.

Motley was the fullback for the Browns from 1946 to 1953. During those years, Cleveland won the All-America Conference championship four straight times and the National Football League title once while taking their division championship the other three seasons. Then the Browns were often referred to as "a pass and trap team." The passer was Otto Graham, and the man who ran the traps, to keep the defense "honest," was Motley. But as important as Motley was carrying the football, he was just as important protecting Graham, who has said many times that a major reason for his success was the confidence gained because Marion was blocking for him.

Motley did not carry the ball as often as Jim Brown, but he averaged more yards per carry for his career. Against Pittsburgh in 1950, he set an NFL record with 181 yards in 11 carries. Brown replaced that one-game record by running up 237 against Los Angeles, but he did it on 23 carries. Never in his career did Motley average under 4.27 yards per try for a season. He once averaged 8.23 yards, and in all but two years he topped the five-yard-per-carry mark.

A native of Canton, Ohio, the birthplace of professional football, big Marion played high school football at Canton McKinley High School, where the big rival was Massillon, then coached by Paul Brown. He played college football at Nevada and during World War II competed for Paul Brown at the Great Lakes Naval Training Center. When the war ended, he joined the Browns, then a new team, along with Bill Willis. The two men were the first Negroes to play major league professional sports after World War II. In that season of

1946, when they were with the Browns, Jackie Robinson was performing in baseball for the Montreal Royals of the International League; he did not move up to the major leagues with the Brooklyn Dodgers until the next spring.

After his retirement, Marion wanted to remain in pro football as a coach, but the old barrier against Negroes in command positions helped prevent that. He assisted his old teammate Otto Graham in coaching the College All-Stars one year (against the Browns), and he served as a part-time scout for the Washington Redskins after Graham became head coach and general manager. Otherwise, he worked as a mailman and in public relations. For a while, he coached a girls' tackle football team.

Motley likes to say that he came along too early in pro football. His best salary as one of pro football's reigning stars was $12,000 a year; now that is a minimum salary in the league.

But Marion's contribution to professional football is not forgotten. In 1968, he was voted into pro football's hall of fame, which is sited, appropriately, in his home town of Canton.

Joe Perry

Fletcher Joe Perry was signed by the San Francisco 49ers in 1948—their first Negro player. But no one remembers him as a pioneer. He is remembered now as a fullback who led the National Football League in ground-gaining twice, in 1953 and 1954, with more than one thousand yards each season. And the man who, until Jim Brown came along, had gained more yards rushing than any other back in pro football history. They used to call Joe Perry "the jet": he had run the 100-yard dash in 9.7 seconds, and he weighed only 208 pounds.

Perry started with the 49ers by borrowing five dollars from owner Tony Morabito. With his casual regard toward money—he never quibbled over salary—Joe wasn't especially worried about a contract when he and Morabito chatted on a foggy, fall morning in the bleachers of San Francisco's Golden Gate Park polo field where the 49ers were practicing. "My biggest problem was whether I wanted to turn pro or finish college," Perry recalled. He was then in the Navy, still playing for a Navy team but about to be mustered out.

Of course, Morabito and coach Buck Shaw, the latter with the "show-me" cynicism that is the hallmark of most football coaches, wanted proof of the young sailor's power before they signed him. They recognized the name Perry only as a potentially great sprinter who had raced against Mel Patton, among others, and lost to him by only a stride. "We watched him in two games," Morabito says. "In the first, Perry carried the ball four times and scored four touchdowns. His shortest run was fifty-five yards. In the second game, he played only the first six minutes and scored two touchdowns. We left. How much convincing do you need?"

In 1949, after Perry had been established as first-string fullback, Frankie Albert, then the 49er quarterback, tagged Joe with his nickname. "I'm telling you, when that guy comes by to take a handoff, his slip-stream darn near knocks you over. He's strictly jet-propelled."

Track was Perry's first athletic love. He was running the 100 in 9.7 seconds even while attending David Starr Jordan High School in Los Angeles. He also was sprinting the 200 in 21.9, broad-jumping 23 feet-5 inches, high-jumping 6 feet-3 inches and shot-putting 55 feet.

He played football on the sly as a high school sophomore. His mother had vetoed the game for him. But Joe checked out a uniform anyhow. And in his first scrimmage, he broke his ankle. "I walked the five blocks home on that broken ankle," Joe says smilingly, "trying to hide the fact that I was hurt, afraid of what

Marion Motley

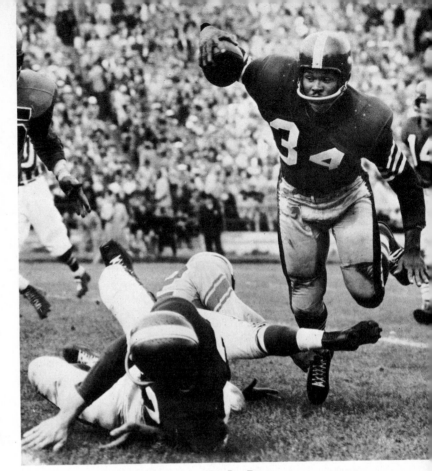

Joe Perry

Joe Perry follows the blocking of Bruce Bosley to pick up a nice gain against the Los Angeles Rams.

my mother would say. As it turned out, after her initial shock, she decided as long as I'd made that kind of a sacrifice, I might as well continue playing. She was my greatest rooter from then on."

After high school, Perry followed a harried life of maritime service and Navy duty, interspersed with odd semesters at Compton Junior College in southern California. At Compton in 1944, he scored twenty-two touchdowns to lead the nation's colleges.

It was also while at Compton, because of the various military interruptions, that Perry was forced to abandon a planned career in electrical engineering. He always regretted that necessity.

But he nonetheless made a fancy career out of football. He was a part of some great backfields that featured such quarterbacks as Frankie Albert and Y. A. Tittle and such running backs as Hugh McElhenny and John Henry Johnson. And Perry was all-pro at his position. End Gordy Soltau once described what it was like blocking for Perry's runs. "Blocking on one of those wide Perry pitchout sweeps is a breeze," said Soltau. "You merely nod 'hello' to the inrushing opponent, and if he's courteous enough to take the time to nod back, Perry is long gone around him."

Gale Sayers

"Gale Sayers," in the opinion of Green Bay Packer linebacker Ray Nitschke, "is the fastest back in the league, fastest at getting to the sideline, fastest at turning the corner, fastest all ways." Sayers, a nifty halfback for the Chicago Bears, was also fastest at establishing himself as a professional star.

Fresh out of Kansas in 1965, Gale scored twenty-two touchdowns (a league record) and led the league in scoring with 132 points. Fourteen of his touchdowns came on runs, six on pass receptions, and two on kick runbacks. Sayers rushed for 867 yards at 5.2 yards per carry—which placed him second to Jim Brown. He was second also in punt and kick-off returns and he caught twenty-nine passes for 507 yards. Sayers completed two of the three option passes he threw and one went for a touchdown. He was naturally the rookie of the year and no one has yet found a way to contain him. He came right back in his second year and set the league's total offense record with 2,240 yards.

Just how explosive 6ft.-1in., 200-pound Gale Sayers can be was demonstrated one soggy Sunday in his rookie year. The day was December 12 and the Bears were playing host in Wrigley Field to the San Francisco 49ers. The first time Chicago got the ball, on its 20-yard line, quarterback Rudy Bukich called a screen pass to Sayers. It is a play in which the receiver is surrounded not only by blockers but by defenders as well.

Sayers caught the ball in the crowd, spotted a narrow alley through the wall of unfriendly flesh closing in on him, and instinctively dashed through. A wiggle, a squirm, a feint, then nothing but sheer speed, and he was alone. He didn't stop running for eighty yards, scoring the first touchdown of the dreary afternoon.

The Bears were leading, 13–7, with less than five minutes remaining in the half, when Sayers got another opportunity. The ball was on the San Francisco 21. He was off around end, staying behind his blockers until they threw light in front of him, then shifting into high gear and dashing unmolested into the end zone. He did the same thing, from seven yards out, in the closing minute of the half, scoring his third touchdown, and sending the Bears off the field with a 27–13 lead.

At midfield, early in the third quarter, Bukich tossed him a pitchout. This time he had daylight from the start, and easily outsprinted the San Francisco secondary to the goal line. The game was no longer a contest, but the crowd remained enthusiastic. Sayers had four

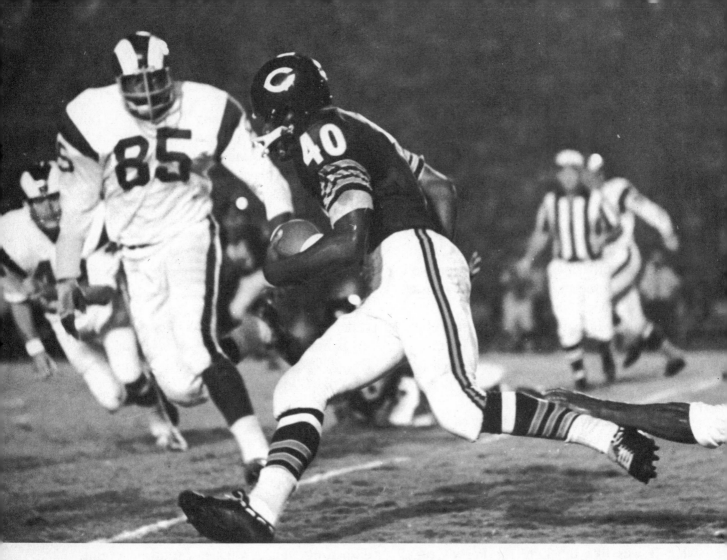

With the retirement of Jimmy Brown, Gale Sayers stepped up as the most dynamic and explosive ball-carrier in the NFL. Combining blazing speed with balance and agility, Sayers is virtually unstoppable if he has a step on the defense. Here he is seen turning the corner against Los Angeles (above), cutting sharply away from a Green Bay tackle (below right), and getting a few pointers from Bear owner George Halas.

touchdowns. One more and he would tie the Chicago team record. He did so late in the third quarter. The Bears were only a yard away from another score and Bukich handed the ball to Sayers. Nothing fancy this time. He just smacked into the center of the line and into the end zone for touchdown number five.

The fourth quarter was half over. San Francisco, now trailing 47–20, was forced to punt. Sayers stood at his own 15-yard line and watched the ball tumble down at him. He caught it, popped straight upfield, swerved to his left away from the mob, then somehow darted around the deeper tacklers without losing a split second's speed and emerged in the clear. Only the cheers chased him into the end zone.

It was his sixth touchdown, a team record, and it tied him with Ernie Nevers and Dub Jones for the National Football League record for most touchdowns in a single game. This was too much, even for a self-contained sort like Sayers. The first five times he'd scored, he had turned quietly and handed the ball to the nearest official. But this time he flipped it into the air, clapped his hands, skipped back toward his teammates on the field, then sprinted to the Chicago bench.

Sayers has always been a marvelous athlete. He was all-state in football two years in a row at Omaha Central High School, in Nebraska, and received almost one hundred scholarship offers before deciding on the University of Kansas. In three varsity seasons there, Gale rushed for 2,675 yards (6.5 yards per carry) and caught thirty-five passes for 408 yards. Once, against Oklahoma State in 1962, he picked up 283 yards rushing in one afternoon's work.

After Kansas, it was instant stardom in Chicago for Sayers. "I don't know exactly how I do it," says Sayers. "I mean, I don't run up to a tackler and say to myself, 'you are now going to fake left and cut right.' I just let instinct take over and I go along for the ride. It just happens, that's all." It just happens that Gale Sayers is now the most exciting and dangerous ball carrier in pro football.

Claude "Buddy" Young

Claude Young never had any business playing football. He grew up to be only 5 ft.-4½ in., weighed 166 pounds in his prime and seemed to merit the nickname of "Buddy." Yet because of his unusual speed, and especially because of his exceptional determination, Buddy Young proved that a good little man is hard to keep down.

Born on the South Side of Chicago in a family of nine children, Buddy Young grew up during the Great Depression. But thanks to help from his family and determination that was to see him through struggle after struggle, he enrolled at the University of Illinois as a seventeen-year-old freshman in 1944. Buddy tried out for football although only he thought he had a chance to compete in the tough Big Ten Conference.

All Buddy did that freshman season was to score thirteen touchdowns, matching the school record set by the most heralded Illini of all, Harold (Red) Grange. He averaged 9.2 yards carrying the ball, and he scored on runs of 92, 82, 74, 63, 40, 31 and 24 yards.

When Buddy turned eighteen, he entered the Navy and starred with the Fleet City team composed of college and professional players. After the war, he returned to Illinois in time for the 1946 season—in time to help lead the Illini to the Big Ten championship and a stunning 45–14 victory over UCLA in the 1947 Rose Bowl game.

Buddy Young was a man now, with a wife and son to support. So he gave up his final year of college eligibility to sign a professional football contract with the New York Yankees of the All-America Conference. After the professional leagues' merger, he continued his brilliant career with the Baltimore Colts of the National Football League. In six seasons in the NFL, he rushed for 1,275 yards and caught passes for a total of 1,978 yards.

All this time, he never weighed more than 170 pounds. Young was hit again and again by 250-pounders, yet bounced up without a whimper or a concession of hurt. This ability to absorb punishment and come back had always been his way. When he entered college at Illinois, he found that he could not be served at one of the popular campus snack shops. His coach, Ray Eliot, advised him, "Get on the scoreboard." That was Eliot's way of saying that if Buddy proved himself he would be able to move in any circles. Buddy did, and later found that he could, indeed, patronize that snack bar; soon, though, he left it far behind.

When Buddy retired, the Colts "retired" his jersey number 22 in a rare tribute for a sport that has so many stars. He rejoined the Colts as a public relations representative. Then the National Football League appointed him a special assistant to the commissioner. His chief assignment was to work with young men.

It was a talent he had always had. Buddy helped many players in the league. One of them was Gene (Big Daddy) Lipscomb, the antithesis of Buddy in many ways. Lipscomb was the league's giant, a 290-pounder, an opposite of Young in size. He was almost an opposite, too, in temperament, tending to be rough. Young's careful handling turned Lipscomb into a gentleman and helped him become one of the finest defensive players in the league.

Now in retirement, Young was helping college boys make the adjustment to the professional ranks, advising them on such things as business opportunities for the years ahead. Buddy was in constant demand as an after-dinner speaker as well. At one banquet given in honor of the 1965 All-American team, the former Oklahoma football coach "Bud" Wil-

kinson approached Buddy after his talk and said, "That was the greatest thing I've ever listened to."

In 1968, Buddy Young, who had played only two years of college football, was voted into the Football Foundation Hall of Fame. It was a tribute to the player and the man.

New League—New Stars

The play was often ragged when the American Football League began in 1960, but two very slick ball carriers came out of that season with star quality written all over them—Abner Haynes and Paul Lowe.

Abner, 6 feet and 190 pounds, came to the Dallas Texans with impressive credentials. He had been a much-publicized breakaway back as a Texas schoolboy and became the first Negro to play for a major Texas college when he enrolled at North Texas State. He led his school to two Missouri Valley Conference titles and twice won designation as the league's back of the year.

That first year in the AFL, while the Texans were finishing second in the Western Division, Abner supplied the dash. He scored three touchdowns against Buffalo, gained 157 yards rushing against New York, carried twenty-seven times against Denver, and caught seven passes against Los Angeles. In a league where no other player led in more than one department, Abner led in both rushing and punt returns, finished fifth in pass-catching, seventh in scoring, and eighth in kickoff returns. He ran 156 times for 875 yards (5.6-yard average), returned fourteen punts for 215 yards (15.4 average), caught fifty-five passes for 576 yards (10.5 average), returned nineteen kickoffs for 434 yards (22.8 average) and scored twelve touchdowns for seventy-two points.

Abner Haynes became the AFL's first player of the year. With great speed, nimble feet and sufficient power, he next had seasons

Paul Lowe

Abner Haynes

Relying more on elusive moves and changes of speed than raw power, Paul Lowe established himself as one of the greatest runners in the history of the AFL.

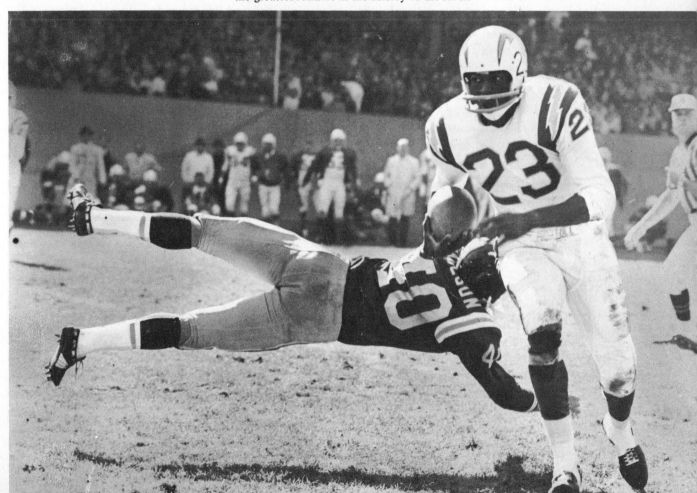

of 841 and 1,049 yards rushing and established himself as a superstar. There were injuries and other problems thereafter—as the Dallas franchise moved to Kansas City—and Abner's play would be good at times and ordinary at others. He moved on to Denver, Miami and New York with the end in sight. But he had been very, very good.

Paul Lowe was a big star in high school, yet few scouts noticed him. He was never all-anything in college, so the pros didn't even draft him. He tried out for the San Francisco 49ers of the National League, and was turned loose. Then he was signed by the newly formed Los Angeles team of the American League, which was desperate for football players.

Paul sat around a year waiting for the league to begin play, and when football started he went unnoticed. It is hard to figure. He has a unique running style. He holds himself straight up and down and raises his knees high and prances around like a man trying to hold his head above tall grass and his feet away from snakes. Seeking running room, he glides like a skater. Moving into a crowd, he hops. Springing into the open, he shifts into high like a racer turning down the home stretch at Indianapolis.

He is not particularly big or strong and he does not have great balance, but he is quick and fast, he changes speed deceptively and he is very elusive. Time after time, he will hit into a line and be stopped cold. But the next time, he will find daylight and be gone. He has had years like 1963, when he broke loose for 1,010 yards and a 5.7 average, and 1965, when he gained 1,121 yards and was the AFL's player of the year. Lowe already ranks as one of the AFL's all-time greats.

Haynes and Lowe were the AFL's first super ball carriers, but now two new men—Mike Garrett and Jim Nance—have risen as the glamor runners in the league.

At 5 ft.-9 in. and 190 pounds, Garrett was considered questionable as a pro prospect when he reported to Kansas City in 1966. True, he was the 1965 Heisman Trophy winner and an All-American from Southern California, but he didn't even have exceptional speed to compensate for his lack of size. All Garrett did was tie for second in the AFL in rushing, with 801 yards in 1966, make the year's longest run from scrimmage (seventy-seven yards), and lead the league with his 5.5 yards-per-carry average. His cutting, feinting and balance made him one of the most exciting runners in football. He capped a fine season by scoring two touchdowns against Buffalo as the Chiefs romped to the AFL title, 31–7.

In 1967, halfback Garrett continued on his march to greatness. He rushed for 1,087 yards, caught forty-six passes for 261 yards and scored ten touchdowns. He carried for 192 yards against New York for the best single-game performance of the AFL season.

Boston Patriot fullback Jim Nance needs none of Garrett's finesse. Jim is 6 ft.-1 in. and 245 pounds and he is a tough man to wrestle to the ground. He floundered as a rookie in 1965 because he was carrying too much weight. But in 1966, the former Syracuse University star trimmed down and started to roll. He advanced 1,458 yards on the ground for an AFL record and was named player of the year. In 1967 he rushed for more yards—1,216—than anyone in pro football.

Garrett and Nance are the kind of rising stars who help make the fans forget the older stars, like Haynes and Lowe.

Leroy Keyes and O. J. Simpson

The 1967 college football season produced a pair of junior halfbacks with two things in common—rather unusual first names for athletes, and rather extraordinary ability on the football field. Rarely do two runners as talented as Leroy Keyes and O.J. Simpson turn in such spectacular performances in one season.

The 1967 season unveiled Leroy Keyes as the most versatile college football player of his time.

O. J. Simpson holds the Player of the Game trophy after Southern Cal's 14–3 Rose Bowl victory over Indiana.

Purdue's Leroy Keyes eludes a tackle to score a TD against Illinois.

How many athletes do you know named Marvin? Well, Marvin Leroy Keyes of Newport News, Virginia, is an athlete all right, probably the most versatile, if not the best, college football player of his time. In 1966, as a sophomore at Purdue, Keyes was a defensive back and a good one. In 1967, Keyes started out on defense, then began playing offense exclusively, winding up as the highest scorer in college football and everyone's All-American. Leroy had nineteen touchdowns on a mixed bag of runs and pass receptions, and he also finished eleventh in the nation in rushing, with 986 yards on only 149 carries (in one game, against Illinois, he set a school rushing record by slashing for 225 yards). Keyes also kicks off on occasion and, according to Purdue sources, would be the school's best punter if he were needed. He does well, too, in other sports. Keyes was a regular in basketball at Newport News' Carver High School, he was a good enough shortstop to interest major league scouts and he still holds the Virginia school broad-jump record. But football is his game: "I laugh most all the time when I play. It's not that I'm laughing at anyone. It's just that football to me is such a fun game."

Orenthal James Simpson doesn't get many laughs over his given name, but the All-American halfback from Southern California couldn't be happier with his nickname: "Orange Juice." "Some day," he once said, a smile lighting his handsome face, "it could make me a lot of money."

Not as much as O.J.'s skills on a football field, though. Professional football teams say the 6 ft.-1 in., 202-pound Simpson is a larger Gale Sayers. Since Sayers is one of the outstanding runners in pro football, this means Simpson has the potential to be even better. In 1967, as a junior, O.J. was voted the player of the year by the National Sportscasters and Sportswriters Association, and by United Press International. He led the nation in rushing —gaining 1,415 yards and scoring eleven touchdowns— and he led Southern Cal to a ranking as the No. 1 college football team in the country. In the Rose Bowl he scored twice and was named the outstanding player as SC beat Indiana, 14–3. A tough kid from a tough neighborhood in San Francisco, O.J. might have ended up with a longer number than 32 on his shirt if it hadn't been for football. He played two years at the City College of San Francisco, then transferred to SC and became an All-American with a money-making nickname—and future.

Bobby Mitchell

Though Bobby Mitchell had a brilliant career as a halfback at the University of Illinois, the pros didn't seem interested in him when they started drafting for the 1958 season. They knew he was swift—he was capable of the 100-yard dash in 9.5 seconds—and elusive. But they wrote him off because even Mitchell's college coach was saying things like, "Mitchell is a good running back who would be okay if you could ever teach him not to fumble.

Nearly eighty players were selected before coach Paul Brown of the Cleveland Browns decided to take a chance on Mitchell. He knew about Bobby's reputation as a fumbler but chose him because he had, said Brown, "tremendous speed, the ability to shift his weight without faltering and he could stop and start at full speed." Paul put Mitchell in at halfback next to his star fullback, Jim Brown, and sat back to let NFL defenses cope with the power and speed of that combination. As a rookie, Bobby gained 500 yards rushing and averaged a stunning 6.3 yards per carry. Brown ran for 1,527 yards and the Cleveland club led the NFL in rushing yardage.

Mitchell picked up 743 yards on the ground his next year and pretty soon experts were raving about him. Said one coach: "Mitchell is the most dangerous and exciting player in football today. He can beat you by going one hundred

Bobby Mitchell gets behind New York's Erich Barnes to haul in a long scoring pass.

Making one of his spectacular catches, Mitchell takes the ball away from Cardinal defender Norman Beal.

Serious and intent, Mitchell waits along the sidelines for his chance to get back into the game.

yards at least four different ways—taking a pass, returning a kick, going off tackle, or turning an end. He hasn't even reached his peak yet, but he is already one of the game's top all-round stars."

"His secret," said Paul Brown of his halfback, "is his exceptional balance. I know of no runner who is more elusive." Bobby had four strong years as Jim Brown's running mate, and then, in 1962, Cleveland traded him to Washington for the Redskins' first draft choice. Paul Brown did it so that he could draft Syracuse halfback Ernie Davis; the Cleveland coach had apparently decided he wanted a huskier man in his backfield alongside Brown.

Bobby had more to adjust to than just a new club. Washington wanted the 6-ft., 190-pound speedster to play at flanker and concentrate on catching passes. He said he felt like a rookie since he had to learn a new set of moves for his pass patterns, and he had to practice catching different kinds of passes. The first time he went up against his old teammates, Mitchell was covered so well he didn't even touch the ball for most of the game.

There were two minutes left and Washington was down 16–10 when Bobby was supposed to go deep for a Norm Snead pass. But he was bumped at the line of scrimmage and didn't get far. Snead threw for Bobby anyway and Mitchell, still spinning from the bump, caught the ball somehow. He bolted to the left sideline, dodged through a circle of tacklers, then shot between two safetymen to run fifty yards and score the winning touchdown. "It was an impossible run," Mitchell said later. "I had nowhere to go, but I found somewhere. It was the greatest run I've ever made and I've made many a run, caught many a pass."

Remarkably, Mitchell caught seventy-two passes and scored eleven touchdowns in his first year as a receiver. He has been one of football's premier flankers ever since. Bobby Mitchell has intimidated the defenders now.

He has come a long way since the day no pro team really seemed to want him.

Charley Taylor

When Washington's Charley Taylor came into the National Football League as a ball carrier in 1964, Dallas coach Tom Landry called him "the best-looking back to come into the NFL since Jim Brown." From Arizona State University, big at 6ft.-2in. and 210 pounds, Charley started out by rushing for 755 yards and finishing sixth in the league in that department. Also, he was eighth in the NFL in pass-catching, with fifty-four receptions, the most any rookie had ever caught. It was no surprise when Taylor was named 1964's rookie of the year.

But in the opening preseason game of 1965, Charley chipped a bone in his right ankle. He came back for the season's opener and sprained an ankle. After that he wasn't the same Charley Taylor. His rushing average dropped from 3.8 yards a try in 1964 to 2.8 in 1965. Lots of people, Charley included, blamed the poor yardage on the bumbling ways of a young offensive line. Early in the 1966 season, in fact, Charley was named by fellow professional players in a magazine story as one of the most underrated players in pro football.

The only trouble was, Redskin coach Otto Graham wasn't one of those who thought Charley underrated. Otto, in fact, thought Charley an overrated halfback. "Charley is a great athlete," Graham said later. "But the more I looked at him, the more I was convinced he would never be a great running back. Charley doesn't have the temperament; he's too impatient. He wouldn't wait for the pattern of a play to develop. He'd run ahead of the interference." So, early in the 1966 season, Graham began alternating Charley at both split end and halfback. "I didn't expect him to be overjoyed," said Graham.

Big and fast, Charley Taylor has provided the Washington Redskins with their greatest offensive threat in years. Combining blazing speed with instinct and agility, Taylor has become one of the most feared pass-receivers in the NFL. Here he cuts sharply away from an Eagle defender (above) and hauls in a Sonny Jurgensen pass (below).

Charley wasn't. He wanted to be a running back and worried about his ability to adjust to the job of pass-receiver. But in the Redskins' ninth game of the 1966 season—against the Colts—Graham made Taylor a full-time split end and Charley caught eight passes for 111 yards and one touchdown. The next week against Dallas, he hauled in eleven more passes, including one over the middle on which he shucked off three tacklers and ran seventy-eight yards for the score. By the end of the season, Charley Taylor had seventy-two receptions, and that was good enough for the NFL pass-catching title.

In 1967, even though enemy defenses keyed on him and he missed three games with injuries, he again led the league in receiving, this time with seventy catches. He had come to camp to learn the fundamentals and he proved to be an apt student. Combined with his instinctive moves and quickness, his additional knowledge made him, at times, almost unstoppable. In one game against Philadelphia, Taylor took a short pass and shed seven tacklers as he turned a five-yard pass into a breathless thirty-nine-yard gain. He does it often enough to infuriate defenses. "He annoys them so much they're looking to give him a good hit and they fire in on him," Eagle tackle Floyd Peters said. "Just when they're committed, Taylor takes that half-turn and step and away he goes."

Charley Taylor is definitely going places as a football player—and he doesn't mind it a bit now that he is doing so as receiver. He likes being number one.

Otis Taylor

Otis Taylor, flanker for the Kansas City Chiefs, is a receiver who seemingly can do anything. He catches passes one-handedly and with both hands. He catches them off the grass and in the air. He catches them long and he catches little five-yard tosses, then turns his 6ft.-3in., 211-lb. frame downfield, with his good speed and strength, to add on hard yards.

In his rookie season with the Chiefs in 1965, Taylor saw only limited action. It was no warning for the way he exploded against the American Football League in his sophomore season. For in 1966 Otis Taylor caught fifty-eight passes for 1,297 yards and a league-leading average of 22.4 yards per catch. He scored eight touchdowns. During the next season, he caught fifty-nine passes, eleven of them for touchdowns.

Taylor was born on August 11, 1942, in Houston, the only son of Otis Taylor, a custodian, and his wife. Otis, Jr. has an older sister, Florence O'Dell Taylor, who is a nurse. Taylor's mother ran the family and still does. "She used to tan me," Otis says, "if I came home with a bloody nose from a football game, or if I tore my clothes."

Tannings and all, at no time was it harsh. "I never needed anything. My mother never refused me anything. The best of pants, suits, shoes. I've always been a clothes freak. I always wanted something new when I was a kid. She'd get it for me. Today, my mother is my greatest fan, my greatest love. I am my mother's baby. It seems I play best when she's there."

As a kid, Taylor played all kinds of ball. He cannot recall wanting to be anything but a professional athlete. In the beginning it was baseball. Then he played forward on his high school basketball team, and one day scored forty-one points; he played college basketball, hitting 16–17 points most nights. He began football as a high school quarterback, but liked catching better.

So Taylor became a receiver, good enough to lure the college scholarship givers. He accepted a full scholarship to Prairie View A&M, forty-five miles above Houston, where he became a physical education major. Mostly, he was a football player. By now, all football fans know that.

Bob Brown

Bob Brown, all-pro tackle for the Philadelphia Eagles, hits with memorable force. "He sort of awes me," said Cleveland's defensive end Paul Wiggin after dueling with Brown one Sunday afternoon. "His strength is fantastic. Brown really doesn't have a weakness. You have to play him without gimmicks, just as hard and tough as you can."

Brown enjoys the testimonials from his opponents. "I don't want to ever be considered just another tackle in this league," said Brown once. "You know the way intelligent football people talk? Somebody mentions blockers and Jim Parker is sure to be talked about. Well, someday when they discuss blocking tackles I want them to say, 'What about Bob Brown?' In a sense I want to become a household word around the league."

He has all the tools to do it. Determination, strength, size and speed—truly spectacular speed. He was once timed in 4.9 seconds over forty yards and his coach, Joe Kuharich, said: "Nobody else gets out in front of outside running plays like Brown. Nobody caves in 250-pounders the way Brown does." Most important, Bob has the right attitude. "The first time I spoke to him," said Dick Stanfel, the Eagles' offensive line coach, "he said he wanted to be the best. He never has stopped striving for that goal. There is not an ounce of complacency in his entire body. He always figures there is something to learn."

Bob wants to be best because of latent talent and not just because he's so big. His size has been both a blessing and a problem for him as long as he can remember. He grew up the second son of a middle class couple on Cleveland's East Side. His father owned a delicatessen on busy Quincy Avenue, and as a boy Bob was guilty of over-sampling the calorie-rich cheeses, corn beef, pastrami, coleslaw, assorted tunas and fattening dressings. He grew wider long before he grew taller and when he walked the streets girls yelled, "Hey, fat boy, how did you get here—you walk or somebody bounce you." Bob Brown has been sensitive about his size ever since.

"I was the victim of some cruel and humiliating talk by the neighborhood kids," he recalled once. "I didn't mind it so much with the boys, but when the girls started heckling me, I had it. When I was sixteen I weighed 290 pounds and, naturally, I had a horrible social life. Who wants to date a fellow 290 pounds? So I decided to do something about it. I quit eating. For five days I took nothing but vitamins and water, and the weight just rolled off. I was so hungry I was in pain, but I found out that you can stand pain if you really want something. I wanted to lose weight and in three months I lost seventy-five pounds. My social life picked up, but when I went to Nebraska (from Cleveland's East Tech High) the coach told me I had to put on more weight. So I just started hitting the calories again."

By his senior year at Nebraska, the 6ft.-4½in. Brown was back up to 285 pounds. He was also everybody's All-American guard. His size and unbelievable speed had pro scouts stuttering. And in 1963 he was the first draft choice of both the Denver Broncos and the Eagles. He signed a three-year contract with the Eagles after the 1964 Orange Bowl game.

Brown has proved his skill as a hitter ever since. He is superior and does not become discouraged or let up when his team is losing. He has too much pride. "When our team can't command respect as a whole," he said, "I have to command it as an individual. I want the man who played opposite me—sometimes during their victory celebration—to sit down and remember I handled him."

Roosevelt Brown

They don't come like Rosey Brown any more; at least they don't usually come to training camp the way he did back in 1953. The

Bob Brown

Rosey Brown

New York's Rosey Brown (#79) prepares to make contact in order to protect the Giants' quarterback.

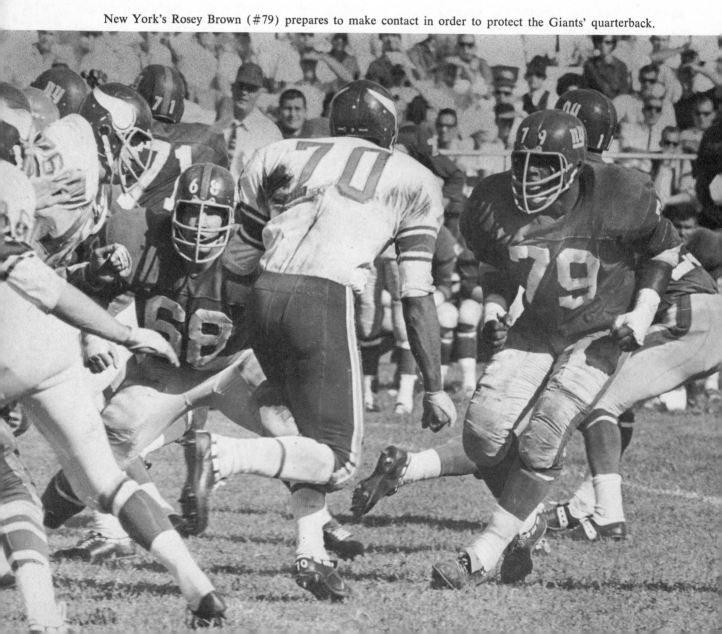

scene was the campus of Gustavus Adolphus College in St. Peter, Minnesota, where the New York Giants were getting ready for the season. Onto the scene stepped rookie Roosevelt Brown, dressed in a neat dark suit, white shirt with winged collar and dark fedora. He wore horn-rimmed glasses and carried a suitcase under one arm; under the other, he held a tightly rolled umbrella.

"He carried that rolled-up umbrella around with him all weekend," recalled Em Tunnell, then a Giants player. "I didn't know whether he was a football player or not." Neither did Steve Owen, then the Giants' head coach. But Brown was 6ft.-3in., weighed 245 pounds and had a 29-inch waist, so Owen had to find out. He matched the rookie offensive lineman against Arnie Weinmeister, a mountain of a man who was rated the best defensive tackle in football. "Steve put him on Weinmeister," said Tunnell, "and Weinmeister almost killed him. Rosey kept going after him even though he couldn't see straight any more and when it was all over he took a couple of laps around the field. Boy, was he green!"

He was green and no one really expected much from him since he had been the team's twenty-seventh draft pick. But before he would retire after the 1965 season, Rosey Brown developed into one of pro football's most respected offensive tackles. He was all-pro more than a half-dozen times, became the Giants' first Negro captain and joined the coaching staff when he quit as an active player. He helped bring the Giants six Eastern Conference titles and one NFL championship.

"The team always looked to Rosey for inspiration," recalled Jim Lee Howell, one of his former coaches. "He got extra tough under heavy pressure and he had the kind of desire and spirit that are hard to beat."

Rosey was playing the trombone in his high school band when the football coach spotted him and convinced him that with his size he should be playing football, not music.

Rosey's father had had a brother who died from injuries received playing football and he hated the sport. He did not want Rosey to play. But Rosey's mother said it was all right and since Rosey's father was a railroad man who was away most of the time, Rosey managed to get in a year of football without his father's being aware of it. The next year his father learned of what was going on and offered strong resistance. Rosey had already played a year without injury, however, and eventually that fact convinced his father to approve his playing.

When Rosey finished high school, he had many scholarship offers and chose Morgan State. Four years later, he was named to the Negro All-American team. The Giants, who had never seen him play, spotted his name and his vital statistics in a newspaper and decided to take a chance on him. The rest is history. Rosey Brown was indeed a gentleman and a football player.

Jim Parker

It was Saturday night in East Macon, Georgia, and the Parker kids sat around the living room all scrubbed and neat while Charles Parker, Sr., who had left the pick and shovel back at the railroad yard for another weekend, held the open Bible on his lap and reminded them of the wages of sin.

He read to them every Saturday night and on Sunday they all walked down the road two miles to the Mt. Moriah Baptist Church, where the six kids attended Sunday School. In the evening, there was prayer meeting and in between, they sat around in their best clothes and made small talk because the children of Charles Parker, Sr. did not wrestle in the dusty street or play football on the Lord's Day. If they did and he caught them, the old man, who often read to them from Revelations about the lake of fire, delivered a swift and merciless punishment worthy of the angry prophets.

There is a theory, heavily subscribed to among the National Football League's defensive linemen, that James Parker, a sort of latter-day avenging angel with the Baltimore Colts, was never handled again on the Lord's Day after leaving his father's home in East Macon.

One of the finest sights in football was Jim lowering his 20-inch neck and burying his helmet into the belly of a 300-pound lineman, or Jim wheeling his 273 pounds laterally behind the line of scrimmage to deliver little pinwheels of light into the skull of an overeager defender. He was, perhaps, the best offensive interior lineman this violent game has ever produced. First as a tackle and then as a guard he was a textbook blend of agility and strength. It was behind Parker's wide frame that Lenny Moore swept to so many touchdowns, and it was to Parker's tender, loving care that the Colts of Baltimore entrusted the safety and well-being of John Unitas' strong right arm. Greater responsibility had no man.

A two-time All-American at Ohio State University, Parker was the Colts' first draft pick in 1957. He was an all-pro tackle for five straight years, then switched to guard and was voted all-pro there, too. In short-yardage running situations, opponents knew the Colts would rely on Parker to clear the way. Still, Parker did the job—even though the defenders were braced for his charge.

Parker was the big man up front for the Colts when they won NFL championships in 1958 and 1959 and a division title in 1964. Don Shula, one of Parker's head coaches at Baltimore, called Jim "the greatest who ever played this game." Unitas, the star quarterback, was certainly in a position to appreciate Parker's work up front. "He's the best passblocker around," Unitas said. "He's so strong and wide, and then he has this immense pride. You know he's going to do a job for you." Jim Parker certainly did a job every Sunday—that is, once he left East Macon, Georgia.

Willie Davis

Think of Willie Davis, defensive captain of the Green Bay Packers, and one remembers big plays and championships. Always big number 87 rushing passers and breaking up end sweeps in games that were bringing championships to Green Bay almost every year.

"He can handle a tackle and fight off a block as well as anyone in the game," said Vince Lombardi, his Packer coach until 1968. Willie plays with a fierce pride and, as defensive captain, feels it is his responsibility to make sure that every man on the squad has the same approach to his work. Willie learned his lesson about attitude in 1960. He had been the seventeenth draft choice of the Cleveland Browns in 1956, had spent two years in service, and then, just as he was becoming a regular in 1960, he was traded to Green Bay. The Packers that year lost the title game to Philadelphia, 17–13, and Davis will always remember one play.

It happened in the fourth quarter with Green Bay leading, 13–10. Van Brocklin threw a quick pass to Bill Barnes who raced thirteen yards to the Packer 14. Eagle momentum was restored and Philadelphia got the winning score. Davis blames himself for not chasing Barnes hard enough. Later, he looked at the films over and over and decided he might have caught him and saved the day for Green Bay. "I made up my mind right then and there," said Willie, "that from then on I would give everything I had all the time." And so he has.

Willie Davis grew up in Texarkana, Arkansas, one of three children of Nodie Davis. His parents split up while he was a youngster and it was left to his mother to raise the children.

If you wanted to be a big man at Booker T. Washington High School, you could do one of two things. You could play in the band or you could play on the football team. Willie Davis tried the band. He tried it for a whole week. The brass horn baffled him.

Jim Parker (left) and Gene "Big Daddy" Lipscomb, two great stars for the Baltimore Colts.

Even resting on the sidelines, Green Bay Packer All-Pro defensive end Willie Davis makes an awesome sight.

He was shooting up and gaining weight, so he went out for the football team. He made it as an end on offense and a tackle on defense. Davis won a scholarship to Grambling College, and he caught the eye of the pro scouts in the Orange Blossom Classic against Willie Galimore's Florida A&M team in 1955. Davis made nineteen tackles and was given credit for assisting on sixteen others. The Browns drafted him when the season was over.

And thus began the professional career of Willie Davis, a determined man who made it all the way to the top in a very tough business.

Gene "Big Daddy" Lipscomb

Around the National Football League, when they used to say, "Big Daddy will get you if you don't watch out," nobody did much laughing. For the reference was to Eugene "Big Daddy" Lipscomb, 6ft.-7in. and 290 solid pounds of defensive tackle, who had a habit of gobbling up quarterbacks and halfbacks carrying a football. "Going in on a running play," someone once said of him, "he sorts the backs out quickly and when he comes to the ball carrier, that's the one he keeps." Big Daddy moved swiftly and could knock a grown man down with one sweep of his huge paw.

He was at the height of his game in the 1958–1959 period when his Baltimore Colts won two straight NFL championships. In 1959, he led the Colts in number of tackles and was generally considered the top defensive lineman in the game. Big Daddy had a gift for diagnosing a play and had the speed and drive to run down the ball carrier wherever he might range. He was also skillful at blocking punts and field-goal attempts. His coach, Weeb Ewbank, bought him a new hat every time Big Daddy blocked one, and Lipscomb always had a good selection of hats.

He is one of the few pros who never attended college. Big Daddy left Miller High in Detroit to join the Los Angeles Rams for the 1953 season. He developed a reputation for having a mean streak and his use of the forearm in the line was known around the league.

The change in his career and life came in 1956 when he was traded to the Baltimore Colts. There the giant met Buddy Young, the round, 5ft.-4in. halfback and learned to play football. "I didn't realize what I was doing was wrong until after the second league game, against Detroit," Big Daddy said later. "I played a lousy game and I was looking for sympathy. But Buddy chewed me out and I went out to prove something to him afterwards. If Buddy had given me sympathy, I would have been the same kind of player. He was the main reason I got somewhere."

From then on, Big Daddy discarded meanness for hardness and even tried to be "a nice guy." When he knocked down a ball carrier, he would pick him up after the whistle. "There was no gimmick," he said. "I thought it was my duty. Lots of guys have families. Why try to hurt them?"

The change was good for him and for his team. Big Daddy joined with some other hard-bitten defensive stars, like Art Donovan and Gino Marchetti, and he began to play the kind of football his magnificent physical equipment made possible for him. He was an indispensable part of the championship Baltimore teams. Later he played for the Pittsburgh Steelers, and after his pro football career had ended he toured as a professional wrestler. Then, while still in his 30's, one night he took an overdose of drugs and died, not long after he had begun to learn how to live.

Big Men of the AFL

Three of the biggest and most successful defensive linemen developed by the American Football League have been Ernie Ladd (6ft.-5in., 313 pounds), Earl Faison (6ft.-5in., 265 pounds), and Buck Buchanan (6ft.-7in., 287 pounds).

With Ernie Ladd (left) at one tackle and Earl Faison (right) at the end, the San Diego Chargers had the nucleus of one of the greatest defensive lines ever put together on a football field.

Buck Buchanan (right) demonstrates (left) why he is regarded as one of the finest defensive linemen in the game. Here he smothers Green Bay quarterback Bart Starr during the 1967 Super Bowl Game.

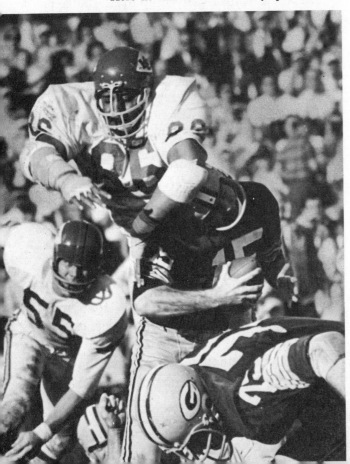

Ladd has led a stormy career both on the field and off. He put in some good years as defensive tackle for San Diego—when the Chargers were a championship team. With his immense strength and surprising agility, Ladd constantly kept the pressure on rival quarterbacks. "I don't believe I would have made it as a rookie if I wasn't big and strong," Ladd said later. "But I've become smart. The coaches show you the moves and techniques, but you have to do it yourself to learn. It took me years to learn how to execute the basic fundamentals without using brute force. I've picked up a few tricks. A guy that has to use brutality, I've got no use for him."

But Ernie, who played his college ball at Grambling College, has a temper and it has driven him to violent action, as when he ripped off Ed Husmann's helmet and began beating the Houston lineman over the head with it. Ladd also had trouble with the league because he had a beard and the AFL ruled that players couldn't wear them.

There were money troubles between San Diego and Ernie Ladd so the big lineman moved on to the Houston Oilers. And from there he was shuffled off to Kansas City. Though people have criticized his attitude, no one has ever denied that Ernie Ladd could hit —and play havoc with a rival's offense.

Faison, a defensive end with enormous strength, had his best years while teaming up with Ladd on that San Diego line. Charger coach Sid Gillman, who made the former Indiana University star his first draft choice, said of Earl: "They shouldn't ever run over Earl Faison. At his best he's the absolute best in the league. He's quick, strong, intelligent; he hits." A Charger teammate who had played against Faison in college described the experience this way: "Earl's got such fantastic balance. If you didn't hit him just right, I swear it was like hitting a tree."

Alvin Roy, who supervised the weight-lifting and isometric training of the Chargers,

said, "Faison has the potential to be the strongest man in the world. If Earl had started lifting weights at seventeen, the Russians would have had to give up the sport."

A brooding sort, Earl would admit that before a game, "I wake up very mean." Coach Gillman once said his All-AFL end hit with "sadistic zeal," and quarterbacks and running backs were painfully aware of it.

Earl suffered from knee trouble—it got to be both physical and mental—and his career of enormous potential was trimmed. But measured against almost anyone else on a football field, Earl could not be found lacking.

Buchanan was a raw young football player when he started out at Grambling College and he learned an immediate lesson from an upperclassman named Ernie Ladd. Ladd bowled Buck over once and Buchanan later admitted it was the first time anyone had ever done that to him. Buck devoted himself to becoming a better defensive tackle than his friend Ernie, and many say that he did, indeed, surpass Ladd.

Buck was Kansas City's top draft choice in 1962 and in four years developed into an All-AFL performer. He was always determined, always hustling. Chief coach Hank Stram recalls Buchanan's first day on the practice field: "We had heard all these reports on his speed, so we timed him in the 40-yard dash. He ran it in 4.9 seconds. We were amazed but he was disappointed; he asked to run it two more times."

Buck worked after practice and during the off-seasons to learn the fundamentals and a few tricks, and he made himself into a formidable defender against both the run and pass. Teams found they had to double- and triple-team him to keep the big guy away from their quarterbacks and running backs. Buck was certain he had arrived when the Chiefs played the Green Bay Packers in the 1966 Super Bowl. "He dominated Fuzzy Thurston [the Packers great offensive guard]," said Coach

Stram. "No question about it." Buck Buchanan had surely arrived.

"Deacon" Jones and the Fearsome Foursome

David is built like Goliath. He stands 6 ft.-5 in. and weighs 255. He is broad and square. He is also fast. He can run 50 yards in 5.6 seconds and 100 yards in 9.8 seconds. When he gets rolling, he is awesome, like a railroad train plummeting downhill. You would not want to get in his way. Yet people are paid to get in his way.

He is a football player. He is David Jones of the Los Angeles Rams and he is called "Deacon." Most times he says he doesn't remember why and when he began to be called Deacon. Sometimes he says it began when he led his college team in prayers. His opponents need the prayers; he is not saintly.

He has a small head and small, bright eyes, which give him an ominous expression. He looks mean and, on the football field, he is mean. Off the field, he is a gentle, good-natured man. He speaks with a soft, deep voice and he laughs a lot, his little bit of a mustache bobbing.

Though he does not laugh on the football field, he is often happy there. "If I can hit a man clean, but hard enough he has to be carried off the field, I'm happy," he says."

"He has more natural ability than any defensive player I've ever known," says Harland Svare, who once coached the Rams. "He is a finished player, a complete player, the best there is."

He played football at Mississippi Vocational and at South Carolina State and the training there was not superb. But after apprenticeship as a pro, he has learned a great deal. He and Willie Davis are the best defensive ends in football.

Cleveland's Frank Ryan rolled out to the opposite side of the field to avoid Jones in one game, but when he looked up he was down and Jones was on top of him. "Please," said Ryan, "admit you were hiding out here waiting for me all the time." Pittsburgh's speedy, 195-pound Marv Woodson once had the ball and a twenty-yard lead on Jones. Deacon hauled him down from behind. "Oh, no, baby," said Marv, "say it's not you." Said Deacon: "It's me, baby, it's me." Another time Jones caught up with Bobby Mitchell, then ran alongside the speedster for several yards before knocking him out of bounds. The Ram coaches asked why he hadn't stopped Mitchell immediately. Said Deacon: "I just wanted to see if I was as fast as he was."

With Deacon and Lamar Lundy (6 ft.-7 in., 260 pounds) at the ends and Merlin Olsen (6 ft.-5 in., 270 pounds, and the only white man on the line) and Roosevelt Grier (6 ft.-5 in., 290 pounds) at the tackles, the Rams developed the best front four in football. When an injury forced Grier out in 1967, big, 300-pound Roger Brown—an All-NFL tackle—was secured from Detroit to plug the hole. The group has been called "The Fearsome Foursome," and the fans love them.

"We are so tall that when we stand at the scrimmage line or go running in with our arms up, the quarterback needs a stepladder to see his receivers," Grier once said. "We are so heavy we would flatten a car if we climbed on the roof." Adds Jones: "And we are so fast that there is not enough room to get away from us."

Lundy, from Purdue, is a more cautious end than Jones, but he is still effective. Grier had an outstanding career with strong New York Giants teams, and is especially good in the pressure games. Brown has long been recognized as a first-rate pass-rusher.

Deacon Jones and his ample associates took the league by storm. When Jones talks about the reception he gets, he might as well be talking for all of them: "I don't look for fights, except on the football field. Guys run away

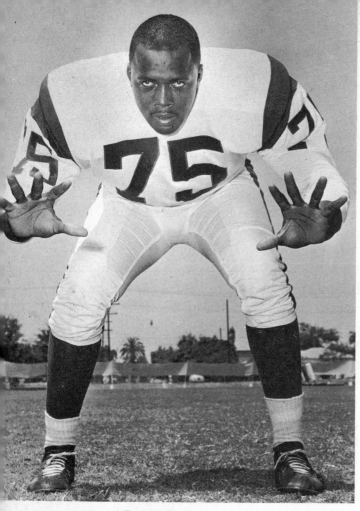

Deacon Jones

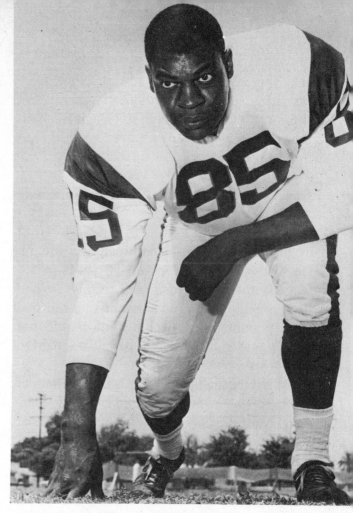

Lamar Lundy

Roosevelt Grier in action.

Roger Brown

from me there. Not the blockers. But the quarterbacks. But I catch them. Man, they're always running away from me. You'd think they were scared of me." The Fearsome Foursome put the league on the run.

Bobby Bell

The story goes that Bobby Bell, the 6 ft.-4 in., 228-pound Kansas City Chiefs linebacker, once raced a horse—and won. Afterward, Bell apologized: "I had a thirty-yard head start, and, besides, it was a poor horse." People around football accept the story as true because they look on Bell as some sort of physical marvel. "This guy," said teammate Buck Buchanan of Bobby, "is the best all-round football player I ever saw. He can throw eighty yards. He can center the ball back farther and more accurately than anyone in the business. He's the fastest runner you'll ever see (he could run fifty yards in 5.4 seconds). He can block. And he's the best defensive end, corner linebacker, or anything else defensively in the whole universe."

Bell has the quickness and strength to pour through on the quarterback and he has the agility to drop off on potential pass-receivers when that is necessary. Early, he showed what he could do as a linebacker by intercepting four passes in 1965. Too, Bell has that urge to hit, so essential to his job.

In high school Bobby was actually a quarterback. He got a scholarship to the University of Minnesota without anyone on the Gophers' staff ever seeing him play. They took him on the recommendation of the late Jim Tatum. Tatum was coaching North Carolina when he first saw Bell as a high school quarterback at Shelby, North Carolina. He couldn't recruit Bell because North Carolina was still segregated. But Tatum knew that at least forty colleges wanted him, including Notre Dame and Michigan State. Both were on North Carolina's schedule, while Minnesota wasn't. So Ta-

tum phoned Jim Camp, then the Minnesota backfield coach, and said, "I don't want any 225-pound quarterback wrecking my boys, and either Notre Dame or Michigan State will get this one. So why don't you take him?"

Camp called Shelby and asked to see movies of Bell, but nobody had ever taken any. He checked with about a dozen other coaches in the area, and every one of them raved about Bell. That was how Bell got the Minnesota scholarship. When Bobby reported to the Gopher varsity after his freshman year at quarterback, he was shifted to halfback, then to fullback by Murray Warmath. But Warmath needed a tackle more than anything else and Bobby became a top one. He made All-American at the position his junior and senior seasons, and won the Outland Trophy as the nation's best college lineman in 1962. He was drafted by both the Minnesota Vikings of the NFL and by the Chiefs, with whom he signed a contract.

When Bell joined the Chiefs, he made an immediate big impression. There are many things people said he might be—like a basketball player (he was the first Negro to play varsity basketball for Minnesota), a baseball player (scouts were interested in signing him out of high school), or a track star (track coach Jim Kelly, the 1956 Olympic team coach, said Bell could have been a point winner in the shot, discus, high jump, and middle-distance races). Instead, he chooses to be all-pro at backing up the Kansas City line.

Dave Robinson

As the Green Bay Packers built up one of the great dynasties in football history during the 1960's, Dave Robinson not only contributed to it but built up his own reputation as one of the strongest defensive players in the game. He played left linebacker and National Football League authorities rated him, year after year, the best in the league.

He stands 6ft.-3in. and weighs 240 pounds, yet with this size he moves like a cat. His reaction time is almost incredible. He can be fooled at the start of a play, yet react quickly enough to save it. And he has the champion's instinct of coming up with the big play at the crucial moment.

In December 1965, it was the Packers against Baltimore, the western division title on the line. With Green Bay ahead 14–13, and only one minute left in the first half, the Colts pushed to the Green Bay two-yard line. Gary Cuozzo went back to pass. Robinson was looking for the run, but then backtracked as he realized he was wrong. Cuozzo tried to loft the ball over him, but Dave snatched the pass and raced eighty-seven yards to the Colt 10. The Packers promptly scored, and now led, 21–13. "It was a fourteen-point play and the turning point," Packer coach Vince Lombardi said later. The Packers went on to crush Baltimore, 42–27, and took the western title.

A year later the Colts and Packers again were nose-to-nose for the western crown. With less than a minute to play and Green Bay ahead 14–10, Johnny Unitas passed the Colts to the Green Bay 23. On the next play Unitas faded to pass. But he did not throw. He ran up the middle. Unitas was hit and fumbled. There, at the right spot at the right time, was Robinson. He captured the ball and, in effect, another championship for Green Bay.

Glory by this time was nothing new for Dave Robinson. A native of Mount Holly, New Jersey, he starred in baseball, football and basketball in high school. Choosing Pennsylvania State University from a host of colleges which offered him scholarships, he played end on three fine teams and concluded with All-American ranking. And unlike many athletes who spend so much time competing in sports that they do not make the grades to finish college, Robinson left Penn State with an engineering degree. He is the kind of man to have around when the going is tough.

Herb Adderley and Willie Wood

Almost symbols of Green Bay Packer style, cornerback Herb Adderley and safetyman Willie Wood can be pushed just so far—and then, whoosh, they make the big play and rack up the other team again.

Take that first Super Bowl ever played, the one pitting Green Bay against the Kansas City Chiefs in 1966. The Chiefs surprisingly trailed only 14–10 at the half. People began to wonder if perhaps Kansas City could pull an upset. The Chiefs took the ball at the start of the second half and moved to their own forty-nine-yard line. It was third and five to go as quarterback Len Dawson dropped back to pass. In swooped Willie Wood, a little guy who grabbed the toss and sprinted to the Chiefs' five-yard line. Green Bay went in to score and the romp was on. Following the Packers' 35–10 victory, Kansas City coach Hank Stram said, "Wood's interception changed the personality of the game."

There was the game earlier that year when Baltimore receiver Jimmy Orr beat Adderley on a fifty-seven-yard pass play to set up a Colt field goal. The next time Colt quarterback Johnny Unitas threw to Orr, Adderley swiped the pass and returned it forty-two yards. The third time Unitas went to Orr, Herb intercepted and raced forty-two yards for the touchdown. For good measure, with the Colts down by three, 20–17, and on Green Bay's twenty-three with fifty-five seconds remaining, Herb recovered a Tom Matte fumble to preserve the Packers victory. "Adderley," said losing coach Don Shula after the game, "always comes up with the big play. Just look at his history."

The record shows that Adderley and Wood have combined nicely to terrorize the opposition. In 1962, for example, they intercepted sixteen passes between them—nine for Wood and seven for Adderley. Herb finished that year as the league's third-best kickoff-return man with a 27.9 average, and he took one 103

Poised for action, Green Bay's Dave Robinson (left) and Kansas City's Bobby Bell (right) wait for the ball carrier. Even on the bench between plays, both Robinson and Bell act like rookies—impatient to return to the field.

Herb Adderley

Willie Wood

Green Bay's Herb Adderley takes off downfield after intercepting a pass.

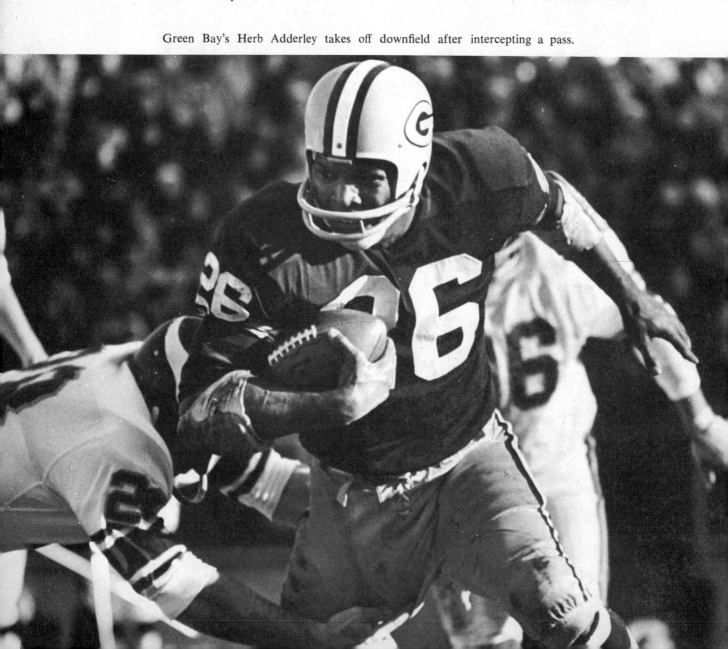

yards against the Colts. Wood was second in punt returns with an 11.9 average.

Both have won all-pro ranking, but each has taken a different road to get to the top. Adderley, 6 ft.-1 in. and 210 pounds, came to Green Bay in 1961 as the first draft choice and the Michigan State All-American was slated to become an offensive halfback. But he got hurt and when he came back, Green Bay decided to try him as a flanker. He did indifferently at that post, but late in the season got a chance at cornerback when Hank Gremminger was injured. That Thanksgiving against Detroit, Herb intercepted a pass that set up the winning touchdown and from then on he was a regular—and a guy who made the clutch plays.

Wood, at 5ft.-9in. and 190 pounds, is smaller than Adderley, but he seems just as exceptional roaming the Packer secondary. There was a time, however, when no one seemed to want him. After three years of quarterbacking at the University of Southern California, Wood was not drafted by the pros. But a friend wrote the Packers a letter, and Green Bay agreed to give Willie a tryout in 1960. In his first big chance, Willie saw Unitas throw two scoring passes over him and he figured he wouldn't last long with Green Bay. But the coaches and his teammates encouraged him, and his biggest thrill was coming back against Baltimore in a later game to intercept a Unitas pass and also return a punt for a seventy-two-yard touchdown. Wood was on his way, and it wasn't long before he and Adderley together were hard to beat.

Grambling College

In 1936, Dr. Ralph Waldo Emerson Jones took over six frame buildings, 120 students, and a pile of debts—and thus signalled the real beginning of Grambling College. Dr. Jones became president of the school, located 300 miles north of New Orleans, and more than thirty years later he was still president, but the school had changed significantly. Now the Grambling campus sprawls over 380 acres of Louisiana countryside and it accommodates 4,000 students. The buildings are of handsome colonial brick and Dr. Jones is particularly proud of his 70,000-volume library.

But what has brought the all-Negro college its greatest recognition has been the remarkable success in turning out scholar-athletes who have gone on to star in professional sports. Only a third of the students are male, and yet an impressive percentage of them have competed for Grambling and then signed up to play pro basketball or pro football.

Football coach Eddie Robinson trained such standouts as Willie Davis of the Green Bay Packers, Buck Buchanan and Ernie Ladd of the Kansas City Chiefs, Lane Howell of the Philadelphia Eagles, Willie Young of the New York Giants, and Rosey Taylor and Frank Cornish of the Chicago Bears. (President Jones also has served as coach to the football team; he occasionally still offers assistance.) Since 1948, more than sixty Grambling men have played pro football in the United States and Canada, and, in 1968, for example, twenty-two Grambling graduates reported to pro football training camps. Coach Robinson is considered a pioneer in getting Negro kids into pro football—especially boys from the all-Negro schools such as Florida A&M, Jackson State, Prairie View, Morgan State, Maryland State, Tennessee State and others. Both the boys and the sport have been better off for his efforts.

Proudly displaying the medals they won in the Decathlon event at the 1956 Melbourne games are Americans Rafer Johnson (second place), Milt Campbell (first place) and Russia's Vassii Kouznetsov (third place).

Arthur Ashe

High jumper John Thomas.

In the USA-USSR track meet at Kiev in 1965, America's Wyomia Tyus beats Russia's Lyudmila Symotesova across the finish line to win the 400-meter relay.

CHAPTER TEN

Breakthrough–Track, Tennis and Golf

IN the world of track and field, the names of Negro stars parade through the championship and record books. Negro athletes dominate the sprints, relays, hurdles, long jump, broad jump and triple jump. It is often an American Negro who is called "the world's fastest human."

It has long been this way. Track and field, an amateur sport, never openly barred Negroes as major professional sports did. Before World War I, Howard Drew was a star, and between the wars Eddie Tolan, Ralph Metcalfe, Dave Albritton and Jesse Owens were champions.

Since World War II, however, United States Olympic teams would have been hollow shells without Negroes. The Olympic Games of 1948 in London and 1952 in Helsinki were the games of Harrison Dillard and Mal Whitfield; the 1956 games produced Milt Campbell; the 1960 games, Otis Davis, Ralph Boston and Rafer Johnson; and the 1964 games, Hayes Jones, Henry Carr and Bob Hayes, among many others.

In this area, Negro women also have produced superlative performances—for example, Wilma Rudolph at Rome in 1960 and Wyomia Tyus and Edith McGuire at Tokyo in 1964. There is no end in sight, not with performers like Jim Green, Jim Hines, Tommie Smith and many more battling for success.

By contrast with track and field, tennis and golf are two sports in which amateurs have always been significant, but not Negro amateurs. For these are "country club" sports, and Negroes have rarely been welcomed to compete at these sites. Young Negro men and women did not benefit from the caliber of coaching and competition that white performers had and thus could not raise their performances to competitive levels. Still, a start has been made—by Charley Sifford and Lee Elder in golf, Althea Gibson and Arthur Ashe in tennis. There is reason to believe that other outstanding Negro performers are on their way up.

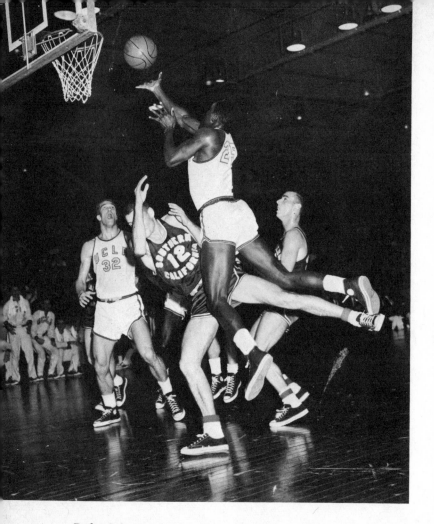

Rafer Johnson, holder of the world Decathlon record, is an all-round athlete. Whether he's driving for a lay-up, putting the shot or running the 100-meter dash, he's a tough man to beat.

...g every ounce of strength in his body, Rafer ...s the discus during the Decathlon event in Rome.

Russia's Vassii Kouznetsov leads Rafer Johnson into the final lap of the men's Decathlon 1500-meter event during the 1958 Track and Field Meet in Moscow.

Leonid Khomenkov, track and field chairman for the Moscow Meet, presents Johnson with the Gold Medal.

Rafer Johnson

When Rafer Johnson attended Kingsburg High School in California's San Joaquin Valley, he was a star halfback on the football team and an exceptional basketball player. During his junior year he tried baseball, played center field and batted .512. His football prowess earned him a scholarship to University of California at Los Angeles, but he decided not to play football so as not to risk an injury that might hurt his track career. Even then he had the desire to qualify for the U.S. Olympic team.

A few years later, Rafer was considered by many to be the best athlete in the United States, if not in the world. In 1956, he represented the United States in the Olympics in the decathlon and, in fact, was favored to win the gold medal. He finished second to Milt Campbell, however, and doggedly set his sights on a gold medal in the 1960 games. Then a determined Rafe swept by all the competition and finished with the previously unheard-of total of 8,392 points.

If any single nation was not surprised by his victory, it was Russia. In August 1958, he had set a world decathlon record of 8,302 points in the "Little Olympics" in Moscow when he defeated the USSR's "man of steel," Vasily Kuznetsov, by 505 points. During the course of that meet, the Russian had leaped ahead in the high jump and broad jump. On the final day, Johnson set a new decathlon discus mark of nearly 161 feet, whipped the javelin 238 feet and vaulted almost 13 feet. He also ran the 400-meter race in an impressive 48.2 seconds.

When the Russians were told that the world record had gone back to the Americans, there were no excuses offered. They held the new champion in the highest esteem. They respected Johnson as a man, too, because he has always carried himself "with invincible humility," as one viewer put it.

Like many great athletes, Johnson is an exceptional performer in events outside his field of specialization. In a 1956 triangular meet, he ran the hurdles in 22.7 seconds, the nation's fastest collegiate time of the season, and only half a second off the world's record then held by Dave Sime. His high hurdle best time was 13.8 seconds, .2 of a second off the NCAA mark at the time. In the 1956 Olympic trials, he also made the team as a broad jumper, at 25 feet-5¾ inches.

Rafer does many other things well. He had almost an A average at UCLA, was president of the student body, starred in basketball, was the first Negro to pledge a white fraternity and headed three campus honorary societies. He also toured Africa, Australia and Europe for the State Department, was a baritone in two church choirs, and served on California's State Recreation Commission.

All these activities were somehow squeezed in between track workouts. The sport was more than just exercise to Johnson; it was a way of expression. He said that everyone is equal when he starts out, but once actual competition begins, the sense of equality disappears. Never in the history of track and field had there been an all-round performer equal to him. In Moscow, for example, competing in the decathlon—ten strenuous events in two days, with almost no time to prime himself for each separate event—Rafer performed so magnificently that, had he been in the 1908 Olympic Games, seven of his ten marks would have taken first place in individual events.

With the close of his athletic career, Johnson became a sportscaster on the West Coast and also was involved in politics. He was at the side of Robert F. Kennedy when the senator was assassinated in June of 1968 and helped apprehend the suspect.

It is clear that Rafer Johnson is more than just one of the greatest athletes of his time. He has proved himself to be a human being of surpassing quality.

Milt Campbell

Swift and powerful, Milt Campbell was one of the most precocious and versatile athletes the country has ever had. Track, football, swimming, wrestling—name it, and Milt could do it with surpassing skill. He could have gone in many directions, but became an international celebrity by demonstrating his all-round track-and-field skills to the world—and he did it before he had even reached college.

Prior to the 1952 Olympic Games, Milt had built up a reputation as one of the finest high school athletes in the nation. Everyone seemed to know about the kid from Plainfield, New Jersey. Then one day his track coach saw an article in a newspaper comparing the track records of Bob Mathias and Jim Thorpe, and felt that Campbell was better than either of them. It was decided to train Milt for the decathlon at the 1952 Olympics in Helsinki. Milt had previously competed in the high jump, sprints, hurdles and shot put, but knew nothing about the pole vault, broad jump, discus, javelin, or 400- and 1,500-meter runs—which are also included in the decathlon.

The training was no secret project since the town had to send Campbell and coach Hal Bruguiere to the West Coast for the tryouts. The community raised $1,500 to cover expenses. Despite the national publicity about the eighteen-year-old Campbell and how his town was behind him, few track experts believed he had enough experience and versatility to make the squad. But he amazed the skeptics by qualifying for the decathlon with a point total second only to that of Bob Mathias—and for good measure he made the final tryouts in the hurdles and the 100-meter dash.

In the actual Olympic contests Campbell further shocked the observers by finishing second, again to Mathias. He returned home to a welcome that would be fitting for any conquering hero.

In 1956, in Melbourne, Milt was again the underdog. The predictions were that he had a chance to finish third. Rafer Johnson of UCLA, the point record holder in the event, was the strong favorite. But Milt beat the field in the 110-meter hurdles, 100-meter dash and the shot put, and almost had the world record until he came to the pole vault, where he cleared only 11 feet-2 inches. Still, his 7,937 points were 350 ahead of Johnson and exceeded Mathias' Olympic record by fifty points. Right after he had tucked away his gold medal, Milt said that he was through with the decathlon. He did not go back on that promise to himself.

Had he not devoted his training strictly to excelling in the Olympics, it is possible that Milt could have been one of the greatest in several other sports. In high school football in Plainfield, for example, he scored a total of 140 points in nine games, leading all New Jersey schoolboys in scoring. On one occasion he offered to substitute for the heavyweight wrestler who had become ill. The opponent, who was later to become the state champion, was pinned by Campbell in a minute and a half. He was on his high school swimming team but quit to spend all his time on track. But after avoiding a pool for a year, he competed in one meet in the 40-yard free style and tied a seventeen-year-old pool record of 19.6 seconds. He was also known to drive a golf ball 300 yards.

Milt accepted a college scholarship to Indiana University where he became a football regular and, of course, a track star. When he had completed his intercollegiate career, he signed with the Cleveland Browns. His pro football career was disappointing. The Browns used him effectively to return punts and kickoffs, but Milt had trouble adapting himself to the complex maneuvers of the modern pro sport. Thus he was deprived of the big money professional sports would have meant. But in the amateur world of sports, where he represented his country, the name of Milt Campbell holds a permanent place of honor.

With muscles straining and spikes flying, Milt Campbell runs with Australia's Ian Bruce during the Decathlon 1500-meter event in 1956. After finishing the race, Campbell clinched the Gold Medal for the United States.

Always concentrating on his upcoming performance, Ralph Boston displays the form that cleared over 27 feet in a track meet with Russia in 1961.

Utilizing his jumping ability, Boston (second from right) clears the last hurdle and sprints to the finish line to win the 60-yard high hurdles event in the Athens International Indoor Track Meet in 1967.

Ralph Boston

Jesse Owens and Ralph Boston are separated in age but united by the fact that they are two of history's greatest broad jumpers. One summer night during the 1960 Olympics in Rome, Owens, the old master, sat down with the young Boston for a heart-to-heart talk.

Ralph told Jesse that he wanted to win the broad jump very badly, but felt guilty about going after Owens' record. He especially admired Jesse's brilliant performance in 1936, when Jesse showed such poise and skill in Berlin, while Hitler and a tense world looked on.

Owens, who had jumped 26 feet-5⁵⁄₁₆ inches in the 1936 Games, replied that the record had served its purpose at the time. Now— in 1960 —the times were different and Boston had an obligation to go out and do his best.

The next day, in the Stadio Olimpico, Ralph fairly flew. Twice he jumped over twenty-six feet, but neither leap broke the record. Ralph was standing near the track just prior to his third try when George Brown, a 1952 Olympian, told him he was not jumping high enough. Boston shed his flannel sweat clothes and got ready to jump. As he walked over to his starting point, he saw Brown place a piece of white paper at the side of the pit far enough from the spring board to match the record. Now Ralph was ready. The eyes of the international crowd, attempting to sift every bit of excitement from the vast panorama, were directed to him by the PA announcer.

Boston gulped in all the air his lungs would hold and heaved his taut-muscled shoulders. Then he took off. His skinny legs pumped high, knees nearly to his chest, and as he approached the pit, he reached top speed. His left foot slammed the board and he left the ground, but his legs kept pumping. His arms reached skyward, he took three and one-half airy steps, then stretched his legs out almost parallel with the ground. Finally, the landing, with his heels no more than six inches apart, burrowed into the sand. And with a final lunge, Boston fell forward onto the canvas padding at the end of the pit.

The piece of white paper lay well behind him as he sprang up and brushed away the sand sticking to his sweaty skin. The officials huddled near the pit area, measuring and re-measuring the distance as Boston jogged around the field waiting for the decision. And then it came: 26 feet-7¾ inches, an Olympic record.

In Laurel, Mississippi, a few hours later, Mrs. Eulalia Boston received the news of the victory of the "baby" of the family, the youngest of ten children. It was quite a victory for Mrs. Boston, too, for she remembered the years she had spent as a housemaid, struggling so that her children could go to college.

As for Ralph, it was the culmination of years of work. In 1954, at the age of fifteen, he had begun improving his personal record by a foot a year. He started at 20-10 and reached a peak in August 1961, in Moscow, when he jumped 27 feet-1¾ inches, to set a new world record.

Unbeaten until the fall of 1961, when an injury threw him off, Ralph never regained his peak form. In the 1964 Olympics at Tokyo he was still favored, but he finished a disappointing second to a British jumper who had never done as well as Ralph, before or after. Still he kept competing, armed with an iron determination. And never to be forgotten was that golden moment in Rome.

John Thomas

The first time John Thomas cleared a high-jump bar at seven feet, he touched off a hot controversy in track-and-field history. His seven-foot leap, the first ever achieved indoors, failed to get into the record books because of an oversight by the officials, and everybody was concerned except John Thomas.

John Thomas shows the technique that made him known as one of the greatest high jumpers in the world.

It happened at the 1959 Millrose Games in Madison Square Garden, New York. All high jumpers except Thomas, then a seventeen-year-old Boston University freshman, and Charlie Dumas, then the world record holder, had been eliminated. The bar was placed at seven feet, measured by officials and then cleared by Thomas. For a moment there was complete silence in the Garden, and then an ear-splitting roar. There was a rush for Thomas as many of those gathered on the infield of the track scrambled to shake his hand. Then, as Dumas prepared to jump, everyone grew quiet. Charlie hit the bar, knocked it over and all of a sudden everyone realized that the officials had not measured the height after Thomas' first jump.

According to regulations, a bar must be measured after a man clears it or the leap cannot go into the record book. The officials were taken to task in the nation's newspapers for their mistake.

Thomas got everybody off the hook two weeks later in the New York Athletic Club games. And that time, the bar was properly measured. After that, John Thomas cleared seven feet so frequently that it was no longer news. He went over 7 feet-2 inches twice during the 1960 indoor season.

Thomas had known defeat only through other people. From the last day of January 1959 until the first day of September 1960, he outclassed every high-jump rival. He competed with infinite grace, seemingly without effort, apparently without nervousness. In seven lengthening strides, strong and sure, he approached the bar from a 37-degree angle. He soared upward with matchless spring while using the orthodox straddle roll.

Thomas reached the height of his skill during the trials for the 1960 U.S. Olympic team when, under extreme pressure, he jumped, without a miss, 7 feet, 7 feet-1¼ inches, 7-feet-2½ inches and, finally, 7 feet-3¾ inches, a world record. John was considered the safest bet America had for a gold medal. During practice, he soared over seven feet with monotonous regularity.

On September 1 the competition started. Thomas went 7 feet-¼ inch, no higher. Robert Shavlakadze and Valeri Brumel, both Russians, finished higher and John had to settle for a bronze medal in his first taste of defeat.

In December 1960, John resumed indoor competition. He regained his old form and soared to 7 feet-3 inches, a personal high. Then Brumel came to the United States to participate in a series of meets. Thomas lost in each competition, with his jumps getting lower and lower.

John Thomas was a superb athlete, gifted with strength and stamina and agility. No high jumper in history had set so many records or leaped so high, so often. Yet today all his brilliant accomplishments—his victories, his records—seem shaded by defeat.

Apparently, something inside Thomas had crumbled after the Olympic defeat. But throughout the series of disappointments, he never made excuses. He just kept jumping—doing what he loved—always with the inner satisfaction of knowing that he once was the best jumper in the world.

Harrison Dillard

In a track coach's book, Harrison Dillard should have failed. At 5ft.-10in. and only 152 pounds, he was much shorter and lighter than other top hurdlers. But these other top hurdlers had one major problem: they couldn't catch him at the finish line.

Smashing meet records and world hurdling marks, the slim Baldwin-Wallace College (Ohio) ace astounded track buffs in the late 1940's. Sure, the experts conceded, Dillard had speed and form, but the best high hurdlers of the times, Fred Walcott and Forrest Towns, towered over six feet.

Harrison Dillard, former Baldwin Wallace track star and 1948 100-meter Olympic dash champion, clears the final hurdle to win his seventh straight 45-yard high hurdles crown at the annual K. of C. track meet in Cleveland in 1952.

Harrison Dillard, shy and hardly affected by his fame, kept one eye on the 1948 Olympics. He vowed that nothing would stop him from winning a spot on the U.S. team. Though pressured to compete at every major meet in the country, Dillard never lost his poise. He made each move like a champion. In one meet in 1946 he churned over the low barriers for 220 yards on a straightaway to tie the world mark of 22.5 seconds. Later, on a 220-yard, one-curve course, he set another record of 23 seconds flat.

Dillard could run the 100-yard dash in 9.6 and was considered to have the fastest leg whip in hurdling. Surprisingly, he took a high hurdle in 13 feet, while most other—and taller—hurdlers cleared the barrier in 10½ feet.

As public interest mounted in the United States prior to the 1948 Games, sportswriters and broadcasters repeated over and over that America was sure of winning at least one gold medal—in the high hurdles, because it could rely on Harrison "Bones" Dillard. He was alone in his field. No one could touch him. In fact, he was unbeaten in eighty-three straight meets covering a two-and-one-half-year span.

But in the Olympic trials Dillard overstrode, hit the second hurdle, stumbled, draped himself over the last hurdle, and finished last. A man who knew only victory had been shut out of his specialty. In apparent defeat Dillard demonstrated the heart and drive of a champion. He walked across the track to where the sprints were starting and entered himself in the race. Straining mightily, he beat Ed Conwell by a quarter-inch for third place and made the Olympic team in an event he seldom ran.

On July 31, in London's Wembley Stadium, the twenty-five-year-old speedster flew over the 100-meter dash in 10.3 seconds, equaling the record that had been set by Eddie Tolan in 1932. He sprinkled dust in the eyes of the world's fastest sprinters and won an Olympic victory that stunned track-and-field experts throughout the world.

A crowd of 83,000 people saw Dillard win the first gold medal for an American track-and-field competitor in the 1948 Olympics. Then came four years of waiting and working. In the 1952 Olympics he won another gold medal—in his own high hurdles.

Hayes Jones

The first time Hayes Jones ran the 120-yard high-hurdle course, he tied a record despite knocking down each of the ten hurdles in his lane. Three years later, Jones was beating such notable hurdlers as Lee Calhoun (the Olympic champion) indoors and was recording times just over the world record outdoors.

He had been a sophomore in high school at the time of his record-tying performance; he was a college freshman when he began beating Calhoun and all other hurdlers indoors. By 1963, he was still beating everyone indoors, having tied or broken all four of the major indoor hurdles records.

One of his major personal goals was to win a gold medal in the Olympics. Although that might not seem too difficult for a man of his talent, Hayes had to work harder than most hurdlers because of his physical size and weight. At 5 ft.-10 in. and 160 pounds, he didn't have the classic build of a hurdler and had to depend on speed and stamina. Hayes didn't have to worry about natural quickness since he had been timed in 9.4 seconds in the 100-yard dash. But stamina was always a problem. Throughout his career, he kept to a vigorous training schedule to build up his endurance.

Hayes had other physical problems, too. His eyes were so weak he could hardly see past the first hurdle when he was in the blocks. And his right leg was three-quarters of an inch shorter than his left leg. His worst handicap, though, was a disease that he called the "case of the wandering eye." Hayes said it bothered him only outdoors, in the longer races.

Using a powerful leap, Hayes Jones clears the final hurdle (above) and prepares to make a sprint for the finish line (below). Jones won the event, with William Johnson placing second and Russell Rogers third.

Twice in the Los Angeles Coliseum, Hayes had shot out of the blocks in his patented perfect start. He would have the lead, and then Calhoun would start to catch up. Anxious, Hayes would turn his head slightly to catch a glimpse of Calhoun and that would slow him down just enough to cost him the race.

In 1960, Jones had his chance to win the gold medal in the Olympics. But Calhoun was still there, and Hayes finished a disappointed third for a bronze medal.

Calhoun retired in 1961, Hayes' first year out of college. That season, Hayes, well rested, won the Amateur Athletic Union's outdoor title at New York City and made a clean sweep of the hurdles in the United States' dual meets against the Russians, the Poles, the Germans and the British. He beat everyone to the tape by at least a yard.

Then, it was on to the 1964 Olympics in Tokyo. Once more Hayes lined up for the finals of the 110-meter high hurdles. Once more this man, who had been so invincible in indoor meets and sometimes disappointing outdoors, had his chance to win a gold medal.

The race began and Jones was running well, clearing hurdles faultlessly, running with speed and rhythm between hurdles. He was inches in front of his U.S. teammate, Blaine Lindgren, but as they hit the eighth hurdle he lost the inches. Lindgren and Jones were abreast going to the ninth hurdle and, as they went over it, Lindgren went up a bit high and came down a bit off balance. When the two hit the tape, no one knew who had won. The judges studied the photo-finish picture and the electric timer for a full half-hour before awarding Jones the gold medal in 13.6 seconds and Lindgren the silver for second place.

With his dream achieved, Hayes Jones retired from competition. But that athletic experience and recognition had given him the foundation for a career of service. He went back to Detroit, his home town, where he became a public relations official for American Airlines and an active worker for the city's youth. After the riot of 1967, Jones was appointed chairman of the athletic division of the New Detroit Committee, which had as its goal better and more understanding treatment for all of its citizens.

Jones' work drew national attention. Near the end of 1967, Mayor John Lindsay invited him to New York City and appointed him the city's first Commissioner of Recreation, with responsibility for all recreation facilities of the nation's largest metropolis. It seems clear that Hayes Jones' career in sports, and his role as a leader of his race, are far from over.

Henry Carr

In the 1960 Olympics in Rome, one of the major disappointments was the failure of the United States to retain its supremacy in the sprints and the relays. In the 1964 Games in Tokyo, the United States regained this supremacy, thanks to the achievements of Henry Carr and Bob Hayes. Carr set an Olympic record by racing the 200 meters in 20.2, and then starred in the relays with Hayes as the United States won both the 400-meter and 1,600-meter relays in the record times of 39 seconds and 3 minutes, .7 seconds, respectively.

Like Hayes, Carr's early days were spent in poverty. Henry lived with his mother in an upstairs flat in Detroit, where only a few of the twelve Carr children lived together. In the ninth grade he joined the track team at Southwestern High School so that he could get off the streets and not be lured into "borrowing" trinkets from local stores. He didn't win anything, but grew to love track. He worked especially hard in the hope that his ability would someday provide a future for him.

By the time his family moved across town, Henry had become a proficient runner, and he continued his track career at Northwestern High School, where he also began playing football and basketball. It was during his two years

International Olympic Committee Chairman Avery Brundage congratulates Ollan Cassell of the U.S. as he presents Gold Medals to the team that won the men's 400-meter relay in Tokyo. Other members of the team are (from left to right) Michael Larrabee, Ulis Williams and Henry Carr (also above left).

Henry Carr applies the final kick as he moves out ahead to win the 200-meter dash in a 1964 meet with Russia. Teammate Paul Drayton finished second, and Russia's Boris Zubov took third.

at Northwestern that Henry started to mature as an athlete.

On May 18, 1961, Carr established himself as one of the great runners in the country, even though he was still a senior in high school. In a meet against Henry Ford High School, Carr ran the 100 yards in 9.4 seconds to tie the national interscholastic record set by Jesse Owens in 1933. Then he dazzled everyone by running the 220 yards in 20 seconds flat, equalling the world record. Unfortunately, since no one had expected such performances, and no wind gauge had been brought along, neither mark went into the books.

Now Carr had a name and he won a scholarship to Arizona State. He was eligible to compete in his freshman year and was almost an instant success. Carr shattered meet records in the 220, his best event, and even in the 100-yard dashes almost everywhere he went. He teamed up with three other speedsters—Ulis Williams, Mike Barrick and Ron Freeman—and together they formed the most feared mile-relay team in the country.

Going into the Tokyo Olympics, Henry was recognized as the world's fastest human in the 220-yard and 200-meter sprints. Straightaway or around a curve, he was considered just about unbeatable. He became the world's record holder in both events, running the 220 in 20.3 seconds and the 200 in 20.2 seconds. He had beaten the Russians in the 100 meters. He had been a three-sport star in high school. He had accomplished nearly everything he had attempted in sports.

Following his success in the Tokyo Games, Carr decided to try out for professional football and signed with the New York Giants. Unlike many other sprinters who have tried the game, Carr, at 6ft.-3in. and 190 pounds, had the size. He remained with the Giants as a defensive back until the end of the 1967 season when he was traded to the Baltimore Colts. Whatever his accomplishments in football, however, Henry Carr will be remembered as one of the great sprinters of his time.

Otis Davis

The Olympic Games of 1960 did not go well for the United States, especially in track and field. In all the races from 100 meters to 10,000 meters and the marathon, the Americans won only one gold medal—in the 400 meters. It was a surprise that the United States won that race at all, but an even bigger surprise was the man who won it. That American was Otis Davis and his triumph was one of the most thrilling of the games.

The setting was a clear Rome afternoon. The favorite was a German, Carl Kaufman, and a threat was the fine Indian runner, Milka Singh. Otis Davis was an outside choice, but he sprinted to an early lead and held it until past the 200-meter mark. Then he appeared to tire and the field came at him. First one runner, then a second and a third passed him, with Kaufman moving to the front. Davis was clearly out of contention.

Then, all of a sudden, he wasn't. He chased Kaufman, closing the distance as the field came down the straightaway. Davis burst to the front ten strides from the finish, but still the race was not over. Now Kaufman rallied and the two men, the blond German and the black American, hit the finish tape at almost the same instant.

There was no immediate way to tell who had won. Men in the press box looking down on the finish line argued with each other. Excruciating minutes went by while officials waited for the finish picture to be developed and to study it. Otis Davis sat by a railing, absolutely worn out—having run the race of his life. His shoulders heaved and he had not the strength to put on his sweatshirt.

Then came the announcement: first, Davis, USA. The pictures separated the men by a single inch. The winning time: 44.9 seconds, a new Olympic and world record.

Someone rushed to tell him. At first he just looked up wonderingly. Then the reality of this moment he had waited for all his life hit him.

Otis Davis (second from the left) wins the 400-meter run in the 1960 Games at Rome.

Tommie Smith of San Jose wins the 200-meter dash in 20.2 seconds. Jim Hines (right) of Oakland was second in this 1967 U.S.–British Commonwealth Meet.

He leaped up, began to jump up and down, again and again. Then he ran in circles, waving his sweatshirt, throwing it in the air, saluting the crowd which was giving him a momentous cheer. Finally, he raced around the track again in an Olympic salute lap. Then he went to the podium; the band played the "Star-Spangled Banner" and Otis received his gold medal.

Otis had thought his dream of a gold medal was impossible. He was then twenty-eight years old—much too old, everyone thought, to be a world champion. But he had made it.

Until those Olympics, Otis had been a fine runner for years but never an outstanding one. He was long and lean; he worked and trained hard; he made the most of his abilities. But he did not compete much in athletics. He was a good student and a good school teacher.

Now he had achieved his dream. Except for a few exhibitions, he did not compete again. He returned to the classroom—a champion.

Bob Hayes

With his powerful legs, broad shoulders and trim waist, Bob Hayes was hardly the picture of a track star when he went to Tokyo in 1964 as a member of the U.S. Olympic team. He would bolt down the track—a tangle of arms and legs—with the grace of a man falling off a horse. But he did bolt.

Before the Olympics, he had lost only two races (one in which he ran despite a 103-degree temperature) and he held three world records—in the 60-yard indoor dash (5.9 seconds), the 70-yard indoor dash (6.9 seconds) and the 100-yard dash (9.1 seconds).

In Tokyo, the youngster from Florida A&M was almost unbelievable. An infamously poor starter, Hayes won the 100-meter semifinal in 9.9 seconds, pure fantasy for the judges who disallowed it because of an aiding wind. Unperturbed, Hayes stepped out and won the final in 10 seconds flat. He was even more amazing in the 400-meter relay. At the final exchange of the baton, France's Jocelyn Delacour had a four-yard lead. Hayes was sixth. No one is quite prepared to describe what happened next, except that Hayes won by three yards.

Track immortal Jesse Owens watched from the press box that day, and his description of Hayes' running style was prophetic: "He looks like a guy catching a ball in back of the line of scrimmage and dodging people." By the Fall of 1965, Bob Hayes was doing just that—and doing it with astonishing skill for the Dallas Cowboys of the National Football League.

Hayes had grown up in a tough section of Jacksonville, Florida. His father, a disabled war veteran, and his mother, a domestic worker, were separated. Hayes was close to his mother. "She says I was a lazy baby," he says, grinning, "and the slowest dishwasher in northern Florida." He shined shoes to earn money for school clothes, and his first competition was running for nickels.

His brother Ernest wanted to be a boxer, and Bob apparently wanted to be a punching bag. He needed to prove himself even then. "I'd fight and fight," Bob says, "but I never had the strength to knock no one down. But I got up every time and fought some more." Hayes would later tell Jake Gaither, his football coach at Florida A&M, "I got my kicks from football. I like to see a guy get hit hard and get up and try again. That proves he is a man."

Bob went to Florida A&M on a football scholarship, and the coaches there realized they had something special when an assistant coach noticed Hayes sprinting by such swift players as Bob Paramore and Hewitt Dixon (who both became professional football players). They stopped practice to scold the two upperclassmen. "Coach," said Dixon, "I never ran faster in my life."

"I ran 9.3 as a freshman," says Hayes. "That's when I first realized the Olympic were

Bob Hayes receives some advice from Jesse Owens before running in a qualifying event for the Tokyo Games. The advice was apparently well heeded as Hayes tied the world record of 10 seconds flat in the 100-meter dash at Tokyo to bring home a Gold Medal.

In a preliminary heat for the 100-meter dash, Hayes breaks the tape ahead of Venezuela's Aruimedes Herrera and Germany's Heinz Schumann.

four years away." And Hayes pointed for the Games and made his reputation as a sprinter, not as a football player.

There were, therefore, doubts when Bob reported to the Dallas Cowboys—doubts that he could take the physical pounding (although he is a sturdy 5ft.-11in. and 185 pounds), that he could hold passes in heavy traffic, that he could maneuver upfield in anything but a fast, straight line.

When the 1965 season drew to a close, people weren't doubting Bob Hayes any longer. He had been the top offensive player for an explosive Dallas club. He had scored 13 touchdowns, had caught 46 passes for 1,003 yards and had led the league with an average of 21.8 yards per reception.

In 1966, the defenses were rigged to stop him, but Bob poured it on for 64 receptions, 1,232 yards and 13 touchdowns. In 1967, he caught 49 passes for 998 yards and 10 touchdowns. He averaged 20.4 yards per catch.

Tommie Smith

During one period in the spring of his senior year at San Jose State College in California, Tommie Smith turned in some of the finest running in track history. First, he ran an anchor leg of 19.6 seconds in leading his school's 880-yard relay team to a world record time of 1 minute, 22.1 seconds. A week later, he himself set a world record of 44.5 seconds in the 440-yard dash.

Tommie is a slow starter, but this does not seem to detract from his record-breaking performances. In May 1966, he set his sights on the oldest records in the books—the 200 meters and 220 yards on a straightaway. Tommie went after both records in a minor meet at the San Jose State campus. Overcoming a slow start, he surged into the lead at seventy-five yards and began to stretch out, flashing across the finish line with a 19.5 clocking for the 220 yards.

Smith admits he could not be a successful distance runner. He can punish himself for the quick bursts, but doesn't have the temperament for the pain and agony of distance events. As he runs, he pumps his knees up high, yet his stride is a half-foot longer than that of most other sprinters and lengthens even more toward the finish. Most sprinters explode in a tangle of churning arms and legs, but Smith glides so smoothly his times are surprising. He shifts into higher speeds with what has been called his "Tommie-jet gear" so that one track expert has said he seems to have three gears where other sprinters are stuck with two.

Tommie was born on June 12, 1944, in Acworth, Texas, the seventh of twelve children of a poor farmer. When he was six, the family moved to Lemoore, a small city thirty miles from Fresno in northern California. Since several of the Smiths were athletically inclined, Tommie had a natural interest in sports. In high school he was good in basketball and a breakaway runner in football. However, he gave up basketball after his freshman year at San Jose and never did play football in college. When he is finished with track, Tommie may ultimately try to make pro football a career.

Tommie realizes that fame in sports comes only through hard work, and he is putting in the time to prove his worth. He knows that one cannot be the best for very long, but he wants to make the most of his time on top.

Mal Whitfield

In the late 1940's, Mal Whitfield worked diligently to establish his credentials as a world-class track star. Touring South America under the colors of the U.S. Air Force in 1947, and also taking part in the Pan-American Games that summer, he impressed many track enthusiasts below the Equator by running the 400 meters in 46 seconds.

The next year provided him with the perfect international showcase. It was time for the

Mal Whitfield breaks the tape
to win the 400-meter race
of the 1951 Pan-American
Games at Buenos Aires.
Whitfield, who earlier had won
the 800-meter run, was clocked
at 47.8 seconds, beating
teammate Hugh Maiocco.

1948 Olympic Games and Mal rose to the challenge. In perhaps the greatest individual performance since that of Jesse Owens in the 1936 Games, Mal set a new Olympic record in the 800-meter race by clocking in at 1 minute and 49.2 seconds; ran anchor in the victorious 1,600-meter relay; and took third in the 400 meters. When they added up the points, Whitfield had the highest individual total of the 1948 Games.

But it wasn't always the glamor of track and medals and college life for Mal. There was a time when he saved for months to buy his first pair of shoes. His father, a fairly prosperous truck driver in Los Angeles, died when he was only four, and his mother, brother and sister had to go to work to insure the family's survival.

Mal's mother worked in the movie studios, his sister Betty in a drugstore. His brother Bob held a part-time job in a service station while school was in session and worked full-time during vacations. As soon as Mal was old enough, he sold papers and later became a delivery boy and a clerk in a drugstore.

When Mal was seventeen, his mother died of heart failure. Mal continued the running he had begun years before, starting first in the neighborhood and then in the playgrounds and parks around East Los Angeles. He also competed at the 49th Street Public School, where he was the champion in the high jump and the 100-yard dash. In junior high he became a quarter- and half-miler and won the city championships in both events.

As news of his victories spread, scholarship offers began to pour in. Mal, however, had decided to go to Ohio State. He was impressed by the fact that this was the school that had nurtured Jesse Owens, and he looked forward to running for coach Larry Snyder, considered one of the nation's outstanding track tutors.

There was a slight delay in enrollment at OSU. World War II was in progress and the day after graduation in 1943, Mal decided to enlist in the Army Air Force. Before he was shipped overseas, however, the war ended and Whitfield's outfit was transferred to Lockbourne Air Base. It was a lucky break for him because the base was located in Columbus, Ohio, the home of Ohio State.

Mal, therefore, attended Ohio State while he was in the Air Force and, under the wartime rules, was permitted to compete in varsity events during his freshman year. From there he went on to the 1948 Olympics and later to the 1952 Olympics. In 1952, he again won the 800-meter race in the identical 1 minute, 49.2 seconds. He has the distinction of being one of very few athletes ever to win his specialty at two successive Olympic competitions.

Wilma Rudolph

The 1960 Olympics in Rome provided major disappointments for American sports enthusiasts who had traveled there to see the United States earn gold medals. They were shocked when the great John Thomas was beaten by two Russians in the high jump, and were equally stunned when the Americans lost the 100-meter dash to a German.

But just as totally unexpected were the magnificent performances of one member of the United States Olympic team, and a young lady at that. Wilma Rudolph proved conclusively that she was the fastest woman runner in the world.

As she came out with the other four finalists for the 100-meter dash, there was a hushed expectancy over the Olympic stadium. Wilma had previously astounded people with her clockings in the preliminary heats and the enormous crowd had gathered to see the marvel from America. The starter, in his orange jacket and white straw hat, raised his gun and the girls went down on their marks. The gun barked and they shot off the blocks, with Wilma flying ahead immediately. She lengthened her lead with almost every stride until it was Wilma Rudolph all alone and the other girls fighting for second place. With her arms pumping in classic style, her long strides eating up ground, Wilma sped the 100 meters at least three full yards ahead of the field.

It was her first Olympic gold medal, but not her last. She repeated her performance in the 200 meters when she set an Olympic record of 23.2 seconds and won again by three yards. Then, running with three of her Tigerbelle teammates from Tennessee State, Wilma anchored the winning 400-meter relay team and became the first American girl ever to win three gold medals in track.

For these superb performances she was voted the female athlete of the year by the Associated Press. She picked up medals and keys to the cities in various states all over the country. She was in demand everywhere. She was Wilma Rudolph, the Jesse Owens of mid-century America.

The gold-medal victories were magnificent in themselves, but they had special meaning for Wilma. They helped her forget the years of torment and discouragement, the torture of double pneumonia and scarlet fever that had left her crippled at the age of four. These memories faded into the past as beaming smiles replaced frowns. Wilma had earned a happiness that seems to come only from conquering the odds.

For in addition to the illness, the odds seemed to have been stacked against Wilma. She was the seventeenth of a family of nineteen children and grew up in the poverty-stricken tobacco and corn country of Tennessee. And with her illnesses, she was not able to walk until she was eight years old; then she had to wear corrective shoes.

But by high school, Wilma's recovery was complete. She became a top basketball player before going to Tennessee State and the famous track teams of coach Ed Temple.

After the Olympics, Wilma decided she would not return in 1964 to defend her victo-ries. Her reason was that the "best I could do if I went back is win three gold medals again. If I won two, there would be something lacking. I'll stick with the glory won—like Jesse Owens did in 1936."

Wyomia Tyus

The afternoon was hot, the sun was bright and Ed Temple was weary. Day after day he had been watching hundreds of high school girls run. All he wanted was three or four who could help Tennessee State A & I University keep its perennial women's national track-and-field championship.

On this day, at the 1961 Georgia high school championships, a gangling fifteen-year-old girl caught his eye. Her name was Wyomia Tyus. She wasn't the fastest runner there, but Ed Temple thought he saw a special determination and a future for her.

A year later, under Temple's coaching, Wyomia won three national girls' titles. By 1964 she was an Olympic champion—four years ahead of schedule. By 1965 she was a world-record holder and one of the speedsters who had helped lift American women's track and field from obscurity.

Wyomia Tyus is a quiet, shy girl, 5ft.-7in. and 134 pounds. She is lean but runs with power. Everywhere that Wyomia runs she is compared to Wilma Rudolph. She is flattered but she wishes the comparisons would stop.

"I know Wilma," she once said, "I trained with her one summer, and I have seen her run. She was very good, very smooth. But I don't pay any attention to comparisons. I'm not her. I can't be her. I'm just Wyomia."

Wyomia was born August 29, 1945, in Griffin, Georgia, to Willie Tyus, a dairy worker (he died when she was fifteen), and Marie Tyus, a laundry worker. There were three older boys in the family, only one of them an athlete (he played tackle on the high school football team).

Wyomia Tyus

Wilma Rudolph

Wyomia Tyus (second from left) wins the women's 60-yard dash final in the Millrose Games at Madison Square Garden in 1965. Crossing the finish line behind her are Debbie Thompson, Pamela Kilborn and Edith McGuire.

In 1961, before Temple first saw Wyomia, she was a sophomore in Griffin excited about basketball. The only sport available after the basketball season was track and field, so she went out for track, as a high jumper. After a monumental struggle, she high jumped four feet and wisely concluded that she wasn't getting anywhere. It was then she decided to run.

In 1961, Wyomia wasn't even dreaming about world competition. She was thrilled that Temple thought so much of her that he put her in his month-long summer training program. He took her to the Amateur Athletic Union girls' national championships that year in Gary, Indiana. She won nothing but she was learning.

The next summer, Wyomia tried again in the girls' nationals at Los Angeles, and this time she won all her heats. Then she won the 50-yard final in 5.8 seconds, the 75-yard race in 8.3 and the 100 in 11.0, breaking two American records along the way.

In 1963 at Dayton, Ohio, Wyomia won the AAU girls' 75 yards in 8.3 seconds and the 100 yards in 10.9. The next day, she ran in the women's meet for the first time, winning her 100-yard heat and finishing second to Edith McGuire in the final. That earned her a trip to Moscow for the meet between the United States and the Soviet Union. Four girls—two from each nation—ran in the 100-meter dash at Moscow. Wyomia finished fourth in 12.0. She was disappointed, but not Temple. He felt she would get experience in the 1964 Olympics and would win in the 1968 Games.

Wyomia wasn't waiting. She entered Tennessee State in September 1963 on a track scholarship and got the benefit of daily coaching from Temple. She learned her lessons well. In the 1964 women's nationals at Hanford, California, she won the 100-meter dash in 11.5 seconds, just beating Edith McGuire. Two weeks later, against the Russians, she ran second to Edith, who had become her close friend in college.

Two weeks after that came the United States Olympic trials in New York. She wanted to go to Tokyo so badly that she tried too hard and tightened up. She managed third place in the trials by inches, but at least she made the team.

In Tokyo her nervousness left her. She won her heat in 11.3 seconds, her quarter-final in 11.2 and her semi-final in 11.3. She won the final by two yards in 11.4 seconds and became the world's fastest female.

Wyomia won the 1965 national 100-yard title in 10.5, and then she went back to Russia. "I wanted to win so bad there," she said. "All I could remember was finishing last in 1963." This time, Wyomia won in 11.1, equaling the world record set two weeks before by Irena Kirszenstein and Ewa Klobukowska of Poland. She ran second to Edith McGuire in the 200, a brand-new event for her. Then, in a 400-meter relay, seen by millions of Americans on television, she turned a seemingly hopeless four-yard deficit into a smashing five-yard victory. Wyomia's performance in Russia that day wiped out any lingering doubts. Everyone knew then that she was the fastest.

Arthur Ashe

One man who doesn't like to see Arthur Ashe win important tennis matches is Harry Hopman. Not that Hopman has anything personal against Arthur; it is that Hopman is coach of the Australian Davis Cup team, and he says this: "Arthur Ashe is without doubt the most promising player in the world and the biggest single threat to our Davis Cup supremacy." Bringing back the Davis Cup, symbol of world amateur tennis leadership, to the United States from Australia, and keeping it here are goals of Arthur, who is the first Negro ever to play for the United States in Davis Cup competition.

Arthur Ashe has moved faster in the world of tennis than either he or anyone else dreamed

"Arthur Ashe is without doubt the most promising player in the world and the biggest single threat to our Davis Cup supremacy."

The above quote from Australian Davis Cup team coach Harry Hopman fully describes this man.

he could. Within three weeks in the summer of 1968, he pulled himself indisputably into the front rank of the world's players. He was no longer "promising." He had arrived.

First it was the United States Amateur Championship tournament at the Longwood Cricket Club in Brookline, Massachusetts. Arthur had to contend with all the best amateur players in the world but he knew he had a chance. His big serve and power clicked, and he won with surprising ease—the first Negro man ever to win the U.S. amateur title.

That left the big one, though, the United States Open at the fabled West Side Tennis Club in Forest Hills, New York. It was the first U.S. "national open," for this was the first year tennis amateurs and pros had been allowed to play in the same tournaments. This time, Arthur Ashe was just another good amateur competing against the world's greatest pros. He said before it started that he didn't think he was good enough to win this tournament.

Yet win it he did, in what was acclaimed one of the most striking sports performances in years. His service was compared to "Pancho" Gonzales', his agility to a panther. In a rousing five-set final, he defeated Tom Okker of the Netherlands, his 26th consecutive singles match victory. Thus Arthur Ashe became the first American man to win the U.S. national title since 1955; the first Negro man to win the U.S. national title ever; and the first man ever to win the U.S. Open championship. This was Arthur Ashe at his best.

At his best, Ashe can seem unbeatable with his booming serve, fancy backhand and deft volley shots. Late in 1965, for instance, he swept through the best players Australia had in winning a tournament there. In one hour and fifteen minutes, he disposed of the tough Fred Stolle, 6–4, 6–4, 6–4. "He aced me twenty-one times," lamented Stolle, "and that's never happened to me before." Then, in the semifinals, Ashe defeated John Newcombe,

6–4, 6–4, 6–3, in an hour and seven minutes. The finals matched him with the great Roy Emerson and Ashe won a gruelling five-set match, 3–6, 6–2, 6–3, 3–6, 6–1.

America's Vic Seixas, a former champion and knowledgeable in tennis, insists that Ashe will one day be the top player in the world. "I don't see how he can miss," Seixas once predicted. "He has the speed, the power, the agility and the relaxed attitude about the game necessary to go all the way. He has the strokes and is not the nervous type."

Ashe began playing tennis at the age of seven. By age ten, tennis was his life. He forgot about baseball and basketball, used a borrowed racquet and became one of the most dedicated members of a local club for Negroes known as the Richmond Racquet Club. It wasn't long before Dr. R. W. Johnson, the Lynchburg, Virginia, physician who had aided Althea Gibson, noticed that Ashe possessed an unusual ability at tennis. Dr. Johnson included young Arthur in the group of players he coached and trained. He replaced Ashe's heavy racket with another of the proper weight and, over ten years, spent close to $3,000 and hundreds of hours developing Ashe's game.

"Art improved his skills as fast as any boy I had ever coached," Dr. Johnson recalls. "There was nothing I taught him that he didn't do well. I'm not selling him as a superman, you understand; he made mistakes. But he rarely made the same ones twice. Years ago, I realized he would become one of the world's great players. I was not surprised back in 1963 when he was first named to the Davis Cup team. I could see it coming for the previous six years."

Dr. Johnson pushed Arthur along quickly. At fourteen, Ashe was entered in the National Junior Championships. In 1958, he went to the semifinals in the under-fifteen division, and in 1960 and 1961, he won the Junior Indoors singles title.

At seventeen, Ashe's game attracted the attention of Richard Hudlin, a tennis official in

St. Louis, who invited the boy to live with him in St. Louis and to play tennis during his senior year at Sumner High School. Desegregation in tennis tournaments had come about and Ashe improved his game playing against the best young players in the nation. At eighteen, Ashe was placed No. 28 in the United States Lawn Tennis Association's men's rankings.

Next, he accepted an athletic scholarship at the University of California, Los Angeles, and enrolled there as a student of business administration. The factor which influenced Ashe to accept the UCLA offer over so many others was location. In California he would have a warm climate which would allow him to play year-round and he would be a long way from the racial discrimination of Richmond. In addition, Pancho Gonzalez, Ashe's idol, lived only a quarter mile from the UCLA campus. "I was naturally very color conscious because they made such a thing of color in Richmond," Ashe recalls, but with a tinge of bitterness. "Skin-wise, Gonzalez was the nearest thing to me. And to boot, he was the greatest player in the world. That was a heck of a combination, a combination I couldn't resist."

Under the direction of his UCLA coach, J. D. Morgan, Ashe climbed in the national rankings from twenty-eight to eighteen, from eighteen to six and from six to two.

Arthur Ashe has displayed the guts, the stamina, the will, and the thick hide to survive in a world long closed to Negroes. And he has broken barriers without doing injury to his own personality. He speaks kindly of Cliff Richey, a white southerner he has lived with on tours. "When people see two guys from the South like Cliff and me, one white and one Negro, sharing a room and being close friends, it must do a little good," he says.

He realizes the social significance of what he has done, but feels that what he really wants to prove is how good a tennis player he is. He has kept working at his game—even when in the armed forces. He has all the physical skills and knows exactly what he wants. "When I say I want to be best," Ashe maintains, "I don't mean the best Negro player. I mean the best player—period! I don't consider myself a Negro player, although almost everyone does. I'm a tennis player who happens to be a Negro. I want to be number one without an asterisk next to my name." And he shows every sign of getting what he wants before he is through.

Althea Gibson

To go, as Althea Gibson did, from the world of poverty to the world of comfort, this rangy, brooding daughter of a black sharecropper had to do in tennis what Jackie Robinson did in baseball. She had to be not merely good but sensational simply to get a chance. She had to endure the humiliations Jackie did—more subtle, perhaps, less profane, because tennis prides itself on being a sport of ladies and gentlemen. But the demeanings were just as scarring to this proud girl's sensitive spirit. She had to win the important matches carrying a double load of tension—the kind that grips every athlete competing for a grand prize and the more crushing kind that grips only pioneers. Althea wasn't playing for herself alone, but for all the brown- and black-skinned boys and girls who would follow her through the door —if she could shove it open so firmly that nobody could close it behind her.

A magnificent athlete, Althea Gibson delivered under the most intense pressure. She was the top-ranked woman tennis player in the country in both 1957 and 1958, the first Negro to achieve this honor. She won tournaments like the French women's singles championship in 1956 and the United States and Wimbledon singles competition in 1957 and 1958. Althea was spectacular to watch. Lean and strong, she uncorked a whizzing serve with the sweep and power of a man. Then she would charge forward and score heavily with her slashing net game.

Althea's childhood was brutal. No money, no clothes, only the most primitive kinds of fun, and, worst of all, no hope. She was born on August 25, 1927, in the little South Carolina town of Silver, but her father went to New York to find work a year or so later and her mother followed with the children as soon as there was fare money. They knew there would never be any money for them in South Carolina. "I got a bale and a half of cotton out of my sharecrop the last year we were there," Daniel Gibson, a big, powerful man, remembered. "Cotton was $50 a bale that year, so I got exactly $75 for working all year."

Yet in New York money was still so tight that Althea spent far more of her childhood away from her family than with it. She stayed first with an aunt in New York and then with one in Philadelphia, and no matter where she was living, she hated school. Even when she was at home and her father gave her some memorable whalings for truancy, she persistently played hooky. Althea somehow graduated from junior high school, but she says, "I don't know how I did it. I think those teachers just made up their minds to pass me on to the next school and let them worry about me."

As a teen-ager Althea cleaned chickens in a butcher shop, ran deliveries, waited on counters at a restaurant, worked as a mail clerk, in a five-and-ten, a dressmaking shop and a button factory. During one long stretch between jobs, the City Welfare Department paid her rent for a comfortable room in a private home and supplied her a weekly allowance. "When I was supposed to be looking for a job," she says, "I was playing basketball and paddle tennis, shooting pool and going to the movies."

It's ironic that if Althea had cared enough about any job to really work at it, she might never have played tennis. But instead of working she played paddle tennis. And a young musician, Buddy Walker, who was working part-time as a city play-leader, saw her slamming the ball. It struck him—a tennis fan—

that she might play tennis just as well. He bought her a couple of second-hand tennis rackets and soon made a date for her to play a few sets with a friend of his at the Harlem River Tennis Courts.

Juan Serrell, a Negro school teacher who was a member of the Cosmopolitan Tennis Club, a private club to which the wealthier Harlem tennis players belonged, saw Althea's workout. He agreed with Walker that she had rare ability and helped provide her with a junior membership in the club and formal instruction by Fred Johnson.

Johnson became the first of a long line of tennis coaches, patrons and officials to try to bend Althea's stubborn will and fiery temperament. They clashed early and often. Althea was willing to take his advice on how to hit a tennis ball but not on how to live her personal life.

Althea played in her first tournament in 1942. She was fifteen, the tournament was the all-Negro American Tennis Association's New York State Open Championship, and she won it. She won the national ATA girls' singles championship in 1944 and 1945 and went to the final round of the women's singles in 1946.

The important thing that happened to Althea in that tournament was meeting two tennis-playing doctors from the South, Dr. Robert W. Johnson of Lynchburg, Virginia, and Dr. Hubert A. Eaton of Wilmington, North Carolina. "My two doctors," Althea has affectionately called them ever since. Professionally and financially successful, and alert to any opportunity to encourage Negro participation in tennis, the doctors suggested that Althea devote the next few years to an intensive tennis training program, preferably as a scholarship student in a good Negro college. Obviously, Dr. Johnson and Dr. Eaton saw in Althea their dream of a Negro tennis player good enough to break the color line in the major national and international tournaments. To Althea the idea of spending all her time playing tennis was

Althea bends low to return a tough net shot during a match at Wimbledon.

Althea Gibson

Althea poses with Louise Brough after a match at Forest Hills. The twenty-two-year-old Gibson was the first Negro ever to play at Forest Hills.

great. But the college part of their proposal stopped her. "I never even went to high school," she said. "How can I go to college?"

The doctors were resourceful. The things they wanted Althea to do couldn't be done by an ignorant girl, no matter how hard she could wallop a tennis ball. So it was arranged that Althea would go to Wilmington for the school year, live with Dr. Eaton and his family, go to high school with the Eaton children and practice her tennis with Dr. Eaton on his backyard court. In the summer, she would move to Dr. Johnson's in Lynchburg and, using his home as a base, travel the Negro tournament trail with him.

Her school work progressed well, better than she had dared hope, and her tennis progressed even more. That summer Althea won her first ATA national women's singles title—the first of ten in a row. For whatever it was worth, and Althea knew it wasn't worth much, she was the best Negro woman tennis player in the country.

Graduating from high school in June 1949, she accepted a scholarship to Florida A&M The following years were difficult ones as she fought for—and gradually won—the right to compete against white players in the big tournaments. She was ranked number nine nationally in 1952, number seven in 1953, and dropped to number thirteen in 1954.

She took her first major title in 1956, winning the French championships and then, in her eighth year of competing against the best white players, she triumphed at Wimbledon —the world's most important tournament —in 1957. She whipped Darlene Hard in straight sets, and then the tough kid from Harlem stepped up to Queen Elizabeth to accept her trophy. For 1957 and 1958 Althea was the best woman player in the world. She had pioneered and won out. Later, she would turn to golf and do creditably. But people will remember Althea for her power tennis and her unyielding drive. That was the combination that broke through the color line in tennis and took her all the way to the top.

Lee Elder

In August 1968, Lee Elder passed up the chance to defend the United Golf Association championship, the most important tournament for Negro players, even though it was on his home course, where he would have been a heavy favorite. But no one could really blame him. The UGA crown, one of the steps on his way to proving himself the best player on the Negro circuit, would have been worth about $2,000 to Lee. He chose instead to compete in the Westchester Gold Classic, where the total purse was $250,000.

The decision for Lee had been settled a week before in the American Golf Classic at Akron, Ohio, on the Firestone course that golfers call the "green monster." This is one of the major events on the annual Professional Golfers' Association tour, and a national television audience in the millions was watching. Lee came to the 72nd and final hole of the tournament needing only a par four to win, but he took a bogey, forcing him into a three-way play-off against Frank Beard and Jack Nicklaus. Beard fell by the wayside on the first play-off hole, which left Elder, the rookie pro, and Nicklaus, considered by many the finest golfer ever, battling each other. Instead of the veteran Nicklaus dominating play, Elder was setting the pace, forcing Jack to make excellent putts to stay in contention. Then Nicklaus made a birdie on the fifth extra hole, giving him the $25,000 first prize. Lee settled for $12,750—far and away the biggest purse he had ever collected.

It wasn't bad for a golfer who had had to make most of his money "hustling" as the players call it—winning on bets or playing against lesser golfers while under severe stroke handicaps. For Elder, it had long been that way, just as it had been that way for Lee Trevino, the Mexican-American who had won the 1968 United States Open championship.

A native of Dallas, Texas, Elder is a lithe, wiry man of 5ft.-8in. who weighs 165 pounds. He began playing golf while a caddy in Dallas, then moved to Los Angeles, where he was tutored by Ted Rhodes, one of the first fine Negro golfers. In the early 1960's, Elder moved to Washington, D.C. and perfected his game at the Langston Public Golf Course, played almost entirely by Negroes, in the city's northeast section. He also played often at the nearby University of Maryland course, where he was helped by the golf coach, Frank Cronin. Elder doesn't hit a golf ball as far as some stars, in the 240-yard range, but he is straight and sound. The Langston course, while not long, is full of doglegs around the Anacostia River, and four of the holes are on a narrow island. Thus Elder's iron shots have become well controlled.

The main trouble with Elder's game, just as with most Negro golfers, is that it has never been challenged enough. Barred because of his race from the best country club courses, he has had to spend most of his time playing on public courses that didn't ready him for the big tournaments.

Lee dominated the United Golf Association circuit, once winning eighteen of twenty-one tournaments, but his winnings could be counted in the hundreds, not thousands, of dollars. Then he decided to try his hand in the big time. He went to the Professional Golfers' Association school, a requirement for any one seeking to play the tour, and earned his credentials. By mid-summer, he had won more than $25,000 in his first year on the tour.

Elder's defeat by Nicklaus, disappointing as it was, still established his national reputation. Lee and his wife, Rose, were feted almost the entire night at Akron, then had to get up early to catch a plane home, where they hoped to get some rest. They couldn't. Friends kept calling all day to congratulate them. Rose and Lee didn't care.

Lee Elder received a well-earned kiss from his wife after winning the 1968 American Golf Classic at Akron, Ohio.

After years of practice and many disappointing rounds, Charlie Sifford, probably the best Negro golfer ever developed in the United States, finally cracked the win column on the PGA tour. Sifford broke down at the cup presentation after coming in seven under par to win the Greater Hartford Open, his first victory after fourteen years on the tour.

Charlie Sifford

Charlie Sifford is probably the best Negro golfer ever developed in the United States, perhaps in the world. He has proven himself in week-after-week competition on the professional golf circuit, usually in the money, sometimes a winner. There is no tougher test for a golfer, and Sifford has shown that he belongs.

Sifford learned to play golf on a public course in Charlotte, North Carolina. He began as a caddy and, in those days, it wasn't common for a Negro to be allowed on a Charlotte public course. But Sutton Alexander, who managed the course, and Clayton Heafner, the professional, saw Sifford swinging a club, took an immediate liking to the young caddy, and provided him with every opportunity for practice. Sifford caught on to the game quickly. He was shooting in the seventies when he was thirteen. Two years later, young Charlie Sifford was able to break seventy.

Not very long afterward, he moved to Philadelphia, still obsessed by the golf bug. His first job was as a private golf instructor to Billy Eckstine, the singer. For several years this was his main source of income. Today, Sifford and the singer remain close friends. "Eckstine's a real good golfer now," Charlie says. "We play together sometimes. Billy's always been a real good friend of mine. I had a lot of fun teaching him the game."

When he wasn't busy teaching, Sifford worked on his own game, sharpening his putting, lengthening his drives and pinpointing his iron shots. Once in a while he won some money in a tournament, but more often he relied on winning bets in pickup matches. Then, in 1952, at the age of twenty-eight, Sifford began playing the professional tour.

It was in 1957 that he won his first major tournament. He took the Long Beach (California) Open and came back later in the year to finish second in the Pomona (California) Open, losing a 19-hole play-off to Billy Casper. That year, Sifford earned more than $8,000 on the professional golf tour.

Charlie Sifford has come a long way since he started making the golf tour. Places he once couldn't play are now open to Negroes. And he has made business arrangements to endorse particular brands of golf clubs, golf balls and other products. Sifford is the first Negro golfer in history to have such opportunities.

Out on the course he has also made progress. In 1967, for example, he shot rounds of 69–70–69–64 and won the Greater Hartford tournament with a 272. By year's end, Charlie Sifford was listed as twenty-fifth among the leading official money-winners; his total for the year was $47,025.55, not counting endorsement and exhibition income. Charlie Sifford had pulled himself into the front rank of golf.

Bibliography

GENERAL SOURCES

"Armageddon To Go," *Time,* LXVI (December 12, 1955), 24.

"Blind Athletes," *Ebony,* X (September 1955), 63–66.

BONTEMPS, ARNA W. *Famous Negro Athletes.* New York, 1964.

BOYLE, ROBERT H. *Sport: Mirror of American Life.* Boston, 1963.

BRAWLEY, BENJAMIN. *Negro Builders and Heroes.* Chapel Hill, N.C., 1937.

DAVIS, JOHN P. (ed.). *The American Negro Reference Book.* Englewood Cliffs, N.J., 1966.

DEFORD, F. "The Power of the Press," *Sports Illustrated,* XXII (March 29, 1965), 21–24.

DEMARCO, M. *Great American Athletes.* Menlo Park, Calif., 1962.

DURANT, JOHN, and BETTMANN, O. L. *Pictorial History of American Sports.* New York, 1965.

EBONY (eds.). *The Negro Handbook.* Chicago, 1967.

"Entertaining Athletes: Negro Sports Stars," *Ebony,* XXI (December 1965), 39–40.

GUZMAN, JESSIE P. (ed.). *The Negro Year Book, 1952.* New York, 1952.

HARLOW, ALVIN F. "Unrecognized Stars," *Esquire,* X (September 1938), 75.

HENDERSON, EDWIN BANCROFT. *The Negro in Sports.* Washington, 1949.

HUGHES, LANGSTON. *Famous American Negroes.* New York, 1954.

———, and MELTZER, MILTON. *A Pictorial History of the Negro in America.* New York, 1963.

The Negro in American Sport. New York, 1960. [Special issue of *Sport.*]

"Negro Stars on the Playing-Fields of America," *Literary Digest,* CXIX (March 2, 1935), 32.

NELSON, ROBERT L. *The Negro in Athletics.* New York, 1940.

"Off-Season Athletes in Off-Beat Jobs," *Ebony,* XVII (May 1962), 68–69.

RIBALOU, H. U. *The Negro in American Sports.* New York, 1954.

RICHARDSON, BEN. *Great American Negroes.* New York, 1956.

"Round Table Discussion: The Negro in American Sport," *Negro History Bulletin,* XXIV (November 1960), 27–31.

SLOAN, IRVING J. *The American Negro: A Chronology and Fact Book.* Dobbs Ferry, N.Y., 1965.

"Sports," *Negro History Bulletin,* XVIII (February 1955), 120–22. [A general article on the status of Negroes in sports.]

"Sports: They Set the Pace in 1947," *Opportunity,* XXVI (Spring 1948), 83.

WHITLOCK, E. F. "Gary Athlete Builds Union: Herman Mac Anderson," *Opportunity,* XXV (April 1947), 110–11.

YOUNG, ANDREW S., "Doc." *Negro Firsts in Sports,* Chicago, 1963.

BASEBALL

"Al Smith, White Sox Outfielder," *Ebony,* XV (October 1960), 85–88.

"The Amazing Willie Mays," *Ebony,* XIII (September 1958), 45–52.

"Are There Too Many Negroes in Baseball?" *Our World*, IX (August 1954), 42–46.

"Are They Ganging Up on Jackie?" *Our World*, VI (September 1951), 56–60.

"Armless Athlete: Lewis Watts Pitches Softball," *Ebony*, IX (November 1953), 41–45.

"Ashford Arrives," *Ebony*, XXI (June 1966), 65–66. [An article on the major league umpire.]

"Backbone of the Chicago White Sox," *Our World*, IX (September 1954), 70–73.

BARBEE, B. "Annual Baseball Roundup: 1965—The Year of the Pitchers," *Ebony*, XX (June 1965), 152–58.

———. "Baseball's Untouchables," *ibid.*, XIX (June 1964), 153–54.

"Baseball Business," *Crisis*, LXI (October 1934), 301.

"Baseball's Comedy Kings: Indianapolis Clowns," *Ebony*, XIV (September 1959), 67–70.

"Baseball's Fastest Player; Hustling Sam Jethroe . . .," *Ebony*, V (October 1950), 55–56.

"Baseball's Young Turks," *Sepia*, XV (September 1966), 56–60.

BENJAMIN, P. "Then and Now: Jackie Robinson," *New York Times Magazine* (April 15, 1962), 84.

"A Big Man Conquers a Big Fear: Don Newcombe Overcomes Fear of Flying," *Ebony*, XIII (March 1958), 101–2.

"Big Man from Nicetown: Roy Campanella," *Time*, LXVI (August 8, 1955), 50–55.

"Big Newk in Japan," *Ebony*, XVIII (November 1962), 115–18.

"Bill Bruton; Milwaukee's Golden Boy," *Our World*, VIII (October 1953), 70–73.

BOYLE, ROBERT H. "The Latins Storm Las Grandes Ligas," *Sports Illustrated*, XXIII (August 9, 1965), 24–30.

———. "The Private World of the Negro Ballplayer," *ibid.*, XII (March 21, 1960), 16–19.

Brainiest Man in Baseball; Leroy 'Satchel' Paige Is One of the National Game's Smartest Players Both on and off Field," *Ebony*, VII (August 1952), 26–28.

"Branch Breaks the Ice: Brooklyn Signed Jack Roosevelt Robinson, Negro Shortstop," *Time*, XLVI (November 5, 1945), 77.

"Branch Rickey Discusses the Negro in Baseball Today," *Ebony*, XII (May 1957), 38–44.

BRODY, T. C. "Giant Shot That Forced a Playoff between the Giants and the Dodgers," *Sports Illustrated*, XVII (October 8, 1962), 18–19. [About Willie Mays.]

———. "Snake-Sliding Dodger Tries To Steal the Pennant," *ibid.*, (October 1, 1962), 22–23. [About Maury Wills.]

BROSNAN, J. P. "Good Pitch Is Better than a Wild Swing," *National Review*, XII (June 1962), 446–48. [About Satchel Paige.]

———. *Great Rookies of the Major Leagues*. New York, 1966.

"Brothers Three of Baseball: Frank Robinson and His Brothers," *Ebony*, XX (September 1965), 73–74.

BROWER, W. A. "Barehanded Catcher," *Negro Digest*, IX (October 1951), 85–87.

———. "Time for Baseball To Erase the Blackball," *Opportunity*, XX (June 1942), 164–67.

BROWN, D. "Negro in Baseball," *Negro Historical Bulletin*, XV (December 1951), 51–52.

BROWN, J. D. "The Onliest Way I Know: Willie Mays," *Sports Illustrated*, X (April 13, 1959), 130–38.

"Brown Bombers," *Time*, LXXVIII (July 21, 1961), 60.

BURLEY, D. "Mother of Negro Baseball," *Sepia*, VII (August 1959), 51–54.

CAMPANELLA, ROY. "How I Catch a Ball Game," *Saturday Evening Post*, CCXXVIII (May 26, 1956), 33.

———. "I'll Walk Again," *ibid.*, CCXXXI (July 26, 1958), 13–15; (August 2, 1958), 26–27.

———. *It's Good To Be Alive*. Boston, 1959.

"Campy Swings, Dodgers Win," *Life*, XXXIV (June 8, 1953), 136–40.

"Can Campanella Come Back? His Injured Hand," *Ebony*, X (April 1955), 91–97.

"Can Jackie Make the Hall of Fame?" *Negro History Bulletin*, XVII (October 1953), 6.

"Can Minoso Beat the Sophomore Jinx?" *Ebony*, VII (June 1952), 15–18.

CANTWELL, R. "Invasion from Santo Domingo: Dominican Big Leaguers," *Sports Illustrated*, XVIII (February 25, 1963), 54–61.

"A Catcher Talks about a Catcher," *Negro History Bulletin,* XVIII (December 1954), 71.

COHANE, T. "Ancient Satchel," *Look,* XVII (April 7, 1953), 65–66.

———. "Mystery of Willie Mays," *ibid.,* XIX (May 3, 1955), 69–72.

———. "Portrait of a Hitter: Hank Aaron," *ibid.,* XXIV (July 19, 1960), 40b–40d.

———. "Tony Oliva: Twins' Lonely Star," *ibid.,* XXIX (June 1, 1965), 83.

COUSINS, N. "His Life Is the Greatest Game: Roy Campanella," *Saturday Review,* XLII (November 21, 1959), 46–47.

CREAMER, R. "Subject: Don Newcombe," *Sports Illustrated,* III (August 22, 1955), 48.

DAVIS, L. "First in Baseball: Negro Umpire," *New York Times Magazine* (June 13, 1954), 59.

DEFORD, F. "Happy Start for a Happy New Willie," *Sports Illustrated,* XX (April 27, 1964), 22–27.

"Delayed Call: First Major League Negro Appointed," *Newsweek,* CLI (March 11, 1966), 79–80. [Negro umpire.]

DODSON, D. W. "Integration of Negroes in Baseball," *Journal of Educational Sociology,* XXVIII (October 1954), 73–82.

"Don Newcombe: The Biggest Dodger," *Ebony,* X (October 1955), 108–14.

DONOVAN, R. "Fabulous Satchel Paige," *Collier's,* CXXXI (May 30, 1953), 62; (June 6, 1953), 20–24; (June 13, 1953), 54–59.

"Duke with Willie," *Sports Illustrated,* II (June 27, 1955), 17.

EINSTEIN, CHARLES. *Willie Mays: Coast to Coast Giant.* New York, 1963.

"End of an Era for Negroes in Baseball," *Ebony,* XVI (June 1961), 36–40.

"Fact Chart on Negro Major League Players," *Ebony,* XIX (June 1964), 156.

FOX, W. B. "Conversation with Satchel Paige," *Holiday,* XXXVIII (August 1965), 18.

FRANK, S. "Nobody Loves Baseball More than Campy!" *Saturday Evening Post,* CCXXVI (June 5, 1954), 25.

"From Banks to Baker to Fame," *Ebony,* XI (May 1956), 100–105.

"From First to Fame: Jackie Robinson," *Ebony,* XVII (October 1962), 85–86.

"The Funny Men of Baseball," *Sepia,* XIV (August 1965), 60–64.

FURLONG, W. B. "Panther at the Plate: Hank Aaron," *New York Times Magazine* (September 21, 1958), 43.

"Garrett Mays: One-Armed High School Pitcher," *Ebony, VIII* (August 1953), 76–78.

GELMAN, STEVE. *Young Baseball Champions.* New York, 1966.

GROSS, M. "Visit with Willie Mays," *Saturday Evening Post,* CCXXXIV (May 20, 1961), 32–33.

———. *Willie Mays.* New York, 1966.

HANO, ARNOLD. *Willie Mays.* New York, 1966.

———. *Willie Mays, the Say-Hey Kid.* New York, 1961.

HICKS, J. H. "St. Louis: Is It the Toughest Town for Negro Baseball Players?" *Crisis,* LVII (October 1950), 573–76.

"The High and the Mired: Hank Aaron," *Sports Illustrated,* X (May 25, 1959), 24.

"History of the Negroes in the World Series," *Ebony,* XII (October 1957), 93–96.

HOWARD, ELSTON. *Catching.* New York, 1966.

———. "It's Great To Be a Yankee," *Ebony, X* (September 1955), 50–54.

HOWARD, LISS. *The Willie Mays Album.* New York, 1966.

"Hurray for Jackie Robinson," *Negro History Bulletin,* XVIII (January 1955), 93.

"It Comes Naturally: Hank Aaron," *Newsweek,* LIII (June 15, 1959), 94.

"It's Good To be Back in the Majors," *Sepia,* XII (August 1963), 63–66.

"It's Good To Be Traded: Don Newcombe, Bill White, Sam Jones," *Ebony,* XIV (October 1959), 46–48.

"Jackie Robinson's Double Play," *Life,* XXVIII (May 8, 1950), 129–32.

"John (Buck) O'Neill; First Negro Coach in Majors," *Ebony,* XVII (August 1962), 29–30.

"John Lewis, Kid Baseball Pitching Whizz," *Ebony,* VI (April 1951), 39–43.

"A Kid and an Old-Timer," *Ebony,* XII (June 1957), 41–46. [About Frank Robinson and Brooks Lawrence.]

"Lady Ball Player, Toni Stone, Is First Woman To Play in Negro Baseball," *Ebony,* VIII (July 1953), 48–52.

"Larry Doby's Symbolic Left Hook," *Ebony,* XII (September 1957), 51–54.

"Last Year for Big Bonus Babies," *Ebony,* XXII (November 1966), 120–22.

"The Law Tells Satch 'Win or Jail,' " *Ebony,* XIII (September 1958), 77–82.

LAWSON, E. "Frank Robinson Comes of Age," *Saturday Evening Post,* CCXXXV (August 25, 1962), 77–78.

LEGGETT, W. "Maury Wills, the Mouse Who Builds the Mountains," *Sports Illustrated,* XXIII (June 12, 1965), 38–42.

———. "The Rampaging Twins Want the Series, Too," *ibid.* (October 4, 1965), 26–28.

Marichal," *ibid.* (September 13, 1965), 36–37.

"Life Goes to Jackie Robinson's Jam Session: $15,000 for Civil Rights," *Life,* LV (July 5, 1963), 79–81.

"Lift the Latch for Satchel," *Sports Illustrated,* XVIII (March 11, 1963), 7.

LINN, E. "Trials of a Negro Idol: Willie Mays," *Saturday Evening Post,* CCXXXVI (June 22, 1963), 70–72.

———. "Woes of Willie Mays," *ibid.,* CCXXIX (April 13, 1957), 31.

LIPMAN, D. "Maybe I'll Pitch Forever: Satchel Paige," *Saturday Evening Post,* CCXXXIV (March 11, 1961), 38–39.

"Man Nobody Wanted: Tony Oliva," *Time,* LXXXIII (June 12, 1964), 80.

MANN, ARTHUR W. *The Jackie Robinson Story.* New York, 1951.

———. "The Truth about the Jackie Robinson Case," *Saturday Evening Post,* CCXXII (May 13, 1950), 19–21; (May 20, 1950), 36.

MANN, J. "The Battle of San Francisco," *Sports Illustrated,* XXIII (August 30, 1965), 12–15.

———. "They Love Herman and Willie: Juan Marichal and Willie Mays," *ibid.* (September 27, 1965), 24–31.

MAYS, WILLIE. *Born To Play Ball.* New York, 1955.

———. *My Life in and out of Baseball.* New York 1966.

———. "What Kids Have Taught Me," *Coronet,* XXXVIII (May 1955), 91–94.

"Money Pitcher: Don Newcombe," *Newsweek,* XLV (June 20, 1955), 86.

"Negro Baseball Players in Japan," *Ebony,* VIII (October 1953), 101–2.

"The Negro Comes of Age in Baseball," *Ebony,* XIV (June 1959), 41–46.

"Negro in Baseball: 1962, Year of the Big Money," *Ebony,* XVII (June 1962), 81–82.

"Negro on the Farm," *Newsweek,* XXVI (November 5, 1945), 94–95.

"Negro Players in Major League Baseball," *Crisis,* XLIV (April 1937), 112.

"Negroes in the Major Leagues," *Ebony,* XV (June 1960), 99–106.

"New Mr. Yankee: Elston Howard," *Ebony,* XIX (October 1964), 39.

NEWCOMBE, DON. "I'm Not a Quitter," *Saturday Evening Post,* CCXXIX (March 9, 1957), 27.

"Oldest Active Umpire," *Ebony,* XII (September 1957), 91–94.

"Out of the Circle: Campanella's Injury," *Newsweek,* LI (February 10, 1958), 81–82.

"Philosopher's Consolation," *Sports Illustrated,* XX (January 27, 1964), 17. [About Satchel Paige.]

"Pitcher Goes to Bat against the Catcher: Marichal—Roseboro Fight," *Life,* LIX (September 3, 1965), 34–35.

"Place in the Sun: Negro Players," *Time,* LVII (May 14, 1951), 91–93.

"Player of the Week: Cincinnati's Reds Outfielder Frank Robinson," *Sports Illustrated,* XXI (August 17, 1964), 85.

POLLACK, J. H. "Meet a Family Named Robinson," *Parents' Magazine,* XXX (October 1955), 46–47.

REDMOND, D. E. "It Happened in Harlingen: Negro in the Little League Team," *Christian Century,* LXXI (February 10, 1954), 175–76.

REYNOLDS, QUENTIN. "More than a Ball Player: Jackie Robinson," *Saturday Review,* XLIII (June 11, 1960), 33.

"Rickey and Robinson," *Crisis,* LIV (May 1947), 137.

ROBINSON, JOHN ROOSEVELT [JACKIE]. *Baseball Has Done It*. Philadelphia, 1964.

———. "Best Advice I Ever Had," *Reader's Digest,* LXXII (May 1958), 214–16.

———. *My Own Story*. New York, 1948.

———. "Speaking Out," *Saturday Evening Post,* CCXXXVI (August 10, 1963), 10.

———. "There's Only One Way To Beat the Yankees," *Life,* LV (October 4, 1963), 106A–12.

———. "Why I'm Quiting Baseball," *Look,* XXI (February 22, 1955), 78.

ROBINSON, L. "World's Greatest Diamond Thief: Maury Wills," *Ebony,* XVIII (May 1963), 35–36.

ROBINSON, MACK. "My Brother Jackie," *Ebony,* XII (July 1957), 75–82.

"Robinson Makes Good," *Crisis,* LIII (October 1946), 277.

ROEDER, BILL. *Jackie Robinson*. New York, 1950.

ROWAN, CARL T., and ROBINSON, JOHN ROOSEVELT. *Wait till Next Year*. New York, 1960.

"San Francisco's Most Colorful Team," *Ebony,* XV (July 1960), 103–7.

"Satchel Paige, the Brainiest Man in Baseball," *Ebony,* VII (August 1952), 26–28.

SCHOOR, GENE. *Roy Campanella: Man of Courage*. New York, 1959.

———. *Willie Mays: Modest Champion*. New York, 1960.

"Scouting Reports: American and National Baseball Leagues," *Sports Illustrated,* VI (April 15, 1957), 45–83.

"Scouting Reports: American and National Baseball Leagues, 1960," *Sports Illustrated,* XII (April 11, 1960), 28–62.

"Scouting Reports: Baseball 1959, American and National Leagues," *Sports Illustrated,* X (April 18, 1959), 32–87.

"Scouting Reports: 1958 National and American Baseball Leagues," *Sports Illustrated,* VIII (April 14, 1958), 39–77.

SHAPIRO, MILTON J. *The Hank Aaron Story*. New York, 1961.

———. *The Roy Campanella Story*. New York, 1958.

———. *The Willie Mays Story*. New York, 1963.

SHARNIK, M. "Moody Tiger of the Reds: Frank Robinson," *Sports Illustrated,* XVIII (June 17, 1963), 32–34.

SILVERMAN, A. *Heroes of the World Series*. New York, 1964.

"Slow: Satchel Paige," *New Yorker,* XXVIII (September 13, 1952), 32–33.

"Small Men, Big Bats: Ernie Banks and Hank Aaron," *Ebony,* XV (May 1960), 85–90.

SMITH, KEN. *The Willie Mays Story*. New York, 1954.

SMITH, R. M. *Baseball's Hall of Fame*. New York, 1965.

"Speed School for Baseball Stars: Harrison Dillard Teaches Cleveland Indians How To Run," *Ebony,* XIII (May 1958), 121–26.

SPORTING NEWS. *Baseball Register*. St. Louis, 1968.

SPORTS ILLUSTRATED. *Sports Illustrated Book of Baseball*. New York, 1960.

"Team To Beat," *Time,* LXVIII (August 20, 1956), 77. [About Don Newcombe.]

TERRELL, R. "Murder with a Blunt Instrument: Hank Aaron," *Sports Illustrated,* VII (August 12, 1957), 8–11.

———. "Reds at the Crossroads," *ibid.,* VII (March 10, 1958), 39–42. [About Frank and Lawrence Robinson.]

———. "Young Men at Work: Vada Pinson, Willie Tasby," *ibid.,* X (April 6, 1959); 44–49.

"Terrific Tony," *Ebony,* XIX (August 1964), 36–38. [About Tony Oliva.]

"Thief of the Bags," *Newsweek,* LX (July 23, 1962), 67. [About Maury Wills.]

"*Time* Magazine Tells the Willie Mays Story," *Negro History Bulletin,* XVIII (October 1954), 13–16.

"Vada Pinson of the Cincinnati Reds," *Ebony,* XV (September 1960), 86–87.

WARD, W. "Low and Inside: Views from the Arena," *Nation,* CC (May 10, 1965), 509–10.

WEBBER, H. B., and BROWN, OLIVER. "Play Ball!" *Crisis,* XLV (May 1938), 136–37.

"What's Ahead for Willie Mays?" *Ebony,* X (August 1955), 35–40.

"When Batters Wobble: Satchel Paige," *Newsweek,* LII (July 14, 1958), 57–58.

"Where the Giants Grow: Willie Mays Moves West," *Newsweek,* LI (June 9, 1958), 52–53.

"Will Jackie Robinson Crack Up?" *Ebony,* VI (September 1951), 23–28.

"Willie the Whoop," *Newsweek,* XXXVIII (September 10, 1951), 63.

WILLS, MAURY. *It Pays To Steal.* Englewood Cliffs, N.J., 1963.

WINTERICH, J. T. "Playing Ball: Negroes in Organized Baseball," *Saturday Review of Literature,* XXVIII (November 24, 1945), 12.

"World Series, 1958," *Sports Illustrated,* IX (October 13, 1958), 14–21.

YOUNG, ANDREW S., "DOC." *Great Negro Baseball Stars: And How They Made the Major Leagues.* New York, 1953.

———. "The Jackie Robinson Era," *Ebony,* XI (November 1955), 152–56.

YOUNG, DICK. *Roy Campanella.* New York, 1952.

"Your Temper Can Ruin Us! Jackie Robinson," *Look,* XIX (February 22, 1955), 78.

FOOTBALL

"Addison Hawthorne: West Coast Football Star," *Ebony,* VII (October 1952), 89–93.

"Alonzo 'Jake' Gaither," *Ebony,* XVI (November 1960), 162.

"Artful Dodger: Lenny Moore," *Time,* LXXVI (December 5, 1960), 45.

"As the Pros See Them: *Time's* Propicked All-America," *Time,* LXXXVIII (December 9, 1966), 65–66.

"Big Daddy from Baltimore," *Life,* XLVII (October 26, 1959), 141.

"Big Daddy Lipscomb," *Ebony,* XV (January 1960), 37–40.

"Big Time Football at Florida A. and M.," *Ebony,* XI (January 1956), 17–20.

"Biggest Man in Pro Football," *Ebony,* XVII (January 1962), 63–68.

BINGHAM, W. "A Season for Sophomores," *Sports Illustrated,* XIII (October 31, 1960), 53–54.

"Bob Gaiters and Pervis Atkins, Negro Backfielders of New Mexico State . . . [top] Blanchard-Davis Army Mark of 223 Points," *Jet,* XIX (October 27, 1960), 54–55.

BROWN, JIM. "How I Play Fullback," *Sports Illustrated,* XIII (September 26, 1960), 53–57.

———, and COPE, MYRON. "Jimmy Brown's Own Story," *Look,* XXVIII (October 20, 1964), 104–12.

———. *Off My Chest.* Garden City, N.Y., 1964.

"Brown Bombers," *Time,* LXXVIII (July 21, 1961), 60.

BROWER, W. A. "Has Professional Football Closed the Door?" *Opportunity,* XVIII (December 1940), 375–77.

———. "Negro Players on White Gridirons," *ibid.,* XIX (October 1941), 307–8.

"Cleveland Browns: Football's Most Democratic Team," *Ebony,* XI (December 1955), 104–8.

"Coach Cracks Color Barrier," *Ebony,* XIX (March 1964), 77.

DALEY, ARTHUR. *Pro Football's Hall of Fame.* Chicago, 1963.

DAVIS, ERNIE, and AUGUST, BOB. "I'm Not Unlucky," *Saturday Evening Post,* CCXXXVI (March 30, 1963), 60–62.

"Ernie Davis: Everybody's All America," *Ebony,* XVII (December 1961), 73–74.

"First Negro Pro Football Coach: Emlen Tunnell," *Sepia,* XV (October 1966), 20–22.

"Floyd Little on the Run," *Ebony,* XXI (December 1965), 86–88.

"Football Coach's Dream Player: Ollie Matson," *Ebony,* XII (January 1957), 28–32.

"Football Honor Roll," *Crisis,* XLVI (November 1939), 337.

"Football Twins: Robert and Richard Haines of Montclair [N.J.] High School," *Ebony,* XIII (December 1957), 75–80.

"Ghostly Power of Old 44: Floyd Little," *Life,* LIX (November 26, 1965), 111–12.

GILMAR, S. "All-Star Pro Team: A Prediction for 1966," *Esquire,* LXVI (October 1966), 88–90.

HAND, JACK. *Heroes of the NFL.* New York, 1965.

HENDERSON, E. B. "The Season's Football," *Crisis,* X (February 1915), 193–95.

"The Horizon: Fred (Duke) Slater," *Crisis,* XXIII (January 1922), 121.

HUNTER, R. G. "1966, Year of the Quarterbacks: Ten Tan Signal Callers," *Ebony,* XXII (December 1966), 39–40.

"Jim Brown in Rio Conchos," *Sepia,* XIII (December 1964), 22–25.

"John Westbrook Cracks Color Bar in Southwest Conference Football," *Sepia,* XV (November 1966), 72.

"Johnny Bright, Drake Halfback, Is Top College Ground-Gainer," *Ebony,* VI (October 1951), 54–58.

JONES, P. W. L. "All-Time Negro Football Team," *Crisis,* XLIV (January 1937), 16–21.

———. "Football in Negro Colleges in 1924," *ibid.,* XXIX (February 1925), 171–73.

———. "Football in Negro Colleges in 1925," *ibid.,* XXXI (March 1926), 221–24.

———. "Football in Negro Colleges in 1926," *ibid.,* XXXIV (March 1927), 7–8.

———. "Football in Negro Colleges in 1927," *ibid.,* XXXV (February 1928), 44–45.

———. "Football in Negro Colleges in 1928," *ibid.,* XXXVI (March 1929), 81–82.

"Kid Football: Midget Negro Team," *Ebony,* VI (December 1950), 61–63.

KLEIN, LARRY. *Jim Brown; The Running Back.* New York, 1965.

LINN, E. "Sad End of Big Daddy Lipscomb," *Saturday Evening Post,* CCXXXVI (July 27, 1963), 73–74.

LIPSCOMB, EUGENE, "Big Daddy: I'm Still Scared," *Saturday Evening Post,* CCXXXIII (November 12, 1960), 36.

"Look Out, Man, He Went That-Away: Warren McVea," *Sports Illustrated,* XXIII (September 20, 1965), 80.

MASIN, H. L. "Gale of Hurricane Force," *Senior Scholastic,* LXXXV (October 21, 1964), 22. [About Gale Sayers.]

MAULE, T. "Extravagant Outing for a Rare Rookie: Gale Sayers," *Sports Illustrated,* XXIII (December 6, 1965), 97–99.

———. "Run for the Money: Pro Football Superstars," *ibid.,* VII (November 7, 1957), 20–25.

———, and SHARNIK, M. H. "National Football League," *ibid.,* XXIII (September 13, 1965), 46–71.

"Men in the Middle: University of Illinois Football Stars J. C. Caroline and Mickey Bates," *Sports Illustrated,* I (October 18, 1954), 64–68.

NACE, E. "Negro Grid Stars, Past and Present," *Opportunity,* XVII (September 1939), 272–3.

"New Record Set for 'Joltin' Joe'," *Ebony,* XIV (December 1958), 28–30.

NIPSON, H. Wizard of the Winged-T," *Ebony,* XVI (January 1961), 90–94. [About Wilburn Hollis.]

"One-Legged Football Player: Artis Rucker," *Ebony,* XII (December 1956), 34–38.

"Oze Simmons, Football Star," *Crisis,* LXI (November 1934), 329.

"The Pigskin Club: A Washington 'Who's Who'," *Negro History Bulletin,* XXXVI (March 1963), 191–94.

"Pro Football Roundup," *Ebony,* XIX (November 1963), 70–72.

"Pro Football Stars from Negro Colleges," *Ebony,* XX (October 1965), 57–58.

"Pro Patient: Ernie Davis," *Newsweek,* LX (October 22, 1962), 76.

Pro, Pro, Pro: Stories of Pro Football's Greatest Stars. New York, 1963.

"The Quarterback from Little Rock: Sidney Williams of the University of Wisconsin," *Ebony,* XIII (January 1958), 46–48.

RIGA, ROBERT. *The Pros.* New York, 1960.

"Rookie and the Vet," *Ebony,* XX (January 1965), 56–58.

"The Roughest Man in Football: Paul 'Tank' Younger of the Los Angeles Rams," *Ebony,* IX (December 1953), 55–60.

RUSSELL, FRED. *Big Bowl Football.* New York, 1963.

SCHMIDT, J. G. "Lenny Moore: Colt's 'Sputnik,'" *Sepia,* X (December 1961), 56–59.

"Scouting Report: 1958 Collegiate Football Season," *Sports Illustrated,* IX (September 22, 1958), 36–114.

SHRAKE, E. "American Football League," *Sports Illustrated,* XXIII (September 13, 1965), 72–79.

———. "Thunder out of Oakland," *ibid.* (November 15, 1965), 86–89. [Includes Art Powell.]

SMITH, R. M. *Pro Football.* Garden City, N.Y., 1963.

"Sooner Hopes Hinge on Negro Back: Prentiss Gautt," *Ebony,* XIV (November 1958), 28–29.

SPORTING NEWS. *Football Register.* St. Louis, 1968.

" 'Spot Shot' Galimore," *Ebony,* XIV (January 1959), 72.

STAINBACH, BERRY. *Football Stars of 1965.* New York, 1965.

STREATOR, G. W. "Negro Football Standards," *Crisis,* XXXVIII (March 1931), 85–86.

"Top Negro Stars in Pro Football," *Sepia,* XII (November 1963), 75–78.

"Touchdown Twins: J. C. Caroline and Mickey Bates of the University of Illinois," *Ebony,* IX (October 1954), 111–15.

"The Toughest Man in Football: Emlen Tunnel of the New York Giants," *Ebony,* XIII (November 1957), 99–104.

TRUE MAGAZINE. *Football Yearbook.* New York, 1968.

UNDERWOOD, J. "How Fast Is the Fastest Man Alive?" *Sports Illustrated,* XX (May 18, 1964), 26–29. [About Bob Hayes.]

WALLACE, W. N. "Left Tackle: Roosevelt Brown," *New York Times Magazine* (November 8, 1964), 137–41.

"When He 'Sacrifices,' Watch Out: Football Star Wilmer Cooks!" *Sports Illustrated,* XXIII (September 20, 1965), 51.

WILKINS, ROY. "Negro Stars on Big Grid Teams," *Crisis,* XLIII (December 1936), 362–63.

"Wilmith Sidot-Singh, Football Star," *Crisis,* XLV (November 1938), 350.

WRIGHT, A. "Ernie Davis: A Man of Courage," *Sports Illustrated,* XVIII (May 17, 1963), 24–25.

BASKETBALL

"All the Credentials: Bill Russell," *Time,* LXXXVII (April 29, 1966), 104.

BALTIMORE, C. H. "Negro in Basketball," *Negro Historical Bulletin,* XV (December 1951), 49–50.

"Basketball's Hottest High School: Crispus Attucks [Indianapolis]," *Ebony,* XV (February 1960), 45–46.

"Bill Russell, Basketball's Leaning Tower," *Ebony,* XI (April 1956), 50–54.

"Bill *vs.* Wilt," *Life,* LI (December 1, 1961), 51–52. [About Bill Russell and Wilt Chamberlain.]

BRESLIN, J. "Can Basketball Survive Wilt Chamberlain?" *Saturday Evening Post,* CCXXIX (December 1, 1956), 33.

"Cafe Society Rediscovers Harlem," *Ebony,* XVII (June 1962), 35–36. [About Wilt Chamberlain.]

"Cazzie Russell: Sophomore Cage Phenomenon," *Ebony,* XIX (April 1964), 101–2.

CHAMBERLAIN, WILT. "Pro Basketball Has Ganged Up on Me," *Look,* XXIV (March 1, 1960), 51–55.

———. "Why I am Quitting College," *ibid.,* XXII (June 10, 1958), 91–94.

———, and OTTUM, B. "My Life in a Bush League," *Sports Illustrated,* XXII (April 12 1965), 32–34; (April 19, 1965), 38–41.

"Coach Russell," *Newsweek,* LXVII (May 2, 1966), 72–73.

"The College Scoring Goes to Cincinnati's Oscar Robertson," *Sports Illustrated,* VIII (June 20, 1958), 22.

DALEY, ARTHUR. "The Education of a Basketball Rookie: Bill Russell," *New York Times Magazine* (February 24, 1957), 22.

DEFORD, F. "Another Big Bluff by Big Wilt Chamberlain," *Sports Illustrated,* XXII (January 25, 1965), 18–19.

———. "How K. C. Won an Oscar in the NBA," *ibid.,* XX (March 16, 1964), 22–23. [About Oscar Robertson.]

———. "The Name of the Game Is Cooty's Turnabout: Guy Rogers," *ibid.,* XXIII (December 13, 1965), 26–28.

"Elgin Baylor: Basketball's Mr. Versatility," *Sepia,* XIII (March 1964), 74–77.

"Elgin Baylor Comes Back," *Ebony,* XX (February 1965), 35–36.

"For All the Marbles: Bill Russell," *Time,* LXXXXI (February 24, 1967), 57–58.

"George Wilson and Connie Hawkins, Two Negroes on *Parade* Magazine's All-America High School Team," *Jet* (April 14, 1960), 58.

"Globetrotting Globetrotters," *Ebony,* IX (February 1954), 42–47.

GOTTEHRER, BARRY. *Basketball Stars of 1965*. New York, 1965.

"Graceful Giants: Oscar Robertson," *Time,* LXXVII (February 17, 1961), 54–56.

GROSS, M. "Basketball's Mood Marvel: Oscar Robertson," *Saturday Evening Post,* CCXXXII (December 26, 1959), 19.

"Harlem Magicians: 'Goose' Tatum and Marques Haynes Form Basketball Team," *Ebony,* XI (February 1956), 51–54.

HIRSHBERG, AL. *Basketball's Greatest Stars*. New York, 1963.

"How Do You Stop Him?" *Time,* LXXXI (January 25, 1963), 40–41. [About Wilt Chamberlain.]

"Illinois' Unheralded Champions," *Ebony,* XX (March 1965), 125–28.

"In Cincinnati They Call Him the Big O," *Life,* XLVIII (January 25, 1964), 69–70.

LARDNER, R. "Can Basketball Survive Lew Alcindor?" *Saturday Evening Post,* CCXL (January 14, 1967), 70–73.

LEGGETT, W. "The New Kid on the Block Takes On the Champ," *Sports Illustrated,* XIII (November 14, 1960), 24–25. [About Oscar Robertson.]

LINN, E. "I Owe the Public Nothing: Bill Russell," *Saturday Evening Post,* CCXXXVII (January 18, 1964), 60–63.

McGUIRE, F. "How We Become Champs," *Saturday Evening Post,* CCXXX (December 14, 1957), 25. [About Wilt Chamberlain.]

McHUGH, R. "Hot Rod and the Best," *Sports Illustrated,* II (January 31, 1955), 20–25. [Outstanding college players.]

McKEAN, W. J. "High Lew Alcindor: Basketball's Mt. Everest," *Look,* XXIX (February 9, 1965), 86–90.

"The Man Who May Change Basketball: Wilt Chamberlain," *Ebony,* XII (March 1957), 27–30."

"The Man Who Won't Give Up; Junius Kellogg," *Ebony,* XII (April 1957), 17–24.

MASIN, H. L. "Greatest of Them All: Wilt Chamberlain," *Senior Scholastic,* LXXVI (March 23, 1960), 26.

———. "Green for Danger: Si Green!" *ibid.,* LXVIII (February 23, 1956), 18–19.

———. "Nothing but the Best: Bill Russell," *ibid.,* LXXXVII (December 9, 1965), 36–37.

———."Russell of Spring," *ibid.,* LXVII (January 12, 1956), 29.

———. "Wonderful O," *ibid.,* LXXIV (February 6, 1959), 25.

MASSAQUOI, H. "The Big O," *Ebony,* XV (March 1960), 115–21.

"Negroes in Pro Basketball," *Ebony,* XIV (February 1959), 55–58.

"New Look for All-America: Oscar Robertson," *Life,* XLIV (March 10, 1958), 99.

"Nose to Chin Whiskers: Wilt Chamberlain," *Time,* LXXXIX (January 13, 1967), 51.

"Not a Muscle, Just Russell," *Time,* LXVII (April 2, 1956), 55.

"Notre Dame's First Negro Basketball Stars," *Ebony,* VII (February 1952), 22–25.

" 'Ol' Massa Russell?" *Nation,* CC (March 1, 1965), 211.

"Oscar Robertson: The Hottest Hands in Basketball," *Look,* XXIII (February 3, 1959), 57–58.

OTTUM, B. "Panic Is on Again," *Sports Illustrated,* XXI (November 9, 1964), 18–19. [About Bill Russell.]

"Pro Basketball," *Sports Illustrated,* XXV (October 24, 1966), 40–52.

"Pro Basketball, 1957–1958," *Sports Illustrated,* VII (November 7, 1957), 48–51.

"Pro Basketball Roundup," *Ebony,* XIX (January 1964), 71–72.

"Professional Basketball's Dream Team," *Ebony,* XVI (March 1961), 54–56.

REYNOLDS, QUENTIN. "Nobody's Better Off Dead: Junius Kellogg," *Reader's Digest, LXXII* (March 1958), 160–62.

ROBINSON, LOUIS. "Cincinnati's Stricken Giant: Maurice Stokes," *Ebony,* XIV (April 1959), 38–42.

ROGIN, G. "We Are Grown Men Playing a Child's Game," *Sports Illustrated,* XIX (November 18, 1963), 74–78. [About Bill Russell.]

RUSSELL, BILL. "I Was a 6' 9" Babe in the Woods," *Saturday Evening Post,* CCXXX (January 18, 1958), 25.

———, and McSWEENEY, W. *Go Up for Glory*. New York, 1966.

————, and OTTUM, B. "Psych, and My Other Tricks: Stars of World Champion Boston Celtics," *Sports Illustrated,* XXIII (October 25, 1965), 32–34.

"Scouting Reports: Collegiate Basketball 1960–1961," *Sports Illustrated,* XIII (December 12, 1960), 35–75.

"Scouting Reports: Preview of 135 Collegiate Teams in 17 Major Basketball Conferences Plus Men To Watch," *Sports Illustrated,* VII (December 9, 1967), 44–73.

"Scouting Reports: Westley Unseld of the University of Louisville," *Sports Illustrated,* XXIII (December 6, 1965), 57–58.

"*Sport* Selects Si Green of Duquesne as All-America Cage Choice," *Negro History Bulletin,* XVIII (January 1955), 93.

SPORTS ILLUSTRATED. *Book of Basketball.* Philadelphia, 1962.

STAINBACH, BERRY, and GELMAN, STEVE. *Basketball Stars of 1966.* New York, 1966.

SULLIVAN, G. E. *Wilt Chamberlain.* New York, 1966.

TAX, J. "A Brave Man and a Good Friend: Maurice Stokes," *Sports Illustrated,* XII (February 1, 1960), 10–15.

————. "Bunyan Strides Again: Elgin Baylor," *ibid.,* X (April 6, 1959), 18–19.

————. "Chamberlain's Big Mistake," *ibid.,* XII (April 4, 1960), 58–59.

————. "The Man Who Must Be Different," *ibid.,* VIII (February 3, 1958), 29–32. [About Bill Russell.]

————. "The Test of the Nation's Best: Basketball Title Tournament," *ibid.,* XII (March 14, 1960), 39–42.

————. "Two Big Men in a Tight Pennant Race," *ibid.,* XII (February 22, 1960), 46–47. [About Bill Russell and Wilt Chamberlain.]

————. "Up for Grabs at the Cow Palace: National Collegiate Basketball Title," *ibid.,* XII (March 21, 1960), 38–42.

————. "What Price Glory for Oscar?" *ibid.,* X (January 26, 1959), 18–20.

"What It Took To Get Wilt," *Life,* XLII (January 28, 1957), 113–17.

YOUNG, A. S. "Basketball's Most Perfect Player," *Sepia,* IX (February 1961), 75–79.

ZINKOFF, DAVE. *Around the World with the Harlem Globetrotters.* Philadelphia, 1953.

TENNIS

"Althea Gibson," *Ebony,* VI (November 1950), 96–100.

"Althea's Odyssey," *Life,* XLI (July 2, 1956), 88.

ASHE, ARTHUR. "I'm Simply Me," *Newsweek,* LXIV (September 7, 1964), 53.

BRUNE, JOAN. "Althea the First," *Sports Illustrated,* VII (July 15, 1957), 12.

DEFORD, F. "Service, but First a Smile," *Sports Illustrated,* XXV (August 29, 1966), 47–50.

————. "An Understudy Takes Charge: Arthur Ashe," *ibid.,* XXIII (August 9, 1965), 18–19.

"First Negro Davis Cupper: Arthur Ashe," *Ebony,* XVIII (October 1963), 151–52.

GIBSON, ALTHEA. *I Always Wanted To Be Somebody.* New York, 1958.

"Gibson Girl," *Nation,* CLXXXV (July 20, 1957), 22.

GORDON, H. "Pioneer in Short White Pants," *New York Times Magazine* (January 2, 1966), 6–7. [About Arthur Ashe.]

"Has Althea Finally Arrived?" *Ebony,* XI (August 1956), 35–38.

JARES, JOE. "Arthur Was King for a Day," *Sports Illustrated,* XXIII (September 20, 1965), 36–37.

"Ladies and Gentlemen: Althea Gibson," *Time,* LVI (July 17, 1950), 74.

"Lorraine Williams: Girl Tennis Star," *Ebony,* VII (July 1952), 41.

"New Tennis Threat: Althea Gibson and Others," *Life,* XXVIII (April 3, 1950), 32.

NORMAN, G. F. "The American Tennis Association," *Crisis,* XXIX (November 1924), 22.

————. "Colored Tennis Champions," *ibid.,* XXXI (November 1925), 18.

PALFREY, SARAH. "Althea," *Sports Illustrated,* VII (September 2, 1957), 28–30.

————. "A Champion Looks at Althea Gibson," *Ebony,* VI (November 1950), 101.

"Power Game: Wimbledon Matches," *Time,* LXX (July 15, 1957), 61. [About Althea Gibson.]

REYNOLDS, QUENTIN. "Long Road to the Center Court: Althea Gibson," *Saturday Review,* XLI (November 29, 1958), 16.

"Tennis Queen from Harlem: Althea Gibson," *Ebony,* XII (October 1957), 54–58.

"That Gibson Girl," *Newsweek,* XLVII (May 28, 1956), 62.

"Triumph of Althea," *Newsweek,* L (July 15, 1957), 64.

BOXING

"Alas, Poor Cassius," *Ebony,* XX (July 1965), 144–45.

"All of a Sudden: Ezzard Charles," *Time,* LVI (December 18, 1950), 69–70.

"Amazing Career of Sam Langford, Boxer," *Ebony,* XI (April 1956), 97–105.

"Archie Moore," *Ebony,* VIII (April 1953), 52–56.

ARMSTRONG, HENRY. *Gloves, Glory and God.* New York, 1956.

ASTOR, G. "Sonny Liston: King of the Beasts," *Look,* XXVIII (February 25, 1964), 67–68.

ATKINSON, L. *Joseph 'Joe' Louis.* [Famous American Athletes of Today; 6th series by Harold Kaese and other sportswriters.] Boston, 1938.

BATCHELOR, DENZIL. *Jack Johnson and His Times.* London, 1956.

BELL, NORMAN. *The Fighting Life of a Fighter: How Joe Louis Became the World's Greatest Heavyweight,* London, 1943.

"Bob Satterfield: Boxer or Bum?" *Ebony,* IX (November 1953), 136–40.

BOWEN, E., and KANE, M. "Conversation Piece: Archie Moore," *Sports Illustrated,* III (September 19, 1955), 18–21.

"Boxing Coach Chuck Adkins," *Ebony,* VIII (July 1953), 98–100.

"The Boxing Monopoly Puts On the Squeeze," *Sports Illustrated,* II (January 24, 1955), 24–26.

"Boxing's Biggest Bout," *Ebony,* XVIII (November 1962), 36–38. [Patterson–Liston fight.]

"Boxing's Feet of Clay," *Saturday Evening Post,* CCXXXVII (April 18, 1964), 86.

"Boxing's Rookie of the Year: Floyd Patterson," *Ebony,* LX (March 1954), 38–43.

BOYLE, ROBERT H. "For Boxing: A Year of Decision," *Sports Illustrated,* XXII (January 4, 1965), 20–21.

———. "Sonny Stands Alone," *ibid.,* XIX (July 29, 1963), 12–15.

———. "Taking Stock on Sonny Liston," *ibid.,* XX (April 6, 1964), 24–27.

———, and SHARNIK, M. "Heavyweight Muddle," *ibid.,* XVIII (March 25, 1963), 12–15. [About Sonny Liston.]

BRATTEN, J. J. "Lament for a Fighter: The Wasted Years," *Sports Illustrated,* V (July 9, 1956), 28–31.

BRESLIN, J. "Be a Champ, Act a Champ," *Saturday Evening Post,* CCXXXV (September 22, 1962), 62–63. [About Sonny Liston.]

———. "Last Days of Sugar Ray," *ibid.,* CCXXXV (March 17, 1962), 106–9.

"Budgeted Beakbusting: Louisville Businessmen Promote Heavyweight Cassius Clay," *Business Week* (November 24, 1962), 30–31.

BURLEY, DAN. "Why Walcott Won't Fight," *Ebony,* VII (December 1951), 64–66.

BURNES, R. L. "Heavyweight with a Past: Sonny Liston," *Saturday Evening Post,* CCXXX (August 13, 1960), 28.

"C. Marcellus Clay, Esq.," *Sports Illustrated,* XVIII (June 10, 1963), 18–25.

"Cassius Clay: Weak on Tests, Strong on Finances," *U.S. News and World Report,* LVI (March 30, 1964), 10.

"Cassius—Still Champ!" *Sepia,* XV (January 1966), 80–81.

"Champion Is a Feeling: Ezzard Charles," *Newsweek,* XXXVII (January 22, 1951), 78.

"Champ's African Love Affair," *Ebony,* XIX (September 1964), 85–86. [About Cassius Clay.]

CHARLES, EZZARD. "How I'll Beat Rocky Marciano," *Ebony,* IX (June 1954), 27–32.

———. "I Was Jinxed by Joe Louis," *ibid.,* VI (October 1951), 114–16.

CLAY, CASSIUS. "Hare Was No Rabbit," *Life,* LVIII (February 12, 1965), 97–98.

———. "I'm a Little Special," *Sports Illustrated,* XX (February 24, 1964), 14–15.

COPE, MYRON. "Muslim Champ," *Saturday Evening Post,* CCXXXVII (November 14, 1964), 32–34.

"Depends on How You Look At It: Foreign Press Reports on Sonny Liston," *Sports Illustrated,* XIX (August 5, 1963), 9.

DIAMOND, WILFRID. *How Great Was Joe Louis?* New York, 1950.

DURANT, J. *The Heavyweight Champions.* New York, 1964.

EARLE, ALICE MORSE. *Colonial Days in Old New York.* New York, 1899. [Includes Tom Molineaux.]

"Ezzard Charles: Winner and New Champion!" *Time,* LVIII (July 30, 1951), 66.

"Ezzard Charles: Winner and Old Champion," *Life,* XXXI (July 30, 1951), 66–67.

FARR, FINIS. *Black Champion: The Life and Times of Jack Johnson.* New York, 1964.

"Fighting Family: Cleveland's Nate Brooks and Brothers Are Boxers," *Ebony,* IX (July 1954), 70–74.

"Final Bell: Ray Robinson," *Time,* LXV (January 31, 1953), 42.

FLEISCHER, N. S. *Black Dynamite: The Story of the Negro in the Prize Ring from 1782 to 1938.* New York, 1938.

———. *The Louis Legend: The Amazing Story of the Brown Bomber.* New York, 1956.

FOX, R. K. *The Black Champions of the Prize Ring: From Molineaux to Jackson.* New York, 1890.

"From Ring Killer to Saver of Souls," *Negro History Bulletin,* XVIII (January 1955), 93–94.

"The Gentle Champion: Hogan Bassey," *Ebony,* XIV (December 1958), 66–68.

GOTTEHRER, B. "Reluctant Dragon: Floyd Patterson," *Newsweek,* LVIII (December 18, 1961), 71.

"Grace under Pressure: Ray Robinson," *Newsweek,* XLIX (January 14, 1957), 54.

GREENFELD, J. "Power of a Positive Left Hook to the Jaw: Sugar Ray Robinson," *Reporter,* XVI (May 30, 1957), 41–42.

GRIGGS, L. "Fame and Heartbreak in the Golden Gloves," *Sports Illustrated,* II (March 28, 1955), 24–28.

HAMILL, P. "Floyd's Fight To Save His Pride," *Saturday Evening Post,* CCXXXVII (June 27, 1964), 76–78.

HEINZ, W. C. "Mystery of Archie Moore," *Saturday Evening Post,* CCXXVIII (September 17, 1955), 26–27.

———. "Strange Case of Ezzard Charles," *ibid.,* CCXXIV (June 7, 1952), 34.

HOBAN, R. "An Artist Looks At His Subject: Floyd Patterson," *Sports Illustrated,* VI (March 18, 1957), 34.

HORN, H. "Comeuppance for the Cocksure Cassius: Clay–Jones Fight," *Sports Illustrated,* XVIII (March 25, 1963), 16–17.

———. "First Days in the New Life of the Champion of the World, Cassius Clay," *ibid.,* XX (March 9, 1964), 26–27.

———. "Rueful Dream Came True: Liston–Clay Championship Fight," *ibid.,* XIX (November 18, 1963), 26–27.

"How Cassius Clay Lost His Cool," *Sepia,* XV (June 1966), 16–21.

JACK, B. "Maybe Somebody Did Rob Me, but I Don't Know Who," *Sports Illustrated,* I (November 29, 1954), 18–20. [Boxer's purse and discrimination.]

"Joe Louis and the Negro Press," *Crisis,* XLIII (August 1936), 241.

"John Lester Johnson: The Man Who Broke Jack Dempsey's Ribs," *Ebony,* XV (January 1960), 80–85.

JOHNSON, JACK. *Jack Johnson in the Ring and out.* Chicago, 1927.

JONES, CLAUDIA. *Lift Every Voice for Victory!* New York, 1942. [Biography of Joe Louis.]

JONES, L. "In the Ring: Cassius Clay," *Nation,* CXCVIII (June 29, 1964), 661–62.

KANE, M. "And the Veep Sat Down," *Sports Illustrated,* VII (September 2, 1957), 15–16. [Patterson–Rademacher fight.]

———. "Beyond Endurance: Patterson *vs.* Jackson," *ibid.,* VII (August 7, 1957), 12–13.

———. "Breathing Easy: Archie Moore–Besmanoff Fight," *ibid.,* XII (June 6, 1960), 58 .

———. "Cleveland Clincher: Basilio-Saxton Fight," *ibid.,* VI (March 4, 1957), 26.

———. "EE-Yah: Johansson-Patterson Fight," *ibid.,* XII (June 27, 1960), 16–19.

———. "The Greatest Meets the Grimmest: Clay-Liston Fight," *ibid.,* XXIII (November 15, 1965), 26–28.

———. "Handicap, My Eye!" *ibid.,* VIII (April 7, 1958), 18–20. [Robinson-Basilio fight.]

———. "Last Chance for Old Arch," *ibid.,* V (November 26, 1956), 34–36.

———. "The Man the System Could Not Beat," *ibid.,* V (December 10, 1956), 8–14. [Moore-Patterson fight.]

———. "A Mighty Peculiar Fight: Johnny Saxton Defeats Basilio," *ibid.,* IV (March 26, 1956), 31–32.

———. "Overmatched, the NBA Concedes to Archie Moore," *ibid.,* XII (March 14, 1960), 47–48.

———. "Patterson by a KO," *ibid.,* VII (July 29, 1957), 24–29.

———. "Speedy Floyd Outsped: Patterson–Harris Fight," *ibid.,* IX (August 11, 1958), 39.

———. "Springfield Rifle Takes the Title: Davey Moore Defeats Hogan Bassey," *ibid.,* X (March 30,1959), 34–39.

———. "A Surprise Party with a Punch: Virgil Akins Welterweight Champion," *ibid.,* VIII (June 16, 1958), 34–36.

———. "Terror: 342 Seconds with Basilio–Saxton," *ibid.,* VI (March 4, 1957), 22–23.

———. "Why Ingo Will Do It Again: Johansson–Patterson Fight," *ibid.,* XII (June 20, 1960), 16–22.

———. "Willie Ran Out of Pep," *ibid.,* IX (September 29, 1958), 46.

———. "Young Body over Old Mind," *ibid.,* VII (September 30, 1957), 10. [Robinson–Basilio fight.]

KEMPTON, M. "I Whipped Him and I'm Still Pretty," *New Republic,* CL (March 7, 1964), 9–10. [About Cassius Clay.]

"Kid Chocolate, the Boxer Who Listened to Mother," *Ebony,* XII (April 1957), 49–52.

"Kid Gavilan, Boxing's Happiest Champ," *Ebony,* VIII (October 1953), 122–27.

KIERAN, JOHN. "A Champion All the Way: Joe Louis," *Opportunity,* XX (February 1942), 48–49.

KING, L. L. "Sugar: Down but Not Quite Out," *Sports Illustrated,* XXIII (September 6, 1965), 58–66.

KIRSON, S., and AROND, HENRY. "The Occupational Culture of a Boxer," *American Journal of Sociology,* LVII (March 1952), 460.

"Kitchel's Dream of Glory," *Sports Illustrated,* I (October 18, 1954), 80–81. [About Jack Johnson.]

LAFONTAINE, B. "He's Just Got That Look: Sonny Liston," *Sports Illustrated,* XXII (April 26, 1965), 32–34.

LARDNER, J. "And He Can't Play a Comb," *Newsweek,* XLIV (August 23, 1954), 73. [About Archie Moore.]

———. "Bloodshed Overdue: Ezzard Charles," *ibid.,* XLIII (June 14, 1954), 64.

———. "How History Is Made: Joe Louis," *ibid.,* XLIX (April 29, 1957), 66.

———. "King of the Sharecroppers: Archie Moore," *ibid.,* XLVI (August 8, 1955), 75.

———. "No Scar, No Memory: Sugar Ray Robinson," *ibid.,* XLIX (May 13, 1957), 77.

———. "Old Man's Price: Archie Moore," *ibid.,* L (July 1, 1957), 73.

———. "Plain Guy Wins: Johnny Saxton," *ibid.,* XLVIII (September 24, 1956), 72.

"Last Prizefighter: Ray Robinson," *Newsweek,* L (September 23, 1957), 106.

"Last Seconds of a Champion: Sugar Ray Robinson," *Sports Illustrated,* VI (January 14, 1957), 8–10.

LAWRY, R. "For the Middleweight Championship: Blood Wedding in Chicago—Ray Robinson's Fight," *American Mercury,* LXXII (May 1951), 578–92.

"Left Hooks and Tenterhooks: Clay–Liston Title Fight," *Sports Illustrated,* XIX (August 12, 1963), 5.

LEGGETT, W. "An Angry Tiger Jumps on Joey," *Sports Illustrated,* XXIII (November 1, 1965), 20–21.

LEWIS, CLAUDE. *Cassius Clay.* New York, 1965.

LIEBLING, A. J. "Reporter at Large: Cassius Clay," *New Yorker,* XXXVIII (March 3, 1962), 104.

———. "Reporter at Large: Charles–Marciano Fight," *ibid.,* XXX (July 10, 1954), 44.

———. "Reporter at Large: Charles–Marciano Fight," *ibid.,* XXX (October 2, 1954), 75–82.

———. "Reporter at Large: Joe Louis," *ibid.,* XXVII (June 30, 1951), 31–32; (November 17, 1951), 102.

———. "Reporter at Large: Marciano–Walcott Fight," *ibid.,* XXVIII (October 11, 1952), 81–88.

———. "Reporter at Large: Marciano–Walcott Fight," *ibid.,* XXIX (May 30, 1953), 33–34.

———. "Reporter at Large: Moore–Johnson Fight," *ibid.,* XXX (September 4, 1954), 44.

——. "Reporter at Large: Sugar Ray Robinson," *ibid.,* XXVII (September 29, 1951), 76; XXVIII (July 12, 1952), 62.

——. "Sporting Scene: Clay *vs.* Jones Fight," *ibid.,* XXXIX (March 30, 1963), 122.

——. "Sporting Scene: Patterson *vs.* Liston Return Fight," *ibid.,* XXXIX (August 10, 1963), 62.

——. "Sporting Scene: Sonny Liston," *ibid.,* XXXVIII (July 7, 1962), 78; (October 6, 1962), 103–10.

LIPSYTE, R. "Cassius Clay, Cassius X, Muhammad Ali," *New York Times Magazine* (October 25, 1964), 29.

LISTON, SONNY. "Famous Last Words: Interview," *Esquire,* LVIII (October 1962), 104–7.

"Little Joe Louis, Joe Brown," *Ebony,* XIII (July 1958), 88–91.

LOUIS, JOE. "Fidel and the U.S. Negro," *Time,* LXXV (June 6, 1960), 36.

——. *How To Box.* Philadelphia, 1948.

——. "I'd Do It All Over Again," *Ebony,* XI (November 1955), 65–70.

——. *The Joe Louis Story.* New York, 1953.

——. *My Life Story.* New York, 1947.

——. "Oh, Where Did My Money Go?" *Saturday Evening Post,* CCXXVIII (January 7, 1956), 22–23.

LYON, P. "Archie Moore, the Oldest Youth," *Holiday,* XXVI (December 1959), 133–35.

McKINNEY, J. "Sonny Liston: A Smell of Rain and Victory," *Sports Illustrated,* XVII (August 27, 1962), 50.

MacLEOD, R. "Hysterical Calm Grips Toronto: Patterson–McNeeley Fight," *Sports Illustrated,* XV (December 4, 1961), 62–63.

MAGRIEL, PAUL. "Tom Molineaux," *Phylon,* XII (December 1951), 329–36.

MAILER, NORMAN. "Ten Thousand Words a Minute: Floyd Patterson," *Esquire,* LIX (February 1963), 109–20.

MALEY, R. "Joe Louis' Greatest Fight," *Newsweek,* XXXVIII (November 12, 1951), 116.

"The Man Who Came Back: Sugar Ray Robinson," *Ebony,* XI (April 1956), 31–34.

"Man with a Sock: Sonny Liston," *Time,* LXXIV (August 17, 1959), 46.

MASSAQUOI, H. J. "Should Boxing Be Abolished?" *Ebony,* XVII (June 1962), 44–46.

MAULE, T. "Cassius To Win a Thriller," *Sports Illustrated,* XXII (March 24, 1965), 22–25.

——. "Fight in Sweden between Boxing's Forgotten Men," *ibid.,* XXI (July 6, 1964), 50–52. [About Floyd Patterson.]

——. "Liston's Edge: A Lethal Left," *ibid.,* XX (February 24, 1964), 18–21.

——. "No Place To Wear His Crown: Ernie Terrell," *ibid.,* XXII (March 15, 1965), 28–29.

——. "A Quick, Hard Right and a Needless Storm of Protest: Clay–Liston Fight," *ibid.,* XXII (June 7, 1965), 22–24.

——. "Sting of the Louisville Lip," *ibid.,* XX (February 17, 1964), 50–51. [About Cassius Clay.]

——. "Yes, It Was Good and Honest," *ibid.,* (March 9, 1964), 20–25. [Clay–Liston fight.]

"Meet Young Mr. Anthony," *Sports Illustrated,* VI (April 15, 1957), 20–22.

MILES, H. D. *Pugilistica: Being One Hundred and Forty-Four Years of the History of British Boxing.* London, 1880.

MILLER, MARGERY. *Joe Louis, American.* New York, 1951.

MILLSTEIN, G. "In This Corner, at Long Last, Archie Moore!" *New York Times Magazine* (September 11, 1955), 26.

MOORE, ARCHIE. *The Archie Moore Story.* New York, 1960.

——. "My Rocky Road to Rocky," *Look,* XIX (September 6, 1955), 94–99; (September 20, 1955), 80–82.

——. "The Secret of My Diet," *Sports Illustrated,* XIII (July 4, 1960), 27–29.

MOORE, G. "Boxing Killed My Husband," *Ebony,* XVIII (July 1963), 31–32.

MORRISON, ALLAN. "Boxing's Most Misunderstood Champion: Floyd Patterson," *Ebony,* XIV (April 1959), 78–81.

——. "Sonny Liston: Boxing's Angry Man," *ibid.,* XVII (August 1962), 46–48.

"Muhammad Ali in Africa," *Sports Illustrated,* XX (June 1, 1964), 20–25.

MURPHY, J. "Champ behind the Mask," *New York Times Magazine* (July 21, 1963), 18. [About Sonny Liston.]

————. "Profiles: Archie Moore," *New Yorker,* XXXVII (November 11, 1961), 61–62.

MURRAY, J. "Put Away the Flowers: Ray Robinson's Comeback," *Sports Illustrated,* XIII (December 12, 1960), 17–19.

"Negroes Make Clean Sweep of Boxing," *Ebony,* XIII (October 1958), 90–94.

NEWCOMBE, JACK. *Floyd Patterson, Heavyweight King.* New York, 1961.

"Night Floyd Patterson Wept," *Sepia,* XIV (April 1965), 52–55.

NIPSON, H. "How Good Is Cassius Clay?" *Ebony,* XIX (April 1964), 77–80.

"Obituary: Sam Langford," *Newsweek,* XLVII (January 23, 1956), 71.

"Old Folks: Charles–Walcott Fight," *Newsweek,* XXXVIII (July 30, 1951), 45.

OLSEN, JACK. *Black Is Best: The Riddle of Cassius Clay.* New York, 1967.

"One of the Great Ones: Archie Moore," *Newsweek,* LIII (February 23, 1959), 92.

O'NEIL, P. "Meet the Next Heavyweight Champion: Floyd Patterson," *Sports Illustrated,* IV (January 30, 1956), 19–21.

"*Pageant* Salutes Joe Louis," *Negro History Bulletin,* XVI (June 1953), 201.

PATTERSON, FLOYD. "Cassius Clay Must Be Beaten," *Sports Illustrated,* XXIII (October 11, 1965), 78–88.

————. "The Floyd Patterson I Know I Am," *ibid.,* XIV (March 27, 1961), 28–33.

————. "I Live with Myself: Patterson–Liston Fight," *ibid.,* XIX (August 5, 1963), 27.

————. "I Want My Title Back: Johansson–Patterson Rematch," *Ebony,* XIV (September 1959), 47.

————. "I Want To Destroy Clay," *Sports Illustrated,* XXI (October 19, 1964), 42–44.

————. "My Greatest Ambition, Financial Security," *Ebony,* XII (March 1957), 59–62.

————. *Victory over Myself.* New York, 1962.

————. "With a Bit of Fear," *Sports Illustrated,* XVIII (September 17, 1962), 18–23.

"Philadelphia Fiasco: Johnny Saxton," *Time,* LXIV (November 1, 1954), 57.

PLIMPTON, G. "Miami Notebook: Cassius Clay and Malcolm X," *Harper's Magazine,* CCXXVIII (June 1964), 54–61.

"Portrait: Ezzard Charles," *Newsweek,* XXXVII (April 2, 1951), 59.

"Portrait: Ezzard Charles," *Time,* LVI (October 16, 1950), 42.

QUARLES, BENJAMIN. "Peter Jackson Speaks of Boxers," *Negro History Bulletin,* XVIII (November 1954), 39–40.

"A Real Champion: Joe Louis," *Opportunity,* XVII (October 1939), 290–91.

RICE, HAROLD. *Within the Ropes: Champions in Action.* New York, 1946.

ROBINSON, RAY. "Why I'm the Bad Boy of Boxing," *Ebony,* VI (November 1950), 72–74.

ROGIN, G. "Billy Fox: Just Riding into Evening," *Sports Illustrated,* XIII (July 11, 1960), 30–34.

————. "Campaign Is Ended for an Ancient Warrior: Archie Moore–Cassius Clay Fight," *ibid.,* XVII (November 26, 1962), 18–21.

————. "Cautious Comes of Age," *ibid.,* XV (October 16, 1961), 22.

————. "Champion as Long as He Wants: Cassius Clay," *ibid.,* XXIII (November 29, 1965), 20–25.

————. "The Death of a King: Sugar Ray Robinson," *ibid.,* XII (June 20, 1960), 54–55.

————. "Drama in Miami: Johansson–Patterson Fight," *ibid.,* XIV (March 20, 1960), 16–21.

———— ."Facts about the Big Fight: Liston–Patterson Fight," *ibid.,* XVII (October 8, 1962), 20–27.

————. "Heavyweight in Waiting: Liston KO's Zora Folley," *ibid.,* XIII (August 1, 1960), 49–50.

————. "Man in the Champ's Corner: Cassius Clay," *ibid.,* XXII (May 24, 1965), 32–36.

————. "Mild Champion Beats an Inferior Brawler: Patterson–McNeeley Fight," *ibid.,* XV (December 11, 1961), 24–25.

————. "Sugar's Show Goes On," *ibid.,* XII (February 1, 1960), 31–33.

————, and SHARNIK, M. "Can't a Fellow Make a Mistake?" *ibid.,* XV (July 17, 1961), 22–24. [About Sonny Liston.]

ROXBOROUGH, J. W. "How I Discovered Joe Louis: Ex–Manager's Insight into the Character of the Former Champ," *Ebony,* IX (October 1954), 64–76.

"Run, Cassius, Run," *New Yorker,* XL (March 7, 1964), 43–44.

SANFORD, N. *Stand Up and Fight.* New York, 1962.

SCHOOR, GENE. *Sugar Ray Robinson.* New York, 1951.

SCHULBERG, B. "Boxing's Dirty Business Must Be Cleaned Up Now," *Sports Illustrated,* I (November 1, 1954), 11–12.

———. "Charles *vs.* Marciano," *ibid.,* I (September 13, 1954), 62–63.

———. "Rematch Is No Match," *ibid.,* I (September 27, 1954), 58–60. [Marciano–Charles fight.]

———. "Sugar Ray: A Will and Five Inspired Seconds," *ibid.,* III (December 19, 1955), 36–37.

SCOTT, NEIL. *Joe Louis: A Picture Story of His Life.* New York, 1947.

"Should Boxing Be Abolished?" *Ebony,* X (January 1955), 34–36.

" 'Silent' Hariston: Deaf Mute in the Boxing Ring," *Ebony,* VI (June 1951), 80–84.

SKELTON, B. "Sparring Partner Looks Them Over," *Sports Illustrated,* XVII (September 24, 1962), 26. [About Sonny Liston and Floyd Patterson.]

STEWART-GORDON, J. "Boxing's Old Man River: Archie Moore," *Rotarian,* XCV (July 1959), 18–19.

"Sugar Ray Dares the Odds: Basilio–Robinson Fight," *Sports Illustrated,* VIII (March 24, 1958), 20–24.

"Sugar Ray's Farewell to Boxing," *Sepia,* XV (March 1966), 50–55.

SULLIVAN, GEORGE. *The Cassius Clay Story.* New York, 1964.

SUTTON, I. "Intimate Look at a Champ: Cassius Clay," *Ebony,* XXII (November 1966), 148–54.

"Sweet Sugar the Great," *Ebony,* XIII (June 1958), 150–54.

"Symposium: Opinions on Liston's Right to Fight," *Sports Illustrated,* XVI (February 12, 1962), 10–11.

TALESE, GAY. "Joe Louis: The King as a Middle-Aged Man," *Esquire,* LVII (June 1962), 92–98.

———. "Loser: Floyd Patterson," *ibid.,* LXI (March 1964), 65–68.

———. "Portrait of the Ascetic Champ: Floyd Patterson," *New York Times Magazine* (March 5, 1961), 34.

"Television's Most Successful Slugger; Tiger Jones Has Current Record of 42 TV Bouts," *Ebony,* XV (September 1960), 55–56.

"The Ten Biggest Lies about Joe Louis," *Ebony,* VIII (August 1953), 52–60.

TERRELL, R. "And Down Went Number One: Johnny Saxton!" *Sports Illustrated,* XV (November 27, 1961), 22–25.

"This Is What Charles Took from Marciano," *Life,* XXXVI (June 28, 1954), 16–17.

"Tiger Jones: TV's Most Successful Slugger," *Ebony,* XV (September 1960), 55–59.

"Time Runs Out for Archie Moore," *Sports Illustrated,* XIII (November 7, 1960), 20.

"Truman Gibson: Boxing's New Brainbuster," *Ebony,* VII (November 1951), 52–58.

TUCKNER, H. M. "Man, It's Great To Be Great," *New York Times Magazine* (December 9, 1962), 47–48. [About Cassius Clay.]

"Tuning Up for Ingo in Indiana: Patterson–Johansson Fight," *Sports Illustrated,* X (May 11, 1959), 34–36.

TURPIN, GUY. *Forgotten Men of the Prize Ring: A Reference Book of Old-Time Boxers.* San Antonio, 1963.

"Twice Is Once Too Often: Second Marciano–Charles Fight," *Life,* XXXVII (September 27, 1954), 32.

VAN DEUSEN, JOHN G. *Brown Bomber: The Story of Joe Louis.* Philadelphia, 1940.

VAN EVERY, EDWARD. *Joe Louis: Man and Super-Fighter.* New York, 1936.

"Violent Paws in the Cow Palace: Zora Folley," *Sports Illustrated,* VIII (April 21, 1958), 30–32.

WARD, ARCH. "Negroes in the Golden Gloves," *Ebony,* VI (March 1951), 86–92.

"Was Jack Johnson Boxing's Greatest Champ?" *Ebony,* XVIII (January 1963), 67–70.

WATSON, E. "Really a Hug Fest: Liston–Machen Fight," *Sports Illustrated,* XIII (September 19, 1960), 111–12.

"Who Can Beat Him?" *Newsweek,* LXII (August 5, 1963), 68–69. [About Sonny Liston.]

"Why Sugar Ray Broke His Promise to God: His Return to the Ring," *Ebony,* X (February 1955), 51–53.

WOLFE, TOM. "Marvelous Mouth Cassius Clay," *Esquire,* LX (October 1963), 146.

YOUNG, ANDREW S., DOC." "Boxing's Elder Statesman, Archie Moore," *Ebony,* XIII (January 1958), 63–72.

———. *Sonny Liston: The Champ Nobody Wanted.* Chicago, 1963.

———. "What Happened to Jersey Joe's Money?" *Ebony,* XI (July 1956), 51–54.

"Youngest Champ of Heavyweights: Archie Moore," *Life,* XLI (December 10, 1956), 54–55.

TRACK AND FIELD

"The Americas' Biggest Sports Meet: Pan American Games 1959," *Ebony,* XIV (September 1959), 40–45.

"Andy Stanfield; The World's Fastest Human," *Our World,* VI (March 1951), 64–65.

"Big Man on Campus: Rafer Johnson," *Ebony,* XIV (May 1959), 53–58.

"Boston Marathon: New York Team Finishes First in Toughest Race," *Ebony,* X (July 1955), 103–6.

BRELIS, D. "Young Man on the Way Up: John Thomas," *Sports Illustrated,* X (February 9, 1959), 40–41.

BROWER, W. A. "Jean Betty Lane, Wilberforce's Mercurial Maiden," *Opportunity,* XIX (June 1941), 172–73.

BURLEY, D. "America's Fastest Female Athlete," *Sepia,* VII (March 1959), 62–66.

BUSH, J. B. "Grandest Olympian: James Cleveland 'Jesse' Owens," *Negro History Bulletin,* XXV (May 1962), 191–93.

"Can Negro Athletes Stop the Russians?" *Ebony,* VII (May 1952), 66–72.

"Can Whitfield Run the Four-Minute Mile?" *Ebony,* IX (May 1954), 36–40.

"Champion: Rafer Johnson," *Time,* LXXVI (September 19, 1960), 75.

COBB, W. MONTAGUE. "Race and Runners," *Journal of Health and Physical Education,* VII (1936), 3–6.

"College Track Champs; Morgan State Is First Negro School To Crack Bigtime Track," *Ebony,* VI (May 1951), 102–05.

"Color-Blind Stopwatch," *Nation,* CXCI (September 3, 1960), 101–02.

CREAMER, R. "The Riotous Wannamaker Mile," *Sports Illustrated,* II (February 14, 1955), 9–13. [Includes Harrison Dillard and Arthur Bragg.]

"Diplomat in Short Pants: Mal Whitfield," *Sports Illustrated,* II (February 7, 1955), 12–15.

"Don Newcombe and Jesse Owens Featured in *Sport,*" *Negro History Bulletin,* XVII (April 1954), 150.

DONOVAN, W. *All-Time Indoor Track and Field Record Book.* Liberty, N.Y., 1960.

"Dues Did It: Miller High School Track Team," *Newsweek,* XXXIII (June 6, 1949), 72.

"Famous Athlete's Diplomatic Debut: Jesse Owens," *Life,* XXXIX (October 31, 1955), 49–50.

"Fastest Female: Wilma Rudolph," *Time,* LXXVI (September 19, 1960), 74–75.

"The Fastest Men in the World: Willie Williams and Ira Murchison," *Ebony,* XII (November 1956), 102–7.

"Fastest Women in the World: Negro Women Win Fame at Pan American Games," *Ebony,* X (June 1955), 27–32.

"Field Day in Plainfield: Milt Campbell," *Time,* LXII (July 13, 1953), 50.

FINLAGSON, ANN," *Decathlon Men: Greatest Athletes in the World.* Champaign, Ill., 1966. [About Rafer Johnson.]

"Five for the Book," *Sports Illustrated,* X (March 2, 1959), 20–21. [Includes John Thomas.]

"Giant on the Track: Rafer Johnson," *Time,* LXVIII (July 23, 1956), 56.

"Girl on the Run: Wilma Rudolph," *Newsweek,* LVII (February 6, 1961), 54.

"Girls' Track Coach in Hawaii," *Ebony,* XVIII (March 1963), 53–54. [About Donnis Thompson.]

GREENSPAN, B. "Champion's Reward: Jesse Owens," *Coronet,* XXXIV (September 1953), 103–4.

HALEY, A. "Girl Who Wouldn't Give Up: Wilma Rudolph," *Reader's Digest,* LXXVIII (May 1961), 140–42.

HEILMAN, B. "Wilma and Ed," *Sports Illustrated,* XIII (November 11, 1960), 48–58.

"High School of Champions: McClymonds of Oakland, California," *Ebony,* XVIII (April 1965), 25–28.

HORNE, F. "Running Fools," *Crisis,* XXXVII (November 1930), 375–76.

"Hustlers: Arnie Sowell," *Time,* LXIX (February 18, 1957), 83.

JARES, JOE. "Off to Russia, without Love," *Sports Illustrated,* XXIII (July 2, 1965), 20–21. [Includes Wyomia Tyas.]

"Jefferson High [Los Angeles] Best High School Track Team in the U.S.," *Ebony,* VIII (June 1953), 106–10.

"Joe Louis and Jesse Owens," *Crisis,* XLII (August 1935), 241.

"John Thomas: Boy Wonder from Boston," *Ebony,* XIV (April 1959), 109–12.

"John Thomas: Brumel Drives a Rambler and Gets His Apartment Free," *Life,* LVIII (June 18, 1965), 72a.

"John Thomas: Higher and Farther," *Time,* LXXVII (February 24, 1961), 54.

JOHNSON, RAFER. "Our Olympic Chances," *Senior Scholastic,* LXXXV (October 7, 1964), 54.

"Jumper on the Mend: John Thomas," *Newsweek,* LV (January 18, 1960), 44.

"King of the Hurdlers," *Ebony,* XIX (April 1964), 63–66.

"Mae Faggs; The Human Rabbit," *Our World,* IX (July 1954), 80–81.

"Magnificent Obsession: Jim Brewer," *Sports Illustrated,* VI (April 15, 1957), 23.

"Mal Whitfield: Athletic Ambassador," *Time,* LXV (February 7, 1955), 32.

"Mal Whitfield: Champion with a Plan," *Time,* LXI (February 16, 1953), 75.

"Mal Whitfield: Out of the Mirror," *Newsweek,* XLI (March 16, 1953), 96.

"Mal Whitfield: U.S. Ambassador of Sports," *Ebony,* XVI (October 1961), 82.

MARTINEZ, A. "No Tears for David," *Ebony,* XV (December 1959), 92–98. [About David Hughes.]

MASIN, H. L. "Campbell Is Coming!" *Senior Scholastic,* LXII (February 25, 1953), 22.

———. "Jumping for Joy: John Thomas," *ibid.,* LXXVIII (April 5, 1961), 20–21.

MAULE, T. "An Explosion That Sputtered U.S.–Russian Track Meet," *Sports Illustrated,* IX (August 4, 1958), 8–10.

———. "Faster, Ever Faster: Outdoor Track Team for U.S.–Moscow Meet," *ibid.,* VIII (May 2, 1958), 44–49.

———. "The Midwest Has It," *ibid.,* X (May 18, 1959), 61.

———. "Moment of Record: AAU Championships," *ibid.,* VIII (June 23, 1958), 16–19.

———. "Power *vs.* Perfection: The U.S.–Europe Track Meets," *ibid.,* XV (July 17, 1961), 16–17.

———. "Racing the Tigers in the Garden: AAU Track Meet," *ibid.,* VIII (February 24, 1958), 14–17.

———. "Ralph Boston: 27′ ½″, World's Longest Jump," *ibid.,* XIV (June 5, 1961), 18–19.

———. "Sky-High for Kansas: NCAA Track Championship," *ibid.,* X (June 22, 1959), 10.

———. "Thirty-Seven Men To Beat the Russians," *ibid.,* X (June 29, 1959), 20–21.

———. "Warm Days, Hot Times, Coast to Coast," *ibid.,* VI (May 6, 1957), 28–29. [College track stars.]

MEADE, G. P. "Negro in Track Athletics," *Science Monthly,* LXXV (December 1952), 366–71.

"Morgan State: College Track Champs," *Ebony,* VI (May 1951), 102–6.

MURPHY, J. "Sporting Scene: Russian–American Track and Field Championships," *New Yorker,* XXXVIII (August 18, 1962), 76.

MURRAY, J. "Big Night for Wilma," *Sports Illustrated,* XIV (January 30, 1961), 48–49.

———. "The Eclipse of Mr. K., by Rafer Johnson," *ibid.,* XIII (July 18, 1960), 32–38.

"Name Your Ticket: Milt Campbell," *Newsweek,* XLI (April 27, 1953), 90.

"Negro Track Athletes," *Opportunity,* XVIII (April 1940), 99.

"New Role for Rafer," *Ebony,* XXI (December 1965), 181–84.

"New Upsurge in Women's Track," *Ebony,* XVIII (June 1963), 115–16.

"None but the Brave: Rafer Johnson," *Ebony,* XIX (October 1964), 110–112.

"Olympian Quintessence: Wilma Rudolph," *Life*, XLIX (September 19, 1960), 115.

"On Track and Field," *Opportunity*, XVII (July 1939), 162–63.

O'NEIL, P. "Blazing the Way at Boulder: Arnie Sowell," *Sports Illustrated*, III (July 4 1955), 17.

"Others Worthy of Honor, Sports 1960: Wilma Rudolph," *Sports Illustrated*, XIV (January 9, 1961), 34.

OWENS, JESSIE. "They Will Never Run the Miracle Hundred," *Ebony*, XIV (September 1959), 110–112.

"Phil Reavis," *Sports Illustrated*, VIII (February 24, 1958), 17.

PHINIZY, C. "Busy, Busy Jumbo: Villanova Track Team," *Sports Illustrated*, VI (June 3, 1957), 20–23.

———. "Four Garden Duels: Track," *ibid.*, VI (February 18, 1957), 38–39. [Includes Milt Campbell and Lee Calhoun.]

POLING, J. "Team To Beat: The Pioneers," *Sports Illustrated*, IV (February 13, 1956), 19. [About Joe Yancy.]

QUERCETANI, R. L. *A World History of Track and Field Athletics*. London, 1964.

"Rafer Johnson: One Man Track Team," *Ebony*, XI (July 1956), 46–48.

"Rafer, the Versatile," *Newsweek*, XLVIII (November 19, 1956), 126.

"Ralph Boston: Walking on Air," *Time*, LXXVIII (August 4, 1961), 57.

RUDDEEN, K. "Seven Feet Up: John Thomas," *Sports Illustrated*, XII (January 25, 1960), 14–17.

"Runner Up to Sportsman of the Year 1959: Ray Norton, Track and Field," *Sports Illustrated*, XII (January 1, 1960), 33.

RUTLEDGE, D. "Tennessee's Tigerbelles Don't Lose . . .," *Sepia*, VIII (September 1960). 47–49.

"The Saga of Jesse Owens," *Crisis* XLIII (September 1936), 267.

"Schooling for a Fourth: National AAU Championships," *Time*, LXXX (July 9, 1962), 50.

"Soundtrack: Arnold Sowell," *Sports Illustrated*, II (March 7, 1955), 21–22.

"Southern University: New Kings of Track," *Ebony*, XXI (July 1966), 69–70.

"Sportsman of the Year 1958: Rafer Johnson," *Sports Illustrated*, X (January 5, 1959), 19–25.

STEWART, C. R. "Negro in Track and Field," *Negro Historical Bulletin*, XV (December 1951), 45–46.

"Summit for Rafer," *Life*, XLV (August 11, 1958), 91–92.

TERRELL, R. "Rome via Eighth Avenue: Millrose Games with John Thomas and Jim Grelle," *Sports Illustrated*, XII (February 8, 1960), 59–60.

———. "Very Good, Very Tired and Winners All the Way," *ibid.*, XV (July 31, 1961), 12–15.

———. "With the U.S.–1956 Olympic Track and Field," *ibid.*, V (November 19, 1956), 55–58.

"To Do a Little Better: Rafer Johnson," *Time*, LXXVI (August 29, 1960), 52–55.

"Top Man: John Thomas," *Time*, LXXV (January 25, 1960), 76.

"Two-Man Attack on Harlem's Asphalt Jungle: John Thomas," *Ebony*, XVI (June 1961), 27–30.

WALL, C. B. "Solid Gold Champion: Jesse Owens," *Reader's Digest*, LXXIII (July 1958), 97–100.

"Wilma Rudolph: Storming the Citadel," *Time*, LXXVII (February 10, 1961), 57.

"Wilma's Home Town Win," *Life*, XLIX (October 17, 1960), 110–12.

"World's Greatest Athlete: Milton Campbell," *Ebony*, IX (November 1953), 121–26.

OLYMPICS

ABRAHAMS, H. M. *XVII Olympiad, Rome 1960*. London, 1960.

"All-Time U.S. Olympians," *Sports Illustrated*, I (October 18, 1954), 22–23.

BELL, J. N. *Olympic Thrills*. New York, 1965.

BELL, W. N. "Next the Olympics," *Opportunity*, XVI (September 1938), 268–69.

BRODY, T. C. "At Last the Girls Are Ours: Women's Olympic Track and Field Team," *Sports Illustrated*, XXI (August 17, 1964), 68–69.

BUSHNELL, A. A. *1964 United States Olympic Book*. (XVIII Olympiad, Tokyo, Japan). Providence [R.I.], 1964.

———. *United States 1952 Olympic Book*. New York, 1952.

———. *United States 1956 Olympic Book*. New York, 1956.

DURANT, J. *Highlights of the Olympics*. Philadelphia, 1961.

GELMAN, S. *Young Olympic Champions*. New York, 1964.

"Golden Melbourne: 1956 Olympics," *Sports Illustrated*, V (December 10, 1956), 19–29.

GROMBACH, J. V. *The 1964 Olympic Guide*. New York, 1964.

———. *Olympic Cavalcade of Sports*. New York, 1956.

———. *The Olympics, 1960*. New York, 1960.

HIGDON, HAL. *Heroes of the Olympics*. Englewood Cliffs, N.J., 1965.

HUGHES, W. S. K. "Olympiad XVI," *Rotarian*, LXXXVIII (February 1956), 36–38.

KIERAN, JOHN, and DALEY, ARTHUR. *The Story of the Olympic Games*. Philadelphia, 1965.

LECHENPERG, H. *Olympic Games 1964*, [Innsbruck, Tokyo]. New York, 1965.

LENTZ, A. G. *United States 1960 Olympic Book* (XVII Olympiad, Rome, Italy). New York: United States Olympic Association, 1960.

LIEBLING, A. J. "Letter from the Olympics," *New Yorker*, XXXVI (September 10, 1960), 85–86; (September 17, 1960), 186–89; (September 24, 1960), 152.

LONG, L. "The Day a Nation Remembered: Germany Erases Hitler's Snub of Jesse Owens," *Ebony*, XV (April 1960), 77–82.

MASIN, H. L. "Our Olympic Chances: Interview with Rafer Johnson," *Senior Scholastic*, LXXXV (October 7, 1964), 54.

MAULE, T. "Dead Aim on the Olympics," *Sports Illustrated*, XII (June 27, 1960), 20–23.

———. "Olympics 1960," *ibid.*, XIII (September 12, 1960), 17–25.

"A Mixed Bag of Medals: 1956 Olympics," *Sports Illustrated*, V (November 19, 1956), 86–87.

"Olympic Athletic Records," *Science News Letter*, LXX (August 11, 1956), 85.

"Olympic Rivals: Everyone Is Equal," *Newsweek*, LVI (August 29, 1960), 81.

OWENS, JESSE. "My Great Olympic Prize," *Reader's Digest*, LXXVII (October 1960), 132–35.

PARRIS, W. A. "American Negro in the Sixteenth Olympiad," *Negro History Bulletin*, XX (May 1957), 179–80.

PHINIZY, C. "The 1956 Olympics Preview," *Sports Illustrated*, V (November 19, 1956), 41–51.

POTTS, D. H., and QUERCETANI, R. L. *The Association of Track and Field Statisticians Olympic Handbook*. Los Altos, Calif., 1956.

RUBIEN, F. W. *United States 1936 Olympic Book*. New York, 1936.

SCHAAP, RICHARD. *An Illustrated History of the Olympics*. New York, 1963.

TERRELL, R. "Olympians Are Your Neighbors," *Sports Illustrated*, V (July 9, 1956), 6–9.

"Track and Field Winners at Melbourne, 1956 Olympics," *Sports Illustrated*, V (December 10, 1956), 54–62.

"Watch the Women: 1956 Olympic Track and Field," *Sports Illustrated*, V (November 19, 1956), 56–59.

"White Man's Burden in the Olympic Games," *Negro History Bulletin*, XVI (October 1952), 2.

WHITFIELD, M. "Let's Boycott the Olympics," *Ebony*, XIX (March 1964), 95–96.

WILLIAMS, C. H. "Negro Athletes in the Eleventh Olympiad," *Southern Workman*, LXVI (February 1937), 55–60.

———. "Negro Athletes in the Tenth Olympiad," *ibid.*, LXI (November 1932), 330–34.

OTHER SPORTS

ASHE, ARTHUR, JR. *Advantage Ashe*. New York, 1967.

"Blind Sports Announcer: Joe Walker," *Ebony*, XIV (November 1958), 91–93.

"Bobsled Brakeman: Clarence Sutton," *Ebony*, XII (May 1957), 71–74.

"Boy Jockeys," *Ebony*, VI (December 1950), 43–44.

"Bullfight . . . American Style," *Sepia*, XIII (September 1964), 30–34.

"Channel Swimmer; Willie Hanks Tries To Become First Negro To Swim the Channel," *Our World,* VIII (December 1953), 60–64.

"Charley Sifford: Top Negro Golfer," *Ebony,* XI (June 1956), 81–84.

"Cricket's Best Batsman: Garfield Sobers," *Ebony,* XV (October 1960), 43–46.

"Daredevil Doctor: Dr. Wells Forde, Sport Car Race Driver," *Ebony,* XIII (August 1958), 46–49.

"Democracy on the Race Track," *Sepia,* X (September 1961), 30–33.

"Dixie's Daredevil on Wheels: Stock Car Racer Wendell Scott," *Ebony,* XV (May 1960), 61–64.

"Don Scott Clicks on TV Bowling Show," *Ebony,* XX (December 1964), 87–88.

"Eddie Henderson of San Francisco, Member of Denver Figure Skating Club To Compete in Midwestern Figure Skating Championships at Minneapolis; First Negro Competing in Figure Skating Events," *Jet* (January 28, 1960), 54.

"Eddie Spann; The Boy Who Swims like a Fish," *Sepia,* X (November 1961), 70.

"Expert on Ski Slope: David Lucy, Varsity Star at Denver University," *Ebony,* XV (May 1960), 50–53.

"Father-Son Speedboat Team: Art and Butch Kennedy," *Ebony,* X (October 1955), 49–51.

"Flint Tees Off; Vehicle City Golf Club Interracial Tourney Is Biggest in the U.S.," *Our World,* IX (November 1954), 28–33.

"Fox Hunt in Virginia: Negro Riders Display Expert Horsemanship," *Ebony,* XI (July 1956), 72–78.

GAVER, J. R. "Wrestling Rings Down the Color Curtain," *Negro* Digest, XI (February 1962), 9–15.

"Ghana Booters Spark Spartans: Two African Students Soccer Stars at Michigan State," *Ebony,* XIV (February 1959), 77–80.

GIBSON, ALTHEA, and CURTIS, RICHARD. *So Much To Live For.* New York, 1968.

"Girl Fencer; New York Student Is First Negro Woman Accepted into Amateur Fencers League; Wins Intercollegiate Title," *Ebony,* VII (November 1951), 8, 82.

"Girl Who Throws Men Around," *Ebony,* XI (May 1956), 26–29.

"Golf Course Discrimination," *Crisis,* LXVII (August-September 1960), 440–41.

"Great Rider Trains a Tiny Tyke," *Ebony,* XIII (November 1958), 96–100. [About Henry Jennings.]

"Harvard Coxswain, Mario Bryan," *Ebony,* XIV (July 1959), 79–82.

"High Flying Water Skier: Alfonso Woodall," *Ebony,* XIII (October 1958), 26–28.

"Hosea Lee Richardson: Young Jockey Bids for Racing Fame," *Ebony,* VII (February 1952), 52–54.

"Hot Ice; Brooklyn's Joe Vanterpool Is a Whiz on Ice," *Our World,* VII (May 1952), 56–57.

"Ice Hockey's Willie O'Ree," *Ebony,* XVI (April 1961), 49–50.

"Illinois' Unheralded Champions," *Ebony,* XX (March 1965), 125–28.

"Is Golf Necessary? The Atlanta Decision," *Time,* LXVII (January 2, 1956), 14.

JOHNSON, T. F. "Swimming in Negro Colleges and Universities," *Journal of the American Association of Health and Physical Education and Recreation,* XX (June 1949), 379.

"Ju Jitsu Teacher; Los Angeles Ex-dancer Teaches Ancient Combat Techniques to Hollywood Stars," *Ebony,* V (June 1950), 94–96.

"Lady 'Robin Hood'," *Our World,* VII (October 1952), 52–53.

"Lady Wrestlers," *Ebony,* IX (June 1954), 64–70.

LEACH, G. B. *The Kentucky Derby Diamond Jubilee.* Louisville, 1949. [Includes Negro jockeys.]

"Leon Gainess, Oldest Jockey," *Ebony,* VII (August 1952), 76–82.

"Life Saver on Skis: Bryce Parks of the Ski Patrol," *Ebony,* XI (January 1956), 33–38.

"Little Giants of Table Tennis: Negro Contenders Win Junior Championship," *Ebony,* XV (June 1960), 71–76.

"Mabel Fairbanks: Top Professional Ice Skater," *Ebony,* VII (March 1952), 105–9.

"Monumental Hand Walk: Russell Nesbit, Acrobat," *Ebony,* XIV (June 1959), 99–102.

"Motorcycle Racers," *Ebony,* X (June 1955), 47–48.

"Negro Bullfighters," *Ebony,* X (April 1955), 51–56.

"Negro Matadors," *Negro Digest,* XIV (May 1965), 78–81.

"Negro Wrestlers," *Ebony,* XVII (May 1962), 43–44.

"Negroes in Bowling: Maurice Kilgore Is Negro America's First TV Bowler," *Ebony,* XIII (April 1958), 95–98.

NETLO, A., and MELLO E SOUZA, C. "Pelé: King of the Booters," *Reader's Digest,* LXXXV (October 1964), 203–5.

"New York's Busiest Swim Expert: Charles Smith," *Ebony,* X (October 1955), 19–25.

"Only U.S. Negro Bowman Club," *Ebony,* XIII (February 1958), 69–72.

"Pete Brown: A Golf Champion at Last," *Sepia,* XII (July 1964), 62–67.

"Peewee Hockey Player, Leslie Franklen," *Ebony,* IX (February 1954), 99–102. [Ice hockey.]

"Quarter-Midget Racer: Randy Ashbourne, Jr.," *Ebony,* XV (December 1959), 101–2.

"Queen of St. Louis Golf," *Sepia,* XII (February 1963), 45–48.

"Roller Derby Demon: Darlene Anderson," *Ebony,* XIV (January 1959), 60–65.

"Roller Derby Star: Quintana Cosby," *Ebony,* IX (May 1954), 56–61.

"Rookie Golf Champ: Bill Wright Wins National Public Links Crown," *Ebony,* XIV (October 1959), 127–30.

"Seasoned Skier Shows Them How," *Ebony,* XX (April 1965), 148–52.

"A Shot at $25,000: Wilbert Sims Attempts Bowling Prize," *Ebony,* XV (April 1960), 85–89.

"Social Side of Golf," *Sepia,* XI (September 1962), 53–56.

"Sophronia Stent: Girl Fencer," *Ebony,* VII (November 1951), 81.

"Sore Thumb Wins a Championship," *Sepia,* X (May 1961), 58.

"Spain's Negro Bullfighter," *Our World,* VII (January 1952), 44–46.

"Speed Demon of the Roller Derby," *Sepia,* XIII (January 1964), 78–81.

"Sport of the Speed Demons," *Ebony,* XIX (November 1963), 113–14.

"Sports Car Racer LaRuth Bostic," *Ebony,* XIII (December 1957), 107–10.

"Stock Car Racer; Only Negro in Sport Is Also Oldest Driver in Fast Races at Chicago's Soldiers Field," *Ebony,* VI (September 1951), 49–53.

"Supersonic Matador: Eugene Gilmore," *Ebony,* XV (February 1960), 99–101.

"Surfing: Frank Edwards," *Ebony,* XX (April 1965), 109–13.

"Top Negro Golfer," *Ebony,* XI (June 1956), 81–84.

"Underwater Expert: Lee Prettyman," *Ebony,* XIV (May 1959), 87–92.

VASBURGH, F. W. *Famous American Jockeys.* New York, 1884.

"Water Ski Instructor: Coleman Taylor," *Ebony,* IX (September 1954), 63–67.

WHALL, H. "Race Problem at Howard Is How To Win: First Negro Institution To Crash Exclusive College Rowing," *Sports Illustrated,* XX (April 27, 1964), 72.

"Wilber Gaines: Stock Car Racer," *Ebony,* VI (September 1951), 49–53.

WILLIAMS, L. J. "Negro in Golf," *Negro History Bulletin,* XV (December 1951), 52-53. [Also has a bibliography.]

"Willie O'Ree" [*Sepia* Salutes], *Sepia,* XI (May 1962), 66.

"Woman Sports Car Racer," *Ebony,* XIII (December 1957), 107–10.

"World's Highest-Paid Athlete: Pelé," *Ebony,* XVIII (February 1963), 62–64.

INTEGRATION IN SPORTS

BUCKER, C. A. "Sports Are Color-Blind," *Journal of Health, Physical Education and Recreation,* XXVIII (December 1957), 21–22.

CLAY, CASSIUS. "Integration: As a Negro Champ Views It—Excerpts from a News Conference," *U.S. News and World Report,* LVI (March 16, 1964), 20.

CLEMENT, R. E. "Racial Integration in the Field of Sports," *Journal of Negro Education,* XXIII (1954), 222–30.

DEFORD, F. "The Negro Athlete Is Invited Home," *Sports Illustrated,* XXII (June 14, 1965), 26–27. [The Butch Beard case.]

"Deliberate Speed in Sports," *Commonweal,* LXXIII (February 17, 1961), 81–82.

JOHNSON, CHARLES S. *Patterns of Negro Segregation.* New York, 1943.

LARDNER, J. "Fifty Per Cent Color Line," *Newsweek,* XLIII (May 10, 1954), 95.

———. "Old Emancipator," *ibid.,* XLVII (April 2, 1956), 85; (April 9, 1956), 84.

LAWSON, E. "Who Will Be All-American?" *Opportunity,* XVI (October 1938), 300–301.

MIX, R. "Was This Their Freedom Ride? Negro All-Stars of the AFL Boycott All-Star Game in New Orleans," *Sports Illustrated,* XXII (January 18, 1965), 24–25.

"National Game, Birmingham, Alabama," *Time,* LXIII (June 14, 1954), 46.

"Negro Athletes and Civil Rights," *Sepia,* XIII (June 1964), 35–39.

"A New Orleans Baseball Park," *Crisis,* XXIII (November 1921), 20.

"No Rambling Wreck," *America,* XCIV (December 17, 1955), 321.

PARRIS, W. H. "Integration of Athletics in the District of Columbia High Schools," *Negro History Bulletin,* XIX (October 1955), 14–15.

"Rebels at Georgia Tech," *Newsweek,* XLVI (December 12, 1955), 104.

REDDICK, L. D. "Why Georgia Lost," *Crisis,* XLIV (June 1937), 186–87.

"Segregation Snafu in Louisiana," *Newsweek,* LXVIII (July 30, 1956), 79.

TOBIN, R. L. "Sports as an Integrator," *Saturday Review,* L (January 21, 1967), 32.

"When Symbols Clash," *Commonweal,* XLIII (December 16, 1955), 274.

EDUCATION, RECREATION AND SCHOOL SPORTS

BOOKWALTER, K. W. *College Facilities for Physical Education, Health Education, and Recreation.* Flushing, N.Y., 1947.

BROWER, W. A. "Dolly King: Great Collegiate Athlete," *Opportunity,* XIX (May 1941), 138–40.

CARTER, ELMER A. "The Negro in College Athletics," *Opportunity,* XI (July 1933), 198–200.

"CIAA Celebrates Golden Anniversary," *Ebony,* XVIII (December 1962), 93–94.

DANZIG, A. "Progress towards Sanity in Intercollegiate Athletics," *Educational Record,* XXXV (October 1954), 261–74.

DUNCAN, R. O. "Teamwork for Fitness," *Journal of Health, Physical Education and Recreation,* XXVIII (November 1957), 23.

DWIGHT, F. C. "Recreation," *Crisis,* XLIX (January 1942), 38. [Facilities for Negroes.]

"Five Athletes, Five Hundred Scholarships," *Ebony,* XIX (October 1964), 57–61.

HENDERSON, E. B. "Famous Colored College Athletes," *Crisis,* II (July 1911), 115–18

JOHNSON, C. O. "Intercollegiate Athletics," *North Central Association Quarterly,* XXVII (October 1952), 180–85.

METHENY, E. "Some Differences in Bodily Proportions between American Negro and White Male College Students as Related to Athletic Performances," *Research Quarterly of the American Association for Health, Physical Education and Recreation,* X (December 1939), 41–53.

MITCHELL, E. C. "Adult Health Education and Recreational Programs: National, State and Local," *Journal of Negro Education,* XIV (July 1945), 363–73.

MUMFORD, A. W. "Present Status of Health and Physical Education in Negro Senior Colleges," *Research Quarterly of the American Association for Health, Physical Education and Recreation,* XIX (October 1948), 190–97.

NATIONAL COLLEGIATE ATHLETIC ASSOCIATION. *1950 Yearbook and Proceedings of the 45th Annual Convention.* Chicago, 1951.

"NCAA Concerned with Youth Fitness: Recommendations Made at 1957 Annual Convention," *Journal of Health, Physical Education and Recreation,* XXVIII (April 1957), 20.

"Physical Education in the Summer School [Hampton Institute]," *Southern Workman,* XLIX (Spring 1920), 397–98.

TOBIAS, C. H. "The Colored YMCA," *Crisis,* IX (November 1914), 33–35.

"Vacation Days," *Crisis,* IV (August 1912), 186–88. [Discrimination and integration in recreation areas.]

Picture Credits

The authors are grateful to the many libraries and special collections whose personnel have aided in the search for unusual and interesting photographs.

The following list of abbreviations has been used in indicating the collection where each picture was found and, where necessary, the picture's placement on a given page. Following these abbreviations is a list, by chapter, containing the page number, location on page and the contributor for each picture.

Those pictures which have not been listed are the property of The Association for the Study of Negro Life and History, Washington, D.C.

FHF	Football Hall of Fame, Canton, Ohio.
HG	Harlem Globetrotters, Chicago, Ill.
NYPL	New York Public Library, New York, N.Y.
NYPL-S	New York Public Library-Schomberg Collection, New York, N.Y.
S	Sport Magazine, New York, N.Y.
UPI	United Press International, New York, N.Y.
WW	Wide World Photos, New York, N.Y.

t: top; b: bottom; l: left; r: right;
c: center

Frontispiece
tl,bl:UPI, tc,tr,br:WW, lc,bc:S.

Chapter Two
6,all:UPI; 9,all:UPI; 12,all:UPI; 13,all:UPI; 18,all: UPI; 19,t:UPI; 20,l:UPI; 21,r:NYPL-S; 23,all:UPI; 26,all:UPI; 28,all:UPI.

Chapter Three
30,all:UPI; 34,all:UPI; 35,all:UPI; 38,all:UPI; 40, all:UPI; 42,all:UPI; 44,all:UPI; 48,tl,bl,br:UPI, tr: NYPL; 50:UPI; 51:UPI.

Chapter Four
54,all:UPI; 59,all:UPI; 62,tl:HG, tr:UPI, b:WW; 63,t,bl:UPI, br:WW.

Chapter Five
68:S; 73,tl,b:UPI, tr:WW; 76,tl:S, tr,b:WW; 77,t,bl: UPI, br:WW; 80,t:WW, bl,br:S; 81,all:WW.

Chapter Six
84,tl,tr,br:S, bl:WW; 87,tl,br:UPI, tr:WW, bl:S; 89,tl,b:WW, tr:UPI; 91:WW; 94,tl:S, br,tr:UPI; 96, tl,b:S, tr:WW; 98,tl,tc,tr:WW, b:UPI; 99,tl,tc,tr:WW, b:UPI; 102,t,c,b:WW; 105,tl,bl,br:S, tr:UPI; 107,t: UPI, b:WW; 110,tl:WW, tr:S, bl,bc,br:UPI; 111,t: UPI, bl:S, br:WW; 114,t:WW, b:UPI.

Chapter Seven
116:UPI; 119,t,bl:WW, br:S; 121,tl:S, tr,bl,br:UPI; 124,tl,tr:S, b:UPI; 125,tl,bl,br:WW, bl:UPI; 128,all: UPI; 129,all:WW; 131,tl,tr:UPI, b:WW; 133,tl:WW, tr,b:S; 134:WW; 136,tl:UPI, b,tr:S; 139:UPI; 141,tl: UPI, tr:S, b:WW; 143,tl,b:S, tr:WW; 145,all:S; 146, all:S; 149,all:UPI; 152,t,br:S, bl:UPI; 153,all:S, 155, b:UPI.

Chapter Eight
156,tl,bl,br:UPI, tr:S; 160,t,bl:UPI, br:WW; 161,all: UPI; 163,t:UPI, b:WW; 166,all:UPI; 168,tl:WW, tr,b:UPI; 170,t:UPI, b:WW; 174,t:WW, b:UPI; 176, tl,tr:WW, b:UPI; 180,all:WW; 181,tl:WW, bl,br:UPI; 184,all:UPI; 186,all:WW; 188,all:UPI; 190,all:UPI; 192,all:UPI; 195,all:UPI.

Chapter Nine
198:UPI; 201,tr:UPI, b:S; 205,t,br: UPI, bl:S; 207,t: WW, b:UPI; 209,all:WW; 212,tl:FHF, tr,b:UPI; 214, t,bl:UPI, br:S; 217,tl,tr:S, b:WW; 219,all:UPI; 221, t,br:S, bl:WW; 223,t:UPI, b:S; 226,all:S; 229,tl:WW, tr,b:S; 231,tl,tr:S, bl,br:UPI; 234,tl,bl,br:S, tr:UPI; 237,all:S; 238,all:S.

Chapter Ten
240,tl,tr,bl: WW, br:S; 242,tl,b:UPI, tr:WW; 243,tl: UPI, tr,b:WW; 246:WW; 247,tl,tr:S, b:WW; 249, all:S; 251:WW; 253,t:WW, b:UPI; 255,all:UPI; 257, t:UPI, b:WW; 259,all:UPI; 261,t:UPI, b:WW; 264, tl,b:WW, tr:S; 266,l,br:WW, tr:UPI; 270,l:S, tr:UPI, tl:WW; 272:UPI; 273,t,br:WW, bl:UPI.

Index

Page numbers in *italics* indicate illustrations.

Aaron, Henry "Hank," 2, 85, 103–104, 106, *105*
Adderley, Herb, 236, 239, *239*
Akins, Virgil, 183, 185, *156, 184*
Akron Pros, 46
Albert, Frankie, 211, 213
Albritton, Dave, 241
Alcindor, Lew, 118, 120, 137, 138, 140, *119*
Alexander, Sutton, 274
Alexander Hamilton High School (Brooklyn), 171
All-America Conference, 2, 199, 210, 215
All-American players (various polls)
  basketball, 49, 122, 142, *62*
  football, 31, 43, 46, 47, 49, 203, 216, 218, 220, 222, 227, 228, 235, 239
All-Eastern boxing title, 171
All-NBA five, 137
All-Pacific Coast Conference, 49
All-star (teams and games)
  baseball, 61, 113
  basketball, 117, 130, 137, 147, 148, 154
  college football, 204, 211
  football, 199
Allen, Richie, 85, 95, 97, *96*
Alston, Walter, 104
Amarillo Colts, 100
Amateur Athletic Union, 37, 39, 41, 158, 179, 254, 265
Amateur sports. *See* College athletics; Olympic Games; *and specific sports and colleges*
Ambers, Lou, 10
American Basketball Association, 138
American Derby (Chicago), 50
American Football League, 199, 204, 216, 218, 224, 230, 232
American Golf Classic (Akron), 271
American League, 2, 56, 57, 58, 61, 85, 90, 106, 113
  See also specific teams
American Sprint Championship (bicycling), 52
Amherst College, 45
Anderson, Eddie, 203
Anderson, Zack, 66, 67
Angott, Sammy, *190*
Antonelli, Johnny, 104, 106
Aparicio, Luis, 113
Aragon, Art, 189
Araujo, George, 187, 189
Arcaro, Eddie, 50

Archer, Joey, 183
Arizona State University, 222, 256
Armstrong, Harry, 8
Armstrong, Henry, 7, 8–11, 157, 182, 193, *6, 9*
Arnett, Jon, 208
Ashe, Arthur, 241, 265, 267–268, *240, 266*
Associated Press, 263
Atlanta Braves, 61, 103
Auerbach, Arnold "Red," 117, 126, 127, 144, 147, 151
Augusta National Golf Club (Georgia), 191
Australia and Afro-American athletes, 17, 19, 52, 53

Babe Ruth Award, 90
Bacon Casino, 14
Baer, Buddy, 16
Bahadur, *51*
Baker, Gene, 100
Baksi, Joe, 164, 173
Bald, Eddie, 52
Baldwin-Wallace College (Ohio), 250
Baltimore Bullets, 120, 140, 142
Baltimore Colts, 5, 202, 208, 210, 216, 228, 236, 239, 256
Baltimore Orioles, 108, 113, 115
Banks, Eddie, 100
Banks, Ernie, 97, 100, *98, 99*
Banks, Howard, 206
Bantamweight boxing, 25
Barnes, Bill, 228
Barnes, Erich, *221*
Baroudi, Sam, 164
Barrick, Mike, 256
Barrow, Joe Louis. *See* Louis, Joe
Barrow, Lillie Reese, 14
Barrow, Munroe, 11
Barry, Rick, 126, 130, 137
Baseball, professional, 1, 2, 56–58, 60–61, 69–115
Basilio, Carmen, 183, 185
Basketball, college, 49, 61, 117–118, 120, 127, 135, 138, 140, 150, 154
Basketball, professional, 2, 5, 55, 61, 64–67, 117, 120, 122–123, 126, 127, 130, 132, 135, 137, 140, 142, 144, 147–148, 151, 154
Bauer, Hank, 115
Baugh, Sammy, 49
Baylor, Elgin, 2, 130, 132, 135, 137, 140, *133, 134*

Beal, Norman, *221*
Beard, Frank, 271
Bearden, Gene, 58
Beau Jack, 189, 191, *190*
Bell, Bobby, 235, *237*
Bell, Clarence "Puggy," 67, *66*
Bell, Tommy, 182
Bellamy, Walter, 120, 122, 137, *121*
Bergesch, Bill, 93
Berra, Yogi, 88, 93
Besmanoff, Will, 158
Bethards, Jackie, 67
Bicycle racing, 52–53
Big Ten football conference, 45, 215
Bing, Dave, 135, 137, 140, *136*
Birmingham Barons, 65, 109
Bivins, Jimmy, 173
Bixler, Paul, 206
Blackburn, Jack, 14, 15, 172
Blackwood, Joe, 167
Bocchicchio, Felix, 173
Booker T. Washington High School (Arkansas), 228
Boozer, Bob, 123
Borchuk, Alex, 14
Bosley, Bruce, *212*
Boston, Eulalia, 248
Boston, Ralph, 241, 248, *247, 249*
Boston Celtics, 5, 117, 122, 126, 127, 137, 144, 147, *153*
Boston Music Hall, 27
Boston Patriots, 218
Boston Red Sox, 58, 85, 90, 92
Boston University, 203, 250
Bouchee, Ed, 112
Boudreau, Lou, 60
Bowdry, Jesse, 175
Boxing, 1, 7–29, 157–197
Boys Clubs of America
  and Armstrong, Henry, 11, 9
Braddock, James J., 15, 24
Bragan, Bobby, 82, 101, 103
Brandeis University (Massachusetts), 148
Breadon, Sam, 83
Brewster Center Gymnasium (Detroit), 178
Brion, Cesar, *13*
Britt, Jimmy, 25
Broadway Athletic Club, 25, 29
Brooklyn Dodgers, 2, 69, 86, 88, 93, 95, 101, 104, 108, 112, 199
  See also Robinson, Jack Roosevelt "Jackie"
Brooks, Pat, 14

Brough, Louise, *270*
Brown, Bill, *63*
Brown, Bob, 225, *226*
Brown, George, 248
Brown, Jim, 2, 199–200, 202–203, 204, 206, 210, 213, 220, 222, *201*
Brown, Joe, 185, 187, *186*
Brown, John, 204
Brown, Paul, 199, 202, 203, 204, 210, 220, 222
Brown, Roger, *xiv, 234*
Brown, Roosevelt "Rosey," 225–226, *226*
Brown University, 31, 46
Bruce, Ian, *246*
Bruguiere, Hal, 245
Brumel, Valeri, 250
Brundage, Avery, *255*
Bruton, Bill, 90
Buchanan, Buck, 230, 232, 235, 239, *231*
Buffalo (AFL), 216, 218
Bukich, Rudy, 213, 215
Buntin, Bill, 154
Burdette, Lou, 112
Burns, Tommy, 17
Butcher, Donnis, 137
Butler, James: *King of the Ring,* 19
Butler, Tom, 52

Calhoun, Lee, 252, 254
California Angels, 3
California Athletic Club, 20
California State Recreation Commission, 244
Camp, Jim, 235
Camp, Walter, 45–46, 47
Campanella, Roy, 2, 85, 86, 88, *54, 87*
Campbell, Milt, 241, 245, *240, 246*
Campbell, Tommy, 187
Canton McKinley High School (Ohio), 210
Capital City cycling track (Indianapolis), 52
Cardiff, Patsy, 20
Cardozo High School (Washington, D. C.), 101
Carnera, Primo, 15
Carpenter, Robert, 83
Carr, Henry, 241, 254, 256, *255*
Carter, Jimmy, 187, 189, *188*
Carver High School (Virginia), 220
Casey, Bernie, 3, 4
Cash, Norm, 90
Casper, Billy, 274
Cass High School (Detroit), 43
Casssell, Ollan, *255*
Castellani, John, 135
Central League, 88
Chamberlain, Wilt, 2, 65, 122–123, 126, 127, 130, 132, 135, 137, 140, 148, *116, 124*

Champ's Gym (Philadelphia), 175
Chandler, A. B., 71
Chapman, Ben, 82
Charles, Ezzard, 16, 162, 164–165, 172, 173, *163*
Chase Athletic Club (Chicago), 39
Chicago American Giants, 56
Chicago Bears, 206, 213, 215, 239
Chicago Cardinals, 206, 208
Chicago Cubs, 100
Chicago Giants, 56
Chicago Packers, 120
Chicago White Sox, 57–58, 108, 115
Children's Aid Society (Harlem), 49
Chuvalo, George, 162, *168*
Cincinnati Reds, 95, 103, 113, 115
Cincinnati Royals, 142, 151, *152*
Choynski, Joe, 24
Clark University (Atlanta), 61
Clay, Cassius Marcellus. *See* Muhammed Ali
Clay, Odessa, 158
Clayton, Jack, 67, *66*
Clemente, Roberto, 92
Cleveland Browns, 2, 199, 200, 202, 203, 204, 206, 210, 211, 220, 222, 225, 228, 245
Cleveland Indians, 2, 57–58, 60, 85, 101, 106, 108, 112
Clifton, Nat "Sweetwater," 65, *62*
Cobb, Ty, 86, 100–101
Colgate University, 200
College athletics, 31, 43, 55, 117
See also specific sports and colleges
Collier, Blanton, 202
Collins, Tommy, 189
Columbia University, 49
Comiskey Park (Chicago), 15
Commissioner of Recreation (New York City), 254
Compton Junior College (California), 213
Conerly, Charlie, 208
Conn, Billy, 16
Convention Hall (Philadelphia), 193
Conwell, Ed, 252
Cooper, Charles "Tarzan," 67, *66*
Cooper, Chuck, 117
Cooper, Henry, 159, 162
Corbett, James J. "Gentleman Jim," 20, 27
Cornell University, 43, 45, 47
Cornish, Frank, 239
Corrales, Pat, 97
Cotton Bowl, 200, 203
Cousy, Bob, 127, 144, 147
Cox, Billy, 112
Crab Orchard track (Kentucky), 50
Cream, Arnold. *See* Walcott, "Jersey Joe"
Creedon, Dan, 24
Creighton University (Omaha), 92
Cribb, Tom, 21
Crispus Attucks High School (Indiana), 150, 151

Cronin, Frank, 272
Cruz, Roberto, 194
Cuozzo, Gary, 236
Cy Young Memorial Award, *94*

Dahler, Ed, *62*
Dallas Cowboys, 204, 222, 258, 260
Dallas Texans, 216
D'Amato, Cus, 171
Dark, Al, 113
Dascoli, Frank, 71
Davis, Ernie, 203–204, 222, *198*
Davis, Lorenzo "Piper," 109
Davis, Nodie, 228
Davis, Otis, 241, 256, 258, *257*
Davis, Willie, 14, 199, 228, 230, 233, 239, *229*
Davis Cup, 265, 267
Dawson, Len, 236
Dean, Dizzy, 60
Dean, Paul, 60
Dee, Johnny, 118
Delacour, Jocelyn, 258
Delaney, Ron, 185
DeMarco, Paddy, 189, *188*
DeMarco, Tony, *184*
Dempsey, Jack, 16, 27
Denver Broncos, 216, 225
Detroit Giants, 56
Detroit Lions, 212, 218, 239
Detroit Pistons, 135, 137, 142, 154
Detroit Tigers, 101
De Vicaris, Louis, 204
DeWitt, Bill, 113
DeWitt Clinton High School (New York City), 49
Dickey, Bill, 56
Dillard, Harrison, 241, 250, 252, *251*
DiMaggio, Joe, 60
Dixie Kid, 24, *26*
Dixon, George, 7, 19, 25, 27, 29, *26*
Dixon, Hewritt, 260
Doby, Larry, 2, 60, 85, 95, 106, 108, *107*
Donohue, Jack, 118
Donovan, Art, 230
Douglas, Robert J., *66*
Drake Relays, *38*
Drew, Howard P., 31, 36–37, 241, *30, 38*
Drysdale, Don, 101
Duffey, Arthur, 37
Duke University, 118
Dumas, Charlie, 250
Dundee, Angelo, 158, 162, 165
Dupas, Ralph, 187
Durelle, Yvon, 177, *176*
Durham, Yank, 169
Durocher, Leo, 69, 71, 83, 93, 109, 112, *76*

East Technical High School (Cleveland), 33
Eastern Conference (football), 200
title games, 227

Eastern Division (NFL), 123, 202
  title games, 126, 130
Eaton, Dr. Hubert A., 269, 271
Ebbets Field, 70, 82
Echeverria, Joe, 182
Eckstine, Billy, 274
Einstein, Charles, 112
Elder, Lee, 241, 271–272, 272
Elder, Rose, 272
Eliot, Ray, 216
Elizabeth II, Queen, 271
Ellis, Jimmy, 165, 167, 166
Elmira Free Academy (New York), 203
Emerson, Roy, 267
Encyclopedia of Sports, 50
Erne, Frank, 25
Esperti, Tony, 158
Europe and Afro-American athletes, 21–22, 25, 27, 36, 51, 53, 65, 194
Evashevski, Forest, 45
Ewbank, Weeb, 230

Fabulous Magicians, 65
Fairfield Industrial High (Alabama), 109
Faison, Earl, 230, 232, 231
Falco, Tommy, 20
Farr, Tommy, 15
Fearsome Foursome, 233, 235, xiv, 234
Featherweight boxing, 8, 10, 25, 27, 29, 157, 194–197
Federal City College (Washington, D. C.), 148
Feller, Bob, 58, 60, 54
Felton, Lester, 192
Fern, Rube, 24
Ferry, Bob, 140, 142
Fiall, George, 67
First
    American girl to win three Olympic gold medals in track, 263
    athletic director at Harvard, 31, 43
    football game in America, 47
    heavyweight to regain championship, 171
    major football league, 46
    man named MVP in American League and National League, 113
    man to win U.S. Open (tennis), 267
    National Leaguer to win MVP award two years in a row, 97
    Negro captain of New York Giants, 227
    Negro football player at Cornell, 43, 45
    Negro heavyweight champion of the world, 17
    Negro in American League, 2, 106
    Negro in National Basketball Association, 117
    Negro in National League, 1, 69

Negro jockey of international fame, 51
Negro named American League's MVP, 90
Negro named National League's MVP, 4
Negro pro basketball coach, 117
Negro to play Minnesota varsity basketball, 235
Negro to pledge white fraternity, 244
Negro to receive Babe Ruth Award, 90
Negro to receive Heisman Trophy, 203
Negro to receive U.S. Amateur title (tennis), 267
Negro welterweight champion of the world, 24
Negro woman top-ranked tennis player in 1957 and 1958, 268
Negroes in major league football, 199, 210
  pro football, 210
Fistiana (magazine), 22
Fitzgerald, Willie, 25
Fitzsimmons, Bob, 27
Fleet City team (Navy), 215
Fleischer, Nat, 24, 27
Florida A&M College (now Florida A&M University), 3, 4, 55, 239, 258, 271
Flynn, Jim, 18
Folley, Zora, 162, 167, 161
Football, college, 31, 43, 45–47, 49, 199, 200–239
Football, professional, 1, 2, 4, 5, 46, 47, 55, 199–239
Forbes, Frank, 66, 67
Fordham University, 47, 206
49th Street Public School (Los Angeles), 262
Foster, Andrew "Rube," 56
Franklin Field (Philadelphia), 45
Frazier, Joe, 167, 169, 168
Freeman, Ron, 256
Frick, Ford, 71, 83
Fullmer, Gene, 183, 180
Furillo, Carl, 112
Furman University, 138

Gainer, Al, 23
Gainford, George, 179
Gaither, A. S. (Jake), 3, 4, 258
Gall, Patsy, 193
Gans, Joe, 7, 25, 27, 6, 26
Garcia, Ceferino, 10
Garcia, "Clix," 67
Gardiner, Arthur, 52
Garrett, Mike, 218
Garrison, "Snapper," 50
Gates, "Pop," 67, 63, 66
Georgetown University, 37
Geraghty, Ben, 104, 106

Gibson, Althea, 241, 267, 268–269, 271, 270
Gibson, Bob, 85, 90, 92–93, 91
Gibson, Daniel, 269
Gibson, Josh, 2, 55, 56–57, 54
Giles, Warren, 80, 99
Gilliam, Jim, 5
Gillman, Sid, 232
Glickman, Bernie, 183, 185
Godfrey, George, 20
Golden Gate Park (San Francisco), 211
Golden Gloves tournaments, 14, 158, 167, 182, 185
Golf, 241, 271–274
Gonzalez, Pancho, 268
Graham, Otto, 210, 211, 222
Grambling College (Louisiana), 55, 232, 239
Gramby, Joe, 175
Grange, Harold "Red," 215
Graziano, Rocky, 182
Greater Hartford tournament, 274
Green, Ernie, 204
Green, Jim, 241
Green Bay Packers, 3, 202, 204, 208, 210, 213, 228, 235, 236, 214
Greer, Hal, 123, 148, 150, 149
Gregory, George, 49
Greminger, Hank, 239
Grier, Roosevelt, 233, 234
Griffith, Emile, 194
Griggs, Dewey, 104
Grimm, Charley, 106
Grispos, Mitsos, 182
Gross, Jesse, 193
Groza, Lou, 202
Gustavus Adolphus College (Minnesota), 227

Halas, George, 214
Hall, Bob, 63
Hall of Fame
  baseball, 83, 81
  football, professional, 199, 211, 216
Hammond Pros, 46, 47
Hampton Institute (Virginia), 43
Hard, Darlene, 271
Harlem Globetrotters, 2, 55, 61, 64–65, 93, 123
Harlem youth projects, 49
Harmon, Tom, 45
Harris, Roy, 171
Harshman, Marv, 118
Harvard Magazine (1859), 43
Harvard University, 31, 43, 46
Hawkins, Tom, 4
Hawkins, Connie, 65
Hayes, Bob, 36, 241, 254, 258, 260, 259
Hayes, Elvin, 120, 137–138, 140, 139
Haynes, Abner, 216, 218, 217

Haynes, Marquis, 55, 65, *63*
Heafner, Clayton, 274
Heavyweight boxing, 1, 7, 11, 14–17, 19, 21–22, 29, 157, 158–173, 177
Heft, Arnold, *141*
Heisman Trophy, 203, 218, *198*
Henrich, Tommy, 88, 93
Herman, Kid, 25
Herrera, Aruimedes, *259*
Hewlett, A. Molineaux, 43
Heyman, Art, *129*
Hines, Jim, 241
Hodges, Russ, 112
Holland, Jerome E. "Brud," 31, 43, 45, *44*
Holman, Nat, 66
Holt, Johnny "Casey," 67
Holy Cross, College of the, 203
Homestead Grays, 2, 57
Hopman, Harry, 265, *266*
Hopper, Clay, 79
Hornsby, Rogers, 60, 104
Horrman, Kurt, 182
Horse racing, 49–51
Houk, Ralph, 90
Houston Astrodome, 138
Houston Astros, 95, 101
Houston Oilers, 232
How to Play Football (Lewis), 46
Howard, Elston, 70, 88, 90, 93, *84, 89*
Howard University, *81*
Howell, Jim Lee, 227
Hubbard, Cal, 71
Huber, Hans, 169
Hudlin, Richard, 267
Huff, Sam, 200
Hundley, Hot Rod, 147
Hunsacker, Tunney, 158
Husmann, Ed, 232
Hutchinson, Johnny, 193

Illinois Athletic Commission, 36
Indiana and high school basketball, 150
Indiana University, 120, 220, 232, 245
Indianapolis ABC's, 56
Indianapolis Clowns, 104
International League, 90
Irish-American Athletic Club, 37
Irvin, Monte, 5
Isaacs, Johnny, 67, *66*

Jackson, "Dynamite," *20*
Jackson, Henry. *See* Armstrong, Henry
Jackson, Inman, 64
Jackson, Lucius, 123
Jackson, Peter, 19–21, 25, *20*
Jackson, Tommy "Hurricane," 171, *170*
Jackson State College, 239

Jeannette, Joe, 29, *26*
Jefferson, Bernard "Bernie," 45, *44*
Jeffries, Jim, 17, 27, *18*
Jenkins, "Fats," 67, *66*
Jenkins, Harold, 67
Jerome Park (New York), 50
Johansson, Ingemar, 171, 172
Johnson, Al, 67
Johnson, Ben, 56
Johnson, Cornelius, 32
Johnson, Fred, 269
Johnson, Harold, 173, 175, *174*
Johnson, Jack, 1, 7, 17, 19, 22, 29, *18, 19*
Johnson, Jim, 22
Johnson, John Henry, 213
Johnson, Dr. Robert W., 267, 269, 271
Johnson, Rafer, 241, 244, 245, *240, 242, 243*
Johnson, Walter, 56
Jones, Bobby, 191
Jones, Deacon, 199, *xiv, 234*
Jones, Doug, 159, 169, 175, *168*
Jones, Hayes, 241, 252, 254, *253*
Jones, K. C., 127, 144, 147–148, *146*
Jones, Dr. Ralph Waldo Emerson, 239
Jones, Sam, 144, 147, *145*
Joyce, Willie, 193
Junior Indoor Singles title, 267
Jurgenson, Sonny, *223*

Kansas City Chiefs, 218, 224, 232, 235, 236, 239
Kansas City Monarchs, 2, 56, 60, 79, 88, 100
Kansas State University, 123
Kaufman, Carl, 256
Keane, Johnny, 92, 93
Kelly, Jim, 235
Kelly, Leroy, 204, 206, *205*
Kennedy, Robert F., 244
Kentucky Derby, 50, 51
Kerlan, Dr. Robert, 132
Ketchell, Stanley, 17
Ketchum, Willie, 187, 194, 196
Keyes, Leroy, 218, 220, *217, 219*
Khomenkov, Leonid, *243*
Kilborn, Pamela, *264*
Kimble, Owen, 52
King, Rev. Martin Luther, Jr., *81*
Kings of the Ring (Butler), 19
Kingsburg High School (California), 244
Kirszenstein, Irena, 265
Klobukowska, Ewa, 265
Komives, "Butch," 140
Koufax, Sandy, 58, 101, 132
Kracken, Jack, 14
Kramer, Frank, 52
Kuharich, Joe, 225
Kutsher's Country Club (Monticello, New York), 144
Kuznetsov, Vasily, 244, *240, 243*

Ladd, Ernie, 230, 232, 239, *231*
LaMotta, Jake, 182
Landry, Tom, 222
Lane, Kenny, *186*
Langford, Sam, 7, 29, *26*
Langston Public Golf Course (Washington, D. C.), 272
Lapchick, Joe, 66
Larkin, Tippy, 191
Larrabee, Michael, *255*
Latonia Derby (Kentucky), 50
Laurinburg Institute (North Carolina), 147
Lavigne, Kid, 25
Lazansky, Judge Edward, 75
League of American Wheelmen, 52
Lees, Tom, 20
Legore, Harry, 46
Lemon, Bob, 58
Lemon, "Meadowlark," 65, *63*
LeMoyne College (Tennessee), 61
Lennon, Jimmy, *195*
Leonard, Benny, 25
Leonard, Bob, 147
Leslie, Charles, 167
Levinsky, King, 15
Lewis, Guy, 118, 138
Lewis, John Henry, 22, 24, *23*
Lewis, William H., 45–46, *45*
Life and Journals of Lord Byron, 22
Light heavyweight boxing, 157, 173–178, 182
Lightweight boxing, 8, 10, 25, 157, 182, 185–194
Lindgren, Blaine, 254
Lindsay, Mayor John, 254
Lipscomb, Gene "Big Daddy," 216, 230, *229*
Liston, Sonny, 159, 162, 167, 171–172, 175, *161*
"Little Olympics": Moscow. *See* United States-Soviet Union games
Logart, Isaac, *184*
Lombardi, Vince, 3, 228, 236
London, Brian, 162, 171
Long Beach Open, 274
Long Island City Boy's Club, *98*
Longwood Cricket Club (Brookline), 267
Lonsdale, Earl of "Foreword" to *Kings of the Ring* (Butler), 19
Lopes, Joey, 187
Lopez, Al, 108
Los Angeles (AFL), 216, 218
Los Angeles Dodgers, 5, 101, 103, 113
Los Angeles Lakers, 4, 126, 130, 132, 135, 142, 148, *141*
Los Angeles Memorial Coliseum, 41
Los Angeles Rams, 49, 200, 208, 210, 230, 233, *xiv, 212, 214*
Los Angeles *Times*, 3, 4
Louis, Joe, 1, 7, 11–16, 17, 22, 24, 27, 33, 157, 162, 164, 165, 172–173, 178, *6, 12, 13, 174*

Louisiana Boxing Commission, 187
Louisiana Recreation League, 104
Lowe, Paul, 216, 218, *217*
Loyola University of Los Angeles, 206
Lucas, Jerry, *63*
Luckman, Sid, 49
Lundy, Lamar, 233, *xiv, 234*

McAuliffe, Joe, 20
McCarthy, Cal, 27
McCarthy, Connie, 193
McCovey, Willie, 112
McCracken, Branch, 120
McCullough, Clyde, 97
McDuffie, Frank, 147
McElhenny, Hugh, 213
McFadden, George, 25
McGraw, John, 56
McGovern, "Terrible Terry," 29
McGuire, Edith, 241, 265, *264*
McGuire, Frank, 126
Machen, Eddie, 162
McKinney, Bones, 147
MacMahon, Don, 112
McNeeley, Tom, 172
McVey, Sam, 29
Madison Square Garden, 16, 27, 37, 135, 150, 167, 182, 191, 250
Maglie, Sal, 71
Manhasset High School (New York), 200
Mann, Natie, 15
Mantle, Mickey, 90, 92, 97
Marchetti, Gino, 230
Marciano, Rocky, 16, 171, 177, *176*
Marigold Gardens (Chicago), 14
Maris, Roger, 90
Maritime Union Upgrading School, *197*
Marquette University (Milwaukee), 39, 41
Marshall University (West Virginia), 148
Martinez, Vince, 183
Maryland State College, 239
Mathews, Eddie, 90
Mathewson, Christy, 92
Mathis, Buster, 167, 169
Matson, Ollie, 206, 208, *207*
Matte, Tom, 236
Mauch, Gene, 97
Mauriello, Tami, 16
Maxim, Joey, 164, 171, 173, 177, 182
Mayers, Harold, 66, 67
Mays, William Howard "Willie," 2, 70, 85, 97, 103, 106, 108–109, 112–113, *84, 110, 111*
Mead, Eddie, 8, 193
Mellody, Honey, 24
Metcalfe, Ralph, 31, 32, 33, 36, 37, 39, 41, 43, 241, *38, 42*
Meyer, Alvah, 37
Miceli, Joe, 185
Michigan State University, 235

Middleweight boxing, 10, 17, 157, 165, 167, 173, 182–183
Mikan, George, 65
Mildenberger, Karl, 162
Miller, Herbert T., 75
Miller, Larry, *119*
Miller High School (Detroit), 230
Milwaukee Badgers, 46, 47
Milwaukee Braves, 90, 103–104
Minneapolis Lakers, 65, 142, 147
Minnesota Vikings, 235
Mississippi Vocational College, 233
Missouri Valley Conference Championship, 150, 216
Mitchell, Bobby, 203, 204, 220, 222, 233, *221*
Mitchell, Jack, 203
Miteff, Alexander, 158
Mobile Bears, 104
Modell, Arthur, 202
Molloy, Ken, 200
Molyneux, Tom, 21–22, *21*
Monde, Leon, 66, 67
Monroe, Earl "The Pearl," 140, 142, *141*
Monte, Hy, 66, 67
Montgomery, Bob, 191, 193, 194
Moor, Buddy, 182
Moore, Archie, 158–159, 171, 173, 175, 177–178, *170, 176*
Moore, Davey, 157, 194, 196, *195*
Moore, Lenny, 208, 210, 228, *209*
Moorehead, Seth, 112
Morabito, Tony, 211
Morgan, Bobby, 112
Morgan, J. D., 268
Morgan State College (Maryland), 55, 206, 227, 239
Most valuable players
  American League, 85, 90, 113
  Cotton Bowl, 203
  National Basketball Association, 130, 148, *149*
  National Football League, 202
  National League, 4, 71, 85, 86, 93, 97, 106, 109, 112, 113, *94, 99*
  Sally League, 104
Motley, Marion, 2, 199, 210–211, *212*
Moyer, Denny, *181*
Muhammed Ali (Cassius Clay), 157–159, 162, 165, 167, 169, 172, 178, *156, 160, 161*
Mulligan, Bowman, 189, 191
Munger, "Birdie," 52
Municipal Stadium (Cleveland), 57, 202
Municipal Stadium (Philadelphia), 191
Murphy, Isaac, 1, 49–50, 51, *50*
Murphy, Mike, 37
Musial, Stan, 69

Nance, Jim, 218
National Association for the Advancement of Colored People, 75

National Basketball Association, 117, 120, 122, 126, 130, 132, 138, 140, 147, 148, 151
  title games, 5, 123, 126, 130, 132, 135, 137, 151
  See also specific teams
National Boxing Association, 16, 162, 164, 165, 175, 193
National Collegiate Athletic Association, 39, 41, 118
  tournaments, 120, 123, 127, 135, 137, 138, 140, 150, 151, *119*
  See also specific colleges
National Football League, 3, 46, 199, 204, 211, 220, 222
  title games, 202, 208, 210, 227, 228, 235
National Junior Championships (tennis), 267
National League, 4, 56, 71, 83, 85, 97, 100, 108, 113, *80*
  See also specific teams
National Negro Baseball League, 56
National Racing Association (bicycle), 52
National Sportscasters and Sportswriters Association, 220
Neal, "Curley," 65
Negro All-American team, 227
Negro American League, 56, 60, 65
Negro athlete, analysis of success of, 3–5
Negro Eastern League, 56
Negro National League, 108, 109
Negro Newark Eagles, 93
Negro World Series, 56
Negroes
  in administration
    college athletics, 5, 31, 43, 46, 148
    professional sports, 5, 56, 126, 211, 216
  and baseball statistics, 85
Nelson, Battling, 25, *6*
New Detroit Committee, 254
New York (AFL), 216
New York, Original Celtics of, 66, 67
New York Athletic Club, 250
New York Athletic Commission, 16
New York City basketball championship, 49
New York *Evening World*, 46
New York Gazette, 37
New York Giants (baseball), 5, 56, 71, 101, 104, 106, 109, 112
New York Giants (football), 208, 225, 227, 233, 239, 256
New York *Herald-Tribune*, 191
New York Jets, 206
New York Knickerbockers, 123, 132, 135, 154–155
New York Mets, 95
New York open class title (boxing), 171
New York Rens, 2, 55, 61, 65–67, *66*

New York State Athletic Commission, 162, 164–165, 169
New York Times, 45, 46
New York Tribune, 37
New York Yankees (baseball), 2, 58, 70, 85, 86, 88, 90, 93, 104, 106
New York Yankees (football), 215
Newark Eagles, 93, 108, *107*
Newcombe, Don, 85, 93, 95, *94*
Newcombe, John, 267
Nicklaus, Jack, 271
Nitschke, Ray, 210, 213
North Carolina College, 144
North Texas State, 150, 216
Northern League, 104
Northumberland, Duke of, 22
Northwestern University, 45
Notre Dame University, 118, 235
Nova, Lou, 16

O'Connell, Tommy, 202
Ohio State University, 33, 36, 41, 228, 262
Ohl, Don, *134*
Okker, Tom, 267
Oklahoma State University, 215
Olderman, Murray, *128*
Olin, Bob, *23*
Oliver, Willie, 64
Olsen, Merlin, 233, *xiv*
Olson, Bobo, 182, 183
Olympic Games
    Australia (1956), 126, 127, 147, 241, 244
    Berlin (1936), 1, 32–33, 36, 37, 41, 248, 262, *34, 35*
    Helsinki (1952), 171, 172, 194, 206, 241, 244, 248, 252, 262
    London (1948), 241, 252, 262
    Los Angeles (1932), 31, 37, 41, 43, *42*
    Melbourne (1956), 245
    Rome (1960), 120, 151, 158, 167, 241, 244, 248, 250, 254, 256, 258, 262–263
    Stockholm (1912), 37
    Tokyo (1964), 167, 169, 241, 248, 254, 256, 258, 263, 265
    See also United States-Soviet Union games
Omaha Central High School, 215
Orange Bowl game, 225
Orr, Jimmy, 208, 236
Ortiz, Carlos, 187
Outland Trophy, 235
Overbrook High School (Philadelphia), 122
Owen, Steve, 227
Owens, Gloria, 36
Owens, Jesse, 1, 31–33, 36, 37, 39, 41, 241, 248, 256, 258, 262, *30, 34, 35, 259*

Paige, Leroy "Satchel," 55, 57–58, 60–61, 109, *54, 58, 59*
Palermo, "Blinky," 193
Pan-American Games, 260
Paramore, Bob, 260
Parker, Charles, Sr., 227
Parker, Jim, 2, 225, 227–228, *229*
Parrott, Harold, 82
Pasadena Junior College, 72
Pate, Harvey, 138
Patterson, Floyd, 158, 159, 167, 169, 171–172, 177, *114, 160, 170, 176*
Patton, Mel, 211
Peacock, Eulace, 39, 41, *40*
Pender, Paul, 183
Penn Relays, *40*
Pennsylvania State University, 208, 236
Pep, Willie, 196
Perry, Fletcher Joe, 211, 213, *212*
Persley, Arthur, 187
Persol, Johnny, 167
Philadelphia Athletics, 56
Philadelphia Eagles, 208, 225, 228, 239
Philadelphia Phillies, 82, 92, 93, 95, 97, 100, 104
Philadelphia 76ers, 123, 126, 127, 130, 148
Philadelphia Warriors, 123, 126, 127
Pierce, Eddie, 27
Pinson, Vada, 113
Pittsburgh Crawfords, 60
Pittsburgh Pirates, 82
Pittsburgh Steelers, 204, 206, 233
Player of the year (AFL), 216, 218, 220
Plimmer, Billy, 27
Podoloff, Maurice, 142
Podoloff Cup, *128*
Podres, Johnny, *87*
Pollard, Frederick, Jr., 46–47
Pollard, Frederick "Fritz," 31, 46–47, 199, *48*
Pollard, Jim, 120
Pollet, Sid, 104
Pollin, Abe, *141*
Pomona (California) Open, 274
Powell, Charlie, *161*
Power Memorial High School (New York City), 118
Prairie View A&M (Texas), 224, 239
Princeton University, 47
Prix du President de la Republique du State (horse racing), 51
Professional Golfers' Association, 271, 272
Providence Steamrollers, 46
Proteus Company, 83
Pruden, Fitzie, *192*
Pullins, Al "Runt," 64
Purdue University, 118, 220, 233

Quarry, Jerry, *166*

Rademacher, Pete, 171
Ramos, Sugar, 194, 196
Rawlings, Luther, 187
Ray, Elmer, 164
Reagan, Richie, 142
Records
    baseball, 100, 101
    basketball, 138, 150
    bicycle races, 52
    and Boston, Ralph, 248
    boxing, 11, 177
    and Brown, Jim, 200, 202, 210
    and Campbell, Milt, 245
    and Carr, Henry, 256
    and Cobb, Ty, 100
    and Davis, Ernie, 203
    and Davis, Otis, 256
    and Dillard, Harrison, 252
    football, 200, 202, 203, 210, 211, 220
    and Hayes, Bob, 258
    and Hayes, Elvin, 138
    and Johnson, Rafer, 244
    and Keyes, Leroy, 220
    and Louis, Joe, 11
    and Metcalfe, Ralph, 39
    and Moore, Archie, 177
    and Owens, Jesse, 32, 33, 36, 248
    and Peacock, Eulace, 41
    and Perry, Joe, 211
    and Robertson, Oscar, 150
    and Rudolph, Wilma, 263
    and Ruth, Babe, 100
    and Smith, Tommie, 260
    and Taylor, "Major," 52
    and Thomas, John, 250
    and Tolan, Eddie, 43
    track and field, 32, 33, 36, 39, 41, 43, 220, 244, 248, 250, 252, 254, 256, 258, 260, 262, 263, 265
    and Tyus, Wyomia, 263, 265
    and Whitfield, Mal, 262
    and Wills, Maury, 101
Reese, Pee Wee, 101
Reiser, Pete, 103
Renaissance Big Five. *See* New York Rens
Rhodes, Ted, 271
Rice, Grantland, 47, 49
Richey, Cliff, 268
Richmond, Bill, 22–23
Richmond Racquet Club, 267
Ricketts, Dave, 142
Rickey, Branch, 1, 69, 71, 74, 75, 78–79, 82, 83, 95, 108, 199, *80*
Ricks, "Pappy," 67
Rigney, Bill, 3
Rinaldi, Guilio, 175
Ring (magazine), 24, 27
Rivlin, Jules, 148
Rizzuto, Phil, 88, *76*

Robertson, Oscar, 2, 137, 142, 147, 150–151, 154, *152, 153*
Robeson, Paul, 31, 47, 199, *48*
Robinson, Bill "Bojangles," 178–179
Robinson, Brooks, 113
Robinson, Dave, 2, 235–236, *237*
Robinson, Ermer, *62, 63*
Robinson, Frank, 2, 85, 113, 115, *84, 114*
Robinson, Jack Roosevelt "Jackie," 1, 2, 57, 69–72, 74–75, 78–79, 82–83, 85, 88, 95, 108, 199, 211, *68, 73, 76, 77, 80, 81*
Robinson, Rachel (Mrs. Jack), 71, *81*
Robinson, "Sugar" Ray, 10, 17, 157, 162, 178–179, 182–183, 185, *180, 181*
Robinson, Willie, 239
Rockefeller, Nelson, 83
Rodriguez, Luis, 194
Rookie-of-the-year
    National Basketball Association, 135, 137, 140, 142
    National Football League, 208, 213, 222
    National League, 71
Roosevelt, Theodore, 53
Rose Bowl, 215, 220
    Player of the Game, *217*
Ross, Barney, 10
Ross, Wirt, 8
Roy, Alvin, 232
Rudolph, Wilma, 241, 262–263, *264*
Runyon, Damon, 14
Rush, Bob, *80*
Russell, Bill, 2, 5, 117, 122, 126–127, 130, 132, 137, 144, 147, *116, 121, 128, 129*
Russell, Cazzie Lee, 135, 154–155, *155*
Rutgers University, 31, 47
Ruth, Babe, 100
Ryan, Frank, 233

Sadat-Singh, Wilmeth, 47, *30, 48*
Saddler, Sandy, 157, 187, 196–197, *114*
St. Louis Browns, 60-61
St. Louis Cardinals, 60, 83, 88, 90, 92, 93, 104
St. Louis Giants, 56
St. Louis Hawks, *134*
Saitch, Eyre "Bruiser," 67, *66*
Salas, Lauro, 189
Salem-Crescent Athletic Club (Harlem), 179, 182
Sally League, 104
San Diego Chargers, 232
San Diego Rockets, 138
San Francisco, City College of, 220
San Francisco 49ers, 211, 213, 215, 218
San Francisco Giants, 3, 101, 112

San Francisco Warriors, 123, 126, 130, 132
San Jose State College (California), 206, 260
Sande, Earle, 50
Sanger, Walter, 52
Saperstein, Abe, 61, 64–65, *62*
Sarette, Dave, 203
Satterfield, Bob, *163*
Sarron, Petey, 8
Sauer, Ed, *80*
Saunders, Walter, 67
Savoie, Armand, 189
Savoy Big Five. *See* Harlem Globetrotters
Sayers, Gale, 204, 213, 215, 220, *214*
Scalzo, Petey, 189
Schafrath, Dick, *205*
Schaus, Fred, 132
Schayes, Dolph, 148
Schmeling, Max, 11, 15, 24
Schoendienst, Red, 90
Schultz, Howie, 79
Schumann, Heinz, *259*
Schwedes, Gerhard, 203
Seattle University, 135
Seixas, Vic, 267
Selvy, Frank, 138
Serrell, Juan, 269
Seymour, Paul, 148
Sharman, Bill, 144
Shatkov (Russian boxer), *160*
Shavlakadze, Robert, 250
Shaw, "Battling," *20*
Shaw, Buck, 211
Sheepshead Bay (New York), 50
Sherman, Allie, 200
Shore Athletic Club (Elberon, New Jersey), 39
Shue, Gene, *141*
Shula, Don, 228, 236, *209*
Sifford, Charlie, 241, 274, *273*
Silas, Paul, *155*
Siler, Herb, 158
Sime, Dave, 244
Simmons, Curt, *80*
Simms, Willie, 50–51
Simon, Abe, 16
Simon Graetz High School (Philadelphia), 204
Simpson, George, 41, *42*
Simpson, Orenthal James, 218, 220, *217*
Singh, Milka, 256
Sinko, Steve, 203
Sisler, Dick, 93
Slavin, Frank, 21
Slocum, Hilton, 66, 67
Smith, Bud, 185, 187
Smith, George, 150
Smith, Jem, 20
Smith, Tommie, 241, 260, *257*

Smith, Walker. *See* Robinson, "Sugar" Ray
Smith, William "Wee Willie," 67, *66*
Snead, Norm, 222
Snyder, Larry, 33, 36, 262
Soltau, Gordy, 213
South Atlantic League, 113
South Carolina State College, 233
Soviet Union. *See* United States-Soviet Union games
Spahn, Warren, 112
Spink, J. G. Taylor, 58
Sporting News, 58
Springfield High School (Massachusetts), 36
Stanfel, Dick, 225
Stanford University, 49
Stanky, Eddie, 82, 103
Starr, Bart, *231*
Stefford, Silent,182
Stengel, Casey, 60–61, 90
Stokes, Maurice, 142, 144, *143*
Stolle, Fred, 267
Stolz, Allie, 191
Stram, Hank, 232–233, 236
Sullivan, Jack, 25
Sullivan, John L., 7, 16, 20, 27
Sumner High School (St. Louis), 268
Super Bowl games, 232–233, 236
Svare, Harland, 233
Sykes, Art, 14
Symotesova, Lyudmila, *240*
Syracuse Nationals, 123, 148
Syracuse University, 47, 49, 135, 137, 200, 203, 204, 218, 222

Tatum, Jim, 235
Tatum, Reese "Goose," 55, 65, *63*
Taylor, Charley, 222, 224, *223*
Taylor, Marshall W. "Major," 52–53
Taylor, Otis, 224
Taylor, Rosie, 239
Tebbitts, Birdie, 83
Tech High (Omaha), 92
Temple, Ed, 263, 265
Temple University, 39, 41
Templeton, Dink, 206
Tennessee State, 239, 263, 265
Tennis, 241, 265–271
Texas Christian University, 200
Texas Western College, 117
Thomas, Frank, 97
Thomas, Harry, 15
Thomas, John, 248, 250, 262, *240*
Thompson, Debbie, *264*
Thomson, Bobby, 106
Thurmond, Nate, 130, 132, *131*
Thurston, Fuzzy, 232
Tittle, Y. A., 213
Tolan, Eddie, 31, 37, 39, 41, 43, 241, 252, *42*
Torres, Battling, 194

Towns, Forrest, 250
Track and field, 2, 31, 32–33, 36–37, 39, 41, 43, 211, 241–265
Trevino, Lee, 271
Tunnell, Em, 227
Turpin, Randy, 182
Tuskegee Baseball Team, *xiv*
23rd Police Athletic League gym (Philadelphia), 167
Twyman, Jack, 144, 151, *143*
Tyus, Marie, 263
Tyus, Willie, 263
Tyus, Wyomia, 241, 263, 265, *240, 264*

Udell, Larry, 14
Unitas, John, 208, 210, 228, 236, 239, *209*
United Golf Association, 271, 272
United Press International, 220
United States Amateur Championship tournament, 267
United States Lawn Tennis Association, 268
United States Open (golf), (1968), 272
United States Open (tennis), 267
United States-Soviet Union games
    Moscow (1958), 244
    Moscow (1961), 248
    Moscow (1963), 265
    Moscow (1965), 265
University of California, 150
University of California (Los Angeles), 31, 49, 72, 74, 118, 120, 138, 140, 215, 244, 267, 268
University of Cincinnati, 150–151
University of Houston, 118, 120, 138, 140
University of Illinois, 215, 216, 220
University of Kansas, 123, 213, 215
University of Kentucky, 117, 135
University of Maryland, 49, 272
University of Michigan, 41, 45, 154
University of Minnesota, 45, 235
University of Nebraska, 225
University of North Carolina, 120, 235
University of North Dakota, 46
University of San Francisco, 126, 147, 206
University of Southern California, 37, 118, 218, 220, 239
University of Washington, 49
University of Wisconsin, 45

Valley Arena Club (Holyoke, Massachusetts), 191
Van Arsdale, Dick, 132

Veeck, Bill, 2, 58, 60, 108
Veldez, Danny, *195*
Vidmer, Richard, 191
Vigeant, Frank, *190*
Villemain, Robert, 182
Virginia Normal and Collegiate Institute, 45
Viscusi, Lou, 187

Waddell, "Rube," 56
Wade, Bill, 208
Wake Forest College (North Carolina), 147
Walcott, Fred, 250
Walcott, "Jersey Joe," 16, 24, 162, 164, 165, 172–173, *12, 174*
Walcott, Joe, 24, *26*
Walker, Buddy, 269
Walker, Chet, 123
Walker, Dixie, 82
Walker, Sidney. *See* Beau Jack
Wallace, Nunc, 27
Warmath, Murray, 235
Washington, Kenny, 31, 49, 72, 74, *30, 48*
Washington Redskins, 200, 204, 211, 222
Washington Senators, 56, 85
Washington State University, 118
Weis, Al, 115
Webster, Joe, 173
Weinmeister, Arnie, 227
Welterweight boxing, 8, 10, 24, 157, 182, 183, 185, 194
Wembley Stadium (London), 252
Wertz, Vic, 112
West, Jerry, 130, 147
West Side Tennis Club (Forest Hills), 267
Westchester Gold Classic, 271
Western Division (AFL), 216
Western Reserve University, 49
Westrum, Wes, 112
White, Bill, 100
Whitfield, Mal, 241, 260, 262, *261*
Wilkinson, "Bud," 216
Willard, Jess, 17
Williams, Cleveland, 162
Williams, Ernie, *186*
Williams, Ike, 187, 189, 191, 193–194, *188, 192*
Williams, Percy, 43
Williams, Ted, 69
Williams, Ulis, 256, *255*
Willis, Bill, 2, 199, 210
Wills, Harry, 7, 29 *26, 163*
Wills, Maury, 85, 100–101, 103, *84 102*

Wiltwyck School for Boys (New York), 169, 171
Wimbledon tournament (1957), 271
Winkfield, Jimmy, 51, *51*
Winston-Salem State College, 140
Wood, Willie, 236, 239, *239*
Woodman, Joe, 193
Woodson, Marv, 233
World Boxing Association, 165
World boxing championships
    featherweight, 8, 10, 25, 27, 29, 157, 194, 196
    heavyweight, 1, 7, 11, 15–16, 17, 22, 157, 159, 162, 164–165, 169, 171, 172, 173
    light heavyweight, 157, 167, 173, 175, 177
    lightweight, 8, 10, 157, 185, 187, 189, 191, 193
    middleweight, 10, 17, 157, 182, 183
    welterweight, 8, 10, 24, 157, 172, 182, 183, 185
World Series
    1948, 60, 106, *59*
    1949, 71, 88, 93
    1953, 90
    1954, 109, 112
    1955, 70
    1956, 93
    1957, 104
    1958, 90
    1959, 103
    1964, 92
    1966, 113, 115
    1967, 92
World War I
    and athletes, 37, 47
World War II
    and athletes, 16, 51, 74–75, 185, 187, 210, 215
Wright, George, 27
Wrigley Field, 213
Wykoff, Frank, 32, 33, *42*

Xavier University of Louisiana, 61

Yale University, 46
Yancey, Bill, 67
Yankee Stadium, 15, 16, 70
Yawitz, Eddie, 183, 185
Yemelyanov (Russian boxer), 167, *168*
YMCA, 49, 75
Young, Bob, *181*
Young, Buddy, 2, 5, 215–216, 230
Young, Willie, 239

Zivic, Fritzie, 10, 182
Zulveta, Orlando, 187
Zurito, Juan, 193